PRAISE FOR ORGANIZATION 21C

"It is probably no coincidence that so many of my closest colleagues and teachers were proteges and co-workers of Dick Beckhard's. We owe him more than we know. Yet, the real work that Dick and the other founders of Organization Development started is just beginning.

Increasingly, large institutions and the networks that interconnect them shape our world, for better and for worse. It is no exaggeration to say that our future depends on their collective intelligence: to see beyond narrow definitions of their interest and to innovate in products and processes commensurate with the health of living systems, large and small. The real work is just now starting and Subir Chowdhury's superb anthology is a great place to begin in grasping its depth and breadth."

Peter M. Senge
Founder, Society for Organizational Learning, MIT
Author, The Fifth Discipline

"A thought-provoking collection from leading thinkers around the world on a broad sweep of issues confronting the 21st century business organization. The emphasis is on how organizations can create a constant learning environment that recognizes and respects diversity. Those who want to understand and shape the future of business should read this book."

Laura Tyson
Dean, London Business School

"This is an essential book for the leader of the future, written by great thought leaders whose vision of the future challenges and inspires."

Frances Hesselbein
Chairman and Founding President
The Peter F. Drucker Foundation

"This book is of the highest importance. The issue of how the modern organization will look in the future is key to many of us. Further, how to operationalize a realistic view of the future organization, how it will work, what the relevant management processes will look like, how people will be asked to function, etc. are key. The book provides invaluable insights regarding this fascinating future."

Peter Lorange
President, IMD Switzerland

ORGANIZATION 21C:
Someday All Organizations Will Lead This Way

ISBN 0-13-060314-7

ORGANIZATION 21C:
Someday All Organizations Will Lead This Way

Subir Chowdhury

FINANCIAL TIMES
Prentice Hall

An Imprint of PEARSON EDUCATION

Upper Saddle River, NJ • New York • London • San Francisco • Toronto
Sydney • Tokyo • Singapore • Hong Kong • Cape Town
Madrid • Paris • Milan • Munich • Amsterdam
www.ft-ph.com

Library of Congress Cataloging-in-Publication Data

Chowdhury, Subir.
    Organization 21C : someday all organizations will lead this way / Subir
Chowdhury.
        p. cm. -- (Financial Times Prentice Hall)
    Includes bibliographical references and index.
    ISBN 0-13-060314-7
        1. Leadership. 2. Creative ability in business. 3. Organizational change. 4.
Corporate culture. I. Title: Organization twenty-first century. II. Title. III.
Financial Times Prentice Hall books

    HD57.7.C52 2002
    658.4'02--dc21

                                                                    2002027065

Editorial/production supervision: *Laura Burgess*
Cover design director: *Jerry Votta*
Cover design: *Anthony Gemmellaro*
Art Director: *Gail Cocker-Bogusz*
Manufacturing buyer: *Maura Zaldivar*
Executive editor: *Jim Boyd*
Editorial assistant: *Allyson Kloss*
Development Editor: *Jim Markham*
Marketing Manager: *Bryan Gambrel*

Printed in the United States of America
10   9   8   7   6   5   4   3   2   1

ISBN 0-13-060314-7

Pearson Education LTD.
Pearson Education Australia PTY, Limited
Pearson Education Singapore, Pte. Ltd.
Pearson Education North Asia Ltd.
Pearson Education Canada, Ltd.
Pearson Educación de Mexico, S.A. de C.V.
Pearson Education—Japan
Pearson Education Malaysia, Pte. Ltd.

Financial Times Prentice Hall Books

For more information, please go to www.ft-ph.com

Dr. Judith M. Bardwick
Seeking the Calm in the Storm: Managing Chaos in Your Business Life

Thomas L. Barton, William G. Shenkir, and Paul L. Walker
*Making Enterprise Risk Management Pay Off:
How Leading Companies Implement Risk Management*

Michael Basch
*CustomerCulture: How FedEx and Other Great Companies Put
the Customer First Every Day*

J. Stewart Black and Hal B. Gregersen
Leading Strategic Change: Breaking Through the Brain Barrier

Deirdre Breakenridge
Cyberbranding: Brand Building in the Digital Economy

William C. Byham, Audrey B. Smith, and Matthew J. Paese
*Grow Your Own Leaders: How to Identify, Develop, and Retain
Leadership Talent*

Jonathan Cagan and Craig M. Vogel
*Creating Breakthrough Products: Innovation from Product Planning
to Program Approval*

Subir Chowdhury
Organization 21C: Someday All Organizations Will Lead this Way

Subir Chowdhury
The Talent Era: Achieving a High Return on Talent

Sherry Cooper
Ride the Wave: Taking Control in a Turbulent Financial Age

James W. Cortada
*21st Century Business: Managing and Working in the New
Digital Economy*

James W. Cortada
*Making the Information Society: Experience, Consequences,
and Possibilities*

Aswath Damodaran
*The Dark Side of Valuation: Valuing Old Tech, New Tech, and New
Economy Companies*

Henry A. Davis and William W. Sihler
Financial Turnarounds: Preserving Enterprise Value

Sarv Devaraj and Rajiv Kohli
*The IT Payoff: Measuring the Business Value
of Information Technology Investments*

In memory of our friend and mentor
Richard Beckhard

ORGANIZATION 21C

SUBIR CHOWDHURY

DEREK F. ABELL	MICHAEL BEER
RICHARD E. BOYATZIS	DAVID L. BRADFORD
W. WARNER BURKE	JAMES A. CHAMPY
ALLAN R. COHEN	JAY A. CONGER
SAMUEL A. CULBERT	CHRISTOPHER DeROSE
DEXTER DUNPHY	DAVID FINEGOLD
ELIZABETH FLORENT-TREACY	ROB GOFFEE
ROBERT L. HENEMAN	HARVEY A. HORNSTEIN
GARETH JONES	ANDREW KAKABADSE
MANFRED F. R. KETS DE VRIES	EDWARD E. LAWLER III
NIGEL NICHOLSON	VLADIMIR PUCIK
EDGAR H. SCHEIN	SCOTT J. SCHROEDER
WENDY K. SCHUTT	SCOTT N. TAYLOR
NOEL M. TICHY	VICTOR H. VROOM

CONTENTS

Chapter 10
The Death and Rebirth of Organizational Development 155

PART 3
21C PEOPLE   175

Chapter 11
The Boardroom of the Future 179

Chapter 12
Power and Influence 193

Tribute to Our Friend and Mentor   329

PREFACE

When I first undertook an international book project involving eminent thinkers around the globe, the first person I called was Richard (Dick) Beckhard, whom I had never met in person. Our meeting on the phone never ended; he challenged my thoughts, inspired me during the project, and supported me continuously. After two years, when the manuscript for *Management 21C* was finally finished, Dick was the first person who reviewed it, and wrote me in a hand-written note: "The book has the fascination of a good novel—plus exposure to the ideas of many of our best futurists. I recommend it to organization leaders, consultants, and academics working on this critical issue for all of us." Dick was so happy about the book that we decided to meet for the first time in New York in January 2000. In December 1999 I returned home from a 40-day book tour in Europe and Asia, and a card was waiting for me that left me speechless for a few minutes. Alas, I would never have the chance to meet my friend and mentor Dick Beckhard. On that night, while reading many of Dick's books randomly, many thoughts emerged: How can I pay tribute to Dick? Where have Dick's works had the major impact? People or organizations? Will people search the organization or will the organization search the people? All these scattered thoughts inspired the birth of *Organization 21C*.

The book you are reading is a gift of collective great minds around the world. This is a true global venture. Australia to America, France to The Netherlands, Britain to Switzerland—from three continents, the very best contemporary organizational behavior thinkers have decorated every page of this book. *Organization 21C* brings together visions for the 21st-century organization in one concise book, allowing the reader to understand the changes going on now and what to expect in the future.

In *Organization 21C*, you can read any chapter at any moment, rather than reading cover to cover. With a vivid description of the emerging global rise, cultures, and people, *Organization 21C* will intrigue, provoke, encourage, and above all, change everyone who reads it. In its introductory chapter you will discover the future of organization and its winning strategy by leveraging talent.

In the first part, read and discover global, world-class, and situational leadership. Part 2, "21C Processes," introduces X-engineering, the power of hierarchy, total rewards management, and shareholder value. This part ends with the rebirth of Organizational Development. Part 3 takes the reader a tour of the boardroom, power and influence, framing, and emotional intelligence, and ends with tips on how to manage the human animal in organizations. In the final part, the sustainability of organizations, organizational culture, and leading organizational change inspire the reader to rethink the 21C organization and also prepares the reader for the future by building organizational fitness.

Organization 21C is for those who inspire others, are peoplistic rather than individualistic, celebrate diversity, constantly search for the dream, and want to reshape the globe of tomorrow. *Organization 21C* was created to help other people, and it also creates a helping attitude among people.

I am extremely proud to announce that every penny of the author's royalties will be donated worldwide in the memory of our friend and mentor Dick Beckhard. Our mission will be successful if you will join us in fulfilling the dream of enhancing Dick's works around the globe.

—Subir Chowdhury
Novi, Michigan
Christmas 2001
email: subir.chowdhury@asiusa.com

ACKNOWLEDGMENTS

I owe a large debt to the 28 distinguished thinkers and authors who have contributed to this book. *Organization 21C* would never have been materialized without the generous support of Derek F. Abell, Michael Beer, Richard E. Boyatzis, David L. Bradford, W. Warner Burke, James A. Champy, Allan R. Cohen, Jay A. Conger, Samuel A. Culbert, Christopher DeRose, Dexter Dunphy, David Finegold, Elizabeth Florent-Treacy, Rob Goffee, Robert L. Heneman, Harvey A. Hornstein, Gareth Jones, Andrew Kakabadse, Manfred F. R. Kets de Vries, Edward E. Lawler III, Nigel Nicholson, Vladimir Pucik, Edgar H. Schein, Scott J. Schroeder, Wendy K. Schutt, Scott N. Taylor, Noel M. Tichy, and Victor H. Vroom. I very much appreciate the donation of time and effort of each of these individuals for the sake of this project. Their dedication and invaluable insights on their work have been a great inspiration for me.

A great colleague, a true friend, and a mentor—Richard Beckhard's works have been a inspiration to us all. I am honored to lead this international book project in his memory.

I owe a tremendous intellectual debt to Peter F. Drucker—a pioneer and the greatest management thinker of our time. His writings inspire me every day.

I am also grateful to all the personal assistants and research associates who represent the direct links to the *Organization 21C* contributors.

I am very lucky to have had the opportunity to work with my editor, Jim Boyd. Also, thanks to my publisher Jeff Pepper, and Richard Stagg at Financial Times Prentice Hall.

I would like to thank Amanda Thompson and Laura Burgess of Financial Times Prentice Hall for their continuous support and assistance.

Special thanks to everyone at my organization, ASI—American Supplier Institute—for their continuous encouragement.

My gratitude to Dick Beckhard's wife, Sandra Barty, who wholeheartedly supported this project from its infancy.

Special thanks to Organization Development Network (*www.odnetwork.org*) for establishing the Dick Beckhard Fund to honor Dick's legacy. Supported by funds from this book, the project will strive to create Organization Development mentorship opportunities in venues throughout the world.

I am grateful to my parents, Sushil and Krishna Chowdhury, for their continuous encouragement.

This book would never have been made a reality without the support of my wife, Malini.

—Subir Chowdhury
Novi, Michigan

1

Toward the Future of Organization

Subir Chowdhury

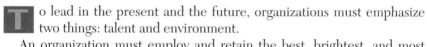 o lead in the present and the future, organizations must emphasize two things: talent and environment.

An organization must employ and retain the best, brightest, and most diversified people in order to innovate. The aim is to create what I call a united talent workforce. Organizations must have people who will work together to bring out better products faster or deploy better processes in the workplace. Organizations need to provide talent with appropriate resources for innovation.

An organization must create (a) a constant learning environment that embraces positive challenge, (b) a fearless environment where people can communicate and collaborate with one another, (c) a diversified environment where people think differently and value each other's thinking, (d) new ways of looking at problems and opportunities and a strong sense of urgency, and (e) a culture that effectively leverages talent.

Organizational Winning Strategy by Leveraging Talent

Whether leading or lagging, in long races those who go fastest win. As General Electric's former chairman Jack Welch said in many different ways, the only sustainable competitive advantage is to innovate and change faster than the toughest competitors.[1] He also emphasized that if the outside is changing faster than you are, the end is in sight. In business, just as in racing, those who go fastest have the combination of the fastest vehicle and the most talented driver. And the fastest vehicle was created by the most talented group of designers, engineers, and fabricators, a winning mix of talented leaders and a strong cast of highly motivated, hard-working doers.

1

The talented driver is the manager–leader who maintains the winning combination of continuous development and on-time obsolescence.

Business is no more than the extension of its key talent in the *value chain*. That's why, over the past two decades, the emphasis in business has shifted from maintenance to meaning, from putting in time to making a contribution, from politics to value-added performance, from labor to talent.

In the business context, *talent* may be defined as "capability applied to create value that is recognized and rewarded by primary stakeholders— owners, managers, and customers." Talented people must know how their jobs fit within the value chain and not only perform the routine tasks well but also excel at the high-leverage components of their jobs.

The high-leverage components usually require some degree of proactivity, creativity, initiative, and ingenuity. If talented people are not regularly operating at the high end of their jobs and being leveraged wisely by management, most of their talent is wasted. In fact, talent is wasted whenever it is not recognized, developed, expressed, refined, and leveraged.

Now let me define what I meant by value chain. A *value chain* connects customers with creators, giving customers the impression (or illusion) of intimacy and identity with the organization and supplying them with the value they want and need to return again and again. In a product-based business, the value chain may have these 10 links.

1. Creative ideas
2. Constructive criticism
3. Concept development
4. Testing/feedback
5. Finished product
6. Managing/marketing
7. Sales
8. Support/service
9. Management systems/processes
10. Leadership

Every business needs top talent at every link because the business will be only as strong as its weakest link. Moreover, the talent at every vital link must feel valued. To the extent that talents feel like victims, performance suffers proportionately.

What talent matters most in your business? Every member of the value chain matters to the customer. Leaders should recognize that the new definitions of talent and value do not exclude any member of the organization. All employees should feel, as should all members of an athletic team, that they play a vital role and might, through diligence and intelligent application of talent, become indispensable (in a here-and-now business sense). This means that on any given day, or on any given shift, their presence and performance not only "matter," but also make all the difference in the world.

I think every person likes the feeling of being a "count-on-me" talent. But people may not stay happy in the system if, after proving themselves, they aren't recognized and rewarded.

How is talent best recognized and rewarded? No one way suits all. To the extent possible, rewards should be personalized, based on the preferences and priorities of each individual talent. Is this too much to ask, you say? Not if you want to be a market leader. The size of the operation is not the critical factor; the critical factor is the habit of showing appreciation.

How is top talent best recruited? Top-performing environments attract top talent. The best talents flow to the best companies to work for. These performers may be influenced by colleagues, peers, and media polls; a lot of recruitment happens by word of mouth in every industry. Talents seek creative freedom, expression, performance options, growth, and a supportive environment with capable owners, managers, coaches, cheerleaders, team members, and pay-for-performance systems.

How is talent best leveraged? I see seven ways.

1. **Teams.** Put top talent with other top talent in teams and give them challenging and meaningful work to do. Make sure this work is valued by the organization and its customers.

2. **Special projects.** There's nothing quite like a special assignment, some "mission impossible" or high-priority project, to bring out the best in talent.

3. **Products.** Pour top talent into products that can be replicated and widely distributed. By creating new products and improving existing products, you gain immense leverage.

4. **Distribution.** Seek wide distribution for the work of top talent. If the world-class work of your top talent is poorly promoted and distributed, you gain little leverage.

5. **Marketing/sales.** Leverage talent through marketing and sales events. This may mean featuring talents in ads or involving them in sales in some way.

6. **Advertising/public relations.** Make your top talents bigger than life. Create an image and identity for them. Invest wisely in advertising and public and media relations to make a brand of the talents' names.

7. **Mentoring/modeling/coaching.** Engage willing, mature talent in the high-leverage activities of mentoring, modeling, and coaching new talent.

What is the new role of managers and leaders? Like management in the sports and entertainment worlds, the primary role of management in business is to support, serve, discipline, and leverage talent. The leader often asks four questions: How is it going? What are you learning? What are your goals now in light of how it is going and what you are learning? How can I help you? In this way, the leader avoids owning the problem and yet offers himself or herself as a source of help. The leader's responsibility is to create conditions of trust, set up performance agreements, allow people to perform, and then hold people accountable—all with the aim of being competitive and making a greater contribution to society.

A talented leader, Sumner Redstone, CEO of Viacom, says: "I've always wanted to win. I think winning is everything. Throughout my life I've had an obsessive drive to be number one. That doesn't mean I've always been number one. But that's what drives me—a desire to be the best at what I do." He tells of the hotel fire in which he was badly burned—and then of being in the heat of negotiating and deal making—and yet of being in perfect health at age 78. "The question isn't whether you are subjected to adversity and conflict during your life," he says. "The question is how you deal with it. If you really want to succeed, you have to be passionate and have a commitment to excellence in performance. If you have both of those, and some intellectual capacity, nothing is impossible. Optimism is not optional in business—it's vital. I believe that optimism is the only philosophy of life that's compatible with sustained success and sanity. So if you want to stay sane, you have to be optimistic and have confidence in yourself and your team."[2]

Redstone is known as the consummate champion of talent and content. "I believe that talent is king because people don't watch TV, they watch talent, content, programming. The way you manage talent is to let them run their business to a large extent. If you have confidence in the talent of your managers, you do not intrude every time they make a decision."

Beyond capability in talent, Redstone looks for character and loyalty. "I look for someone I can trust, and who trusts me. And, I look for confidence, competence, and commitment."

To maintain a culture of innovation and creativity at Viacom, Redstone cultivates creative talent. "Where does great content come from? Creativity. And where does creativity come from? From people who work in creative environments and associate with creative leaders. We maintain a high degree of innovation and creativity because we also have a high degree of financial discipline—and one works right along side the other. But money is never the driver. Most talented people are not motivated primarily by money but by the desire to achieve, to win, to be the best, and to try to make a positive difference through their work every day. They have a sense of mission."

Redstone is a prime example as he continues to lead Viacom. "The word 'retirement' was somehow omitted from my dictionary. I love what I do. I'm surrounded by brilliant people, many of whom could run Viacom. I respect their views, and I want to hear them. If they disagree with me, I want to hear that too. And they don't hesitate to tell me. Naturally if they disagree, I want them to have some solid reasoning behind their position or point of view. But I respect and trust my team. I know I can trust them, and they know they can trust me. Mutual trust is the most important element in running a company. Without it, you lose. I would like to think that I'm making some kind of a dent in the universe for the better. I'm not sure that's the case. I know I try. And if you try, perhaps you succeed. But the best news is—I am not yet finished."

Talents versus Knowledge Workers

Most organizations do not know how to distinguish between their talents and knowledge workers. All talents are knowledge workers, but not all knowledge workers are talents. Talents are more than knowledge workers. To operate successfully, every organization needs both talents and knowledge workers. Knowledge workers may become talents through dedication and a well-defined goal, but most don't make the transformation. The following are seven differences between talents and knowledge workers.[3]

Talents Make and Break the Rules; Knowledge Workers Conserve the Rules

The main difference between talents and knowledge workers is that talents break the rules, create, initiate, invent, direct, and send—talents take initiative, they are proactive. Knowledge workers, in general, do not. Knowledge workers take orders. They are studious and obedient people. Just because a person is brilliant or has a Ph.D. does not mean that person is talented. One need not be a genius to be a talent.

In the 1950s, when W. Edwards Deming begged American companies to improve their quality, they didn't listen. He continued to beg into the 1980s, when corporate America finally listened. Of course, by then Japan had a 30-year head start, from which the Western world has never recovered. Deming identified incredible persistence as a key characteristic of talent. His ideas provided a great service to society but were slow to gain acceptance in the Western world.

Breaking the rules is not necessarily the road to glory and wealth. The dot-bombs broke all the rules of business leadership. Many had no visible means of actually making money by offering something for sale. They simply sold their ideas to people with money who clearly did not use diligence in recognizing unrealistic business plans. They broke the rules and bombed out at the expense of many broken lives.

Talents Create; Knowledge Workers Implement

Talents are your ingenuity source. They are creative. But creative talents need support from knowledge workers to make the products and services and get them to customers. For an example in a different arena, scientists are talents who do research with the help of associates (knowledge workers). In business organizations, knowledge workers help talents to transform ideas into reality.

Talents Initiate Change; Knowledge Workers Support Change

Talents can feel the need to initiate change before it becomes necessary to change. Talents generally initiate change within the organization. But talents need visionary knowledge workers who support the change. Without the support of knowledge workers, it would not be possible for talents to bring about the changes within the organization. Even the rare talents who can intertwine talent behaviors and knowledge worker behaviors as the circumstances demand need the support of additional knowledge workers to implement innovations and changes.

Talents Innovate; Knowledge Workers Learn

Talents innovate, and knowledge workers learn and apply those innovations in the organization. Talents are the teachers; knowledge workers are the good students. A talent may create a programming language and teach it to the knowledge workers, who would then learn, use, and refine the language.

Talents Direct; Knowledge Workers Act

Talents direct knowledge workers to perform the work. Good knowledge workers learn to deal with the idiosyncrasies that seem to be characteristic of talents. With the direction of talents, knowledge workers perform their work. Knowledge workers carry out the visions and marching orders of talents.

Talents Inspire and Lift People; Knowledge Workers Receive Information and Motivation

If you are a talented person, you likely want to help the next generation; you want to lift the people who work around you; you want to see those people become successful. And yet when some of those people fail, you become frustrated. Knowledge workers don't understand this. Often knowledge workers don't understand what talents are after because they are so different. Knowledge workers have to understand what talents are after, what their missions are. Unfortunately, talents are not always good at explaining their ideas and intents to their knowledge workers. No talent is perfect. Talents need to work on their weaknesses as they play to their strengths. If you are a talented manager, and you have 10 knowledge workers reporting to you, you need to take time to get them to share the excitement of the dream with you. Show them your love for what you do and pass that ball to them.

Talent Management System

The Talent Management System (TMS) is an effective tool for creating a symbiotic relationship between talent and the organization to dramatically accelerate performance improvements. The TMS is a distinct function within the organizational management system devoted exclusively to attracting, keeping, managing, and identifying talent.[4] It is administered by the management team in cooperation with the human resource function.

TMS elevates talent to a visible, exalted position to which others aspire. The TMS should be implemented and communicated as a big deal because it promotes distinct tracks for talents and other employees. The introduction of a TMS system could create commotion, gossip about the insensitivity of management to people's feelings, complaints of discrimination, outright rebellion, and work stoppages. But if introduced carefully, TMS can also cause people to recognize special contributors in meaningful ways.

Special tracks are not new. Most corporations identify high-potential employees (hi-pos) and put them on a hi-po track with a higher pay scale. Engineering organizations identify gifted engineers and put them on a "dual ladder" track that can extend upward through several vice presidential levels. The same for gifted scientists. Why not the same for other talents?

The TMS should be a powerful magnet to talents, demonstrating that the corporation cares about talents and their joy-of-work needs. The TMS is structured into four elements.

1. **Attracting Talent** describes how to become a strong magnet for talent. Here are seven ways organizations can attract talent.

   - Treat talent as customers.
   - Have a TMS.
   - Promise future reward and recognition with stock options, other ownership options, and performance-based pay packages.
   - Have a flexible work environment and positive culture.
   - Provide proper training and research facilities.
   - Practice visionary management and leadership.
   - Conduct performance reviews and succession planning.

   The single most important thing organizations can do to become more attractive to talent is to create a flexible work environment. To attract more talent, an organization needs to create an environment that attracts the most talented people to create the knowledge base needed in the organization. Rather than have narrow job functions—"This is the only thing I do and nothing else"—people should feel free to walk around. For example, even though they are working in the marketing organization, talented employees may go to product development and say, "Here is an idea." It may be wild, but the marketing people should still have the freedom to talk about it—and product development should consider the idea. For example, suppose you want to develop a car, and somebody in marketing comes up with a phenomenal car design and concept. There's nothing wrong with that. That's the kind of flexible work environment that attracts talent.

2. **Keeping Talent** describes how to create and maintain daily working environments in which talents can productively pursue the joy of work and financial benefits from contributions. Organizations keep talented employees by doing the following.

   - Treat talents as customers.
   - Compensate talents as preferred suppliers.
   - Offer the right compensation, including proper reward and recognition.
   - Conduct meaningful performance appraisals.
   - Design jobs to appeal to talented people.
   - Assign the right talent to the right jobs.
   - Choose the right location to attract and retain the right talent.

- Provide proper training, development, and succession planning.
- Provide a proper research facility.
- Balance age, race, gender, and color.
- Create a challenging environment or excitement in jobs.
- Communicate candidly without fear of reprisal.
- Provide unassigned time to seed and cultivate ideas.
- Create social bonds with talent through adventures, sports, games, contests, parties, and celebrations. For example, a former IBM manager used to take his 24 managers on a white-water rafting trip down the Colorado River each summer. He says, "When you're in white water together, and someone falls out of the raft, and you have to think how to get him back in, that creates deep bonding. At night, at a campsite that is far removed from cell phones and other distractions, the group can discuss different business strategies."

3. **Managing Talent** describes how to treat talents as customers and create opportunities and freedoms for talents to stretch for their dream, for the things that make big differences for the company and for society. Managing talents may seem a hopeless endeavor. Talents seek freedom and support, not managing. Again, think of talents as customers. You can't manage customers. You can only provide them with the goods and services they want and need. Determine their customer requirements. Ask talents what they believe is the most important thing they can do for the company. If it is within the boundaries of the strategic direction of the company, ask them what they need from you and then provide those needs instantly. Act quickly. Delays in service indicate that you don't care—not a message you want to send to temperamental customers.

   Managing talent has to be learned. Managers must know how to get the best out of people and how to strategically place them in the right position where they are not dragged down by routine work. Managers must provide the setting in which their talents can produce maximum knowledge and maximum innovation and have maximum impact. When strategically managed, talents will generate maximum return. Many companies don't bother to grow their own talent or have talent farms or other ways to grow talent because they don't have anything like a TMS. They think managing talent is the human resource manager's job. Many managers mistake "people who kiss up to the manager" for talents—and they may promote the wrong people. Whom you know becomes much more important than what you know or what you do. This is a common mistake. Don't let politics get in the way of making good decisions. The manager may have a hard time making the proper decision. Often, the employees will know the talent better than the manager does. There are a couple of easy ways to solve this problem. The simplest way is for the manager to get an unbiased read from the employees on who is doing the best work. If the manager does it regularly enough, the employees will let down their guard, and the communication will be best. Absent that level of communication, the manager may need a more formal way of ascertaining who might be most talented. The manager might need an independent unit led by a chief talent officer (CTO) who manages the talent. In addition, the company could establish a "Keep Talent Happy Council" headed by a CTO to provide the guidance and training of the management team. If the organization is having a difficult time analyzing, finding, managing, or keeping its most talented people, something along these lines is a good idea.

Treating talents as preferred suppliers by spectacularly compensating them for their spectacular contributions will also change the behaviors of the managers whom you wish to retain. The demand for talent places new demands on management. Managers who attract talent should be on the talent track. Those who repel talent should be somewhere else.

More organizations should have CTOs and talent management councils whose job will be to manage talent effectively inside and outside the organization. CTOs must hire the best, use the best, and keep the best. They manage talent effectively by treating talents as customers, they compensate talents as preferred suppliers, they choose the right talent for right job, they allow talent to focus on creating and applying knowledge, they create an emotional bond by touching the mind and emotions, they embrace a trust culture, they build trust by talking and listening to each other freely, they present positive challenges to their talents to increase their performance level—where "positive challenges" does not mean criticism or humiliation but rather constructive coaching and encouragement, they provide a continuous learning environment, they focus on performance, they reward talent immediately, they build a culture where talents can turn their dreams into reality, and they create a boundaryless organization where information can flow freely.

4. **Identifying Talent** describes three ways to identify visible and hidden talents: (a) notice and identify the obvious talents, (b) use a performance-based identification tool, and (c) use a test-based identification tool.

Talent shortage is often the biggest obstacle to a company's growth. More companies need to grow their own talent, instead of just hiring talent. Hiring talent away from a competitor creates a war mentality. In fact, the personnel market is often called the "war for talent" because companies are hiring (stealing) talent from their competitors. Some people cast an unmistakable aura of talent. Others are hidden by impersonal company bureaucracies or overbearing bosses. External people may or may not carry a brand as talent. Internal or external, put the obvious talents on the talent track with significant and immediate compensation appropriate to the talent track. When uncertain, go prospecting. Prospecting for scarce, valuable resources is an honorable profession. If your apparent gold turns out to be "fool's gold," throw it back and try again.

Year after year, I come across managers who do not know how to identify talented people. Over the years I have met many bright men and women, but management fails to use them effectively. They are frustrated talents and are therefore unproductive talents. If management does not use these talents properly, someone else will. Big benefits come from identifying talents within the company before hiring new employees.

Identifying your own talents before hiring new talents is beneficial because existing talents already know the strengths and weakness of the organization, they are already familiar with the culture, they already know what corrective steps are needed to improve, they take less time in action or implementation of any strategy or idea, and identifying them eliminates recruitment costs. If you still need to hire talent, and you almost certainly will, visible internal talent will help attract outside talent. Talent attracts talent.

Employees *can* change behaviors: Heads-down, obedient doers of what is asked can explode into dynamic leaders of big ideas that can make big differences to your corporation, if they are given freedom to explore and act; the encouragement to champion new ideas; support in championing ideas when the opposition gets tough; bosses who devote the time and energy to listen for understanding and even work on and add to talent's new ideas; or the experience of being rewarded with a "thank you" for out-of-the-box ideas rather than being chastised for wasting time on dreams—in other words, a whole new environment that fosters creativity, not just the daily grind of executing a project. Such environments have transformed wimps into tigers, really strong, agile talents. The challenge is to find the tigers hiding as wimps. It is certain that there are some such people within your organization. Find them and free them. That is what the TMS is all about.

Conversely, all employees have to be accountable for what they do. If some people don't perform, get rid of them. If you want to move fast, you have to get rid of dead weight. You can't afford people who just go to work from 8 to 5, check e-mail, or surf the Net. This is the flip side of what the TMS is all about.

Talents within the organization often stand out as different. Bosses, peers, and subordinates all recognize obvious talents. However, some talents are hidden by the system. Some talents are quiet, unassuming, and mild mannered. Such people are sometimes difficult to identify as talents. In these instances, other assessment tools can be used. The method of identifying talents is to pay attention, notice, explicitly identify them, and put them on the talent track.

Benefits of the TMS

New management systems that impact human resource practices often frighten management. Management fads don't always work, and getting a management system wrong can take down a company. Enormous benefits and minimal risk need to be shown.

The TMS can quickly transform an organization from an also-ran or a laggard to a world-class leader. The TMS is designed to minimize risk. It is a small overlay on whatever system is in place. The overlay resides primarily with line management, not human resources. Human resources picks up some new administrative responsibilities, such as introducing and maintaining a new system that promotes inequities between talents and others. This is not a new challenge. Hi-po and dual ladder tracks are the norm in manufacturing corporations. The suggested talent track is no different. Special tracks are very manageable when the portion of the population in them is small and clearly distinguished from the general population. By definition, the talent population will always be small because talent is defined by a high level of contribution compared with the level of contribution of the rest of the population. If the overall level of capability rises, the bar for talent status also rises.

The benefits winnow down to winning or losing. In long races, the best talent with the fastest vehicle wins. The vehicle is the corporation. Being fastest means changing faster than the toughest competitors. XYZ analysis, defined in my book, *The Talent Era,* indicates that 60 to 70% of contributions come from 5 to 10% of the employees, the talents. The TMS will create enormous excitement.

1. Management behaviors will immediately change, at least for those you want to keep. The concept of treating talent like customers completely changes the paradigm about the roles of employees and managers. Envision writing a stage play about telling a manager that she is now the supplier of "joy of work" to temperamental customers called talents.

2. The TMS will be a strong magnet for attracting and keeping talent.

3. Nontalents will aspire to become talents. They will seek guidance about how they can improve to be worthy of becoming a candidate for moving to the talent track, hi-po track, or dual ladder track.

4. Hidden talents will become visible. The silent ones will feel safe in coming forward.

5. External talents will be knocking on your door to get in.

6. If you are first or second in creating a significant talent pool among practitioners and managers, then your organization will develop a reputation of being the absolutely best place in the world to work. Then you can further increase your talent pool. Of course, the opportunity to leverage early successes

to spiral up is accompanied by the opportunity to trail behind and spiral down.

7. Talent can go anywhere, and most of them know it. Be the first to make a big splash about your new TMS oriented around treating talent like the customers that they are. Then advertise: "We know that you have more attractive opportunities than you can investigate. So do we. We need more talent. We are truly different. Our very livelihood depends on talent. We are different, we need you, we know we need you, and we will behave in ways that you want us to behave. And that's different."

8. Be first. Catch the best talent.

Challenging Environment

What do talents want and need from your organization? If you already know the answer to this question, then your organization must be brimming with talents. If you enjoy a market leadership position, you have a strong foundation from which you can build faster than your competitors. If, however, you are having difficulty attracting and keeping talents, perhaps it is useful to review the wants and needs expressed by talents from other organizations.

People factors dominate. Talents consistently cite three needs above all others. The first is coworkers and bosses with whom they can develop a mutual respect and trust, learn from, bang around ideas with, and collaborate with. The second most-cited need is freedom from micromanagement. Few people enjoy being overly managed. Talents will not tolerate micromanagement and bosses constantly looking over their shoulder and providing unsolicited "how to" advice. Talents want and need—and often demand—freedom to work, freedom to make mistakes, freedom to learn, freedom to innovate, and freedom to pursue the joy of work. The third key need is freedom from fear. Talents shy away from organizations that exhibit even tiny amounts of fear. Fear is a strong negative attribute, and it instantly repels talent.

Other needs include freedom to pursue ideas and passions; a strong culture of values like honesty, trust, respect, fairness, love, kindness, and compassion; freedom to participate in outside activities such as professional societies or universities to stay current and continue to learn; pay for performance; competitive compensation and in some cases opportunities for large awards for large contributions; and a dynamic, changing organization with a winning attitude.

You can attract talent and manage talent, but the question at the end of the day is, "Are your talented people growing, or do they feel that they don't need to grow?" This is a growth rule that applies to people who are not talented as well as to people who are talented. Many people are too fearful to challenge their bosses. Historically, this has not been a winning move. Sometimes bosses may not challenge talented people due to lack of knowledge.

Most managers talk about challenge, but few really practice it. When I talk to middle and senior managers, they talk about creating a challenging environment, but when I talk to them individually and ask, "How many times do you challenge your boss? How many times do you say, 'We aren't doing this right, this is the way it should be'?" I don't find that. An environment of fear will stifle the creativity of the people and will allow bad processes to continue. Talented people respond well to positive challenge. Talent has a "what's next?" mentality. If somebody challenges me, I can learn something from it, and I can do something better.

Positive challenges enhance the performance of talent. Challenging someone based on knowledge represents a positive challenge. Sometimes bosses criticize their subordinates without the proper knowledge or data—a negative challenge. When colleagues challenge each other, they learn from each other and share their knowledge. This is a positive challenge.

Positive challenges increase the knowledge of talents. Knowledge grows faster within the company. Intellectual assets appreciate faster. A continuous learning environment is created, bureaucracy is limited, and trust is built, allowing talents to share more with each other.

Rather than kiss up to their boss, talents seek to challenge their boss. Some people always want to please their boss by accepting their boss's strategy and directives without question. They always obey their boss—wrong or right. They think that if they blindly follow their boss, they will be rewarded. If talents don't believe what their boss says, they do not accept it.

Every corporation faces competition in every aspect of business, and this competition will only increase in the future. To compete with these outside challenges, organizations need to create an internal challenging environment where talents challenge each other positively and create the right strategy, the right products, and the right services. Positive challenges help a company face challenges from competitive organizations by increasing efficiencies, performance, and knowledge of the people. Positive challenges create better products, strategies, and services. Positive challenges create a sense of urgency to create something better.

To create a challenging environment, organizations must

1. Bury bureaucracy and rigid hierarchy.
2. Try to attract and keep true talents.
3. Create a continuous learning environment.

4. Reward performance.
5. Remove color, race, age, and gender barriers.
6. Create a fearless environment.

As a manager without challenge, you may not know that what you believe is right. What happens if you do not know the solution to a specific problem? If you have been constantly challenged, you will know whom to go to for the right answers, the honest answers. Challenges help validate or refute beliefs. You have a team whose ideas and opinions you value. The team will help you solve your problem. But when you face a challenge, you will have to prove your viewpoint based on knowledge and performance. Challenge is also a way of finding talent or understanding what level of talent you have in the organization. Nontalents avoid challenge because they fear that if somebody challenges them, and they don't have an answer, they might lose their jobs, or their boss won't be happy. You have probably seen the "I don't know" dance. The challenged person dances all around the question or challenge without responding directly to it in an effort to cover his or her ignorance. You can create an environment that has just the right challenge. Every talent has to be held accountable for performance by earning a high talent score, knowing that the organization needs a high return on talent.

Create an environment with little bureaucracy. Yes, you will still have a boss, but you can open your boss's door or send him or her an e-mail anytime. If you believe you have a better idea than your boss, then your boss should be totally open to it. However, much of the time the boss is not so open to new ideas that challenge his own thinking. He may even withhold rewards for exceptional performance. If people do their jobs much better than expected, they should be rewarded for their performance. When nontalents see that talents are bringing challenges to the environment and that they are being rewarded for it, then the nontalents will either improve or self-select out of the environment.

PART 1

21C LEADER

oday's CEOs are deeply concerned about 21st century leadership in global organizations. However, there exists little consensus as to what a 21st century global leader really is, or how to create a *global* organization as opposed to a *multinational* one. In addition, as yet there is little understanding of how 21st century global leaders develop. In an authoritative way, distinguished professor Manfred F. R. Kets de Vries and researcher Elizabeth Florent-Treacy, both of INSEAD's campus in France, open the first part of this book with an excellent chapter that is a broad study of the distinguishing characteristics of a global leader, global leadership development, and the interaction of successful global leaders and "global followers" in global organizations. They also reminded us that even in the 21st century, there is no *leadership* without *followership*.

In the rapidly changing global competitive arena, sustainable competitive advantage depends on the ability of employees across all regions of the world to implement increasingly complex competitive strategies. Does every manager need to be "global?" Who really needs global brains and to what extent? Managers are not "born global"; they acquire "global brains" through a series of experiences, many of them at a substantial cost to the organization. What is the return on investing in developing people with global brains? Eminent IMD Switzerland professor Vladimir Pucik boldly announces that global mindset is not just part of a vision statement, it is the way a company makes strategic decisions and goes about implementing them. In this thought-provoking chapter, he defines what global mindset is, how to develop it through human resource strategies, and finally, how to implement a global mindset.

Why have considerations of leadership now become central to the growth and development of today's corporations? Europe's leading authority on leadership and Britain's Cranfield University professor Andrew Kakabadse makes a strong argument that leadership cannot solely concentrate on the individual. Considerations of leadership, whether concerned with the individual or with the team of which the individual is a member, will need to be linked to a broader concept of enterprise value, be that shareholder or stakeholder value. His analysis focuses on how the development of the corporate organization is likely to demand the application of particular leadership philosophies and practices to ensure the survival and prosperity of the enterprise. He concludes that in the 21st century organization, team-based leadership is an absolute necessity, not a luxury.

The difference between leadership and management is not just semantic. In his chapter, Yale School of Management professor Victor H. Vroom clarifies the ambiguities in the term "leadership," evaluates the principal approaches to understanding it, and explicates his belief in the fundamental importance of a contingency approach to leadership to the effectiveness of organizations in the 21st century. He wraps up the first part of the book with a powerful illustration of a contingency approach by summarizing the highlights of a research program spanning several decades on the age-old problem of styles of leadership. Vroom concludes that the matching of personal qualities and situational challenges is indispensable to the development of viable technologies for helping organizations in the selection and development of effective leaders.

2

Global Leadership from A to Z

Manfred F. R. Kets de Vries
Elizabeth Florent-Treacy

CEOs have downsized, restructured, flattened, networked, and—now more than any other time in history—feel ready to conquer the world. But...are they *really* ready? Although it would be foolish to deny that the global organization is the paradigm for organizations of the future, it is still hard to predict who the winners will be when the dust settles. Though a global orientation appears to be the *sine qua non* for success, the truly global organization—a relatively new phenomenon—lies in largely uncharted territory, despite all the declarative hype.

Not surprisingly, many organizational stakeholders are deeply concerned about leadership in global organizations. In addition, although many organizations put a high priority on identifying potential global leaders among their young managers, as yet there seems to be little understanding of how global leaders develop and how they interact with what we call global followers. We have found that it is only when *global leaders* establish a state of complementarity with *global followers* can we speak of a *global organization* in its truest sense.

In this chapter we intend to look deeper into this state of complementarity. We have identified many questions to be explored in this context. For example, what—if anything—distinguishes an exceptional leader from an exceptional *global* leader? How do (and should) the global leader and the global organization interface? Given that the old "psychological contract"— lifetime employment in exchange for loyalty to the company—is no longer possible, how can contemporary CEOs recreate a modicum of stability, loyalty, and meaning in the cultural diversity of the global organization? What does *excellence* mean in a global organization, and by what criteria should it be judged?

Many factors have a significant influence on the global organization—for good or for ill. Cultural dimensions affect leadership style, but so do followers' wishes, motivational needs, values, beliefs, attitudes, and behaviors. This fact raises another set of questions: How does the global leader defuse the anxiety that rapid change creates in followers? What are the dimensions of the new psychological contract that will allow employees—no matter where they are located in the world—to become fully engaged and productive? Our objective in this chapter is to address this set of questions by drawing on our extensive interventions in global organizations and interviews with global leaders.[1]

The Competencies of the Global Leader

Because the concept of global leadership is fairly new, researchers and global organizations alike are asking similar questions: What exactly is a global organization? Is there such a thing as a truly *global* leader? How should companies in this day and age choose people to be their future leaders? Are there specific qualities or qualifications that indicate high potential for global leadership? How can companies ensure that those chosen will be culturally adaptable and operate competently across borders? What does the term "global mindset" really mean? Are leaders of global organizations born or made?

It has become increasingly clear that leaders cannot be studied meaningfully in isolation from their surroundings. It is essential to differentiate between those leadership characteristics that are nonculturally contingent and those that are valid only in a limited cultural context. Many people would agree that a "leader" could be defined as being a rational, directive, pragmatic, cost-driven, hierarchical, male (or female who "thinks like a man") technocrat with a short-term time orientation. Yet upon closer inspection, we realize that this description is derived from observing the successful behavior of political and business leaders of the most powerful nation in the world—the United States.[2] This is a nearsighted approach, since the value Americans place on extreme individualism and on participatory management is often in opposition to leadership practices in other parts of the world.[3]

For example, as Asian and Pacific Rim countries began to outperform the United States and Europe economically in the 1980s, attention turned toward Asian management practices. Rooted in ancient Confucian tradition, they seemed to provide a significant competitive advantage, appearing (at least for some time) to be more effectively adapted to that region than Western practices. It became obvious that Asian leaders had a different set of values—particularly persistence and perseverance, the ordering of relationships by status (and the preservation of this order), and thrift. Persistence and perseverance indicate tenacity in the pursuit of goals, ordering relationships by status ensures loyalty and interrelatedness, and thrift leads to availability of financial resources.[4]

In addition, some of the most successful male global leaders have traits and values that are often labeled *feminine* in the West. These include interdependence, humility, and a respect for the overall quality of life (including concern for the environment). In our own studies of female leadership, we have observed women's greater willingness to empower people; greater effectiveness in networking; greater realism regarding personal limitations (implying a lesser degree of narcissism); concern about a balanced lifestyle; and their broader, more humanistic vision of how to construe life in organizations.

If we distill the aforementioned observations to arrive at a kind of "essence of leadership," we find that there are some universal leadership characteristics. The most effective leaders take on two roles: a *charismatic* role (consisting of envisioning, empowering, and energizing) and an *architectural* role (designing the organization, setting up structures, and formulating control and reward systems).[5] A set of behavioral characteristics—which contribute to specific emotional and cognitive "competencies"—differentiate exceptional leaders from other people and allow them to assume these roles. These behavioral characteristics include *surgency* (a broad term that embraces competitiveness, achievement orientation, self-assuredness, and dominance), agreeableness, conscientiousness, emotional stability, and intelligence (including emotional intelligence).[6] Exceptional leaders also tend toward controlled extroversion and have a great deal of physical energy.[7] Finally, they feel that they have control over the events in their lives (*internality*).[8]

In our work with top executives, we have found that the new global leaders have all the qualities of exceptional leaders just discussed. However, excellent leadership qualities alone are not enough.[9] The global organization, as we have pointed out, is a fairly new type of organizational structure. Before looking into the specific traits of the global leader, it would be wise to discuss what we mean by the term *global organization*.

The Global Organization

As domestic organizations began to look toward foreign markets in the postwar period, the fundamental challenge that faced them was balancing the economic advantages of global integration with the political imperative of dealing with foreign stakeholders.[10] There were two apparent options: a global strategy or a country-centered strategy. Globalization seemed to be the better choice. There were trends toward increasing homogenization of products across countries, as well as marketing systems and business infrastructure. Transportation was becoming cheaper and more reliable. Improved telecommunications and computer systems sped up all processes.[11] However, organizations were soon faced with a growing counter-trend toward a more nationally oriented strategy, fueled by the growing number of powerful foreign stakeholders. Organizational leaders had to worry not only about their subsidiaries' viability (e.g., meeting profit objectives), but also about their legitimacy (i.e., stakeholder perceptions as to whether the firm's activities are consonant with the values of the host country).[12]

In response, organizations moved from an *ethnocentric* predisposition (all strategic decisions guided by the values and interests of the headquarters and the home country; focus on *profitability*) to a more *polycentric* predisposition (strategic decisions tailored to suit the culture of the various countries in which the organization competes; focus on *legitimacy*). Ultimately, though, this decentralization proved to be difficult to control. For example, in the 1970s, Procter & Gamble came out with a new laundry soap. Unilever's decentralized, national detergent companies responded to the challenge and came up with 13 new soaps—but Unilever soon realized that the development costs were extremely high, and not one of their new products was as good as Procter & Gamble's.[13]

More recently, in the past 15 years or so, a growing number of organizations have become more *geocentrically* oriented, meaning they focus on both profit and legitimacy; governance is mutually negotiated at all levels; communication is vertical and lateral; allocation of resources is decided by both local and headquarters management; strategy focuses on global integration and national responsiveness; the structure consists of a network of organizations; the best people everywhere in the world are developed for key positions anywhere in the world; and finally, the culture is global.[14] Throughout this chapter, when we use the term "global organization," we are referring to this kind of geocentric orientation, and we will focus on the specific skills and qualifications that are demanded of successful global leaders of this type of organization.

A Definition of Leadership

In the context of the global organization, the homegrown, up-through-the-ranks, insular CEO of the past is an anachronism. For example, as we said earlier, standard U.S.-based definitions of excellent leadership fall short in a global context. Everyone knows apocryphal horror stories about "star" CEOs who speak only English, depend on Hilton hotels, and only eat familiar foods wherever they are in the world. What has amazed us in our research and consulting is how often we find real evidence of this kind of behavior and attitude, and how this can seriously affect or derail subsidiary–headquarter relationships, or even once-promising mergers and acquisitions. We find examples almost weekly of top executives who can hardly be considered global leaders, no matter how brilliant their domestic record might be or how many international trips they log in a year. We know of an American Fortune 500 high-tech organization whose French R&D subsidiary executives refer to the American vice presidents' and directors' visits to France as the arrival of the "elephants." In other instances, headquarters-based directors rely on others for information on what is happening in their foreign subsidiaries. They run the risk of alienating foreign employees, who may see their leaders as "corporate cultural imperialists" and feel themselves to be a sort of corporate underclass. As a result, these executives rarely develop the kind of understanding of local markets that will give them an edge over competitors.

It is crucial, then, that companies choose excellent leaders who are also culturally adaptable and able to operate competently across borders. The new organizational paradigm requires cross-functional and cross-cultural process skills. These competencies are essential because global leaders must rise above the particularities of many regions and national cultures while at the same time meeting the expectations of followers in those different cultures. Global CEOs who are dazzled by numbers and neglect to take into consideration the human factor—and that includes the cross-cultural dimension—do so at their own peril.

As an example of that danger, we can point to the 1995 merger between two pharmaceutical firms, one Swedish and one American, that formed Pharmacia & Upjohn. This merger—a likely winner, on the face of things—did not meet expectations for several years. An inability to deal with cultural differences was generally cited as one of the reasons for American chairman John Zabriskie's departure in 1996. It was not until a CEO with a global background—Fred Hassan, born in Pakistan, educated in England, veteran of two other U.S. pharmaceutical companies—came on board in 1997 that Pharmacia & Upjohn began to fulfill its promise. Hassan's first move was one that we have documented many times for other successful global leaders: he visited subsidiaries and listened. He emphasized that, as an outsider, he had no favorites among the Pharmacia or Upjohn people. Hassan then streamlined overlapping departments and functions, which was painful at the time but resulted in increased sales and ultimately improved performance and morale.

In contrast, when British Petroleum faced a dramatic fall in consumer confidence and market share in the early 1990s, then-CEO Robert Horton devised an ambitious program to transform the organization. It looked good on paper, but it quickly became bogged down because employees felt that Horton was *imposing* change rather than *fostering* it. People felt out of touch, and many blamed Horton's "abrasive, American leadership style." (Horton is British, but spent many years in the United States.) Horton was replaced by David Simon, who was known for his friendly, reassuring manner. Simon's first action was to listen and to be accessible. He quickly earned a reputation as being a fair and trustworthy leader. One of the goals of the significant transformation process that followed was to create a very flat, team-based organization, consisting of small business units—grouped according to function not geographical boundaries—in which decision making was pushed down to local levels. Ironically enough, Simon continued the restructuring program designed by Horton—including divesting and downsizing—but this time people had confidence in their leader and the transformation was successful. After this internal transformation had been digested, BP went on to form important mergers in Europe and the United States—an example of global leadership built upon excellent internal leadership. Last but not least, we were not surprised to find that Simon also has a multicultural background; he is Welsh with a French stepfather and speaks five languages.[15]

Another interesting example is Coca-Cola, currently going through a dramatic shift in perspective under CEO Douglas Daft. His predecessor, Douglas Ivester, had underestimated the public relations damage done in Europe by allegedly contaminated cans of Coke found in Belgium in 1999. One of the first tasks Daft set for himself was to regain the confidence of Europeans. He went on a four-week "good-will tour" during which he met with officials to listen to their point of view. He learned that they felt Coca-Cola based its strategy on what was legally acceptable in the United States. Coke used "bulldozer behavior," showed contempt for European officials, and used "abrasive, domineering, and unacceptable American practices."

Daft's approach was unusual in that he deliberately went in not only to *discover* others' perspective on the company, but also to *integrate* this perspective into the organization's culture and future strategy. Inspired by his European tour, he quickly took action. He told executives they should think of the Coca-Cola corporation as a collection of villages, each with its own culture, but all part of one organization. He quickly replaced almost all of Coca-Cola's senior management in Europe with local people. He intends to have offices in Brussels and London as well as Atlanta, and work there regularly.[16]

Daft is aware that a large majority of Coca-Cola's profits are generated overseas, and the organization's continued growth depends on its good standing in foreign countries. Daft sees his most important leadership role as being to change the image of a corporation often considered outside the United States to be arrogant and overly aggressive; he will focus on gaining the confidence of both Coca-Cola clients and employees throughout the world. In a clear example of global as opposed to multinational leadership, Daft has realized that his job as CEO is to create an egalitarian and symbiotic organization in which the whole is greater than the sum of its parts.

From our study of these and many other global leaders, we have found that successful global leaders have certain qualities above and beyond those found in excellent domestic or multinational leaders.

- A strategic awareness of, and deep interest in, the socioeconomic and political scene of the countries in which they operate.
- Excellent relational skills, including verbal and nonverbal communication across cultures.
- Physical hardiness (global leadership requires a great deal of travel and adaptation).
- Resilience and a high tolerance for frustration and uncertainty.
- Cultural relativity, including an awareness of their own biases.
- Curiosity about different cultures, and a willingness to adjust their own behavior where necessary.
- A "teddy-bear" quality that makes them accessible and trustworthy to followers from different cultures; the willingness and ability to *listen*.

It could be argued that excellent domestic leaders also have many of these qualities; these leaders often work with diverse groups with specific identities (e.g., people with firm ties to Hispanic or Asian communities). We observed, however, that global leaders retain these capabilities even when they find themselves in *completely unfamiliar* situations (e.g., on a personal level, functioning effectively in countries where they don't speak the language; on an organizational level, operating in chaotic markets in developing economies). Furthermore, such leaders *search out* unfamiliar situations as a way of continually challenging themselves and their organizations. An oil executive working with subsidiaries in Texas, California, and Alaska will certainly face obstacles, but the executive dealing with guerillas in Columbia or oligarchs in Azerbaijan who are exploring new oil fields will be confronted with difficulties that are in a different category altogether.

The Development of the Global Leader

Though it seems clear that exceptional global leaders have specific competencies and character traits, we think it is important to understand how these qualities develop. Most global organizations have procedures (whether formal or informal) for testing a candidate's aptitude for a global

leadership career. Candidates are often selected according to their performance in the organization in their country of origin, their self-described
desire for an international post, or simply because they have no depen-
dants. Candidates chosen for such training are then nurtured by the prevailing corporate culture, which—at its best—is a kind of ladder, providing
support and encouragement for global leadership development. However,
it is essential to understand that the foundation for the development of the
exceptional global leadership practices described earlier is laid in childhood
experiences, which in turn are affected by cultural socialization patterns, all
of these exposures consecutively building on each other. Early managerial
responsibilities and international projects *foster* (not *create*) global leadership competencies by building on that foundation. We would go so far as to
argue that if the right foundation is lacking in a given individual, "global
leadership" training within the organization will be of little use. In the
selection of future global leaders, global organizations would do well to
look into the backgrounds of potential high-flyers, scrutinizing early childhood and educational experiences.

Tradition, Training, Transfer, Teamwork, and Travel

By *tradition*, we mean the early influences that shape a young manager's
world view. The more intercultural experiences children have early in life,
the more likely they are to develop the kind of cultural empathy necessary
for effective leadership in a global setting. Because of the impact of early
socialization, exposure in childhood to different nationalities and languages
can be a determining factor in how well an adult deals with cultural diversity later in life. Children of mixed-culture marriages, bilingual parents, or
diplomats or executives who move frequently also have an advantage.

Training, Transfer, Teams, and Travel

These four elements most often occur together. At a preliminary stage of a
young executive's career, international executive training courses have
become almost a requirement for future global leaders. Many organizations
send their high flyers to an MBA program such as that offered at INSEAD,
a business school in Fontainebleau, France, that has no national identity
and is a breeding ground for attitudes of cultural relativity. INSEAD students work in mixed-nationality teams over their 10-month course; a typical
group might include one American, one Frenchman, one Russian, one Japanese, one Swede, and one Brazilian. They spend part of the program at
the Singapore campus. As these individuals work together on various
projects, they develop the necessary cross-cultural mindset, minimizing
ethnocentricity.

On-the-Job Training

On-the-job training offers an education of another sort, and it is no less vital. Exposure to international leadership experiences early in one's career is important (by *experiences* we mean concrete project responsibility). This experience should include working with multicultural teams. Such experiences hone a person's capacity to cope with difficult leadership challenges later in the career cycle. Travel, for pleasure and business, is essential, as are transfers that stretch young executives in new ways, especially if they occur in conjunction with an internationally oriented human resource system and an organizational support system conducive to the management of global careers. (This support system must take into consideration the family situation of the global executive, just as the hiring process must include criteria for selection according to that situation. The spouse or partner must be supportive, adaptable, adventurous, and mobile. Children are also an extremely important factor. The hard truth is that the majority of expatriate assignments that fail do so because the family of the executive cannot adapt.) This kind of early international experience is a good test of a young manager's global leadership potential.[17]

Nokia is a good example of an organization that looks for young employees with a firm grasp of cultural relativity and then provides opportunities for people to develop their leadership potential. This organization goes even further, providing continuing opportunities for older executives.

As the number-one maker of mobile phones in the world, Nokia is now a household name. The 136-year-old Finnish company, once a manufacturer of everything from rubber boots and toilet paper to TVs, transformed itself under CEO Jorma Ollila into a producer of cutting-edge mobile phones. A large part of Nokia's success is due to its ability to turn from a provincial organization with 60% of its business in Finland 10 years ago into a truly global organization with only 4% of its activity in Finland in 1999. Of the 44,000 employees hired in the past three years, half work outside Finland. The organization is flat and highly decentralized, with R&D centers in Japan, the United Kingdom, and Finland; factories in Texas and China; and a design center in California.

Innovation on a global scale is a core value at Nokia; not surprisingly, global leadership is a key preoccupation among the members of the board. They take a leading role—as faculty members—in the Panorama Leadership Program, an action-learning program for senior executives. A central feature of the program involves giving executives greater geographical familiarity. Each year, one module of the program takes place in a different area of the world—an area in which the company wants greater market penetration or which is viewed as a potential provider of new technology skills. Thus executives have to spend time in, for example, China, Japan, or the United States. These seminars, which help to create multicultural groups, represent the kind of cross-cultural exposure that has put Nokia at the forefront of the industry.

Companies like Nokia stand out as exceptional organizations that are far-sighted enough to devote time and money to identifying and developing truly global leaders. These organizations are ahead of the game because they already have in place a set of values, attitudes, and behavior patterns that center on cross-cultural empathy. They have gone to great lengths to hire and build up a critical number of globally competent employees—the pool from which leaders of the future will come.

Contrast these leading global firms with companies that use their foreign subsidiaries as parking lots for redundant employees when times are lean at home. Or compare them with companies that send expatriates to take charge when an expensive and important new factory or project is due to come on line in a subsidiary, passing over the local employees who did the initial groundwork. Predictably, the local executives resent such decisions and act accordingly; the expats (and their families) are equally unhappy, stressed by a hasty move to an unfamiliar environment with little prepara-tion (a cursory language program at best) and often culturally isolated in an expat "ghetto," with no guarantee of a job in their home country when the foreign assignment is finished.

The global mindset of the organization, as these examples illustrate, is—and should be—shaped from the top, though that shape will vary from company to company. For Percy Barnevik, former chairman of ABB, a strong corporate culture is a great equalizer. At ABB, the culture was codi-fied—a kind of Rosetta stone—in ABB's policy "bible." This 21-page docu-ment describes ABB's values; among them, how ABB should create a global culture, what can be done to understand others, the benefits of mixed nationality teams, and how to avoid being turf defenders. ABB's official lan-guage is English, although Barnevik used to remind native speakers to be patient with colleagues who are less proficient.

One of the indicators that an organization is truly global is the number of nationalities represented on its board. Most U.S. organizations with global operations still have boards composed entirely of Americans. The same point can be made of many European and Asian corporations. A mixed-nationality executive board shows the outside world that the organization is committed to globalization and integrates different perspectives, and it offers an antidote to signs of ethnocentricity within the organization. It also demonstrates that the top jobs are not the exclusive bailiwick of certain nationalities. Most important, a truly global board can accomplish the func-tion of effective decision making based on diverse perspectives.

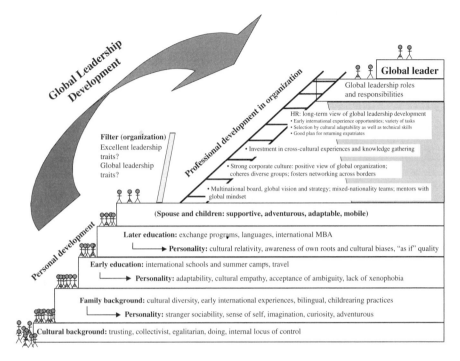

Figure 2–1   An overview of the developmental action steps involved in the making of a global leader.

There is no easy solution to the development of leaders in a global age, but companies that carefully select and strategically develop people with global leadership qualities (like Nokia) and use them at all levels in the organization will have a competitive edge sooner rather than later. (See Figure 2–1 for an overview of the developmental action steps involved in the making of a global leader.)

New Global Organizations

So far we have looked at the development and character traits of the global leader, but we believe that this is only one side of the coin. It is essential to remember that there is no *leadership* without *followership*. As the old saying goes, for want of a horseshoe nail the kingdom was lost. This holds true in global organizations—all employees, down to the shop floor, must feel part of the global team. How can a global leader acquire the loyalty of the thousands or hundreds of thousands of employees in his organization throughout the world? The dilemma facing any leader is how to assemble a solid organization out of many different individuals—different puzzle pieces, as it were. This problem is even more complex on a global scale.

Global Leadership Best Practices

Global leaders draw on their competencies (discussed earlier) to create multicultural organizational communities. Given their own backgrounds and unique perspectives, they are able to establish a corporate culture that transcends differences and establishes a number of "beacons"—values and attitudes—that are comprehensible to employees from diverse cultural groups. We have found that successful global leaders understand there are a number of common denominators, or basic desires, that all human beings have in common. These basic desires include a feeling of *attachment* or human connectedness, taking *pleasure* in learning and doing new things as an antidote to their existential anxiety, and a sense of usefulness or *meaning* to life. The meeting of these universal human desires is the foundation on which global leaders build to foster loyalty, motivation, and exceptional performance.

We have observed on many occasions that when the human desires for attachment, pleasure, and meaning are being met in a global organization, employees feel a greater sense of self-determination, greater sense of impact, greater sense of competence (implying feelings of personal growth and development), greater sense of belonging, greater sense of enjoyment, and a conviction that their individual contribution is valuable. In such organizations, cultural barriers and boundaries fall, and people are motivated to put their imagination and creativity to work. They more easily discover a feeling of total involvement and commitment; they experience a deep sense of meaning about the work they do. In these organizations, the desires for attachment, pleasure, and meaning can also be considered the meta-values that provide the foundation for global leadership best practices.

Attachment

A corporate culture based on trust and mutual respect in turn fosters attachment among individuals in groups. In addition, a *trusting* culture facilitates a *learning* culture—one where people are permitted to make mistakes and to learn from them, and to learn best practices from nontraditional and often unexpected sources (maybe even their own colleagues from a different country). This blend of trusting and learning results in distributed leadership—leadership that is spread throughout the organization and across geographical boundaries, and shared among leaders and followers alike.

We studied a Dutch shipping company in which the meta-value of attachment is easily recognizable. A new leader took the company through a remarkable turnaround from a demoralized loss-maker—one described as "fossilized," "arthritic," and "a snake pit"—to a very profitable, market-focused organization. She surprised people by creating a culture in which trust and open communication were priorities—a focus nearly unheard of in this male-dominated industry.

Even when it comes to meta-values, however, a leader must be culturally sensitive. An example of this is an organization we studied in which the meta-value of attachment took a form that was diametrically opposed to what we found in the Dutch company. We visited a Russian factory that had been acquired by a French multinational. The new CEO sent in to lead the transformation process had gone about it in an unexpected way. Owing to his own French–Russian mixed-cultural background, he knew that the Russian employees were not ready for empowerment or participatory management. Accustomed to job security at whatever cost, their primary concern was for stability, and they looked to strong leadership to protect them from the turbulence in Russia. Although they are in no way "empowered" according to the Western definition, we found that even at the shop-floor level employees spoke of how their new leader is a man they respect and trust, and they are proud to be a part of a French global organization. Their CEO's actions contributed to the establishment of a sense of community.

Pleasure

When pleasure is a meta-value in a global organization, the distinction between work and play is blurred. The leaders of these companies recognize that when people have fun in a pleasant atmosphere, they not only work harder but are also more creative, more innovative, and nicer to customers. An atmosphere of controlled exuberance can be highly motivating.

Insightful executives in high-performance organizations, of whom Richard Branson of Virgin is a prime example, realize that turning work into an exciting adventure can make all the difference to employee attitudes and productivity. Branson said of Virgin, "We've done things differently, and that's made life more fun and enjoyable than if we'd taken a more traditional approach that business schools teach. I've been determined to have a good time."

Fun encourages cross-cultural networks and friendships, helping to break down barriers among people who must get to know and trust each other to accomplish a goal. Good fun is also a release from stress and pressure, allowing people to step back and put things in perspective.

Meaning

Successful leaders of global organizations make it clear that they want their people to feel proud of their organizations and of their personal contribution to something worthwhile. Percy Barnevik once said that he was motivated by a desire to make a better world by creating employment (particularly in Eastern Europe) and by providing clean energy and transportation. BP recently took out full-page color advertisements in major newspapers describing their emphasis on environmental responsibility, closing with their new slogan: BP—Beyond Petroleum. Nokia is in the business of connecting people—and is a major player in China, with projects for taking millions of people from no phones (no infrastructure) to mobile phones, significantly changing lives in the process. When people see their jobs as transcending their own personal needs (e.g., by improving the quality of life for others or by contributing to society)—in other words, when the meta-value of meaning is honored—the impact can be extremely powerful.

Soft Processes, Hard Results

We have found that successful global leaders have fostered the meta-values we described earlier while putting in place a global strategy. In their own search for meaning, the leaders of these companies created a vision that clarifies what the organization stands for, highlights the organization's fundamental purpose for existing, and outlines the values and beliefs that define the organization's corporate culture.

To summarize, the essence of our argument is that the core culture of top-performing global organizations is fundamentally different from those with average performance. A survey of the business press supports this observation. For *Fortune*'s "Most Admired Global Companies," key priorities are teamwork, customer focus, fair treatment of employees, initiative, and innovation. In the more *average* listed companies, top priorities are minimizing risk, respecting the chain of command, supporting the boss, and making budget.[18] Additional criteria for a company's inclusion on *Fortune*'s most admired list are "the level of trust, pride, and camaraderie that employees share with management and their peers, as well as what practices the company has in place to support those things."[19] Not surprisingly, these organizations have very healthy balance sheets as well; hard results based on soft practices. Our own extensive observations have shown that leaders of these organizations are people like Percy Barnevik, Douglas Daft, or David Simon—people with a multicultural background, years of cross-cultural work experience, and the exceptional global leadership traits we discussed earlier.

In their roles as change agent, cheerleader, coach, teacher, mentor, and integrator, these CEOs change the way their people work by helping them to reframe their attitude toward work. They instill in their employees a kind of pride that goes beyond the numbers game. They foster corporate values with a crucial emphasis: their organizations work through team effort, not autocracy. Perhaps a better metaphor for many of these global organizations is that of the jazz combo. All the employees play together, but for each player in these organizations there is ample room to improvise as a soloist. The focus is on *process:* constructing the kind of high-performance, learning organization that encourages innovation based on individual contribution.

Playwright–dissident Václav Havel obviously knows something about the significance of meta-values in the new global world. He made the following comments upon assuming the presidency of Czechoslovakia on New Year's Day 1990:

> The recent past…has shown the enormous human, moral, and spiritual potential: the civic culture that has slumbered in our society beneath the mask of apathy. Whenever someone categorically claimed that we were this or that, I always objected that society is a very mysterious creature and that it is not wise to trust the face it chooses to show you….[P]eople are never merely a product of the external world—they are always able to respond to something superior, however systematically the external world tries to snuff out that ability.[20]

It is our hope that we in the business community can nurture the kind of global leaders who will foster these meta-values in global organizations. Such global leaders, as part of their quest for meaning, will encourage a sense of community in their employees and a sense of continuity in their organizations, allow their employees to "play," give their employees the opportunity to express themselves creatively and fully, and highlight the value of organizational tasks. In addition, they will transmit to their employees a feeling of appreciation as individuals, a sense that their contributions make a difference. This congruence between inner and outer worlds will promote both individual and organizational health, laying the groundwork for a new psychological contract in global organizations.

3

Developing Global Leaders

Vladimir Pucik

A s firms compete globally, they face a multitude of new requirements for their organization and people, often being pushed in several contradictory strategic directions at once. To survive and prosper in the new globally competitive environment, companies are embracing closer regional and global integration and coordination.[1] At the same time, in the markets in which they compete, they face demands for increasing local responsiveness, flexibility, and speed. Consequently, building and sustaining organizational capabilities for global operations is a critical challenge for most firms operating across borders. To quote one of the early proponents of a global organization, the former CEO of ABB, Percy Barnevik: "We want to be global and local, big and small, radically decentralized with central reporting and control. If we can resolve those contradictions we can create real organizational advantage."[2]

In response to these tensions, leading global companies attempt to avoid the pendulum swinging between centralization and decentralization that often results in organizational paralysis. Rather than trying to balance the traditional organizational contradictions (e.g., trading some degree of integration for some degree of responsiveness), the best global competitors are attempting to maximize both dimensions, achieving global integration while remaining locally responsive. This can only be done by shifting away from structural solutions toward an acceptance of the global organization as a fluid and dynamic differentiated network.[3] The new approach is focused on management process, not on organizational structure and procedures. The key to unlocking this process is in the minds of people inside the global organization.

In the rapidly changing global competitive arena, sustainable competitive advantage depends on the ability of employees across all regions of the world to implement increasingly complex competitive strategies. The demands in the transnational vary from one subsidiary to another and from function to function, and one of the challenges is to respond to the need for differentiation. Headquarters rules and policies cannot cope with this differentiated reality, and yet needs for cohesion and fairness must be respected. This requires a particular intellectual orientation to business problems. We call the attitudes that underlie such thinking a "global mindset."

Let us illustrate the issue with an example from a rapidly globalizing European company. Several years ago, this leading provider of telecommunication infrastructure participated in a benchmark study on how managers perceive the company's global strategy. The survey showed that some parts of the organization, such as product business units, had a highly global orientation, whereas other parts, such as the sales companies in emerging markets, were strongly local. The reaction of some of the top executives was initially positive: "This is exactly the type of differentiation we need—strongly integrated product lines worrying about global economies of scale and locally oriented sales units worrying about local opportunities."

On reflection, however, their view changed. They realized that the consequence of this polarization was that conflicts were being pushed up to senior management for arbitration, overloading their own agendas, causing delays in decision making, and leaving little time to focus on institutional leadership. Although the product managers indeed needed to be global, they also had to understand the need to work through conflicts with local sales units—and vice versa. Meeting the organizational challenge of globalization required changes in cognitive processes through which managers framed business problems—to develop a more balanced perspective, the necessary global mindset.

What Is Global Mindset?

This argument is not new. It was proposed more than 30 years ago when researchers began to examine how corporations make decisions about foreign investments, and it parallels other research on managerial cognition.[4] Perlmutter developed the first formal outline of the orientations or mindsets of managers in multinational firms.[5] His now-classic typology of ethnocentric, polycentric, and geocentric orientations formed a framework for subsequent theoretical and empirical work. The future need was clearly for more "geocentric" managers, "the best men, regardless of nationality, to solve the company's problem anywhere in the world."[6] Since then many authors have argued that the cognitive orientation of managers has become a critical issue facing multinationals.

There are two different and complementary perspectives on global mindset, one rooted in a psychological focus on the development of managers in multinational firms, and the other coming from scholars and practitioners with a strategic viewpoint on the transnational enterprise. One concept of global mindset views it as the ability to accept and work with cultural diversity, leading to research that tries to map out the skill or competency sets associated with this. Scholars have observed that people with global mindsets tend to approach the world in ways that differentiate them from domestic managers.[7] Unlike firms with an ethnocentric mindset, a firm with a global mindset "accepts diversity and heterogeneity as a source of opportunity."[8]

Extensive lists of competencies that distinguish successful global managers have been developed.[9] Some examples include the championing of international strategy (visioning the future), acting as a cross-border coach (giving and receiving feedback from international teams), cognitive complexity (the ability to step back and see new patterns), and emotional maturity (being able to handle emotional crises). However, most of these lists are generic; they do not take into account the specific strategic focus of the firm. Although no one can disagree with the general desirability of such qualities and their relevance for managers in multinational firms, such all-encompassing use of the global mindset concept has stripped it of any distinct cognitive meaning.[10]

The strategic perspective on global mindset is more concerned with mirroring the dilemmas of the organization. Rather than focusing on general skill sets, it focuses on a way of thinking that reflects conflicting strategic orientations. Since most multinational firms face contradictions (the determining feature of the transnational enterprise), scholars have emphasized the need for "balanced perspectives," arguing that a critical determinant of success in such firms lies in the cognitive orientations of senior managers.[11]

> Diverse roles and dispersed operations must be held together by a management mindset that understands the need for multiple strategic capabilities, views problems and opportunities from both local and global perspectives, and is willing to interact with others openly and flexibly. The task is not to build a sophisticated structure, but to create a matrix in the mind of managers.[12]

The concept of "the matrix in the mind" vividly captures the notion of global mindset and the idea that contradictions cannot be resolved by structure but need to be built into the way of thinking of leaders and managers in the transnational firm. Thus, the strategic perspective on global mindset refers to a set of attitudes that predisposes individuals to balance the competing business, country, and functional priorities that emerge in international management processes, rather than to advocate any of these dimensions at the expense of the others. It involves recognizing that organizational resources are deployed across all subunits and places high value on sharing information, knowledge, and experience across boundaries.[13]

The concept of global mindset helps to differentiate between expatriate and global managers.[14] Expatriates are defined by *location*, as managers who are working in a different country from their own. Global managers, by contrast, are defined by their *state of mind*. They are people who can work effectively across organizational, functional, and cross-cultural boundaries. They are able to balance the simultaneous demands of global integration and local responsiveness. They are expected to have a hands-on understanding of global business and perceive global competition as an opportunity. Some global managers may be expatriates—most have been expatriates at some point in their careers—but not all expatriates are global managers. International management literature is full of examples of expatriates with an ethnocentric orientation.[15] At the same time, local managers in lead countries may not be expatriates, but they invariably need to have a global mindset.

Global or otherwise, the kind of mindset managers *do* need depends on the competitive position of the firm. Not all companies have to become transnational to do business across borders. A multidomestic or a meganational mindset may be just as appropriate, and a polarized mindset may serve a positive purpose at a particular stage of globalization. What matters is alignment and consistency.

Mapping Global Mindsets

The first step in developing a global mindset is to be able to measure it. Without measurements, it is not easy for organizations to act. Scales for measuring individual and organizational progress toward a global mindset were first developed and validated by Murtha and his colleagues.[16] The aim is to assess the key ingredient essential for the successful implementation of a global competitive strategy: the capacity of individuals to consider complex interactions and differences in the core global strategic process.

The main concepts behind the transnational enterprise are global integration, local responsiveness, and worldwide coordination. *Global integration* refers to the centralized management of dispersed assets and activities to achieve scale economies. *Local responsiveness* refers to decisions on resource commitments taken autonomously by a subsidiary in response to primarily local competitive, political, or customer demands. *Worldwide coordination* refers to the level of lateral interactions within and among the network of affiliates with respect to business, function, and value chain activities. Global mindset scales are used to capture these core dimensions.

The core global mindset scales can be used to investigate a number of critical questions pertaining to the progress of global strategies. For example,

- To what degree do area, country, functional, and business unit responsibilities account for differences among individuals in their understanding of corporate global objectives? Do managers in global product divisions conceptualize the importance of integration and responsiveness in the same way as managers in the country units? What about managers with international experience versus those with purely local careers?
- What is the overall congruence with the global strategic vision? The responses can show the extent to which the thinking of HQ, business units, areas, and countries is in line with the global strategic vision articulated by top management. When necessary, specific actions can be taken to fix the gap, and the effectiveness of these actions can be measured over time.
- What is the perceived impact of organizational policies and practices on differences in attitudes toward globalization (including accountability, job scope, and career and learning opportunities)? For example, to what extent do managers believe that they are held accountable for supporting globalization? Or, which units/groups of individuals see globalization as most promising for their careers?

Over a period of eight years, we carried out a study with three firms that operate internationally with more than 20 different businesses, all successful, but with different ways of thinking about how to compete globally (see Figure 3–1).[17]

Company A (represented by triangles), a major U.S.-based financial institution, takes a laissez-faire approach to globalization. Each division pursues its own strategy—some are transnational, one of them (selling financial IT systems worldwide) is meganational to the extreme, and another (a European brokerage house) places more emphasis on responsiveness. In contrast, company B (represented by dots) is a diversified manufacturing firm, also based in the United States. Its foreign-born CEO has long aspired for the company to operate as a transnational. The data showed that he had achieved this, with all units sharing a balanced view of the need for both responsiveness and integration

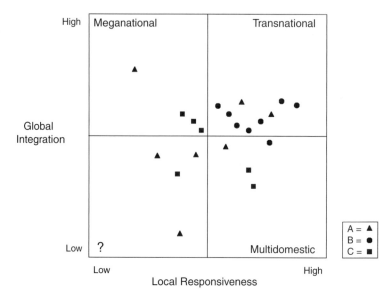

Figure 3-1   Global mindset map.

Company C (represented by boxes) is the European-based telecom equipment firm introduced at the beginning of this chapter. In general, the data showed that the company valued integration more than responsiveness and illustrated a polarity between the global orientation of the business units that were part of worldwide product lines and the local orientation of downstream units responsible for regional sales and customer services. Corporate staff held balanced views, but with a relatively low orientation toward both integration and responsiveness, reflecting difficulties in reaching consensus.

Previously, this rapidly growing company had handled tensions of conflicting polarities through extensive informal dialogue in the close-knit network of leaders who shared common experiences and values. This informal approach to strategy implementation had been extremely successful. However, as the business expanded, the ability of a small network of leaders to address all the issues was increasingly strained. In the view of top management, this global mindset needed to shared by a much larger managerial population of the firm, not remain limited to a few senior old-timers.

What did the company do? Armed with specific data, top management actively communicated the need to increase local responsiveness, rotated the leadership team to give more visibility to executives with downstream experience, decentralized P&L accountability, and sponsored action learning programs for 250 managers to find ways to increase lateral coordination to replace vertical integration. The next round of the survey 18 months later showed a significant shift in the desired direction.

This example shows how measuring mindsets can become a powerful tool for implementing global strategies. Using repeat surveys to evaluate global mindset provides top management with an objective indicator of the effectiveness of globalization activities. Before-and-after scores assist in evaluating the effectiveness of international management training and of communications programs intended to promote global values and priorities in an organization. Individual and group scores can also help to assess the effect of management policies and human resources (HR) tools affecting globalization (e.g., international assignments and rotation, global compensation practices, performance management, and specific training programs).

Developing Global Mindset through HR Strategies

Although it may seem obvious that global firms will need more and more managers with "global brains," translating this attractive vision into an operational reality is not simple. First of all, does every manager need to be "global?" Who really needs global brains and to what extent? Managers are not "born global"; they acquire global brains through a series of experiences, many of them at a substantial cost to the organization. What is the return on investing in developing people with global brains? Making a rational business case concerning the future need for and use of global managers is one of the critical strategic decisions companies face as they expand globally. But once the case has been made, how does one go about developing this global mindset?

Developing and supporting the global mindset is one of the foundations of global HR management. Indeed, data from our research strongly indicate that the presence of global HR policies and practices, as perceived by managers around the world, positively impacts acceptance of globalization. In particular, staffing strategies, leadership development, and performance management are three global HR management tools with the greatest potential for powerful leverage.

Demand-Driven or Learning-Driven Assignments?

Perhaps the strongest mechanism for developing global mindset is international assignments and international experience in general. There is a great deal of evidence that global mobility enhances the opportunities to develop a global mindset (although not everyone who frequently moves across country boundaries necessarily fits the characteristics of a global manager).

The classic study by Edström and Galbraith has already shown how transfers socialize people into the dilemmas and challenges facing the firm, thereby powerfully building the matrix into the mind.[18]

At the same time, socioeconomic and cultural trends around the world point to increasing barriers to cross-border mobility: dual-career families, parental care needs, children's education constraints, the equalization of economic opportunities reducing incentives to move. These are all factors that may diminish the desire of employees to actively seek out international assignments. In response, global organizations will have to become more and more creative in finding suitable alternatives to mobility, especially for senior managers. With flat organizational hierarchy supported by advances in modern communication technology, the traditional country-based job boundaries will begin to disappear, stimulating demand for positions with multicountry responsibilities.

Despite the increasing barriers to mobility, cross-border transfers are likely to remain the critical building block for enhancing global leadership skills. However, the nature of international assignments will change dramatically. In the past, they were mainly demand-driven, filling positions where there was insufficient know-how locally or where the authority of the center needed to be maintained. In other words, international managers were *teachers,* transferring capabilities and maintaining order. Given the expense, the emphasis on limiting the number of "teaching" expatriates was only natural. In future, the international assignments will become much more *learning-driven.* With localization and increasing sophistication of labor markets across the world, there is less need for knowledge transfer from the center. Many expatriates will be *learners,* not teachers. They will learn through experience about market and cultural differences, while developing long-lasting networks of relationships. They are also likely to come from many parts of the organization, not just from the mother country.

Global assignments should therefore become an integrated part of the career planning and development process. However, in contrast to past patterns of expatriation, the learning-driven global assignments should occur relatively early in an employee's professional career, when the learning impact is likely to be greatest. Transfers of young employees are also less costly and easier to implement from a career and family point of view. They will involve rotations across the whole global network, not just the traditional exchanges between the corporate center and country affiliates. Travel, short-term assignments, advisory visits, and best practice and study tours will also greatly increase.

One important caveat on the effects of international transfers: Data from our research showed that expatriates were far more balanced in their perspectives than their domestic counterparts, showing a high degree of understanding of the interplay between global and local forces and of the need for worldwide coordination. However, six months after expatriates returned from an assignment, there were no significant differences in mindset orientation between them and those who had never left home. At the headquarters, the roles, responsibilities, and corresponding performance criteria were heavily skewed to the global at the expense of the local. Repolarization of the mindset appeared to follow quickly. Mobility is not enough for balanced mindsets, if performance management does not support it. Adjusting performance management metrics was therefore one of the key steps taken by top management as they pushed for more balanced perspectives.

Cross-Border Project Teams and Task Forces

Transfers develop the network of critical ties that come to constitute the nervous system of the firm. Much of the communication in the transnational is informal, not prescribed, often based on a cross-border personal network of relationships that came about through international assignments, as well as steering groups, project teams, and action learning. These informal global networks supplement formal communication and can provide managers with rapid access to necessary information and, even more important, resources.

However, although international transfers (increasingly, learning-driven ones) are likely to remain a critical building block for developing global mindset, they are expensive and reserved for the select few with clear technical or leadership potential. An equally important building block, and one that is increasing dramatically, is cross-border project work. In different shapes and forms, project work has become the prime tool for coordination. Because cross-border projects are tools to work through local–global and related problems or opportunities, they are an excellent way of developing global mindset—perhaps the most important instrument for the future. The very purpose of the project group (or cross-border steering group or internal board) is to bring different perspectives to bear on a problem or opportunity.

Through project work, people learn a set of skills that underlie global mindset: the ability to work with people who have very different perspectives, how to set goals on important but ambiguous tasks, how to work through conflicts, and the like. It could even be argued that no one should move into a position of technical or managerial responsibility in a multinational organization without proven experience and demonstrable results in cross-border project work.

Leadership Development for Global Mindset

Many companies today use in-house training as a vehicle to speed up the dissemination of global mindset. At the heart of training in global mindset are projects, experiential methodologies, and action learning. It is the exchange and confrontation of different perspectives that leads to an understanding of the dilemmas of global management. The globalization process at General Electric is a good example.

Part of the GE transformation under Jack Welch was to make GE a company that operated globally, taking advantage of the growth and profit opportunities outside the United States. Recruiting abroad was one obvious response, but it was clear that it would take time to give the new recruits the exposure and experience they needed to be effective as GE leaders. Simultaneously, many GE managers who had operated only in the United States up until then had to master the ground rules of working internationally. To address these two developmental issues, GE's corporate management development staff designed a series of short, intensive, and experiential action learning programs with the aim of fostering the globalization of GE.[19]

As part of these programs, multicultural action learning teams of GE managers were sent to China, the former Soviet Union, and India to work on specific GE problems in these regions as well as to collect information on GE's best and worst practices around the world. The teams immersed themselves in the issues relevant to each region and reported on their findings, outlining business opportunities for GE to the company's top management. Even today, 10 to 15 years since they took part, many of the former participants reflect on their "global leadership" training as one of the most influential events of their careers.

Can people change their way of thinking in such a short period? A typical program lasted only about four weeks, but the stakes and tensions within teams were high—the unspoken perception was that the credibility (and future career prospects) of team members depended greatly on the quality of the final output. It was clear to everyone that reporting to Jack Welch that the team could not reach a common solution was not an option. Pie-in-the-sky planning was also not advisable, as the hottest business prospects were usually assigned to the team members to implement. Why was the training successful? Careful selection of participants, real work, stretch goals, and personal commitment of top management to mentor and coach all contributed.

Global firms will increasingly rely on flexible networks of relationships to foster global integration and coordination. Training that enhances global mindset should therefore be targeted at a broader cross-section of employees. In addition, a significant component of developmental activities should focus on the socialization aspects of leadership development. The purpose should be to create and enhance relationship networks and support the sense of common purpose, trust, and cooperation among employees across the whole global organization. Again, facilitated joint projects are probably the best tools to accomplish this objective.

Performance Management

Just as skill training that is not closely connected to the challenges of a job is unlikely to be transferred, so the development of global mindset through assignments, projects, and training is unlikely to be effective unless it is reinforced by other organizational processes. After all, the old maxim of "what gets measured, gets done" does not change in the global era.

In most global firms, different units of the organization have different strategic priorities, and thus different performance indicators are given different weight. However, having some common performance metrics and at least some common objectives facilitates the resolution of conflicts across boundaries. In the telecom equipment firm introduced earlier, giving managers in local subsidiaries and product managers in global business lines shared P&L responsibility was a major driver for mindset change. But setting targets is not enough. Given its decentralization of accountability to local units, the transnational needs to emphasize the importance of objective setting and appraisal, as well as obtain the buy-in of senior management in the subsidiaries to how it should be executed in practice.

A well-designed performance management system in a global firm is in itself a good example of balanced thinking. Often, measurement and control systems are seen as the opposite of decentralized responsibility. But the polarity is not absolute. For example, the main role of ABB's ABACUS—an acronym for the ABB Accounting and Communication (not control!) System—is to communicate useful operating level information to managers who need it as quickly as possible. In fact, ABB's ABACUS is designed to allow decentralization to work responsibly, providing prompt, timely measurements of all aspects of operational performance. In so doing, its aim is to (a) help local managers identify and diagnose problems and (b) allow top managers to monitor that performance. Their aim then is to help rather than interfere: "What's the problem? What are you doing to fix it? And how can we help?" Help means helping people to help themselves. It is only if they cannot help themselves that the control system leads to intervention.

Finally, to the extent that performance management and appraisal processes are rigorous, a powerful additional pressure for developing global mindset comes from what is called *anticipatory socialization*. As managers move from a local subsidiary role to a regional or global coordination role, they know that they may inherit any problems of excessive localization in their next job. The career prospects of the foreign assignee hang on his or her being able to satisfy the performance requirements of the subsidiary, the demands of headquarters staff, and perhaps those of his or her mother country. It is an excellent training in global mindset.

Implementing Global Mindset

Global mindset is not just part of a vision statement; it is the way a company makes strategic decisions and goes about implementing them. It starts at the top. The first step is top management articulating and reinforcing it, in clear and consistent language, across all levels and units. During his tenure as ABB's first CEO, Percy Barnevik spent over 200 days per year visiting the operating companies around the world, personally presenting his vision of a global enterprise to thousands of managers and employees worldwide. Even today, further down the organization, "Barnevik's slides" serve as a common source of reference. For Barnevik, communicating the business vision, organizational values, and management philosophy was not something that could be delegated. Creating the proper context for the actions of the whole firm was the core of his own leadership responsibilities. The same is true for GE's Jack Welch and other global leaders.

While top management provides the context for how to think about global strategy, it is up to the senior managers (business unit, function, and country leaders) to make global mindset inside an organization a reality. Their respective roles may be different,[20] but they ultimately share the responsibility for the synergy of responsiveness and integration. Accepting this responsibility is not easy or natural. Acceptance of global mindset requires an environment that creates *consistency* across the elements of an organization—the underlying communication network and coordination mechanisms, the requisite clarity of responsibilities and the empowerment linked to responsibility that is necessary for performance management, the attention to leadership development, and the underlying culture and values (see Figure 3–2).

The elements of this model are interdependent. But if one factor perhaps stands out above the others it is the emphasis on horizontal coordination. In our research on global mindset, a high degree of coordination across organizational subunits was the key differentiator between balanced and polarized businesses. Best practices forums, knowledge networks, task forces, project teams, steering boards, and other cross-border coordinating mechanisms are the fundamental building blocks for the successful deployment of global mindset. However, all of these organizational mechanisms rest on a single foundation—person-to-person relationships built on trust and common values.[21]

Having a global mindset implies recognizing the benefits that can flow to the whole organization from encouraging and valuing cultural diversity in people, not just as members of distinct cultural groups, but as individuals. Success in building cross-border networks of relationships—the principal arteries of effective global organizations—depends on understanding and valuing cultural diversity. Yet valuing diversity must go well beyond the traditional emphasis on bridging the distance between clusters of national cultures by focusing on average—and stereotypical—national characteristics.

Cultural knowledge in international management requires understanding differences within a culture as well as across cultures. The barrier that hinders effective cross-cultural interactions is not just the average distance between national cultures. It is also outsiders' lack of comprehension of the diversity within a given culture, because they do not understand the historical, political, and social context of "within-culture" differences, and thus have to rely on often misleading general assumptions and stereotypes. We have stopped stereotyping about gender and race; perhaps we should tackle culture with the same determination. A genuine emphasis on global mindset implies recognizing not only often-quoted cultural diversity but also human diversity.

Figure 3-2   Best practices supporting global mindset.

Equal Opportunity for All—Regardless of Passport

As global mindset is one of the key characteristics of future global leaders, one of the principal tasks of global leadership development should be to create and support an environment where global mindsets can flourish. But where will the future global leaders come from? Will global opportunities be available to employees all over the world, or only to those located in one of a few key countries or regions?

Perhaps the biggest barrier to the development of global mindset is the impression of local staff around the world that one's passport counts more than one's talent. Attracting and developing local leadership is not enough. Often, companies announce with great fanfare a campaign to "localize" management. The intention is certainly right, but what are the consequences? If at the end of the campaign all managers are local, then who is global? Effective localization implies attracting, developing, and retaining local talent with a mindset that can support global strategies. If global development opportunities are restricted to people from the mother country or those from a few lead countries (even if this is not intentional), then local employees will inevitably tend to adopt local perspectives (i.e., the only direction for their own future). Thus a key task for those responsible for international HR development is to ensure equitable access to career opportunities for talented employees worldwide.

From a long-term perspective, the transnational enterprise must satisfy a simple but demanding test: for future success, does it matter where an employee enters the organization? Today, there are probably only a few companies that can meet this benchmark, especially if global really means outside of the northern hemisphere. Among established multinational firms, only a handful, such as Citigroup, ABB, and McKinsey & Company, have developed a cadre of senior executives representing all continents. It took decades of effort to ensure that selection criteria are not biased toward one cultural group and that early identification of talent works equally well in Karachi as in New York. But things are speeding up. The new transnationals of the dotcom variety are totally focused on meritocracy. They are increasingly seen as the new beacons of opportunities for the best and the brightest worldwide. This is partly the challenge of the job and partly the attraction of stock options, but it is also the belief that nothing else but capability matters.

Changing the Globalization Paradigm

At this point, it may be useful to remind ourselves that global mindset is about balancing perspectives that at first glance may appear contradictory.

In their passion to promote global mindset, academics and others writing from a normative perspective sometimes tend to see global or cosmopolitan as superior to local, calling for a "universal way that transcends the particulars of places."[22] What is "local" is seen as parochial and narrow-minded. However, in our view, global mindset requires an approach that may be seen as the opposite to such one-dimensional universalism—it calls for a dualistic perspective, an immersion in local particulars, while at the same time retaining a wider cross-border perspective.

The nature of the whole debate about the benefits and cost of globalization is closely tied to how open we are to the idea that we do not all necessarily share the same preferences. Acceptance of diversity should include tolerance of people who are not "global," perhaps because of lack of opportunities, or perhaps because of personal choice or circumstances. Anything taken to an extreme risks becoming pathological; global mindset is no exception. This is true for companies as well as for individuals. International management textbooks are full of examples of "dumb" multinationals that are not sensitive enough to the cultural differences that the savvy "globals" navigate with ease. But years of successful navigation sometimes make one forget about the rocks below the water line. The difficulties facing Coca-Cola—the ultimate global firm—as the firm tries to rediscover its local roots is one recent example.

During the last decade, a catchy paradigm "Think globally, act locally" has often been used to capture the concept of a progressive global corporation that considers the whole world as its market, but at the same time carefully nurtures and adapts to local priorities and requirements.[23] Implementing this vision is, however, a longer and more difficult process than most companies envisioned.

What is the key problem? In a multinational firm that used this popular slogan on the first page of its annual report, one local subsidiary manager commented on its application in practice: "Our firm is organized on a simple premise. When operating under stress, and that is most of the time, *they* do the thinking, and *we* do the acting." In other words, the thinking and acting are two separate roles, performed by two separate groups. The headquarters takes the strategic initiatives, which the locals are left to implement. Although such a paradoxical outcome may not be what was intended, it may be unavoidable when tensions embedded in managing a business on a global basis are dealt with by separating responsibilities rather than through developing shared ways of thinking about what globalization implies.

Perhaps the way out of this dilemma is to return to the logic of the globalization process. Today, leveraging technologies and service platforms increasingly requires a world-scale approach and global mobilization of corporate resources. At the same time, customer needs are increasingly individualized, and customers worldwide exhibit a strong preference to be treated as individuals—the secret of the business model implemented by Dell, Mercedes-Benz, Ritz-Carlton, and others. What, then, is the competitive advantage of a global firm? In simple terms, it is the ability to tap global knowledge and skills to satisfy local customer needs.

The very specific needs of customers have to be carefully assessed; hence the requirement to be able to learn and understand the local context, the "local" immersion advocated earlier. The ability to satisfy those needs through delivery and execution is, however, dependent on the "global" mobilization of corporate resources. It may be useful, therefore, to rephrase the original paradigm. Creating a global mindset inside an organization is really about developing leaders who *learn locally, but act globally.* Looked at from this perspective, it is not so easy to separate the corporate mind and the body spread out over the globe.

4

World-Class Leadership for World-Class Teams

Andrew Kakabadse

eadership has been one of the most debated topics in history. From military leaders such as Napoleon and Wellington to social movement leaders such as Martin Luther King and Mohandas Gandhi, the debate has raged as to the characteristics of great leaders. Despite the potency of such discourse, the composition of leadership still remains devoid of universally clear criteria and parameters. Leadership can be viewed variously as the innate characteristics of the great men and women of history; as the personal relationship between the individual and the group; as the process of striving toward common goals and values; or as aspects of behavior, whether desired and in control of the individual, or, alternatively, reactive and driven by a number of forces in the environment.

Bearing in mind these varying interpretations, this chapter provides a brief history of the subject of leadership, highlighting why considerations of leadership have now become central to the growth and development of today's corporations. Further, analysis focuses on how the development of the corporate organization is likely to demand the application of particular leadership philosophies and practices to ensure the survival and prosperity of the enterprise. The point is that leadership cannot solely concentrate on the individual. Considerations of leadership, whether concerned with the individual or the team of which the individual is a member, will need to be linked to a broader concept of enterprise value, be that shareholder or stakeholder value. What is becoming increasingly evident is that shareholder, customer, supplier, and media confidence in an organization is affected by the perceived impact of the organization's leadership on the worth of the enterprise. Hence, the psychology of leadership and the economics of business administration have become irrevocably intermingled.

Views of Leadership

The following are among the different interpretations of leadership.

- Leadership is seen as a distinct kind of work that may or may not be required, according to demands of the circumstances.
- Leadership is akin to a strong motivation or drive that spurs the individual to act, and hence has nothing to do with status, authority, or the holding of office.
- Leadership is not always necessary, as steadily achieved success can be equally attained by good management.
- Leadership is linked to the exercise of power, so that a vision can be realized through the mobilization of resources.
- The effective practice of leadership requires broad capability, in that knowledge of products, services, and markets, and the application of functional skills have to be matched by drive, energy, and a wide-ranging intellectual capacity for problem solving.
- Effective leaders need to be powerful motivators of people.
- Effective leaders need to have developed highly attuned conceptual skills, so that they can spot potential opportunities, analyze and verbalize them, and turn them into future opportunities.
- Effective leaders need to have evolved sound judgment, involving attention to detail, conceptualization, and intuition, attributes that do not sit comfortably together.
- Leadership requires the development of key aspects of character and balancing ambition with conscience, so that the individual can harness drive with the desire to be held fully responsible for his or her words and deeds.
- Effective leaders need to engender sufficient humility so as to nurture the wisdom that will enable them to work their way through the ambiguities and paradoxes that they will inevitably face.

Whatever perspective of leadership attracts one person or another, it is clear from the aforementioned list that the handling of opposites is inherent in the pursuit of leadership and that in itself is a prime skill. How can one be ethical and political at the same time? How can one be sensitive to others and yet drive through change with discipline and determination? How can one attend to details and yet grasp and pursue even half-formed possibilities? These contrasts promote the first clue as to the requirements of high-performance leadership, namely the balancing of its transformational and transactional elements.

Such balancing involves working through paradox, between leading and managing; between striving to restructure and yet efficiently administering the day to day in an orderly fashion. The results of a number of studies conducted at Cranfield School of Management emphasizes that balancing between transforming and transacting, leading and managing, is of absolute necessity but difficult to achieve in practice.

Leaders who transform alter the parameters of the status quo, through providing a vision for the future and then investing the time and effort in having others share that vision. Through sharing their vision, they clarify the present, explain how the past has influenced the present, and promote a view of the future. To be effective, transformative leaders need to listen as well as be consistent, persistent, and focused to both empower others and maintain momentum. A leader who exhibits such transformative power deeply penetrates the soul and psyche of others and thereby raises in others a level of awareness that rejuvenates people to strive for ever greater ends.

However, the results of the Cranfield studies indicate that to keep the organization operational, leaders are equally required to perform transactional duties. Transactional leadership requires the application of managerial skills to effectively address the operational, day-to-day aspects of working life. Managing the detail of budgets, reviewing progress, following through on projects and initiatives, keeping meetings on schedule, ensuring that agendas are adhered to, and conducting appraisals are examples of transactional management.

In determining whether and how leaders adopt a more transformational or transactional perspective, we will take a journey through the three key schools of leadership—that leaders are born, leaders are made, and the emerging late 20th-century concept of discretionary leadership.

Born-to-Lead School

The military historian John Keegan identified hunting as a central concern of primitive societies. The deeds of the huntsmen required all to be heroes, for all had to take risks so that the tribe could eat. As all were heroes, the lack of exceptional behavior made all heroes ordinary, thus reducing huntsmen to being no heroes at all. Similarly, in the battlefield, there were no heroes, as the expectation of the primitive warrior was to "fight as you hunt." Exceptional behavior was not exhibited by the warrior, but by the elders who mediated between disputing groups when violence went beyond tolerable limits. So negotiation, the settlement of claims, the cajoling, the persuading, and the pushing led to the emergence of the elders as leaders. The elders represented a transactional philosophy of leadership: reach a status quo position, get into detail when bargaining, and make sure that life can return to an operational, day-to-day normality to ensure survival from those who transformationally used slaughter to alter the course of primitive geopolitics.

However, when it became recognized that physical prowess combined with discipline, cunning, and eloquence could gain far more than the conservatism that arises out of mediation, so was born the era of leadership on the battlefield. The distinguished warrior, the glamorous Prince Rupert, and the brilliant but petulant Napoleon portray the more romantic figure of leader, the one who would physically or intellectually take the extra step to be seen to lead and win. As the settling of boundary disputes moved to clever fighting on the battlefield to take over the land and domain of others, the heroic, transformational leader came to the fore—envied, feared, mysterious, and a role model for others to follow. As such, the transformational concept of leadership became deeply embedded in the psyche of history and for subsequent generations, a prime center of enquiry. The transactional aspect slipped by as a distant memory.

It was Friedrich Nietzsche's interpretation of the glamorous leader through the concept of übermensch (superman) that has lead to a 20th-century quest to identify those extraordinary qualities of leadership that, in the right combination, provide for that unique capability to transform. In the latter half of the 20th century, such perspective has gained favor with two particular groups, the biographers and the search consultants. Glorification, attribution, the highlighting of extraordinary tensions, and the quest and drive for power have been the techniques used by biographers to immortalize their subjects. Based on their analyses, the biographers and biographical historians have had a profound impact on promoting the image of the great leader. Gratefully accepting such perspectives have been the search consultants, the head hunters, whose aim has been to find the right person to fulfill the demands of key positions in organizations. In fact, the very concept of fit—fitting the right person to the right job—adds to the mystique of searching for the "great" person.

Self-Development School

In contrast to the great man/woman interpretation of leadership, which assumes a single, focal point of drive, energy, and inspiration, the self-development school portrays a world of dialogue, in which debate between the leaders and the "common person" is the mechanism that identifies the way forward, and involvement in discussion is the lever to gaining the commitment of others to follow. This more societally based interpretation of leadership provides a broader platform on which to analyze leaders—from the singular great individual to an interaction among so-called equals (or almost equals)!

The ancient Greeks, founders of the wisdom movement in leadership, were deeply influenced by the Socratic question of "what ought one do?" The Socratic paradox demands an account from individuals as to why they choose one goal over another. In so doing, Socrates required each person to articulate what they consider to be good, or at least justify their course of action. The steering through obstacles and the need for justification of actions led to the concept of wisdom, itself an inspiration of finding and shaping pathways through hindrances. By addressing the question of what to do, Socrates combined intellect with humility and rationality with emotive reaction, for the search for ways through life's challenges could not meaningfully proceed without self-examination. As such, Socratic philosophy ruled out the genetic interpretation of born to lead, as no one remained "within a box" unless bounded by their own perspectives.

In a similar vein, Plato's quest for the enlightened leader, who can overcome the convolutions of human conduct through the possession of an intellectual vision, provided the basis for diligent authority. Plato's desire for a defense against those who would rule the state according to whim and fancy was driven by a deep suspicion of arbitrary and capricious leadership. To stand above unproductive emotions and drives, Plato emphasized the leader's development as one of breaking out of perpetual straightjackets, which if unabated would limit and damage the state. Plato's aim was for each leader to nurture his own "one truth."

In contrast to the Socratic and Platonic virtues and values interpretation of leadership, Niccoló Machiavelli focused on the more practical aspects of how leaders ought to behave. Machiavelli asserted that if political anarchy is to be avoided, concerns of rights and morality come second to the struggle and establishment of power. According to the circumstances, the leader should be prepared to employ whatever means are needed to defend and promote the welfare of the state. Similar to Plato, but for different reasons, Machiavelli intertwines the needs of the state with the desires of the individual, but by taking a position at the lower end of the values continuum. In circumstances where different interests prevail, the one who succeeds and dominates the rest of the pack becomes leader, thus establishing the concept of "superior power." The difference between Socrates and Machiavelli is between values on the one hand and pure pragmatism on the other. The similarity, however, is that both imply that for the individual to progress, reading the context in order to identify pathways through challenges is fundamental.

For the ordinary individual, the contextualist interpretation of finding ways through has found great favor in the consumer- and stress-driven 1990s and beyond in the form of spirituality. Self-development, leadership, and spirituality, as a triumvirate of concepts, have deep roots, stemming back to Taoism and Buddhism.

Taoist concepts were introduced into the Western world by Heraclitus of Ephesus, the pre-Socratic Greek philosopher who influenced the work of Hegel, and who in turn guided Karl Marx, the popularly attributed proponent of the dialectic view of reality. Dialectics, however, is not the prerogative of Marx, but is an all-pervading Taoist religious and philosophical concept. Taoism is a description of nature (*tao* means way), which in turn is shaped by the interplay between yin and yang. Yin and yang, which originally denoted the dark and sunny sides of the hill, emphasize how the tao (the way forward) is shaped by the flow of complex and opposite forces. To progress, contrasts have to be reconciled, such as sociality with individuality, order with spontaneity, unity with diversity.

Despite the impractical nature of the philosophy of enlightenment, the expunging of unhelpful and deeply rooted attitudes (Buddhism), journeying, and wholeness, the Socratic and Eastern spiritualist teachings have had a profound impact on the management trainers, management consultants, and organization development and broader client-driven specialists of the final years of the 20th century. Peter M. Senge highlights the need for *metanoia*, meaning a transcendence of mind, whereby a shift of perspective is required if organizations are to be turned into the higher order entity of a learning organization. In a similar view, Stephen Covey advocates philosophical principles as the basis for leadership. Covey outlines how the individual's character is the basis of personal effectiveness, thus leadership denotes taking charge of character development. Covey's seven habits are an attempt to explain how highly effective people become so, through such principles as integrity, humility, and fidelity. The seventh habit, sharpening the saw, includes spiritual renewal, which Covey extends to mean the continual clarification of values and commitment to others as the individual progresses through life.

Discretionary Leadership

Research conducted at Cranfield School of Management and at Brunel University has introduced a third perspective, that of discretionary leadership.

Surveys of top teams conducted at Cranfield, which included over 11,000 organizations spanning 14 countries, have identified three core capabilities required of today's corporate and public services leaders: visioning, dialogue, and the quality of communication between senior management and the rest of the organization.

Visioning

One of the key questions asked in the Cranfield survey was, "Do the members of the top team (e.g., president, chairman, CEO, directors, senior civil servants, etc.) hold different views concerning the future shape, nature, and direction of the organization?" The sample consisted of numerous private sector organizations, the National Health Service (NHS) Trusts (Britain), and the senior civil servants of the Australian Public Service (APS; see Table 4–1).

Table 4–1   Respondents Reporting Discrepancies of Vision, by Nation or Organization

Recognize that fundamental divisions exist within their top team concerning the future	
20% NHS Top Team	32% Germany
21% NHS Board	33% China
20% Sweden	39% France
23% Japan	39% United States
25% Finland	40% Spain
30% Britain	42% Hong Kong
31% Austria	48% Ireland
Feel that top management hold fundamentally different views as to the future direction of their department	
56% Australian Public Service	

The greatest discrepancy at top team level occurs among top Australian civil servants, who believe that members of the senior management group hold fundamentally different views as to the shape and nature of the APS in general, of their departments, and in particular the future pathways that should be pursued. In contrast, in British NHS Trust organizations, only 20%

of the executive team members and 21% of the majority nonexecutive board members highlight that fundamentally different views on the vision, future, direction, and shape of the organization are held by members of their respective groups. Of the private sector respondents, the Irish, Spanish, and French top managers compare with the Australian split of vision and diversity of view. The Swedish and Japanese respondents highlight the least difference of view concerning strategic direction at senior management levels.

Dialogue

For senior management to reduce the level of tension and understand the nature of differences that exist at top management levels, it is essential to create an environment that fosters the airing of views, the asking of questions, and entering into the kind of deep debate that ends with a declaration of intent. This process is vital to shift toward a cohesive top team who could effectively lead the organization. On the basis that meaningful dialogue, as opposed to casual conversation, is crucial to team-based leadership, a second fundamental question was asked in the Cranfield surveys: "Are there issues or sensitivities that merit, but do not receive, adequate attention at senior management levels?" (see Table 4–2).

Table 4–2   Respondents Reporting that Important Issues Go Undiscussed, by Nation or Organization

Believe there are issues that should be discussed but are not

36% France	63% Spain
47% Britain	67% Austria
49% Finland	68% Ireland
50% Sweden	66% NHS Board
58% Hong Kong	70% NHS Top Team
61% Germany	77% Japan
62% United States	80% China

Believe there are issues that should be discussed but are too sensitive; as a result, operation opportunity costs are experienced

66% Australian Public Service	

The Chinese and Japanese top executives voiced the greatest number of concerns, indicating that important but disregarded issues predominate among senior management. The British NHS executive directors also reported high levels of inhibited dialogue at senior levels. The Australian civil servants followed the Irish and Austrians in their concern about issues not attended to, while the Finnish, British, and French senior managers identified the smallest numbers of sensitive issues impacting on the quality of dialogue at senior levels.

The vast majority of business and public service leaders report outstanding issues remaining unaddressed at senior levels, but that need to be addressed for the organization to progress. A vision for the future may be shared, but its translation into practical steps may give rise to operational difficulties in achieving synergy across the enterprise. For example, the concept of global brands may make perfect sense from the corporate center's viewpoint, but may not address consumer desire in particular countries or regions, leaving the local manager vulnerable in terms of meeting targets and promoting brands that do not suit that locality. Hence, how such conflicts of interests are raised and consequently addressed powerfully impacts on the future revenues generated; on costs incurred; and on the motivation, confidence, and development of the staff and management of the organization. The research shows that not being able to discuss such charged issues nurtures an environment of continuous missed opportunities.

Communicating

Within an environment of diversity, effectively communicating across complex structures is no easy matter. Given the different agendas senior managers need to address, and coupled with the varied expectations people have of their managers, it is an inevitability that sooner or later a senior manager will project an inappropriate or undesired message. To minimize the communication of such tensions, the Cranfield surveys identified six key interfacing behaviors that, if well managed, project trust, confidence, a sense of cohesion at senior management levels, and a discipline and consistency for effective follow-through. However, the survey also highlights differences of perception as to what constitutes effectiveness of behavior between top directors and their general manager subordinates (see Table 4–3).

Table 4-3 Interfacing Behaviors: Top Directors' (TD) and General Managers' (GM) Perceptions (in %)

Perception	Japan TD	Japan GM	Britain TD	Britain GM	France TD	France GM	Ireland TD	Ireland GM	Germany TD	Germany GM	Sweden TD	Sweden GM	Spain TD	Spain GM	Austria TD	Austria GM	Hong Kong TD	Hong Kong GM	United States TD	United States GM
Easy to talk to	82	62	73	65	80	76	87		78		84	83	75	77	80	64	80		78	65
Not easy to talk to								41		54								56		
Discuss sensitive issues	69		66		71		52		68	63	66		44		60		67		62	
Address safe issues		47		44		47		60				42		61		51		40		58
Understanding	78	61	68		61		52		41		63		53		58		53		60	
Not understanding		61		70		48		67		68		48		61		51		66		48
Trust each other	73	61	65		66		61		75		71		58		63		71		63	
Not trust each other				68		48		67		69		66		51		57		72		51
Implement decisions made in top team	89	76	72		74	64	91		83	64	79	73	70	69	65		78		78	60
Implement decisions that personally suit				44				50								41		50		
Address long- and short-term issues	75	62	54		58		61		68		56		61		62		64	67	73	60
Address short-term issues				58		48		66		42		50		60		49				

The six key interfacing behaviors are:

- Being easy to talk to
- Being sufficiently robust to discuss sensitive issues
- Displaying broad business understanding of how the organization functions
- Displaying trust of colleagues and subordinates
- Displaying cabinet responsibility in consistently implementing decisions agreed to in the top team
- Displaying sufficient breadth in knowing how to address long- and short-term issues simultaneously

For example, the British sample shows that 65% of top directors consider the way they behave displays a high level of trust in each of the members of the top team and in their general manager subordinates. However, 68% of the key general managers consider that the very same behaviors indicate that the members of the top team do *not* trust each other, nor do they display the necessary levels of trust in them. Across these six core behaviors, the survey results indicate that British and Irish top managers display the greatest level of dysfunctionality in terms of interfacing behaviors.

Diversity

The results of the Cranfield top team surveys highlight that diversity, dissension, and difference are an everyday reality of life at the top of private sector and public service organizations. The survey equally highlights that no individual, no matter how gifted, is likely to fully appreciate the various requirements of different contexts. In fact, many top directors in the survey stated that they could not understand why their colleagues were championing particular viewpoints. Whatever the reasons for individual senior managers adopting different perspectives on key issues, the survey shows that top managers exercise discretion to pursue what they consider to be an appropriate way forward.

Insightful research conducted by Elliot Jacques, originally at the Tavistock Institute and then at Brunel University, categorized two types of executive work—prescribed and discretionary. A *prescribed* role is one in which 51% or more of that role requires the occupant to pursue and complete tasks and objectives that have already been set. This work is structured, leaving the individual little room to exercise judgment. A *discretionary* role is one where 51% or more of that role is determined by the role occupant; considerable judgment is necessary for the individual to function effectively in this role. By this distinction, a prescribed role is more of a struc-

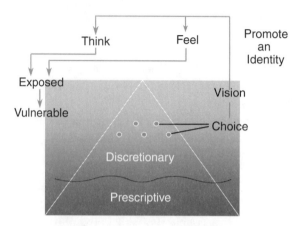

Figure 4–1   Discretionary roles within the organization.

tured, middle-management transactional job, whereas a discretionary role epitomizes the transformational nature of a leadership position.

The degree of discretion may be planned for in the role and/or driven by the role incumbent's capability to influence and determine the boundaries, responsibilities, and accountabilities of his or her role. Different senior managers set different boundaries and responsibility levels according to contextual pressures, their trust in their subordinates, and each individual's wishes and desires. Further, any organization may possess a considerable number of discretionary roles within the overall configuration of the organization (see Figure 4–1).

In theory, the number of discretionary roles that exist in an organization determines the number of visions and ways of operating that can shape, positively or negatively, the future of the organization. Also, the number of discretionary roles will vary from one organization to the next. Further, not all discretionary leader roles need be congregated at the top. Those executives who hold senior management positions—chairmen, CEOs, directors, managing directors, and general managers—are most likely to occupy discretionary leader roles, the difference of leadership responsibility between them being one of degree. However, lower down the organization, younger, key-client account managers may well occupy discretionary leader roles that shape the future of the company, not because of their involvement in strategic debate, but because of their influence on key accounts. If any one or more key-client accounts are damaged, the loss in revenue and the damage to external credibility could severely undermine the image and viability of the corporation. Hence, according to discretionary role analysis, a multitude of views can enter into the strategic debate, a point strongly emphasized by the Cranfield leadership surveys.

The diversity perspective is additionally emphasized by another Cranfield survey exploring the role and contribution of nonexecutive directors (NEDs; see Table 4–4). The quality of interaction between board members varies, but is considerably influenced by the personality and style of the chairman and the relationship the chairman has with the CEO. Equally, how each NED interprets his or her role and consequently the contribution each makes also varies. Some instinctively apply their functional expertise (boards tend to prize financial literacy and experience in marketing and branding). Others make every attempt to appreciate the nature and needs of the organization on whose board they sit and adjust their contribution accordingly. However, few NEDs are identified as making the effort to develop an intimate understanding of their corporation. Equally, different NEDs hold different views concerning the topic of governance. Some perceive governance as little more than procedural box ticking, so as to be seen to be addressing issues of rights, duties, and disciplines in a world haunted by political correctness. Those who make genuine attempts to create a positive governance framework also tend to stimulate debate concerning how to enhance the reputation of the corporation. Some of the more positively inclined NEDs strongly argue that improving the reputation of the corporation would equally elevate share price. To do so, stringent attempts are made to become acquainted with the senior management of the corporation to nurture cohesive team behavior. However, the survey shows that very few organizations display such a degree of integration at board level. In many organizations, NEDs still do not sufficiently challenge current mindsets to help elevate the leadership onto a more productive way of thinking.

Table 4–4   NEDs—Role and Contribution

NEDs and Boards
Critical role of chairman
NEDs relation with CEO/chairman is crucial
Role/contribution varies
Approach to governance/corporate reputation varies
Few understand the corporation
Continuous paradox

World-Class Leadership Means World-Class Teams

According to the role held by each leader and the demands faced by the individual in that role, research shows continuously attempting to resolve tension is an everyday reality. Today's organizations face so many issues and have an order of complexity such that the single leader concept has given way to team-based leadership. The need for team, or more specifically, cadre-based leadership, was not a requirement in the post-World War II era, a period where the level of production could not meet consumer expectation. The single individual directing resources in a growth economy fostered the image of the hero/heroine leader.

However, by the 1970s, the cycle had turned. Markets began to experience an oversupply of goods and services, which led to the first revolution of leadership—to differentiate the organization from its competitors, as the simple production of goods and services could no longer guarantee their sale. Bad habits, such as poor product quality, poor service, and spiraling wage demands based on the expectation of continued growth, needed to be confronted. In response, there emerged such initiatives as quality circles, customer care, personal service, and the downsizing of corporations, as much to remove managers and operatives who lacked the inclination to alter their habits as well as to lower costs. The company with the better quality of portfolio, with improved service at an affordable price, stood out and gained an edge in the battle for consumer attention. The hero corporation of the late 1970s, 1980s, and early 1990s became the epitome of differentiation and sustainability.

However, as more organizations applied high-quality management techniques to the operational/market delivery end of their business, differentiation once again became blurred and survival anxiety began to displace the confidence of sustainability. Most companies today produce high-quality goods, promote high-quality service, and back that by efficient delivery. Hence, as attempting to differentiate at the delivery end of the business has became unsustainable, trying to gain competitive differentiation as a total corporation has now become the challenge. As such, consideration of the needs of consumers has been intertwined with consideration of other stakeholders, principally shareholders, but also the media. In effect, what the organization does in terms of providing goods and services is as important a concern as what it stands for in the eyes of the shareholders and the public at large. As supply side economics has come to dominate virtually every aspect of life, the capacity to meet customer demand is now becoming secondary to the question of total corporate capability.

In attempting to appreciate what differentiation means to different managers, further research conducted at Cranfield School of Management has identified that the term "strategy" holds different meanings for different individuals according to their experience and view as to where the true value of the corporation is located. Corporate value may lie in the cost-driven vertical synergies pursued by the organization, where attention is focused on cost discipline, enhancing the efficiency of corporate structures, and the continuous trimming of overhead so that the organization develops a capability of scale economies (see Figure 4–2). Within such circumstances, senior management's concern would center around issues of overhead—does the organization have too many people? Does the cost base of the organization inhibit competitive behavior? Such questions would predominate senior management's attention as the prime corporate differentiator is based on price. The goods and services offered by the corporation are considered to have reached such commodity status that their only avenue of differentiation is to be less expensive.

In contrast, horizontal-based synergies assume making a difference according to the manner in which knowledge is generated and leveraged across the organization, so as to provide for a sustainable difference in terms of services, brand, and management capability, without necessarily being price sensitive. Cost disciplines exist, but are considered an activity and not a total enterprise capability of scale economy.

To promote corporate value added through scale economies, less attention needs to be given to leadership and more to discipline-based manage-

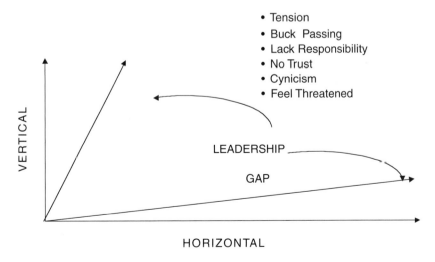

Figure 4–2   Paradox of leadership scope box.

ment systems, as the prime emphasis of the organization is control. Rather than strong leadership, solid management is desired.

Projecting corporate value added through horizontal synergies is likely to require robust debate on vision, mission, and prime purpose. Locating unique knowledge and deciding how it is to be leveraged, determining the level of involvement of the center in the affairs of the operating businesses, and calculating the impact of all that on pricing and competitive capacity—while continuing to satisfy shareholder expectations—requires a leadership fluent in dialogue and with an instinct for cohesion in terms of applying strategy consistently.

However, the Cranfield studies highlight that most organizations, in order to truly stand apart, need to pursue both horizontal and vertical synergies; therein lies the paradox. Can any one top manager control costs and prune expenses, and at the same time promote an internal environment of openness, trust, and cooperation? How can one, as a senior manager, say to a subordinate or colleague, "give me feedback on what our clients think of us, even if it is critical of me," and at the same time expect that person to freely respond when they feel that the very same senior manager who is asking the question may eliminate their job within the next financial year?

It is possible to pursue either vertical or horizontal synergy strategies effectively. However, to pursue both is considerably stretching, and potentially promotes a gap of leadership, a gap that may be filled by strife, buck-passing responsibility upwards, and feeling no sense of identity with one's leadership role (see Figure 4–2).

The tensions highlighted in Tables 4–1, 4–2, and 4–3 concerning the future nature and shape of the organization, quality of dialogue, and effectiveness of communication highlight the dissatisfaction senior managers experience in finding ways through the juxtaposition between vertical and horizontal synergies. The phenomenon of the leadership gap is an experience common to the top management of private and public sector organizations. The question is, which organization today can afford to promote only vertical or horizontal synergies? The answer is, very few—gaining advantage in markets and maintaining the trust of shareholder communities requires the pursuit of both! Team-based leadership is an absolutely necessity, not a luxury.

Promoting a Shared Philosophy

As the management of tension and diversity is an everyday norm that can split an immature management and, in turn, damage the organization, nurturing the necessary level of maturity in each of the leaders in the organization requires engendering a shared philosophy among the members of the top management team. The philosophy the top team shares and promotes throughout the organization is the "corporate glue" of the enterprise, the mechanism that binds together the staff and management of the corporation; it also serves as the identity that promotes confidence in customers, suppliers, and shareholders. The reason that the generation and promotion of a shared philosophy is inextricably linked to the levels of maturity of top management is that the activities that any one or more top managers feel they need to pursue may contradict the overriding philosophy that needs to be promoted by all of top management. The distinction between working on transactional activities while simultaneously promoting a transformation philosophy may not be clear in the minds of the members of the top team. Where conflicts of interest occur, it may be important for any senior manager to subjugate their immediate interests in favor of the greater corporate whole. Hence, the requirement is to develop today's leaders as team players, recognizing that the concept of "team" is likely to mean membership of multiple teams, as senior managers hold functional, line of business, subsidiary, regional, and corporate center responsibilities. In fact, the concept of "leader" needs to be extended to the concept of cadre, meaning the fundamental core of top management.

Certain organizations, such as Bass Brewers, have been deliberate in their efforts to develop their managers according to a cadre-based interpretation of team. For many years, the Bass organization identified its high-potential future leaders as those whose names were placed on the Chairman's List. The brainchild of the chairman, Sir Ian Prosser, the Chairman's List represents the cadre of Bass. Chairman's List managers are the accomplished high flyers who are expected to share the same philosophy and consistently promote best practice and the core values of the organization. Although the Chairman's List represents the next generation of leaders, only some are selected for the top jobs. Despite competing against each other as well as against outsiders for senior positions, Chairman's List managers responsibly act as the present-day and future backbone of the organization.

Conclusion

The fundamental reason that a group-based view of leadership predominates today's organizations is because of an ever growing political, social, and economic diversity. Today, greater acknowledgement has to be given to the demands of multiple stakeholders. In so doing, continuous attention to context is a must, as today's dynamic circumstances force the leadership of the organization to pay attention to, and respect, the particular nature of their circumstances. Responsiveness to context requires a mindset of continuous development, in which the individual, in conjunction with his or her colleagues, needs to be ready to adjust and change his or her skills and approach according to the needs and demands of stakeholders. Searching for leaders who display predetermined capabilities means little in today's world; however, owing to continuous change, a follower in one context can be an influential stakeholder or shareholder/owner in another.

5

Situational Factors in Leadership

Victor H. Vroom

During the last two decades, the term "leadership" has acquired an increasingly important place in the lexicon of management. At the time of this writing, courses in leadership are part of the core curriculum in the MBA programs at Harvard, Yale, and Wharton, to name just a few. A decade or two ago, formal education in leadership was reserved for military officers. MBAs were taught management.

It is my strong belief that the difference between leadership and management is not just semantic. I believe that the change reflects important and necessary trends in the education for those who seek positions of responsibility within organizations, whether they be in the public, private, or nonprofit sectors. In this chapter, I attempt to clarify the ambiguities in the term "leadership," evaluate the principal approaches to understanding it, and explicate my belief in the fundamental importance of a contingency approach to leadership to the effectiveness of organizations in the 21st century. Finally, I illustrate a contingency approach by summarizing some of the highlights of a research program, spanning several decades, on the age-old problem of styles of leadership.

A Definition of Leadership

Leadership is not a scientific term. Rather, it was borrowed from the popular vocabulary. As such, it has many different meanings, varying with the user and the context. It could be argued that the term has been so overused that it should be abandoned altogether. A reasonable case could be made for starting afresh with a new term devoid of the excess baggage of its predecessor. In this chapter, I will retain the term but will try to delineate carefully what I choose to mean by it.

Exercising leadership inevitably involves having influence. One cannot lead without influencing others. Warner Burke writes about an amusing headline in a national newspaper saying, "Afghan leader lacks followers!" Of course, if no one follows, one cannot exercise leadership. Influence over the behavior of others is necessary for leadership but, I will argue, is not sufficient. All forms of influence do not involve exercising leadership.

First of all, the influence must be *intended*. Movie stars, rock musicians, or professional athletes frequently serve as role models for the young. Their influence is profound but it is seldom intended. In most instances the driving force is the desire to be good at their craft; the effect on others is incidental. The inclusion of intention as a qualifier also eliminates influence that is inconsistent with the intention of the leader. A parent is not exercising leadership to a child if the child does the opposite of what he or she is asked.

I also wish to eliminate from the domain of leadership the brand of influence that is coercive. This statement is not intended to deny the potency of coercive pressures but rather to avoid confusing them with leadership. I prefer to restrict the latter term to influence in which the forces driving the action are predominantly voluntary, conforming with what Kurt Lewin referred to as "own forces" rather than induced forces. Thus, threats and indeed bribes, while undoubtedly processes for exercising influence, do not meet my definition.

At the risk of splitting hairs, I wish to make one additional qualifier to the term influence before including it within the umbrella of leadership. This third condition, I believe, is of particular importance in leadership processes within organizations. It refers to the consequences of the influence. Not only must the influence be successful but the *effect* of the influence must benefit the organization and its stakeholders. Thus, the Pied Piper of Hamelin, who led a group of innocent children to their certain death, would not qualify. This usage is consistent with popular treatments of the term. Jack Welch's leadership at General Electric is celebrated because of double-digit profits that have been attained for two decades. Such would not have been the case had the double-digits been losses!

To summarize the working definition employed in this chapter, leadership is an influence process that is noncoercive in nature and produces acceptance or commitment on the part of organizational members to courses of action that contribute to the organization's effectiveness.

Since the influence process inherent in this definition is often difficult to observe directly, measures of effectiveness are frequently used as an indication of leadership. Organizations vary markedly in their effectiveness, whether they be football teams, manufacturing plants, banks, or military units. The question before us is whether, or to what degree, do differences in organizational effectiveness reflect the quality of their leadership.

The Heroic Model of Leadership

One can distinguish three positions, each advocated by different groups of scholars, in an attempt to answer this question. I refer to the first of these as the heroic model since it views leadership as a personal trait that enables those who possess it to inspire and energize others in productive directions. In one form of this model these leadership qualities are genetically deter- mined, and effective leaders may ultimately be determined by their DNA. Thus, leaders are born, not made. More often, those advocating a heroic position view the trait of leadership as originating, at least in part, in life's experiences, perhaps those occurring early in life. The classic "nature ver- sus nurture" debate is independent of the essence of the heroic model; a leader is a leader is a leader—independent of the situation.

The heroic model is reminiscent of what historians have termed the "great man" approach to history. From this perspective, historical events can be traced to the impact of a finite number of people, such as Jesus Christ, Mohammed, Alexander the Great, Adolph Hitler, and Joseph Stalin.

Belief in the heroic model is still strong today, both among social scien- tists and, to an even greater degree, in the general public. For example, Kil- patrick and Locke assert, "Recent research using a variety of methods has made it clear that successful leaders are not like other people. The evi- dence indicates that there are certain core traits which significantly contrib- ute to business leaders' success" (1991, p. 49).

The heroic model speaks to the question of selecting leaders. The best predictor of success in one leadership role is success in another leadership position regardless of how similar or different the two positions. An effec- tive military leader is likely to be effective as a university president, and an effective business leader is likely to be effective as mayor.

The heroic model has also spurred the search for psychological tests that might identify those who have a capacity for leadership. If the traits and skills necessary for leadership could be identified and measured, the task of selecting leaders for tomorrow's organizations would be much simpler and countless errors would be avoided.

To date, we are still far short of a scientifically based technology for selecting leaders. Measures of intelligence have not been very successful in distinguishing leaders from nonleaders or effective from ineffective lead- ers. Claims that emotional intelligence may be much more closely related to leadership than verbal and mathematical proficiency have yet to be substantiated owing to the multidimensional nature of this construct and the absence of valid and reliable measures.

Locating leadership in terms of the traits that people possess rather than their functions or accomplishments makes inferences more equivocal and subject to interpretation. On a recent plane trip, I found myself perusing the airline store catalog in the seatback in front of me. Among the many items was a beautifully framed print titled, "The Essence of Leadership." Underneath the title was the following definition of leadership: "A true leader has the confidence to stand alone, the courage to make tough decisions, and the compassion to listen to the needs of others. In the end, leaders are much like eagles...they don't flock, you find them one at a time." This is an impressive set of traits, but what do they really say? A few hours later I arrived at my destination, turned on CNN, and heard a story about John Walker, the 20-year-old American who had been fighting with the Taliban. Based on the information provided, Walker met the aforementioned definition as a leader. He had the confidence to stand alone, the courage to leave his privileged life in the United States for Yemen and Pakistan, and was motivated by the humanistic side of Islam! But there is not a scintilla of evidence that he had exercised the type of influence over others that was inherent in my definition.

Nonetheless, there remains much popular sentiment for the heroic position. Best-selling books on leadership encourage managers to learn the secrets of leadership from Queen Elizabeth I, Attila the Hun, Jesus Christ, Ernest Shackleton, and countless others. The fact that these individuals' undisputed accomplishments occurred in response to highly specific challenges at earlier points in history does not deter readers from the belief that they are equally relevant to the circumstances they face today.

The Situational Approach to Leadership

In sharp contrast to the heroic model is the situational point of view espoused by some scholars, most notably Jeffrey Pfeffer of Stanford University. To Pfeffer, leadership is an illusion. It is a quality that is attributable to people who are the beneficiaries of unusually favorable external conditions. The general who wins the battle becomes a "great leader," while the one who loses becomes "the goat." Similarly, the CEO whose stock price quadruples is a great leader, while we search for deficiencies in leadership talent in one whose stock tumbles. Pfeffer argues that leaders have little or no control over the key variables that determine organizational performance, and that the discretion they do have is severely limited both by the organization, of which they are a part, and by its external context. We attribute causality to leadership because it enhances our feeling of safety and control. Organizations feed this illusion of potency to leadership through elaborate search and selection processes followed by highly visible ceremonies surrounding the change of control.

To put it succinctly, the heroic model would have us believe that great leaders create the situations for which they are remembered, whereas the situational approach would predict that it is these situations that create the illusion of leadership.

There are at least two properties of situations that seem to support the Pfeffer position. Both typically lead to the attribution of leadership qualities in the absence of compelling evidence of the kind of influence in our definition. The first of these is success. George Bush, Sr., attained a personal high in popular attitudes just after the Desert Storm War, as did Colin Powell and Norman Schwartzkopf. Conversely, Jimmy Carter's leadership image was tainted by the chance juxtaposition of helicopters and a sandstorm.

But success or failure are not the only determinants of good leadership. External threat, for which the leader is not responsible, also contributes to the attribution of leadership. This phenomenon is vividly represented in the aftermath of the terrorism of September 11, 2001. The popularity of George W. Bush skyrocketed from a mediocre 50% to an incredible 93%, probably not because of actions on his part but rather because of our need for heroes in times of threat. Similarly, George Pataki, governor of New York State, and Rudy Guiliani, mayor of New York City, experienced similar gains in popularity. To paraphrase Pfeffer, the more powerful the contextual effects on organizations, the more people feel overwhelmed and the greater the need to invent leadership. It is intriguing to speculate how many of those who go down in history as great leaders were simply beneficiaries of situations extremely well suited to the attribution of leadership.

The situational model sidesteps the issues of leader selection and training. Since leadership does not exist except in the minds of followers, technologies for selecting or training leaders are irrelevant. If it has normative value, the situational model is of principal relevance to those desiring to acquire a reputation as a leader. Positions having a high likelihood of success or changing from negative to positive should be sought, whereas those with opposite qualities should be avoided.

Contingency Models of Leadership

The third model of the role of leadership in determining organizational effectiveness is termed the contingency model. It views effectiveness as largely determined by an appropriate matching of leader qualities and situational factors. It is not the situation alone nor the leader alone, but rather the relationship between the two. Leadership is not a generalized trait but rather a set of situation-specific traits. Similarly, the situation is not a solitary cause but rather corresponds with a set of demands that have the potential of capitalizing on the talents and predispositions of those who are exposed to them.

The contingency or matching theory complicates both the selection and training of leaders by introducing situational components into each. The task of selecting leaders becomes a special case of the classic selection problem of matching job characteristics with applicant abilities. Evidence of past success is less relevant than evidence of past success in dealing with similar challenges. Similarly, leadership training must be tailored to the specific challenges to be faced or oriented toward developing the ability to accurately perceive situational demands and match one's leadership style to these demands.

Illustrating the Three Models

These three contrasting positions constitute different "lenses" for viewing leadership. The differences among them can be illustrated by considering a hypothetical experiment. On one hand, we have an array of people who view themselves or are viewed by others as candidates for a leadership position. On the other hand, we have a set of situations, each requiring the exercise of leadership. These situations could vary markedly in the magnitude and nature of the challenges they pose, including the culture in which the challenge is embedded, the values of those whose energies are to be tapped, and so forth. The people could also vary in such things as their aptitudes, abilities, and other personality dispositions.

Now let us imagine the perfect experiment in which we could observe each person in each situation and we could judge their effectiveness in each. Thus, we could represent the results of our experiment as a matrix, with people represented by rows and situations as columns. Aggregating by rows and then by columns would enable us to test the three positions we have described. If leadership is a generalized trait, we would observe most of the variance in effectiveness occurring among the row means. There would be large differences in the overall effectiveness of different people, meaning that one could predict a person's ability to demonstrate leadership in one situation from his or her performance in a totally different situation. On the other hand, the situational point of view would lead us to expect large differences among the column means. Some challenges would enable all people to shine as leaders whereas others would defy the skills of all.

Finally, the contingency model would be consistent with those observations within the matrix that could not be predicted from either the person's mean score (reflecting a general leadership trait) or the situation's mean score. In other words, the person's success or failure would be a surprise, not explicable by either the pure situational or pure dispositional approach but potentially explained by a contingency theory.

Where then should we look to understand effective leadership—to the person, to the situation, or to both in interaction with one another? All three models have some explanatory value but we shall argue that relative potency depends on the nature of the problem one seeks to answer. In our hypothetical experiment, if the situations are highly similar to one another (and the persons are different), performance in one is likely to be predictive of performance in another. Experiments in which managers have been rotated from highly performing units to poorly performing ones doing the same kind of work shows that they tend to carry their level of performance with them. Personal qualities tend to transcend situational differences when situations are highly similar.

On the other hand, if the situations are highly dissimilar and the persons very similar, we make the opposite prediction. Situational effects will dominate the effects of personal qualities. These are precisely the kinds of situations that Pfeffer cites to support his situational view. Studying cities and towns and athletic teams over substantial time periods, he finds little or no evidence that changes in policies, practices, or achievements are attributable to changes in leadership. Pfeffer concludes that, "If one cannot observe differences when leaders change, then what does it matter who occupies the position or how they behave." But mayors, athletic coaches, and, indeed, most leaders must pass through a strict screening and selection process that greatly limits the variability among those who are finally selected. If the persons are carbon copies of one another, situation effects should be the residual source of variance and leadership effects should disappear.

Leadership effects should also disappear when leaders have minimum discretion in the conduct of their jobs. There are some leadership roles in which leaders' choices are highly constrained by institutional traditions. The leader is, to use Pfeffer's term, an actor, with the script largely written by others or dictated by the organizational context.

I once had a colleague who had a mechanical model of an organization. It was a set of gears assembled in the shape of a pyramid. Turning the gear at the top of the pyramid about 10 degrees produced rapid 360-degree rotations at the pyramid's base. Pfeffer's analysis envisages a drastically different gearing—one in which turning the uppermost gear has little or no effect on the behavior of other gears!

But what about the contingency model? When is it most likely to represent the blueprint for thinking about and acting on leadership? The answer is clear: Wherever there is diversity among leaders and leadership candidates, and whenever there is diversity and fluidity in the kinds of challenges facing leaders, matching of leaders and environments will represent the key to effectiveness. This is precisely the environment that will be experienced by leaders in the 21st century.

In the present rapidly changing and complex world, the heroic model is no longer adequate to guide policies for selecting and training leaders. Similarly, the situational model, while appropriately drawing our attention to the "luck of the draw" in attributions of leadership, gives us no levers by which the quality of leadership may be enhanced. Matching of leadership qualities and behaviors to situational demands has been and will continue to be necessary for optimizing organizational effectiveness. To use an historical example with clear parallels to the present day, Patton and Gandhi may both have had the personal qualities necessary for the immense challenges they faced, but it is very unlikely each could have succeeded in the other's role.

A Contingency Model of Leadership Style

I turn now to a specific contingency model that I have been working on with colleagues for over a quarter of a century. This model deals not with all facets of leadership but rather with what has traditionally been termed leadership style. Historically, this term has been used to refer to the form and degree to which leaders involve their direct reports in decision making. Some refer to this dimension of leader behavior as empowerment. I prefer the term *participation*, which we define as the opportunity afforded direct reports to influence decisions.

The astute reader will note that I have shifted to the term "we" in describing the contingency model of leadership style. I use this term in two senses. First, there is the proximal "we"—my colleagues Philip Yetton and Arthur Jago, with whom I worked closely at different stages in the evolution of these ideas. Then there is the distal "we"—the hundreds of social scientists in different parts of the world who have spontaneously joined us in testing and elaborating these ideas. Thus far, a body of over 100 scientific publications and about 50 doctoral dissertations have laid the foundation of the particular contingency model summarized here. In this chapter I will not be able to do justice to this large body of research, but rather will touch on the highlights including its implications for the leadership challenges in the current century.

Our interests were both normative and descriptive. Normatively, we sought to construct an expert system that would guide leaders to match their leadership style to the situations they face. Descriptively, our goal was to understand when leaders do, in fact, utilize various leadership styles and the factors that influence their choices.

A Taxonomy of Leadership Styles

Both normative and descriptive approaches utilize the same taxonomy of leadership styles. The taxonomy has changed over the life of the research program but the current form is shown in Table 5–1. The terms decide (0), consult individually (3), consult group (5), facilitate (7), and delegate (10), refer to leadership styles, and the numbers in parentheses indicate what most people believe to be the relative amounts of participation that they afford. (A mean score of 2–3 is highly autocratic; a mean score of 6–7 is highly participative.) In the normative model, leadership style is the independent variable and the goal is to understand when each style is likely to be most effective. In our descriptive work, leadership style is the dependent variable and the goal is to understand when each style is likely to be employed.

Toward a Normative Model

Our effort to develop a normative model began with a search of the relevant research evidence on the effects of participation. We identified four outcomes of participation, each relevant to its organizational impact. Two of these, the quality of decisions and the effectiveness with which they are implemented, are components of the effectiveness of the decision. The remaining two outcomes are byproducts of the decision-making process. Any decision-making process incurs costs (principally the time of organization members) and may have benefits (principally the development of organization members).

The nature of these four outcomes and the principal evidence concerning the effects of leadership styles on each has been reviewed elsewhere. Here we will restrict our attention to the way in which our normative model incorporates these outcomes. In developing a normative model, we faced a choice between a model that would prescribe a single leadership style for an organizational position or role or one that recognized differences between the styles required in dealing with different problems or decisions within that role. We chose the latter course as the unit of analysis for both research and for the construction of an expert system.

Table 5–1 Taxonomy of Leadership Styles

0	3	5	7	10
Decide	**Consult (Individually)**	**Consult (Group)**	**Facilitate**	**Delegate**
You make the decision alone and either announce or "sell" it to the group. You may use your expertise in collecting information from the group or others that you deem relevant to the problem.	You present the problem to group members individually, get their suggestions, and then make the decision.	You present the problem to group members in a meeting, get their suggestions, and then make the decision.	You present the problem to the group in a meeting. You act as facilitator, defining the problem to be solved and the boundaries within which the decision must be made. Your objective is to get concurrence on a decision. Above all, you take care to ensure that your ideas are not given any greater weight than those of others simply because of your position.	You permit the group to make the decision within prescribed limits. The group undertakes the identification and diagnosis of the problem, developing alternative procedures for solving it, and deciding on one or more alternative solutions. While you play no direct role in the group's deliberations unless explicitly asked, your role is an important one behind the scenes, providing needed resources and encouragement.

Consistent with the contingency or matching position advocated earlier, we reject the position that there is one leadership style that fits all situations. Instead, we have identified a set of eleven situational factors that should influence a leader's choice. These are depicted in Figure 5–1 in the form of a scale. Factors to the left-hand side should tilt one's choice to the more autocratic alternatives, while those to the right should tilt one's choice to a more participative style. The two factors at the center determine the fineness of the point or fulcrum on which the bar rests. Thus, a high level of decision significance and/or a high level of disagreement among direct reports increases the sensitivity of the scale to factors on either left or right.

Figure 5–1 introduces the logic underlying the model but falls far short of prescribing a unique style for each decision problem. Figures 5–2 and 5–3 contain decision matrices that overcome this limitation. In Figure 5–2, we depict a time-driven model that utilizes the least amount of time to create an effective decision. Its orientation is short-term, since it is concerned with making effective decisions with a minimum investment of time. No attention is placed on employee development. Figure 5–3 shows what we term a development-driven model. It can be construed as long-term since it is concerned with making effective decisions in a manner maximally consistent with employee development. No attention is placed on time. It chooses the most developmental style consistent with creating an effective decision.

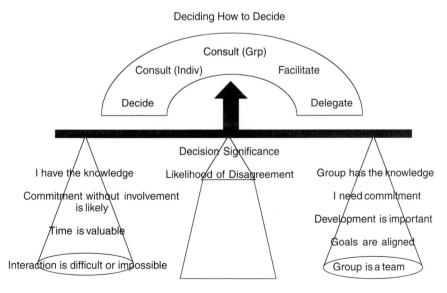

Figure 5–1   Factors that influence a leader's choices.

Decision Significance	Importance of Commitment	Leader Expertise	Likelihood of Commitment	Goal Alignment	Group Expertise	Team Competence	
H	H	H	H	-	-	-	Decide
			L	H	H	H	Delegate
						L	Consult Team
					L	-	Consult Team
				L	-	-	Consult Team
		L	H	H	H	H	Facilitate
						L	Consult Individually
					L	-	Consult Individually
				L	-	-	Consult Individually
			L	H	H	H	Facilitate
						L	Consult Team
					L	-	Consult Team
				L	-	-	Consult Team
	L	H	-	-	-	-	Decide
		L	-	H	H	H	Facilitate
						L	Consult Individually
					L	-	Consult Individually
				L	-	-	Consult Individually
L	H	-	H	-	-	-	Decide
			L	-	-	H	Delegate
						L	Facilitate
	L	-	-	-	-	-	Decide

Instructions: The matrix operates like a funnel. Start at the left with a specific decision problem in mind. Column headings denote situational factors that may or may not be present in that problem. Progress by selecting high or low (H or L) for each relevant situational factor, judging only those situational factors for which a judgment is called for, until you reach the recommended process.

Figure 5-2   Time-driven model.

Use of each model requires a specific decision problem and a specific group or team who could potentially be involved in solving the problem. One enters each matrix at the left-hand side and looks for the presence or absence of each of the situational factors expressed as column headings. If the factor is present, one follows the H (high) path; if it is absent, one follows the L (low) path. Continuing this process (while avoiding crossing any horizontal line) provides a recommended process. Submitting the same problem to both models can be interesting. Sometimes the two models yield identical recommendations. When they differ, the development-driven model recommends a more participative process.

Table 5–2 contains four cases and the results obtained by applying the two matrices to them. The observant reader will note that we dropped four situational factors in moving from the scale in Figure 5–1 to the decision matrices.

Decision Significance	Importance of Commitment	Leader Expertise	Likelihood of Commitment	Goal Alignment	Group Expertise	Team Competence	
H	H	-	H	H	H	H	Delegate
						L	Facilitate
					L	-	Consult (Group)
				L	-	-	Consult (Group)
			L	H	H	H	Delegate
						L	Facilitate
					L	-	
				L	-	-	Consult (Group)
	L	-	-	H	H	H	Delegate
						L	Facilitate
					L	-	Consult (Group)
				L	-	-	
L	H	-	H	-	-	-	Decide
			L	-	-	-	Delegate
	L	-	-	-	-	-	Decide

Figure 5–3   Development-driven model.

Table 5–2 Cases and Results of Matrix Analysis

Setting: Banking
Your Position: President & Chief Executive Officer

The bank examiners have just left, insisting that many of your commercial real estate loans be written off, thereby depleting already low capital. Along with many other banks in your region, your bank is in serious danger of being closed by the regulators. As the financial problems surfaced, many of the top executives left to pursue other interests, but fortunately, you were able to replace them with three highly competent younger managers. While they had no prior acquaintance with one another, each is a product of a fine training program with one of the money center banks in which they rotated through positions in each of the banking functions. Your extensive experience in the industry leads you to the inevitable conclusion that the only hope is a two-pronged approach involving reduction of all but the most critical expenses and the sale of assets to other banks. The task must be accomplished quickly since further deterioration of the quality of the loan portfolio could result in a negative capital position, forcing regulators to close the bank.

The strategy is clear to you, but you have many details that will need to be worked out. You believe that you know what information will be needed to get the bank on a course for future prosperity. You are fortunate in having three young executives to help you out. While they have had little or no experience in working together you know that each is dedicated to the survival of the bank. Like you, they know what needs to be done and how to do it.

ANALYSIS   TIME DRIVEN: H H H L H H L – CONSULT GROUP
                     DVPT DRIVEN: H H L H H L – FACILITATE

Setting: Repertory Theater
Your Position: Executive Director

You are the executive director of a repertory theater affiliated with a major university. You are responsible for both financial and artistic direction of the theater. While you recognize that both of these responsibilities are important, you have focused your efforts where your own talents lie—on ensuring the highest level of artistic quality to the theater's productions. Reporting to you is a group of four department heads responsible for production, marketing, development, and administration, along with an assistant dean who is responsible for the actors who are also students in the university. They are a talented set of individuals, and each is deeply committed to the theater and experienced in working together as a team.

Last week you received a comprehensive report from an independent consulting firm commissioned to examine the financial health of the theater. You were shocked by the major conclusion of the report. The expenses of operating the theater have been growing much more rapidly than income, and by year's end the theater will be operating in the red. Unless expenses can be reduced, the surplus will be consumed, and within five years the theater might have to be closed.

You have distributed the report to your staff and are surprised at the variety of reactions that it has produced. Some dispute the report's conclusions, criticizing its assumptions or methods. Others are more shaken, but even they seem divided about what steps ought to be taken and when. None of them or, in fact, anyone connected with the theater would want it to close. It has a long and important tradition both in the university and in its surrounding community.

ANALYSIS   TIME DRIVEN: H H L L H H H – FACILITATE
                     DVPT DRIVEN: H H L H H H – DELEGATE

Table 5-2   Cases and Results of Matrix Analysis (continued)

Setting: Auto Parts Manufacturer
Your Position: County Manager

Your firm has just acquired a small manufacturer of spare auto parts in Southeast Asia. The recent collapse in the economies in this region made values very attractive. Your senior management decided to acquire a foothold in this region. It was less interested in the particular acquired firm, which produces parts for the local market, than it was in using it as a base from which to produce parts at reduced cost for the worldwide market.

When you arrived at your new assignment two weeks ago, you were somewhat surprised by the less than enthusiastic reception that your received from the current management. You attribute the obvious strain in working relations not only to linguistic and cultural differences but also to a deep-seated resentment to their new foreign owners. Your top management team seems to get along very well with one another, but the atmosphere changes when you step into the room.

Nonetheless, you will need their help in navigating your way through this unfamiliar environment. Your immediate need is to develop a plan for land acquisition on which to construct new manufacturing and warehouse facilities. You and your administrative assistant, who accompanied you from your previous assignment, should be able to carry out the plan, but its development would be hazardous without local knowledge.

ANALYSIS   TIME DRIVEN: H L L L – CONSULT INDIVIDUALLY
                     DVPT DRIVEN: H L L – CONSULT GROUP

Setting: Manufacturer of Internal Combustion Engines
Your Position: Project Manager

Your firm has received a contract from one of the world's largest automobile manufacturers to produce an engine to power their "flagship" sports car. The engine is of Japanese design and is very complex, not only by American but by world standards. As project manager, you have been involved in this venture from the outset, and you and your team of engineers have taken pride at the rave reviews the engine has received in the automotive press. Your firm had previously been known as a producer of outboard engines for marine use, and its image is now greatly enhanced as the manufacturer of the power plant of one of the world's fastest sports cars.

Your excitement at being a part of this project was dashed by a report of serious engine problems in cars delivered to customers. Seventeen owners of cars produced in the first month have experienced engine seizures—a circumstance that has caused the manufacturer to suspend sales, to put a halt to current production, and to notify owners of this year's production not to drive their cars! Needless to say, this situation is a disaster and unless solved immediately could expose your firm to extended litigation as well as terminate what had been a mutually beneficial relationship. As the person most informed about the engine, you have spent the last two weeks on the road inspecting several of the seized engines, the plant in which they are installed, and reviewing the practices in your own company's plant in which the engine is manufactured. As a result of this research, you have become convinced that the problem is due to operation of the engine at very high RPMs before it has warmed up to develop sufficient oil pressure. The solution would be to install an electronic control limiting engine RPMs until the engine has reached normal operating temperature.

ANALYSIS   TIME DRIVEN: H H H H – DECIDE
                     DVPT DRIVEN: H H H H L – CONSULT GROUP

To have retained all 11 factors would have greatly increased the complexity of the matrices and made it impossible to represent them on a single page. To combine the usability of the matrices with the complexity of the model, we developed a computer program that we have dubbed an expert system. The computer model, contained on a CD-ROM, has features not found in the decision matrices. These include (a) use of all 11 situational factors, (b) permitting five possible levels of each situational factor, (c) incorporating the value of time and the value of development as situational factors rather than as separate matrices, and (d) guiding managers through the process of analyzing the situations they face rather than as separate matrices.

Figure 5–4 shows the basic screen of the expert system being applied to the manufacturing problem described in Table 5–2. The case has been evaluated on all 11 factors. Clicking on the Calculate button has produced the bar graph depicted at the bottom. This particular bar graph is labeled Overall. To illustrate the trade-offs among the four outcome variables one can produce bar graphs for each outcome by selecting the tabs on the right-hand side of the screen.

The potential usefulness of a normative model such as this one depends on its ability to predict the odds of effective decisions resulting from the use of the five leadership styles. Since this version model shown here is very recent, it has not yet been subjected to studies of its validity. However, earlier versions of the model have been validated. In summarizing the

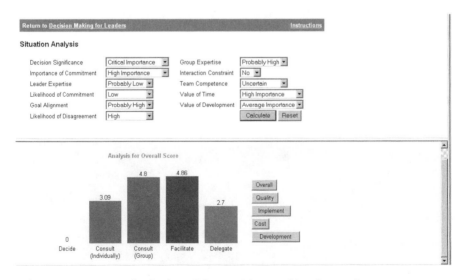

Figure 5–4   Sample display of the Decision Making for Leaders program.

results of six validation studies conducted by different investigators of an earlier version of the model, we have shown that choices made by managers that coincided with the model were about twice as likely to produce decisions deemed to be successful than choices that did not coincide with the model's recommendations. Further evidence relevant to validity is that the model's recommendations on a set of standardized situations correlate very highly with the mean choices made by experienced managers.

It would be a mistake to conclude that use of the model is a guarantee of effective decision-making. The model has a reasonable batting average (indeed, one that is far superior to that of most managers); however, it does not bat "one thousand." Many managers who have used it, in either the decision matrix or CD-ROM form, tell us that the discipline of analyzing a situation on a set of dimensions relevant to effective leadership is in itself useful, regardless of whether one actually clicks on the Calculate button to generate the bar graph.

Toward a Descriptive Model of Leadership Style

Here we turn from our efforts to help managers match their leadership styles to the challenges they face to our second goal—understanding how managers go about deciding when and how to share their decision-making power. The principal method used is a device we call a *problem set*. It is a set of short, real-life cases (usually containing 30, but sometimes as many as 54 cases). Samples of the kind of cases we use are shown in Table 5–2.

Problem sets are not assembled randomly. They are very carefully constructed in accordance with what statisticians call a multifactorial experimental design. Eight of the principal factors that should influence leadership style are varied across the set of cases and the variation of each factor is uncorrelated with each other factor. Managers who are untrained in the normative model are asked to imagine themselves in the role of leader in each case, and to indicate what leadership style they would employ if faced with that situation.

Our data collection efforts have involved well over 100,000 managers from various parts of the globe. All of these managers worked on the problem set as part of a leadership training program that included training in the normative model. They worked on the problem set on their jobs prior to the training with the expectation that they would receive feedback on their leadership style during the training.

These data have taught us a great deal about how managers think about sharing their decision-making power. Here we will address some of the more important parts of our findings.

It should come as no surprise that, like the normative model, all managers vary their style with the situation. No manager is "one size fits all." Furthermore, the average manager tends to respond to each of the situational factors in a manner roughly corresponding to their role depicted in Figure 5–1. However, few managers are like the average manager! Most attend to some of these factors and ignore others. A few attend to a factor but respond to its presence or absence in a manner inconsistent with the model and with what we believe to be effective decision making.

Managers also differ in their overall tendencies to use styles that are autocratic versus participative. This is expressed by their mean score over the entire set of cases on the 10-point scale shown in Table 5–1. A mean score of 2-3 is highly autocratic; a mean score of 6-7 is highly participative.

Of all the demographic variables, culture is by far the most important, accounting for the greatest variance in managers' mean score on this index of participation. Another important factor is gender. In study after study, we have found that female managers tend to use more participative leadership styles than their male counterparts.

Early in our data collection enterprise we began to notice a shift toward more participative styles. In the quarter of a century that we have been tracking leadership styles, we have observed that the average manager has moved progressively toward the right-hand side of the scale. It is interesting to speculate as to what is driving this movement. We suspect that there are many factors that could be involved. One of these is the increased rate of change in the environments of most organizations induced by globalization and deregulation. The enhanced complexity of decisions in a rapidly changing world puts them beyond the capabilities of any one individual and requires blending multiple competencies and specialties.

A second factor may be increased education in the labor force and the greater need for self-expression and development of one's capabilities that are associated with education. Also of potential relevance may be the flattening of hierarchies and the rapid growth of information technology.

Differences among managers in their propensity to involve their associates in decision making and, to an even greater degree, their sensitivity to critical differences in situational requirements, produces large differences in effectiveness. Managers' choices on the problem set reveal the extent to which each uses leadership styles that produce decisions that are high in quality and possess the commitment needed to be effectively implemented. It also reveals differences in managers' time efficiency and in the extent to which their styles are likely to further develop the capability of their work teams.

While problem sets were originally developed for research purposes, they have become very valuable tools for developing leaders. Currently, each manager who completes the problem set receives a five-page, computer-based analysis that compares his or her leadership style with a peer group, and compares the choices with the normative model. It also reveals the situational factors that they attend to, ignores their success in achieving each of the four outcomes affected by participation, and ends with a series of recommendations for increased effectiveness.

Conclusion

The research that we have done on styles of leadership has reinforced our belief in the importance of leadership in building effective organizations and in the value of contingency approaches to its understanding. Influencing others in the pursuit of organizational goals by noncoercive means is too important and too complex to be explained by either situational or personal qualities alone. Matching of personal qualities and situational challenges is indispensable both to our understanding of the leadership process and to the development of viable technologies for helping organizations in the selection and development of effective leaders.

Our focus on participation is but a small part of the leadership terrain, but hopefully will serve as a model for others interested in other aspects of that terrain.

PART 2

21C PROCESS

R eengineering guru James A. Champy introduces a next generation of process change called X-engineering in the introductory
chapter of Part 2. Champy sees the reengineering of the last decade
as only a beginning, and in this decade the nature of work will change
even more dramatically. And the corporation, once a closed enterprise, will become part of a much larger network of customers, suppliers, and collaborators, all working in concert to perform their work at
new levels of efficiency. X-engineering requires a mastery of change
across multiple enterprises and an objective beyond improved efficiencies. He relates the example of how Owens & Minor, Inc.—a $3-bil-
lion, Fortune 500 company—is revolutionizing its industry by applying
the ideas of X-engineering. In fact, it was at work on changing its
industry well before the term was even conceived. By paying attention
to how employees actually divided their time among various processes
and customers, O&M found that costs and profitability depended on a
few key factors, most of them controlled by the customer. Finally,
Champy explains three principles that underlie X-engineering: harmonization, transparency, and standardization.

Bosses and others at the top continue to dominate, exerting subordinate controls that extend far beyond the entitlements and jurisdictions
ceded them by the organization chart. Subordinates continue to
knuckle under, mimicking beliefs from above without openly expressing those courses of action they believe more corporately correct. Uni-

versity of California, Los Angeles, professor Samuel A. Culbert, and Chaminade University professor Scott J. Schroeder unleash the key to getting hierarchy to work in the 21st-century organization. They suggest that the key is changing the system to feature two-sided accountable relationships. The basic conditions are internalization of human-nature facts, appreciation for the politics that derive from self-interests, and a clearly articulated hierarchy that unambiguously delineates responsibilities and authorities so that decision makers are motivated to openly solicit other views prior to taking action.

Robert L. Heneman, a professor at Fisher College of Business at Ohio State University, and HR consultant Wendy K. Schutt propose some fundamental issues that need to be addressed by executives in order for basic reward principles developed in the 20th century to be successfully applied to the rapidly changing nature of work in the 21st century. The issues addressed in their chapter need to be considered if further progress is to be made at developing new principles of compensation applicable to organizations in the 21st century. In this chapter, they explore how to integrate reward systems with organizational learning systems, focus on execution as well as strategy, move from compensation to total rewards, design public sector rewards, revisit the concept of equity, and extend reward systems to new business environments.

The central purpose of enterprise is to create value for its shareholders. IMD Switzerland professor Derek F. Abell proposes a framework for understanding the underlying stakeholder purposes that influence organizational performance, and the leader's role in balancing these purposes and interests to achieve long-term sustainable success. He has raised questions not only about the validity, but also about the long-run efficacy of single-minded attention to shareholder value. Abell makes the convincing argument that what is evident is the need for leadership initiative at the policy, strategic, and operational levels simultaneously, and attention to not only the whats and hows of balanced leadership, but even more importantly to the whys. When any of these are ignored, focusing on shareholder value improvement up front is like pushing on a string; when these are all used in a coordinated fashion, the resulting broad commitment has the combined effect of tautening the string and pulling shareholder value upward.

Eminent thought leader Noel M. Tichy and researcher Christopher DeRose, both from the University of Michigan Business School, take us on a tour of the historical phases of organizational development (OD) in the final chapter of Part 2. They boldly argue that in the 1980s, Jack Welch, chairman and CEO of General Electric, fathered the rebirth of OD and why they believe so. In their well-researched chapter, they provide detailed example of Royal Dutch/Shell that demonstrates how leaders who see their primary role as leader/teachers, who lead change and develop human capital, can transform a business at its core. This case offers a compelling benchmark for OD practitioners everywhere for they have demonstrated solutions for helping leaders become teachers and scale this capability to thousands of people around the world, generating billions of dollars of new revenue and cost savings. The most interesting advances in OD in the future, Tichy and DeRose believe, will come from practitioners who are teaching leaders in their organizations to teach others.

6

From Reengineering to X-Engineering

James A. Champy

When Mike Hammer and I wrote *Reengineering the Corporation* in 1992, we argued that there were compelling forces that required companies to change. We called those forces the *three Cs*: customers, competition, and change itself. Today, those forces are still at work, more powerful than ever. In response, they require a sort of reengineering on steroids—the fundamental redesign of work, not just within the walls of a company, but now between a company and its customers, suppliers, and partners. I call this next generation of process change *X-engineering*. The X denotes the crossing of organizational boundaries.

Back in 1992, customers were already gaining the upper hand. They had more choices, their loyalty was fleeting, and they were becoming more sophisticated. They wanted products of consistent quality, attentive service, and just-in-time delivery; and they wanted all this at a low price. Companies could no longer be just product-driven. The catchwords of the day had become "customer driven," although many companies thought that just meant having a pleasant voice answering the customer service line.

At the same time, competition was increasing, thanks to globalization. No market was safe from a new competitor who either changed business rules or had a dramatically lower cost structure. Wal-Mart was reinventing discount retailing; Japanese automobile manufacturers were delivering quality cars at low prices (and making money); and a few banks had figured out how to process a mortgage application in days, rather than months. And because markets were becoming increasingly open, these new competitors were showing up everywhere, from Anchorage to Ankara.

And the rate of business change itself seemed to be accelerating. Companies that had been market leaders one year were floundering the next. The need to change became a constant. Size was not a clear advantage—

certainly if it slowed down a company's ability to change. Nimbleness became an important corporate quality.

Our answer in 1992 was as follows: Fundamentally redesign work, not around traditional departments or functions, but around processes. Companies had become slow to respond, mired in their own bureaucracies, and overly fragmented. Work was passed from department to department, with no one in charge. Customers were often confused as to where to go if they had a problem. And just applying more automation to bad processes wasn't the answer. That just seemed to make things worse.

We called our approach reengineering. The idea caught on as companies fought to regain their competitiveness. Across the globe, companies sought to reduce cycle times, lower costs, and improve quality by looking at such processes as new product development, order fulfillment, and materials procurement. Few workplaces were untouched by these changes.

Today, however, I see the reengineering of the last decade as only a beginning. In this decade, the nature of work will change even more dramatically. And the corporation, once a closed enterprise, will become part of a much larger network of customers, suppliers, and collaborators, all working in concert to perform their work at new levels of efficiency. Companies like Dell, Intel, and Cisco have been leading the way, fundamentally changing how they do business with their customers and suppliers. The current slowdown in technology spending and the resultant challenge to these companies should not be confused with what is going on within their network of relationships: whole new levels of operating efficiencies are being achieved.

The drivers of this next phase of business change are still the three Cs. Today, however, these forces are intensified by information technology—particularly the Internet. Customers have endless choices just a click away. Almost every product or service appears at risk of becoming a commodity. Competition increases as companies become more transparent and information becomes more available to customers. And the Internet accelerates almost all processes. Business seems breathless.

Inefficiencies and Opportunities Are Exposed

As these pressures intensify, the inefficiencies that still exist in doing business are also becoming increasingly evident. Take, for example, the whole area of logistics—the processes by which goods move from company to company or from company to customers. Globally, approximately two trillion dollars a year are spent on these services, and 40% of those dollars pay for administrative services, sometimes called paperwork. A transoceanic shipment can require up to 26 documents. What if we could improve the efficiency of these administrative processes by 50%? That would result in annual savings of 400 billion dollars.

No industry is free of these intercompany inefficiencies. Take healthcare, for example. Some healthcare providers—such as HMOs—spend 35 cents of every dollar on administrative tasks, like claims processing. That's money that could be spent in the actual delivery of care if we could find ways to reduce the inefficiencies in the transactions between employers, insurers, doctors, hospitals, and patients. And despite the fact that the healthcare industry spends hundreds of millions of dollars on administrative processes, no one is satisfied with the service. Doctors feel overmanaged by payors. Patients are perplexed by the lack of universal healthcare records and the complexity of the care process. Hospitals wait a year to get paid only 75% of what they have billed. And employers complain that healthcare is once again getting too costly.

The potential for X-engineering in healthcare, and in most industries, is enormous. But companies will be challenged in its execution. Reengineering will have seemed simple in comparison. After all, that was work done within a single company whose managers were ostensibly in control. X-engineering requires a mastery of change across multiple enterprises.

X-engineering also requires an objective beyond improved efficiencies. When a company focuses its process efforts only on cost reduction, the opportunity to deliver even more value to customers may get lost. The X-engineer asks two additional questions as she looks for collaborative process opportunities: what new business proposition will I be able to offer my customers and are there other participants who can help me create an ever improving proposition? Together with process, proposition and participation create what I call the *three Ps* of X-engineering.

Although challenging, X-engineering can be done, as the following example illustrates. And as you read the story of this inspired company, contemplate X-engineering's working definition: the art and science of using technology-enabled processes to connect businesses with other businesses and companies with their customers to achieve dramatic improvements in efficiency and create new value for everyone involved.

Owens & Minor, The Quiet Giant

Owens & Minor, Inc. (O&M) is the leading U.S. distributor of medical and surgical supplies to hospital systems. It is a $3 billion Fortune 500 company, and is revolutionizing its industry by applying the ideas of X-engineering. In fact, it was at work on changing its industry well before the term was even conceived.

O&M has long been in the technological and process forefront: It put in its first computerized order system back in 1954, the Jurassic age of computing. In 1990, still well ahead of the pack, the company embarked on an aggressive growth strategy with a commitment to technology and supply chain partnerships. The strategy was successful. As the new century approached, CEO G. Gilmer Minor III, whose grandfather co-founded the company in 1882, could boast that O&M was distributing 300,000 medical and surgical products through 49 distribution centers to 4,000 hospitals across the country. It was one of the largest distributors in the health industry, which was itself growing inexorably, and the future should have looked golden.

But there were snakes in this Eden; as Minor put it, "We saw the world changing around us." As managed care swept the industry, hospitals came under enormous pressure to cut costs. They merged, consolidated, and formed buying groups to increase their market leverage, squeezing down distributors' already thin profit margins. They learned to buy their most expensive goods direct from the makers, cutting distributors out of the loop and paying them only for high-volume, low-profit supplies. And the manufacturers added to the pressure by raising prices and shaving the discounts they had traditionally given distributors. When O&M raised its own prices by 1% across the board in 1995, some of its customers switched to other distributors. O&M chalked up a loss for the year of $11 million.

A basic roadblock to change was the cost-plus pricing system, standard in the healthcare industry for two decades. Distributors traditionally took a markup of 6 to 8% on the manufacturer's price, which was supposed to cover their costs and provide their profit. But as cost pressures grew, hospitals fought to cut inventories by demanding more frequent deliveries. Some converted to "stockless" operation, with just-in-time delivery so finely tuned that O&M was handing over boxes of sutures directly to operating rooms.

This added to O&M's costs not just by multiplying delivery trips, but in carrying more inventory and extra handling of the supplies as pallets were unloaded and goods were repacked in smaller boxes. Managing inventories led to product returns, financing costs, and the special problem of making sure medical products were used before their expiration dates. And since hospitals felt free to hold payment for 90 days, the receivables had to be financed too.

But O&M couldn't even track its own costs with any certainty. Its processes had developed haphazardly, with some clients getting more services than others. "We had gotten into some contracts where we underpriced the service because we didn't know what our costs were," recalls Jose Valderas, divisional vice president. "We knew what our total costs were to run our warehouse for all customers. However, we didn't understand how much it would cost to run one particular account, pick the orders in the fashion the account needed, make the number of deliveries they needed, and so on." What O&M had to do, he concluded, was "to separate the price of the box from the price to move the box."

To solve that problem, O&M set up a pilot program in activity-based costing (ABC) at the distribution center at O&M's headquarters in Savage, Maryland. It is a well-tested, scientific way to follow the money, attaching real costs to real processes. And following the money is one technique for finding X-engineering opportunities.

By paying attention to how employees actually divided their time among various processes and customers, O&M found that costs—and thus profit-ability—depended on a few key factors, most of them controlled by the customer. These included the type of service requested (e.g., traditional bulk deliveries vs. a stockless system); the number of purchase orders per month; the number of lines in each order; the number of deliveries per week; whether the order came in by phone, fax, or electronically; and the interest cost of carrying inventory and receivables. This approach also gave O&M the opportunity to observe more closely the inefficiencies in its cus-tomers' processes.

Using that data, O&M made some progress in cutting its own costs. But it had already been an efficient operation; the real problem was the strait-jacket that cost-plus pricing and managed care had produced and the cost burdens imposed on O&M by its customers' poor processes.

Adding to the pressures, the manufacturers of medical equipment were also pushing for a more efficient supply chain. Their goal was to set up a continuous replenishment process, with a flow of information stretching from raw materials producers to the patient's bedside to ensure the smoothest possible operations. But here again, O&M was frustrated; given the hospitals' lack of attention to process, continuous replenishment was not an option any time soon.

The problems came to a head, and in 1996 the beginnings of a solution emerged. Ideal Health System, a nonprofit hospital chain, had been using a rival distributor but announced that its $30 million annual business was now up for bids. In the past, the competitor had been able to underbid O&M because it was affiliated with a manufacturer and could discount those products. O&M's Valderas knew Ideal wasn't happy with that arrangement because its member hospitals would prefer more choice of product. But how low a bid would it take to get the contract, and how could O&M cover its costs?

Valderas was studying the latest ABC report when the idea hit: O&M could abandon cost-plus pricing and convert to activity-based pricing, taking a markup of zero and charging for the services it actually performed. In that way, customers would see the actual costs of the processes associated with the services they were demanding. (Transparency is an important principle of X-engineering.)

Sizable risks were involved. Activity-based costing was a fairly new concept, difficult both to grasp and to implement. The healthcare industry was used to cost-plus pricing, which was built into the industry's financial and accounting structure from budgeting to the incentive program. How could a distributor's fee be inserted in a hospital budget that didn't have a line for it? How could it be factored into transfer prices on products moving from one department to another? And fundamentally, how could Ideal—and other hospitals in turn—be persuaded that this whole approach wasn't just a fancy scheme to charge higher prices?

The challenge wasn't easy. But O&M found opportunity in following the money because it was looking to reduce hospitals' costs and improve their operations at the same time. Valderas and his colleagues had not merely listened for customers' complaints; they had perceived problems that the customers hadn't yet detected themselves.

In truth, the cost-plus system wasn't working well for the hospitals either. As the ABC data showed, the system masked inefficiencies and costs that were built into hospital operations. O&M's services were largely used to paper over problems that O&M had no power to cure. Even the expedients that the hospitals had found to cut their payments to distributors didn't come without a price. If they bought expensive goods direct from the makers, for instance, they had to buy more than they wanted and swallow the inventory cost. In forcing distributors to lower their margins, they thought they were getting bargains; however, the distributors often found a way to raise the price of less-conspicuous items.

By following the money, hospitals could track their own costs, improve their own efficiency, and actually reduce their payments to O&M, while O&M would perform less service and earn more profit. In X-engineering terms, the total landed cost of the service would be sharply reduced, to everyone's benefit.

But O&M would have to be completely transparent about its costs—and swallowing hard, Minor agreed. O&M opened its books, showing Ideal its detailed costs and its meager profit of less than 1% of revenues. Impressed with the distributor's forward thinking, flexibility, and dedication to customer service, Ideal agreed to make the transition to a modified version of activity-based pricing.

For a long time, the whole concept was a hard sell for the rest of the industry. Early on, says Tim Gill, O&M's director of logistics and support services, there were only blank stares when he asked customers if they knew about activity-based management. O&M put on a series of educational seminars around the country to persuade hospitals that the new way would help their bottom lines. The company also figured out that the pitch worked better with financial officers, who could see the larger picture, than with the purchasing materials people who traditionally dealt with distributors.

Activity-based pricing also involved a continuous process of X-engineering. Over time, O&M developed an array of technological programs to implement activity-based pricing. There was Wisdom, a software program to identify and track the costs of handling O&M goods in a hospital's materials management system, followed by Wisdom 2, a program that could also track products that hadn't been bought through O&M. Those programs, in turn, were incorporated into CostTrack, a three-step program that O&M uses with each client to make a baseline analysis of costs, find out what the system lacks, and provide services that will add value. One such service is OM Direct, an Internet-based purchasing system that lets buyers ascertain availability of products, order goods for delivery to the distributor, manage their inventory with hand-held computers, and make better informed decisions than ever before. At last count, O&M was moving $120 million in goods annually through OM Direct.

What O&M shows its customer, says Gill, is "what you really need and what makes sense for you. Is there anything you're doing internally that we could probably do better for you, or are there any services that we're providing you that maybe you don't need?"

A customer who has been getting six deliveries a week, for instance, might decide to cut O&M's fee by $2,000 a week and get along with five deliveries. That marginal increase in inventory cost is more than offset by cutting the time the customer's own staff spends unpacking and handling goods. Another hospital might assess the costs of its own internal handling system and pay O&M a smaller sum to deliver goods to the point of use. O&M might install its own sophisticated materials handling system in a customer's warehouse, taking over inventory management and hiring some of the customer's former staffers to run the system.

All told, Minor tells his clients, "This is the silver bullet." But he also warns them that it takes a lot of time and work to get the processes to mesh. There is a learning curve of about two years before major results start coming, and many customers need continuing help from O&M to make the system work. But that produces another major benefit: As customers catch on to what the harmonized process can do for them, their relationship with

O&M quickly changes from adversarial wariness to a new trust. "Once they see your costs, and say, 'Hey, these guys are really trying to help,' that's when you really start seeing change," says Gill. And when O&M applies its tools and techniques to the customers' processes, "We can give them information about their own operations that they never saw before."

At last count, 22% of O&M's business had been switched from cost-plus to activity-based pricing, accounting for $764 million worth of goods. Minor's goal was to reach 50% within three years. And the X-engineering will continue. In the next few years, O&M hopes to develop OM Direct into an Internet-based marketplace that connects with other marketplaces and lets customers buy goods from other distributors as well as from O&M.

In the long run, says Minor, the goal is "to make this whole ordering business seamless, from the point of use all the way back to the manufacturer's production line and then back through the supply chain." That's a long trip—but then, he has already gone a good part of the way.

X-Engineering Principles

As the O&M example illustrates, there are three principles that underlie X-engineering: harmonization, transparency, and standardization. Let's take each of them separately.

Harmonization

It should come as no surprise that transactions between companies are inherently inefficient. After all, they usually involve processes that were developed at different times by different players. One company's selling process tries to engage another company's procurement process. Another company's ordering process tries to engage another company's order-fulfillment process. As these processes engage, there is usually more friction than harmony—lost time, lost quality, and lost money. To deal with these problems, companies often build redundancy into their work, adding even more complexity and costs.

Early approaches to dealing with these problems—such as electronic data interchange and customer relationship management—were intended to work at the interfaces of differing processes, moving data and information across corporate boundaries. They did not aim to go very deep in the redesign of processes within companies.

X-engineering goes further. It requires that the processes companies share be jointly redesigned, or harmonized, as I call it. A company, for example, should not see its suppliers as independent entities throwing products or services over its wall, but rather as a set of processes that must be integrated into its own, and vice versa.

Transparency

For companies to harmonize their processes with others, they must become increasingly open. That is, they must show others how they operate, and even what their costs look like. That means letting go of false beliefs that most of what companies do is proprietary, and not to be shared. The hard truth is that most companies in an industry do the same thing. Very little of what they do is distinctive.

For customers and suppliers to connect in harmony with your processes, they must be open and visible. The next step will be to share your knowledge and your good ideas. Just as you propagate goods ideas within your company, you will now discuss them with your customers and suppliers.

Recently, I was explaining this concept of openness to a group of executives at a conference on corporate change. One executive challenged the idea. "You're advocating the death of capitalism as we know it," he argued. "How can we compete if we give all our secrets away?" Of course, if you have real secrets—like a truly proprietary manufacturing process—you don't give that away. But I believe that I am advocating the next phase of capitalism, a time when information flows freely between companies and when the basis of competition increasingly becomes a company's ability to execute.

And remember one other condition as you contemplate opening up and letting the world see how you operate. You can compete on the basis of having superb processes. Your competitors may not be able to copy your processes easily, because of their own behavioral legacies. High-performing companies often share how they do things. For example, take GE's processes for business improvement known as Six Sigma. For years, GE has been telling other companies how to accomplish major process change using Six Sigma techniques. The result has hardly been new competitive threats to GE in its markets, but rather an increasing admiration for how well GE operates.

Standardization

Once you have accepted that most of what you do is not unique, it should be an easy step to accept the benefits of standardization. Why not share nondifferentiating processes and the infrastructure to execute those processes with other members of your industry? This model was accepted many years ago in the financial services industry, when clearinghouses were established for processing multiple kinds of standard transactions. But even the financial services industry has not gone as far as it could. Most banks and brokerage houses maintain large "back room" operations that perform the very same, nondistinctive operations. Billions of dollars a year are spent on these duplicative infrastructures. The duplication benefits neither banks nor their customers.

But standardization cannot just be restricted to processes. Information technology infrastructures must also be standardized. Information, products, and money cannot move from one company to another in an X-engineered environment without systems that can easily work together. Even within single companies, multiple versions of systems, software, and hardware proliferate, making it difficult to communicate and do business internally. Before a company moves to X-engineering, it must reengineer itself—getting itself in order so that it can better collaborate with others.

The O&M story also illustrates several principles to keep in mind as you look for opportunities to X-engineer your own business.

Follow the Money

Knowing the real costs of operating can provide you with great insight as to where process improvement opportunities might lie. But don't stop at your own costs. Look at your customers' total landed costs for your product and services. And find out what it costs your suppliers to deliver materials in the manner you have requested. Also look for opportunities to reduce capital expenditures by managing inventory differently or sharing ownership of fixed assets with your customers, suppliers, and partners.

Go Broad

Excess costs in operations and performance problems generally are not attributable to a single activity or even a single process. The broader your net, the more you will find. Look across your processes and the processes of your customers and suppliers. The further you go, the greater the opportunity and the greater the challenge.

Know What Your Customers are Going Through

The French philosopher, Simone Weil, used to tell her students that when meeting a person they should not ask, "How are you today?" but rather, "What are you going through today?" Weil argued that it was the more authentic question.

Similarly, it is better to ask about the authentic realities and challenges facing your customers than to ask about their immediate needs. You need to have an intimate knowledge of your customers' concerns, not just their buying history, to find business propositions that will work for them and for you.

Chart Breakdowns

Analyzing failure will give you some direct clues as to where you might improve your processes and business propositions. Talk to your customers directly and openly about problems as they occur. It will give you great insight as to customers' expectations and what they really value.

Fish Upstream

The cost of a product, service, or process is substantially determined in its design phase. That is true for you, your customers, and your suppliers. Look upstream with your customers and suppliers into their design processes and see where you can do early harmonization. The farther back you go in the processes of your customers and suppliers, the more efficiency improvements and customer value you are likely to create.

Finally, in your search for X-engineering opportunities, let me suggest that you use a mix of optimism and realism. Pessimists need not apply for this work. They worry too much that if something is broken, their company or their customers may never change.

Optimism is important to see X-engineering's opportunity, and realism grounds you in the scope of the task ahead, dispenses with the hubris around technology, and forces you to confront the capabilities that you will need to develop or acquire.

7

Getting Hierarchy to Work

Samuel A. Culbert
Scott J. Schroeder

When it comes to the conduct of hierarchical relationships and how those with organizational authority are expected to direct and account, the 20th century concluded the way it began—with a steady stream of abuses, scandals, and exposés of hierarchy gone awry. Yes, there were advances in "democracy" and the participation of plebeians in the ranks, but scrutinizing end results does not reveal a system where those in charge conduct themselves differently from how people in charge conducted themselves a century ago. They self-indulge, use power to dominate, and avoid standing straightly accountable for their actions.[1]

To be sure, some changes were made. Today, hierarchical uppers are painstakingly thorough in appearing sensitive to the concerns of people lower down, and self-convincing in their charade of having no desire to dominate. They seek input from the ranks, delegate decision making to people with expertise, express sensitivity to the well-being of everyone on the so-called "organization team," and are immediately responsive to public regulating bodies concerned with safety, product quality, fair business and employment practices, and above-board systems of financial recording. And almost always their motivations are sincere.

But assessing these surface-level enhancements sufficient to constitute "progress" covers up what's still corrupt and taking place today. Bosses and people at the top continue to dominate, exerting subordinate controls that extend well beyond the entitlements and jurisdictions ceded them by the organization chart. Subordinates continue to knuckle under, mimicking beliefs from above without openly expressing those courses of action they believe more corporately correct. This results in bosses having inflated ideas about their knowledge and expertise, feeling supported in their overly indulgent use of corporate resources, and making decisions that those around them believe are severely misguided. And it results in subordinates withholding expression of their alternative viewpoints, justifying their not telling the truth as they know it on grounds that doing so would cost them their jobs. Of course whether or not either party, or both, benefits from this collusion, company interests inevitably lose out. Communication is warped, internal politics is corrupt, teamwork is illusionary, accountability is avoided, and esprit de corps suffers.

The culprit is the faulty system that allows bosses to dominate and take credit for corporate success without standing accountable for squandered resources, unutilized potential, personnel failures, and negative bottom-line outcomes and results. It's a system that forestalls honest dialogue, causing people desiring open and honest interaction to distort, withhold, and doublespeak. A boss who doesn't know better takes at face value what he or she is told. A subordinate concerned with getting a pay raise or a good assignment, or who sees the boss's evaluation as a significant factor in career advancement, naturally spins his or her actions and accounts of real-time events to reflect what he or she thinks bosses want to see and hear.

At one level it's a system problem caused by one-sided accountability. While subordinates are accountable to bosses, bosses are not accountable to subordinates. At a deeper level it's a problem created by a society steeped in a rationalistic mentality that limits the ability of people to internalize and use established principles of human nature or to recognize the basis of the competitive, politicized group dynamics that result from not utilizing these principles. People struggle with hierarchical relationships and lack the correct assumptions to solve the entrapments they create. Fixing the accountability problem and raising corporate-level consciousness of human nature fundamentals and the political dynamics that arise when people form hierarchical relationships are what's required to change how people operate and to improve the system's functioning. The system needs hierarchy; the idea is to eradicate the misconceptions that prevent hierarchy from performing its accountability work.

The key to getting hierarchy to work is changing the system to feature two-sided accountability relationships. The issue today is the same as it was 100 years ago. But interrupting the dynamics that cause people to form one-sided accountable, hierarchical relationships is as daunting an assignment as it has ever been. That's what this chapter is aimed at facilitating. It's the 21st century course on the causes and resistance and what's needed to revise the hierarchical system. We intend it as a stage-setter for implementation.

One-Sided Accountability

The organization chart formalizes the chain of accountabilities people expect in an organization large enough to require hierarchy. The first-order accountability is to hold people with functional and jurisdictional decision-making authority, known as bosses, accountable for getting beneficial results from the individuals and units who report to them. The second order is to hold individuals with specific responsibilities and assignments, known as subordinates, accountable for high-quality functioning and contribution. In both instances the chart should provide a straightforward representation of responsibilities and authorities, with the goal to identify productive and unproductive units and contributors. There's also a third-order accountability; it places adjacent, independently functioning units and jurisdictions on notice that their work orientations and accomplishments are expected to complement and integrate. The intent is to ensure that each unit stand accountable for the fact that how it performs—orientations taken, methods used, and outcomes sought—bears on the ability of other units, also critical to overall organization success, to perform effectively. Delegating responsibility to people with expertise, providing them with sufficient resources to fulfill that responsibility and the authority to orchestrate those resources synergistically, and then holding them accountable for end results is the key to getting hierarchy to work. Conversely, diffused authority on the chart leads to confusion about who has which responsibility and what authority and, ultimately, to no one standing accountable for responsibilities that aren't effectively carried out. The three orders of accountability are summarized in Table 7–1.

But having an organization chart doesn't ensure that people will "correctly" see and/or respect other people's authorities, or that functional and jurisdictional bosses will actively consider other people's endeavors and conduct themselves with an eye toward integrating with and complementing adjacent efforts. When disagreements in perception and motive lead to a competitive moment, which is almost always, people fear they will be held accountable for operations they lack the authority to control. At this point many assert themselves. They explain, lobby, and use whatever power-taking tactics are available in an attempt to take control of resources and jurisdictions they see as critical for delivering on commitments they've made. However, when people doubt their ability to sequester needed resources, they begin distancing themselves from accountability. They accumulate data and logic aimed at showing how other peoples' actions and external factors prevented them from producing the results they've pledged.

Table 7–1   Chain of Accountability Embedded in the Organization Chart

	Accountable Segment of the Organizational Chart	**Accountability Objective**
First Order	Unit heads—Individuals that the chart shows having direct reports	Accountable for directing and supporting the efforts of and getting positive results from the individuals, groups, and units they oversee.
Second Order	Single work units and individual contributors—Individuals that the chart shows having direct or collateral responsibilities	Accountable for assuming specific responsibilities and performing assigned tasks in a cost-effective manner using appropriate and approved methods in producing tangible products and quality results.
Third Order	Integrated work units, departments, and divisions—Individuals that the chart shows leading segmented functions, disciplines, and jurisdictions	Accountable for complementing, augmenting, and assisting adjacent units to perform effectively with an eye toward maximizing overall corporate objectives and goals.

Experience has taught us that functional responsibilities split among groups in different reporting chains, and/or lack of clarity and agreement about who has decision-making authority, almost always lead to accountability disputes. Conversely, when responsibility is fixed within a single reporting chain and it's clear that those with responsibility have the authority to make decisions bearing on the execution of that responsibility, there should be little question about who's accountable for a result. One merely consults the organization chart, sees who has authority to make decisions in the domain producing the disappointing result, and who was supposed to provide oversight. If, in fact, organizations operated this way, then it would be the bosses, not just the subordinates, who received the boot when things didn't work out. But as everyone who has witnessed an organizational activity go sour knows, this is not how one-sided accountability works. Practicing one-sided accountability allows bosses to survive and even prosper while the people they hired—whom they judged sufficiently capable to receive delegated responsibility and whom the chart says they are supposed to direct, oversee, guide, and coach—receive negative evaluations leading to their dismissals.

Thus one-sided accountability is the source of the system's corruption and the main reason why the system does not self-reform. It interferes with the three orders of accountability promised by hierarchical structure as represented by the organization chart. Nowhere does the chart imply that hierarchy is supposed to extend to relationships with lowers deferring to uppers in all point-of-view discussions. In fact, the chart is intended to promote an open and honest exchange of viewpoints by designating who ultimately is the decision maker. Logically thinking, once an individual is assured that it's his or her decision to make and that afterwards he or she will have to stand straightly accountable for actual results, there's no reason for that person to censure open and honest dialogue. Standing accountable provides a motive to decide correctly even if it means implementing a plan suggested by someone else.

It's a perversion of purpose that the chart is used to intimidate lowers to place saying what the boss wants to hear ahead of expressing their own beliefs and doing what they believe in their hearts is right for the company. In fact, we can't think of a single instance of an organization coming out ahead when hierarchical structure was extrapolated to create a deferential, "yes, boss" relationship. Certainly no concept of teamwork proposes such an outrageous feature as a top-down command and control discussion format with one-sided accountable relationships. Of course, people at different hierarchical levels have different roles and functions to perform so that the alternative—a two-sided accountable relationship—seldom means mirror image reciprocity. Role and function dictate the specific obligations for which an individual should have to account.

Why Doesn't the System Change?

The most obvious reason why the system doesn't change is that it protects and benefits the very people who hold the power to fix it. Fixed, it would hold bosses accountable for the success of subordinates and deprive them of opportunities to pass blame downward when an individual or unit within their jurisdiction fails to produce promised results. Fixed, bosses would have more incentive to help subordinates succeed, which, in many instances, they see detracting from and diluting their energy for highly visible, more immediately gratifying functions such as problem solving, networking, marketing, and strategizing—all functions where positive results are apparent and lack of results are easy to hide.

It's been 40 years since Paulo Freire began reporting his insights into the consequences of hierarchical relationships, albeit in a substantially different context.[2] Describing how hierarchical relationships intimidate and disempower, he concluded that only the stifled and oppressed could release their oppressors from the tyranny of oppressing them. Why? Because people enjoying the spoils of oppression are reluctant to surrender the benefits, especially to put their fates in a participatory methodology that subjects them to explicit criticism and give-and-take debate. However, asking subordinates to change the system implodes on conundrums. Not only do subordinates see themselves lacking the power to express disagreement, but the vast majority have already bought into one-sided accountable, hierarchical relationship reasoning.[3] Most subordinates are also bosses trying to acquire and demonstrate the type of thinking that qualifies them to be higher level bosses.

One-sided accountability reasoning is possible only because people overlook, neglect, and deny in others certain human nature traits they readily accept in themselves. At work people expect others to be logical, rational, and objective in their statements and actions despite the fact that, when they take time to self-reflect, they can see emotions, self-interests, bias, and subjectivity in almost every action they, themselves, take. All self-candid individuals recognize that self-interested motives constantly influence what they allege is objective as well as their self-virtuous reports of organization events and critiques of other people's actions. In fact, self-candid people readily accept self-interests and personally convenient motives in the intra-organizational politics they practice when advocating what's best for the company or calling attention to other peoples' self-interests as a means of discrediting positions advocated by those with competing advocacies.

If bosses accepted the inevitability of self-interest, bias, emotions, and omnipresent subjectivity, they would understand that the only effective way of operating is to inquire into other people's views of events to understand the reasoning that underlies the courses of action people instrumentally take and their motives. They would rationally accept bias as a natural fact and seek to identify it as a variable worthy of consideration, not outrage. When tempted to issue command and control directives they would understand that their words are subject to self-interested interpretation regardless of the lip service acquiescence they receive. They would know the inevitability of self-interested motives and perceptions that no directive could more than temporarily supplant.

Thus, we see false objectivity and double standards regarding self-interested politics to be the sponsoring agents of one-sided accountable relationships as people misguidedly extrapolate from hierarchical structure, also known as the chart, to format their relationship with a direct report or hierarchical superior. Cancelled out in the process are teamwork dynamics and the type of accountability that allows hierarchical structure to perform its work. If omnipresent self-interests and inevitable subjectivity were internalized givens in a boss' mind, then open and above-board discussions would be required to get the other person's views out for viewing so that differing intellectual positions could be appreciated, understood, and addressed. Then corporate interests would be served and a major source of system-wide corruption could be checked.

Thus, we see organization traps caused by people falsely extrapolating from the accountability model of hierarchical structure to hierarchical relationships with its telling symptoms: one-sided accountability, boss domination, and system-wide corruption. On the other hand, we see boss domination as a trap that readily dissipates when people break from their unrealistic, moralistic expectations of expecting unbiased behavior— accepting in others what they already know about and accept in themselves. All that is necessary is the internalization of certain human nature principles and tenets, facts we've been calling attention to for years and that are briefly summarized in this chapter.[4] Internalized, these facts equip people to implement the more organizationally constructive two-sided accountable paradigm. In the following sections, we outline the three principles (and three tenets) of two-sided accountability; this material is summarized in Table 7–2.

Table 7–2   Two-Sided Accountability Principles

Principle 1	There's no getting around it, subjectivity is inevitable	Everyone interprets events distinctively according to his or her motives, needs, and means.
Tenet 1	Don't guess what others are doing— ask them	You can't tell for sure what someone is trying to accomplish, or why he or she is proceeding in a certain way, merely from observing that person's actions. This is particularly important to remember when you see someone doing what you would never prescribe. The best way to find out what that person is doing and why is to ask how he or she sees the situation and what they believe their actions will accomplish. Only after you hear the explanation and seek to understand it in the context of the person's intentions and motivations can you voice your opinion in a way that's likely to be accurately heard and possibly well received.

Table 7–2   Two-Sided Accountability Principles (continued)

Tenet 2	Until you can ask, assume others are trying to be "life" competent	When you aren't able to directly inquire, assume the individual is doing what he or she feels must be done to perform "life" competently, the best way that person knows how to do it. Interpret the other person's motives broadly, not restricted to the task at hand.
Tenet 3	Remember that "everyone" includes yourself	You also view organization events self-interestedly, constantly scrutinizing for "life" benefits, opportunities, and threats.
Principle 2	Practice win-win-win politics	At work any statement or action, taken or perceived, that affects someone's ability to function effectively is "political." Conducting one's politics strategically entails active consideration of what each interacting party has at stake. We call the orientation of searching for self-interested outcomes that also benefit others the "win-win-win" orientation to organization politics. The first two wins include what's self-beneficial and what benefits the company; the third win is what others deem important to their interests and success. Leaving out any of the three reduces one's political motives to tactical ones, resulting in a pull back toward hierarchical relationships.
Principle 3	Put two-sided accountability into action	Look for opportunities to initiate, build, and sustain two-sided accountability relationships, particularly in interactions you have with a boss or subordinate.

Principle #1: Acknowledge Inevitable Subjectivity

This principle, embodied in a Culbert and McDonough[5] slogan and emphasized in Culbert's book *Mind-Set Management*,[6] states "organization is an artifact of the mind that views it." Succinctly explained, it holds that all interpretations of an individual's work activities are a matter of individual perception, inextricably influenced by the needs, interests, motives, means, and agendas of the individual viewing it. It's a way of saying, "What you see depends on where you stand." It's the story of the six blind men feeling different parts of an elephant being asked, "What is the object in front of you?" It's the story of the three baseball umpires bragging about the magnitude of their power when determining balls and strikes, with each umpire competing to outdo the others. The first umpire claims, "I call 'em the way I see 'em," the second, "I call 'em the way they are," with the third providing the topper, "They ain't nothing 'til I call 'em." In other words, subjectivity colors every aspect of an individual's life at work. It allows us to finally resolve the question of what constitutes "reality" in a human endeavor. It alleges that each individual sees and interprets events distinctively and differently according to his or her needs, motives, background, and means.

Inevitable subjectivity posits that people are biased perceivers even when giving what they believe are honest accounts of their experience. Internalize this principle and you'll stop fighting human nature. You'll no longer be put off by people who view and think about events differently than you do. And you'll have a way of figuring out where people are coming from when you try to influence them, especially when what you want them to do is not something they naturally think of doing. By considering that each individual lives within a unique reality, inevitable subjectivity is the ultimate diversity approach. It considers all individuals to be unique and distinctive; it treats all categories and stereotypes with suspicion.

This principle has the potential to turn your way of viewing people and organization events inside out. Seeing things differently, you'll act differently. You'll understand the importance of accessing the deeply psychological and personal issues that underlie an individual's perspectives on events and relationships at work. You'll change the way you approach people you want to influence. You'll choose the right people as partners. You'll approach those you choose intelligently and with sensitivity.

The First Tenet of Inevitable Subjectivity

You can't tell exactly what an individual is doing or thinking merely by observing that person and his or her actions. We can go even further. When you are critical of someone's behavior, there's little likelihood that he or she is up to the same thing you would be up to if exhibiting the same behavior.

To understand exactly what someone is doing, you need to ask that person, "What are you up to, and why are you going about it this way?" If what you learn doesn't make sense, it means that you need to inquire further. For all inquiries we recommend you proceed with the tone of asking a "reasonable person." Instead of declaring, "Why are you doing that!" or inquiring, "Don't you know a more effective way?" as if the person is a dope, you need to think—and to express—"I'd really like to understand what you had in mind when you did what, given my ways, I would never think to do."

With a mindset that assumes the other person reasonable, your goal is to uncover the reasoning behind his or her actions. For example, if the person seems unnecessarily suspicious about a deal he or she is making, you might say something like, "In your shoes I would be less suspicious, maybe even naïve. What alerted you that got your guard up? It must have been something I didn't see." If you still don't uncover the sensitivity, it's time to ask for more background. You might continue, "Is your reaction one that's typical for you? What's taking place here that evokes it?" If after asking such questions you still don't understand why this person is reacting with suspicion, it's time to consult a mutual friend. But the bottom line is that it's the other person, not you, filling in the blanks. If it was you, you would probably be stating why, under similar circumstances, you would do what the other person did, which you already know you would not. If you were similarly inclined, this issue would have never become a topic for your inquiry. There would be nothing more you needed to understand.

The Second Tenet of Inevitable Subjectivity

When you're not able to ask people what spurred them to act as you just observed, your best way of understanding their intentions is to assume they are doing what they feel they must to perform competently, the way they know how to be competent. However, beware of tunnel vision. Assuming that people are primarily out to perform work competently is short-sighted. To maintain political face, people talk as if everything they are doing is aimed at producing a competent work performance but what's actually driving them is the idea of performing competently in their life more generally. People are interested in optimizing total life performance, and work events represent only one dimension, however important that dimension may be.

Your reluctance to assume that people whom you judge to be flawed in their dealings with the task at hand are doing their best to perform competently, and to recognize that their focus includes many more issues than the work topic on which you are focused, will cause you to systematically undervalue what people are doing. Thus, when spotting someone whose actions are, in your estimation, insufficient to the work agenda at hand, you should know it's time to start learning. Reflect on everything you know about that person's life and the strengths he or she is endeavoring to display, the flaws the person doesn't want exposed, and his or her personal expressiveness needs. Learn whatever you need to learn to make your understanding of his or her actions compute. Think about how a person with that individual's personal agenda and operating style could reasonably go about accomplishing what you see needing to be done. Whatever you do, don't start thinking that you know enough to get heavy handed. There will be times you feel the urge, but it's an urge that needs resisting. Heavy handedness is a one-way street toward cementing an adversarial hierarchical relationship in which stand-and-be-counted accountability takes a back seat to domination and control.

The Third Tenet of Inevitable Subjectivity

Everyone, including yourself, gives self-interested interpretations to all events, particularly ones that hold important personal consequences. Consistently, we find this to be a principle that many people can't seem to behaviorally comprehend. Incorrectly, people make evaluative statements about the pluses and minuses of another individual's performance, as if those efforts were wholly work driven and their assessments were perfectly objective. But careful scrutiny will show you that all assessments are greatly colored by what the evaluator has at stake personally. People cavalierly portray another person's predilections and biases as flaws that need correcting, not acknowledging that everyone they know views the world with biases and omnipresent self-interests and that the reason they are complaining about this individual's behavior is linked to their own unexpressed self-interested motives. With this principle internalized, no critique of anyone else is complete without the phrase "…and this gets in the way of my self-pursuits and interests." Not accepting this principle implies that somewhere there's a cadre of people whose work behavior is even-handed and objective. Of course, the inevitable subjectivity principle critiques such presumption as spurious reasoning.

You'll find that your IQ for engaging in two-way accountability increases considerably when you internalize the fact that you, just like everyone else, are a self-interested and biased judge of other people's behavior. Given fair-minded values, you'll take this into account when considering your judgments. Instead of contending that the other person is doing something profoundly insufficient, you'll give more consideration to how actions taken by that person make matters more difficult for you. Of course, given your political sensitivity, you'll prudently choose the moments for publicly owning up. There are many times that you'll correctly choose to keep your self-effacing comments to yourself. There will be other times when you'll see that owning up allows others to experience you as someone they're willing to trust.

Principle #2: Practice Win-Win-Win Politics

If organizational behavior was a logical science then all laws would follow from the law of self-interest: People interpret their jobs and perform their work in ways they perceive best for themselves. This premise features self-interests as a given with people seeking win-win outcomes. The first win features outcomes that benefit the individual; the second, outcomes that benefit the organization and/or company. If, hypothetically, there were 6,431 outcomes that could benefit an organization, then each individual pursues a subset of 1,260 that also benefit him or herself. This is why, when asked to explain their actions, people almost always have an explanation that emphasizes benefits to the company.

But because different people possess quite different needs, desires, and capabilities, their self-interested pursuits are different. This quickly gets us to the first implication of the law of self-interests: People with comparable assignments see their jobs differently and, because of this, pursue different avenues of action and reasoning when performing their work. In our hypothesis, this means that two people working on parallel assignments will pursue somewhat different "1,260s." Moreover, when it fits their convenience politically, they will self-interestedly interpret the other person's lack of overlap as neglecting an essential organizational interest. A second implication holds that organizational dynamics leading to conflict derive from different people pursuing different interests in different ways. Others hold that the organization prospers when each member's self-interested pursuits are nested to augment the self-interested pursuits of other members and that enterprise activities are most efficient when staged to accrue rewards to all who participate. Conversely, people and their organizational endeavors stall and suffer when one or more of the constituents' interests are not addressed or served. Of course we're talking percentages because, from time to time, there are many organizational endeavors in which interests left out of the immediate mix receive focus in another endeavor or at a later time.

Simply stated, an organization succeeds when people engaged in self-interested pursuits choose and perform activities in ways that are attentive to the needs of work associates and the organization. In essence, wherever possible, all organization actions ought to be predicated on win-win-win reasoning, with the first win being the interests of the individual taking action, the second being the interests of corporate entity, and the third, the interests of others affected by that action. Of course, practically speaking, people won't always be able to figure out how to act in ways that meet three sets of interests simultaneously. Nevertheless, all three should receive active, intelligent consideration, especially when the end-game goal is two-sided accountable, trusting relationships.

Principle #3: Put Two-Sided Accountability Into Action

Abuses and corruption stemming from one-sided accountability were cited in the opening paragraphs of this chapter and are meticulously described in the book, *Don't Kill the Bosses!* Here it is revisited from the vantage points of antidote and treatment. We've portrayed one-sided accountability as intrinsically hierarchical with the implication that it inevitably leads to corruption and self-inflation and as the anathema to open, honest, above-board, and trusting relationships. One-sided accountability allows uppers to hold lowers' feet to the fire without lowers being able to complain that their feet are too hot. Of course the reason behind our invective is that we favor two-sided accountability. That is, we think every boss's job includes staging for the effective performance of the people he or she oversees. Who is better positioned than the performer to comment on the help and support that's needed and received? We crave partnerships instead of hierarchical relationships, and we eschew situations where a boss gets to say how a subordinate is doing without the subordinate having a voice that counts.

We believe a company prospers most when bosses make it possible for each individual to work at his or her best. And we believe the method for effecting this is the establishment of reciprocal accountabilities. This implies inevitable subjectivity consciousness and win-win-win politics practiced at every level. Subordinates need to stand accountable for alerting all levels of "bosses" to the structural constraints that limit their ability to candidly state what they sincerely believe. Supervisors need to stand accountable for their efforts to fairly and open-mindedly oversee quality and provide coaching that's appropriately formatted for a specific individual. Managers need to stand accountable for their efforts to check and revise systems that are supposed to facilitate the effectiveness of units and groups. And leaders need to stand accountable for coming up with organizational effectiveness initiatives that facilitate people doing what they think the company actually needs done and that leverage the resources of the people performing work. All this requires reciprocity of effort and each individual focusing on how his or her way of tackling an assignment impacts every other person on the organization "team"—win-win-win politics.

Taken as a package, these three principles—with tenets and implications—lead to an accountability mentality that casts one-sided accountable, hierarchical relationships as an invalid default setting.

Human Nature and the Political Processes that Evolve

You will find the world of work looks decidedly different once you have these human nature truths internalized. First, you'll remember not to turn your back on the politics of self-interests and the fact that people are internally wired to look out for themselves. Next, you will realize that subordinates require safeguards to tell it straight to bosses whose judgments affect their security and rewards. And, third, you'll understand that teamwork starts at the top—with bosses and subordinates looking out for one another, searching for ways to enhance one another's personal well being and success.

With subjectivity acknowledged, one immediately sees that all organizational events are open to interpretation, with personal motives and self-interested biases determining how they are experienced and what they are called. Thus, organization politics are the dynamics that unfold when people with different perceptions and motives discuss what is happening and the specific actions required. Faced squarely, there is no corruption—just a difference in interpretation driven by differing self-interested motives.

Corruption takes place when one or more individuals take the negotiation underground, seeking to decide matters in a way that benefits the organization while also benefiting themselves. In the case of bosses, this may merely involve making a decision without seeking sufficient advice and counsel from those responsible for implementation and whose expertise and experience qualify their views as relevant considerations. In the case of subordinates, this may constitute selective spinning and withholding of essential facts in the service of giving the person who decides their rewards what they want that person to think and know. In either instance it entails people seeking self-beneficial rewards at the expense of the open and honest interactive process that produces the best organization result.

When people feel their viewpoints are excluded from a decision made in their domains of responsibility and expertise, they are likely to experience political processes unfair to the extent that they believe the situation justifies rectifying manipulation. This is precisely the consequent dynamic created in a one-sided accountable, hierarchical relationship and why, for an antidote, we advocate two-sided accountability. We seek relationships where people are not afraid to speak their minds or hear what's on other people's minds because, at the end of the day, they know who has the authority to decide the matter and that person knows he or she will eventually be called upon to stand accountable for the result. Standing accountable causes decision makers to listen carefully to what others believe best and to provide the supports necessary for people to candidly deliver their views. Of course, all honest expression comes with a self-interest motive and bias, and decision makers need to learn enough about other people to bracket those interests and make decisions that are not just good for themselves and the organization, but good for others on the team. When you think about it, this is the heart of teamwork.

What Does Two-Sided Accountability Entail?

Two-sided accountability is founded on the teamwork concepts embedded in hierarchical structure, especially as emphasized in the third-order accountability described in Table 7–1. At all times each person has dual responsibilities: first, to make sure that he or she performs assigned responsibilities, functions, and roles effectively; and second, to display initiative and support in helping others to effectively cover their functions, responsibilities, and roles.

Listening to what bosses say they do you'd think that these dual responsibilities were all but universally implemented today. And, everyone can point to a behavior that they think exemplifies an active commitment to staging for others to perform competently. However, if you examine what most bosses actually do, and listen to what subordinates say about what they are doing and not doing, you get a decidedly different perspective on what's mainstream practice in management today. And you'd think most bosses would know about this since we can't think of more than a handful of bosses who report to higher level bosses that they don't consider teamwork deficient.

To provide a picture of where words, deeds, and good intentions fall short, we describe four dimensions of managerial performance in which bosses have the opportunity to pass the practical test but where most fail to understand what is required. Consider what most well-intentioned bosses do and the two-sided accountable enhancements suggested. In our minds each of these dimensions is highly pertinent to affecting individual and team effectiveness.

Getting Informed

Bosses practicing one-sided accountability often put a good deal of effort into getting themselves informed. They ask questions, hold briefings, conduct reviews, and diligently monitor results. In fact, they generally attempt to solicit all points of view prior to making up their minds and stipulating action. However, if a boss were to practice two-sided accountability he or she would do appreciably more.

After getting briefed and making a decision, the boss would present his or her tentative "this is where I'm coming out" conclusions for discussion by the people whose perspectives he or she is drawing upon for a "what problems do you see?" conversation that allows "briefers" to respond to the boss's logic and state their reactions. Afterwards, with authority clearly defined, the boss would be free to decide and act any way he or she saw fit and those with differing opinions would have a basis for continuing the dialogue should ensuing events warrant further pressing of a reaction.

Informing Others

For most bosses, engaging in team play means getting subordinates the information required for them to competently perform their jobs. Once again, bosses who practice one-sided accountability will say they already do this based on front-end information sharing and perspective-setting discussions they hold when assigning a project or responsibility. Their beliefs are reinforced by the information updates they provide and the mid-course corrections they advance. But from where we sit the aforementioned schema is more tactical than strategic because the reference point for all data and perspectives shared is the problem framed and formatted for available resources as seen by the boss.

Practicing two-sided accountability entails giving subordinates a strategic perspective on their assignments and sufficient information about what is expected in the way of results. To be strategic, subordinates need to be present when a project is formulated or at least when key parameters for the project are initially discussed and mapped. To be strategic, oversight involves a "roll-up your sleeves" work session, not just a "Let me sell you on the logic of how we're going about this" presentation. To be strategic, the boss takes the role of learning what subordinates require to "get it right," not just evaluating whether they have it "right," the way that boss wants the work done.

When there's two-sided accountability, the boss' involvement doesn't stop with making sure that subordinates have the information he or she thinks is needed. It includes finding out what information subordinates want and helping them access it. With two-sided accountability, subordinates are accountable for producing results while bosses are accountable for making sure subordinates have what they need to get those results.

Conserving Time and Energy

Next on our list is the boss' utilization of human capital. Here the differences between bosses who practice one-sided and two-sided accountability are particularly obvious. One-sided-accountable bosses are wasteful of other people's time. They engage in self-indulgent acts such as scheduling meetings without giving serious consideration to subordinate commitments and schedules, creating inefficiencies that cascade down. Almost automatically they assume meetings to be at their office location regardless of the number of people who must transport themselves there. They have canned apologies for people they leave waiting in their outer office for an hour or more, re-reading the previous day's news. They assign projects that are considered wasted efforts by the people performing them, ignoring their futile complaints. The list of human effort wasted and opportunities lost is endless.

On the other hand, bosses who practice two-sided accountability are seriously interested in subordinate productivity. They align their self-interests with the total corporate effort by measuring efficiency and productivity in terms of total work unit progress and company results, making these their ego-gratifying accomplishments. They inquire about availability prior to making an assignment; they solicit the other person's viewpoint with a concern for conserving effort. When invoking urgency, they consider off-loading other number one priorities. They display an active interest in each individual's well-being and general morale. In short, they produce asset value by fostering personally rewarding, productive relationships between personnel and company efforts.

Respecting Individuality and Uniqueness

The last item on our boss-as-leader functions is knowledge of the needs of other people and acceptance of one's role in facilitating their pursuits. We're not just talking about what people lower down need to perform their assignments competently; we're talking about what drives them personally, professionally, and corporately—what they must realize to make their company affiliation personally meaningful. This is the "if you're going to be a leader, you need to know what the people you are leading think" mindset that everyone in a leadership position acknowledges. It's another way of putting *inevitable subjectivity* and *win-win-win politics* together, finding out what you need to know to grasp another's perspective and gain his or her enthusiastic participation by seeking outcomes consistent not only with your interests and the company's, but also with the other person's.

Aware of the value of knowing what's on the minds of people below them and how they see organizational events, people high up on the chart often sponsor a stream of activities. These include informal brown bag lunches for interactive discussions, periodic open forums for discussion of controversial topics, encouraging direct reports to submit agenda topics for team meetings, regularly scheduled one-on-one supervisory meetings, and anonymous surveys and 360-degree feedback conducted by third parties, with new modalities on the drawing boards.

Unfortunately, most of these activities are carried out with one-sided accountability. Brown bag sessions intended to be responsive to employee concerns turn into sales sessions where giving the company line supplants listening to how individuals see things differently. Topics nominated for management meetings get "back of the line" treatment as the executive in charge arranges the agenda to ensure that his or her urgent issues are addressed prior to time running out. One-on-one meetings are held only when the boss has something to discuss. Human resources people take control of the open forums, using them to explain proposed changes in benefits and parking. Anonymous surveys are engaged defensively as recipients react as if the objective is to clean up the list rather than to hold focused discussions where perceptions are engaged and both participants explain. Three-hundred-and-sixty-degree feedback is helpful in belling the cat but not in changing underlying beliefs or developing relationships. The reaction is obvious; people stop participating. They protect themselves by quickly adopting a "been there, done that" attitude when coming attractions are announced.

Two-sided accountability changes all this. Personal effectiveness discussions are held face to face, not anonymously, with bosses asking during initial discussions, "What do you need from me in order to feel comfortable speaking honestly?" Recall that two-sided accountability incorporates the principle of inevitable subjectivity and the fact that underlying each person's company affiliation are desires to pursue life needs, maximize rewards and gains, and receive good value for sacrifices made. The boss' listening and learning is emphasized. Any meeting in which the boss does lots of talking is followed up with meetings devoted to inquiring, "What did you hear and where did you come out?" Two-sided accountability requires the boss to work on developing a capacity to live with the tension that comes from differences not reconciled. The modus operandi is power-sharing, not power-taking where the boss unilaterally frames the issue. Neither is it power-denying, where the boss uses the uniqueness of a subordinate's concern to discredit that individual's position.

What Will it Take to Get Two-Sided Accountability?

There's nothing complicated about establishing two-sided accountable relationships for people who are convinced the other person isn't going to unilaterally decide to drop out. Getting there, however, takes someone with muscle to stand up for the company by saying, "From now on we're going to have processes that ensure no one's needs are overlooked." Why do we say stand up for the company? Because in a system of one-sided accountable relationships, where people feel the necessity to indulge in deception and denial in order to succeed, the company always loses out. Next, it's going to take consciousness-raising. People need to expect subjectivity and they need to learn about the bias that characterizes their actions and thoughts, and even some things about the history that underlies that bias. Lastly, it requires a system[7] that protects people lower down so that they don't suffer a personal setback merely from saying what they see and believe.

These safeguards are readily obtained with an evaluation system in which direct bosses select and hire their subordinates and their boss, the subordinates' big boss, provides the performance evaluation review. Of course proximity, time required, and numbers of people to be evaluated will cause direct bosses to provide most of the input and big boss evaluators to focus mainly on troublesome and contested evaluations while rubber stamping the rest. When an evaluation is contested, both individuals' views will need to be sensed. Then, the focus will not just be on the subordinate's performance, it will also be on the direct boss's conduct in helping that person to succeed. Distancing and passing the buck will become more difficult and bosses will have more motivation to ask direct reports, "What do you need from me today?" and to develop relationships where this question can be answered straight. Of course this is the basic two-sided accountable paradigm mandate.

The aforementioned is only one of the ways for achieving two-sided accountability described in *Don't Kill the Bosses!* The basic conditions are internalization of human nature facts, appreciation for the politics that derive from self-interests, and a clearly articulated hierarchy that unambiguously delineates responsibilities and authorities so that decision makers are motivated to openly solicit other views prior to taking action. With these conditions met, the feeling of "being in it together" becomes more reality than slogan and organizations have more of what they need to succeed.

8

Total Rewards Management

Robert L. Heneman
Wendy K. Schutt

uring the 20th century, a significant body of knowledge regarding reward systems was developed. Basic principles were established, such as the need to link pay to performance to increase productivity.[1] Research was conducted that clearly showed the positive impact of reward systems on employee and organizational performance.[2] New forms of reward systems such as variable and skill-based pay were created.[3] The importance of linking reward systems to business strategy to align the interests of employees and owners was emphasized.[4]

Much of this progress took place during unstable business periods such as the turmoil of World War I and II and the Great Depression. For example, many job evaluation methods that are currently used by employers (e.g., the Hay system) were developed during or shortly after World War II.[5]

Turmoil is also likely to exist in the 21st century and this turmoil is likely to further hasten advances in reward systems. The current turmoil faced by employers is the rapidly changing nature of work. Elements of this change include changes in the nature of the employment relationship from permanent to contingent employment, changes in technology that have made it easier for organizations to monitor vast amounts of data about employee and organizational performance, changes in organizational structures from bureaucracies to virtual organizations, and changes in the design of jobs from strict to loose role definitions for employees to follow.[6]

The purpose of this chapter is to propose some fundamental issues that need to be addressed by executives in order for basic reward principles developed in the 20th century to be successfully applied to the rapidly changing workplace of the 21st century. More important, the issues addressed in this chapter need to be considered if further progress is to be made at developing new principles of compensation applicable to organizations in the 21st century. Issues to be explored in this chapter include the following: moving from compensation to total rewards, focusing on execution as well as strategy, integrating reward systems with organizational learning systems, revisiting the concept of equity, public sector rewards design, and extending innovative reward systems to new business environments. These topics will be covered in turn.

Moving from Compensation to Total Rewards

The portfolio of reward programs used by most managers in the 20th century consisted primarily of compensation (wages, salaries, and incentives) and benefits. The portfolio of compensation and benefits was usually homogeneous for occupational groups and controlled by the human resource management department. This approach worked relatively well with the stable business environments that characterized much of the 20th century.

Radical changes in the nature of work in the 21st century require a shift in the paradigm from two forms of rewards to multiple forms of rewards, from homogeneous rewards to heterogeneous reward programs, and from human resource management control to line manager control. In the absence of this shift to total rewards, it is unlikely that managers will be able to successfully align the interests of employees with the interests of the organization.

In terms of the forms that rewards take, the rewards need to be expanded to include learning opportunities and job design. Learning opportunities are now needed given the changing nature of the employment relationship from permanent employment to contingent employment. Learning opportunities help employees to broaden their skill sets to take on multiple roles in the organization. When roles cease to exist temporarily or permanently, employees are equipped to shift from one role to another role that is still being performed in the organization. Ultimately, when the employee no longer works for a particular organization, learning opportunities help employees develop their human capital so that they are desirable to other employers.

In addition to learning opportunities, job design is another aspect of total reward systems for the 21st century. Dynamic rather than static job assignments can be used as a selling point by the organization to align employee and owner interests. Research has clearly demonstrated that for many, but not all employees, work that is characterized as high in autonomy, feedback from the work itself, skill variety, and work significance are more likely to lead to employees committed to their work. These characteristics of work promote a sense of psychological meaningfulness and are more likely to be present with dynamic rather than static work.[7]

The mix of base pay, incentives, benefits, learning opportunities, and meaningful work needs to be carefully matched to the finances of the organization and to the needs of employees at various stages in their lives. Flexible or cafeteria-style rewards plans will be needed to match the interests of employees with owners. Employees are much more likely to perform in a manner commensurate with organizational goals when they have input into the mix of rewards they receive.[8] While the amount of total rewards they receive may remain homogeneous by occupation and performance, the forms in which pay is delivered may be very heterogeneous.

In terms of control over pay decisions, the human resource department of the 21st century will not be able to retain the tight control over pay decisions that they had in the 20th century. Work will be changing so rapidly that line managers—those closest to the changing nature of work—will be the only ones close enough to the changes to be able to make the rapid-fire adjustments in pay that will be required. Certainly, human resource management departments still play a role in setting pay parameters for line managers to follow (e.g., market value), but much more discretion will need to be given to line managers in total reward decisions.[9]

Focusing on Execution as Well as Strategy

In the latter parts of the 20th century, compensation professionals became obsessed with strategic compensation. The focus was on what types of compensation systems work best under certain business circumstances. While this is an extremely important issue, many lost track of the assumption that is made with strategic compensation; namely, that the compensation strategy selected will be properly designed, implemented, administered, and evaluated. Unfortunately, gains made by strategic thinking in the 20th century were often lost because of poor execution. An example of this gain and subsequent loss is the use of employee competencies as a basis for pay. From a strategic perspective, this approach to compensation is very much in strategic alignment with contemporary organizations such as virtual organizations.[10] Unfortunately, the use of competencies as a compensation strategy has fallen into disfavor. To pay on the basis of competencies, many organizations simply copied competencies from a competency catalog made available by consultants and then added these competencies to the merit pay system. No concern was given to the reliability and validity of these competencies in a particular organization. Not surprisingly, many competency pay systems failed, not because of strategy, but because of execution.

For human resource professionals to add value to organizations, they must do a better job at execution than in the 20th century. Basic analytical concepts such as reliability and validity have slipped from the tool kit of human resource professionals and need to be replaced as we go forward in the 21st century. In the absence of basic analytical knowledge by human resource professionals, it is very doubtful that new compensation strategies will be implemented successfully.

Integrating Reward Systems with Organizational Learning Systems

As reward systems become more fluid and flexible in response to the changing nature of work, organizations will be forced to develop, store, and disseminate knowledge about how reward systems most effectively operate. Never has the need for this integration of reward systems and organizational learning been stronger. Not only is the changing nature of work impacting compensation systems, but so too is the current decline in compensation knowledge. Owing to the changing nature of the labor force, experts in rewards will continue to retire at a rapid rate as the baby-boom generation ages.[11] In addition, compensation scholars are retiring for similar reasons and unfortunately, fewer and fewer of the new generation of scholars are doing research in reward systems.

An important technological advancement that should be very useful for the integration of reward systems and organizational learning is expert systems, which capture subject-matter expert's ideas, codify them, and develop them into a software program that can be used after the expert moves on. An example of this approach was undertaken by one of the authors. An expert system was created that shows the appropriate reward system to use depending on the business strategy (prospector vs. defender), organizational structure (organic vs. mechanistic), and organizational culture (high involvement vs. low involvement) of the company. Depending on the configuration of these three variables for a company, the system provides the most appropriate reward system to follow. The system is defined by the reward form (monetary vs. nonmonetary), unit of analysis (person vs. job), value comparison (internal vs. external markets), reward measures (behaviors vs. results), reward level (individual vs. business unit), pay increase (fixed vs. variable), administrative level (centralized vs. decentralized), timing (lead vs. lag), and communications (open vs. closed).[12] Subject matter experts used to create this expert system included practitioners and scholars.

Alliances will also need to be formed to create additional rewards knowledge. One example is the Consortium for Alternative Reward Strategies

Research, which was formed to investigate the effectiveness of incentive plans in over 663 companies for up to a five-year period. Consortium members included private sector companies and the advisory board and research sponsors consisted of consultants, academics, and professional association staff. This monumental undertaking produced a wealth of best practice information on incentive plans.

A similar approach is currently underway and is called the Knowledge of Pay study. This study, coordinated by WorldatWork and the LeBlanc Group, has 25 leading private sector companies in the United States and Canada that are having their white-collar employees surveyed regarding their awareness, understanding, and belief in their compensation systems. The hypothesis being tested is that employees most knowledgeable about their pay systems are more likely to be engaged in their work as evidenced by greater commitment to their work organizations. For practitioners, this study will provide ideas on how to best communicate pay plans for maximum impact on employee attitudes and beliefs.

The major point being made here is that organizations in the 21st century will have to be proactive in generating reward system knowledge for their organization. Expert systems can be created for internal benchmarks and alliances can be formed for external benchmarks. Because of the death of information being created by organizations and by scholars with the retirement of the baby-boom generation, the knowledge being created about reward programs in the 21st century will increasingly become proprietary and a source of competitive advantage for those organizations that actively integrate reward systems with organizational learning.

Revisiting the Concept of Equity

To ease the administrative burden associated with reward decision making, organizations in the 20th century focused on developing pay systems around the job as the unit of pay rather than the person as the unit of pay. This practice dates back to the world wars. To aid the war efforts, it was far easier to design reward systems for thousands of jobs than for millions of people. Job evaluation systems that were created during the world wars became the method that was used to link jobs to pay rather than people to pay. This approach was adopted by industry right after World War II and was used throughout the rest of the 20th century.

This job-based approach focused employees on the description of their jobs, as the job—rather than the person—was the unit of pay priced by the organization. Comparisons between similar jobs both within the organization and between organizations became the basis for employee equity perceptions. Given the rapidly changing nature of work, and the demise of fixed duties in jobs, equity issues become far more complex to manage. Unfortunately, one common response by employers has been to ignore internal equity issues and use the demise of job descriptions as an excuse.

Equity perceptions remain regardless of whether there is a formal job description and may actually become more salient rather than less salient to employees in the absence of a job description. Inequity perceptions are correlated with withdrawal attitudes and behaviors (e.g., turnover). As a result, work still needs to be defined and categorized in order for equity issues and subsequent withdrawal behaviors to be successfully managed.

One of the authors is working on a new procedure to evaluate the worth of work rather than the worth of jobs in organizations. In this new system, attention is given to the many different types of work including jobs, roles, competencies, and teams. In addition, evaluation standards are being developed that take into account the changing nature of work for many employees and give employees credit for those changes on an ongoing basis. Hopefully, efforts such as these will help managers in the 21st century.

Scholars are also developing new ways to manage equity perceptions. The most well-known effort here is to look at what has come to be known as "procedural justice."[13] This concept and the supportive research behind it indicates that how people are paid is just as important as what people are paid in forming equity perceptions.[14] Research shows that procedural justice procedures are strengthened when work is clearly defined for employees, employees have an opportunity to say what work they will perform, and employees have a chance to appeal decisions about their work. Employees are more likely to feel equitably paid, even if their pay is low, when these components of procedural justice are followed. In the 21st century, the process used to pay people will be as important as the amount that is paid.

Public Sector Rewards Design

Much of the focus on compensation research and design during the 20th century has been on private sector businesses, with less attention paid to public sector organizations. This may be due to the fact that traditionally, the public sector has been viewed as a desirable place to work, and is exempt from the usual woes of rewards system design and implementation. This perception is fueled by several components, including the perception of "lifetime employment" (i.e., employment stability with little risk of layoffs, downsizing, or performance-based terminations), consistent and scheduled wage increases, a sound benefits package including guaranteed retirement funds, an environment uninterrupted by global change, and reasonable work hours.

As the working world continues to change and adequately skilled employees are increasingly difficult to attract and retain, the public sector has been forced to review and update its rewards practices. In addition to the factors just mentioned, increased accountability and public scrutiny have also fed into the need to examine public sector compensation systems and their effectiveness.

In a recent study conducted by the authors at a large state agency, several themes were noted in the structure, implementation, and effectiveness of the rewards system. First, the human resources function continues to be the "ruling force" in compensation design and decision making, practically eliminating feedback and decision-making authority from line management employees. Second, pay ranges and practices were outdated and inflexible and therefore not meeting recruitment and retention needs (e.g., no practices in place to address the need for employees with skills in "hot technologies" in the information technology arena). Third, the public sector is just beginning to understand the meaning and importance of total compensation. And fourth, the compensation expertise in labor market trends and basic labor market data is lacking as the focus continues to be internal, rather than external.

The consequences of these four themes are varied and substantial. As a survival technique, front-line managers are forced to manipulate position descriptions to escalate the pay range of an employee to increase pay. The trust of the human resources function is low, and therefore the functional impact is minimal. Attraction and retention are difficult as salaries are not competitive and the environment is undesirable to many in the labor market.

Although this is just one example of public sector rewards system readiness and effectiveness, the authors have been involved in several other studies with public sector organizations that confirm these findings are indeed trends, rather than exceptions.

Public sector organizations are beginning to realize that rewards system design is critical. Therefore, many organizations are commissioning studies to analyze and design skill-based pay plans, knowledge-based pay plans, bonus systems, and pay-for-performance rewards programs. Although this is a positive first step in modernizing public sector pay practices and improving their effectiveness, the acceptance, viability, and sustainability of these concepts is yet to be established.

Extending Innovative Reward Systems to New Business Environments

Traditional reward systems in the early 20th century placed an emphasis on base pay and benefits. A major determinant of the level of pay and benefits was seniority. This approach was developed in private unionized companies and extended to nonunion companies, public sector organizations, and nonprofit organizations.

Table 8-1   Reward System Readiness Checklist for the 21st Century

Organization Readiness
• The rewards philosophy and system dovetails with the business strategy and the goals of the organization (i.e., employee performance and goal achievement leads to organizational success and goal attainment). • The short-term and long-term financial resources of the organization are ample enough to support the rewards system.
Compensation Expertise
• The organization has the in-house compensation expertise to support the current and future rewards system needs. • The organization continually seeks out new information on compensation trends and changing rewards systems and practices and participates in relevant wage surveys and market studies. • Rewards systems fundamentals are updated and in place, including a functional job evaluation system; pay ranges or bands; job descriptions; lead, match, or lag philosophy; and so on.
Employee Readiness
• The front-line management team is informed and educated about the components of the compensation system. They are prepared and understand how to make effective compensation decisions, and they have the authority to make rewards decisions and communicate those decisions as appropriate. • The employees are educated on the components of the rewards system, the pay-for-performance link, and their influence on individual and team pay, and they have a sense of internal and external equity.
System Readiness
• The rewards system is flexible and dynamic and therefore able to meet the needs of exceptional employee circumstances, the changing needs of the organization, and the shifting labor market. • An auditing process is in place to periodically assess if the rewards plan is meeting the needs of the business and tracking with labor market demands. • A scalable rewards plan is in position that adapts as the company grows and diversifies.

At the end of the 20th century, private nonunion companies began to use more innovative reward programs. A common theme to these programs was to focus on pay increases based on performance. Performance was defined in a multitude of ways ranging from performance ratings to output measures at the individual, team, and organizational level. In the 21st century, private unionized companies, public sector organizations, and non-profit organizations are likely to also use innovative reward programs. Resistance to performance rather than seniority as a primary determinant of pay is down in unions because they realize that pay-for-performance results in greater productivity and in turn, greater productivity leads to more job security.[15] The public sector is more receptive to pay-for-perfor-mance because they realize that they must compete with private sector organizations to deliver services to the public. In this new 21st century environment, measures of performance such as customer service are criti-cal to public sector organizations.[16] Nonprofits in the 21st century will not only be responsible for delivering services, but also for doing it at the low-est cost possible. Innovative reward strategies such as gain-sharing are crit-ical to nonprofit organizations as they provide rewards on the basis of cost reductions to the organization.

Summary and Implications

As we move into the 21st century and face a diverse and changing labor market, continuous global transformation, an increasingly fast work pace, mounting technological enhancements and demands, and a shift away from bureaucratic work structures, organizational rewards systems *must* have the ability to meet these challenges and enhance organizational success and achievement. This chapter has addressed several of the components needed to meet these demands, as follows.

- Move from a strict compensation-only viewpoint to a total rewards philosophy, including integrating learning opportunities and job design. Learning opportunities allow employees to broaden their skill and knowledge base, thereby increasing employees' internal mobility and external marketability. Job design refers to the dynamic makeup of positions and job assignments and is characterized by high levels of autonomy, skill variety, work significance, and so on.
- Shift the focus to include both strategy and execution. This focus should include a rewards system that is both strategic in nature (i.e., the system is in alignment with, and feeds into, organization strategy and goals) and reflective of sound

compensation design (i.e., properly designed, implemented, administered, and evaluated).

- Integrate reward systems with organizational learning systems so that the development, storage, and dissemination of compensation system knowledge are an integral part of the organization and are rewarded accordingly.
- Manage equity perceptions by shifting the focus from a job-based-only approach to a dual job-based and person-based method. This allows organizations to assess and address both internal and external equity issues while enhancing employees' perceptions of fairness and proper compensation levels.
- Revisit public sector rewards system design and enhance their effectiveness by implementing contemporary compensation practices, educating employees and line management about pay practices, equity issues, and so on; implementing skill-based, knowledge-based, and bonus-driven pay systems; and ensuring that a system of supports is in place to make certain these changes are successful.
- Extend innovative reward systems to new business environments by implementing performance-based pay systems into private businesses, public sector organizations, and nonprofit agencies, and shift away from seniority-driven rewards systems.

To assist professionals in determining if an organization's reward system is ready for the unique challenges of the 21st century, a comprehensive checklist may be found in Table 8–1.

9

Putting Shareholder Value in the Right Perspective

Derek F. Abell

he 20th century closed with more questions than answers about a wide array of business challenges and ways in which leaders could meet them. On one issue, however, there seems to be a widespread and even growing consensus: The central purpose of enterprise is to create value for its shareholders. And certainly, recent history has clearly demonstrated that increasing attention to shareholder value has allowed many companies to perform better. Recognition of what is essential to the achievement of sustainable long-term growth in cash flows has resulted in more weight being put behind these "value drivers" and, in turn, the creation of more performance-oriented cultures and incentives.[1]

As we move into the 21st century, the question appears not to be whether the concept is theoretically sound, but whether in its application it is correctly realized. Questions are being raised about whether failure to pay proper attention to real customer satisfaction, employee motivation, the way leaders realize their own purposes, and the broader needs of society as a whole might not result in backlashes that may eventually undermine the value-creating process itself, and thus jeopardize shareholder value creation. While this seems intuitively obvious, some managers who are single-mindedly dedicated to the shareholder value concept have seemingly overlooked this important balance. Others, not realizing the complex interactions among different elements of purpose, conclude that performance on one element can only be achieved by sacrifice on another.

A striking example of the aforementioned was Renault's decision to close its car production plant in Vilvoorde, Belgium, in 1997–1998.[2] The closure was probably inevitable, since it followed a history of poor management by the state-run enterprise, failure by the French government to adopt a policy of transition to the new realities of over-capacity in the European auto industry, failure by the Belgian government to manage social overheads so that the company could remain competitive cost-wise, failure of management to streamline and focus its factories, failures to leverage new innovative breakthroughs, and failures to move more expeditiously toward the international marketplace. But when the closure was finally announced, shareholders were the main beneficiaries (the share price rose immediately to FF. 154, a 52-week high, and up almost 50% from its 52-week low of FF. 103). It was the Vilvoorde workforce who took the lumps. Some 3,000 employees were eventually dismissed, and a similar number lost their jobs in the surrounding community as a result. Worker morale at Renault suffered immeasurably, as did broader support in Europe for corporate moves toward globalization (100,000 workers from all over Europe marched in the Vilvoorde streets to support the Renault workers' cause). The importance of worker satisfaction (or lack of it in this case) was underlined when dismissed workers dumped 5,000 keys in the parking lot. These keys were for 5,000 cars which, during negotiations, had been "held hostage." Renault had to make the best of matching cars and keys, to say nothing of making the best of severely damaged morale among those who retained their jobs elsewhere in the Renault system.

While the Renault example points to the hazards of too single-minded a pursuit of (and here also delayed attention to) profit performance at the expense of other stakeholder considerations, it is also true that it is easy to err on the other side also. How many organizations are there with only flimsily defined goals and pathways for creating shareholder value, who cannot perform on other dimensions in the long run because the money to do so is simply not available? The more classic examples come from the so-called nonprofit sector. Familiar are universities, which are near the limit of eating up public funds to ostensibly achieve the broader education and research needs of our society, often failing, however, to clearly satisfy any particular customer constituency. Or museums or organizations in the performing arts, which cannot survive in the absence of continual sponsorship from benevolent patrons. Aren't these institutions sometimes guilty on the other side of putting too much weight on satisfying personal passions and their own understanding of customer satisfaction and societal benefit, and too little on securing financial sustainability?

Renault, on the one hand, and financially strapped universities, on the other, are of course extreme examples—and many readers will already have in mind for-profit companies that are successfully managing with more broadly defined purpose and performance (such organizations as Royal Dutch/Shell, Canon, DuPont, and Nestlé immediately come to mind). It's easy also to think of nonprofit enterprises that manage nevertheless to be financially self-sustaining (later, I use the example of a drug rehabilitation center, San Patrignano, to make this point).

We will see later that some businesses are naturally inclined to balanced consideration of multiple stakeholder purposes, while some are more naturally inclined to imbalance. The bulk of businesses are somewhere between, and in most cases, require a rebalancing of these considerations to succeed in the long term. Many will not, for lack of leadership. When statesmanlike and balanced leadership is absent, other forces necessarily take over and fill the vacuum: Those stakeholders with most clout, seldom fully appreciating the long-term risks of imbalance, carry the day. Rarely do they carry the long term. My point will be that, whatever the natural disposition of the business is, all enterprises, in all businesses, at all times, and in all places, have to achieve balance to attain sustainable long-term performance.

At the root, the real issue seems to be whether shareholder value creation can really be regarded as the central purpose of the enterprise, or whether it is really a measure of a desirable, and in fact essential, result. Is it, in reality, the logical by-product of the successful pursuit of broader purposes involving a broader constituency of stakeholders?

The Value Creation System: Stakeholder Purposes, Contributions, and Derived Benefits

There are five central stakeholders in the value creation system: customers, shareholders, employees (not only within the firm's four walls but in the value-creating business system), leadership, and society. Each has its own purposes, makes its own contributions to the system's functioning, and derives its own benefits. Each, intuitively at least, understands that value creation is a system with multiple stakeholders and that there are interdependencies among each. Because of these interdependencies, and partly because of the system's overall capacity or lack of capacity to create value, the benefits received by each stakeholder may or may not measure up to the original purpose. As with a tandem bicycle, perceived extra effort from one partner may be rewarded with concomitant effort by another; foot dragging may be reciprocated. The result can either be a virtuous circle of mutual commitment to higher output or a vicious circle of less and less output.

The enterprise value-creation process is similarly susceptible to virtuous circles and vicious circles. When the system is in balance and stakeholders perceive equity, value creation is enhanced; when the system is in imbalance and stakeholders perceive inequities, value creation is diminished. Those perceiving inequity may reduce their commitments or even withdraw from the process.

Perceived inequity can arise for one or both of the following reasons: A stakeholder perceives inequity in his own transaction with the system in the sense that actual derived benefits fail to match up to contributions (e.g., when customers perceive that the price they are paying for services rendered is unreasonably high). A stakeholder perceives inequity vis-à-vis other stakeholders, as when employees are asked to accept flat wages while their bosses take home huge bonus payments.

In either case, the result is the same; one or other contributor to the value-creation process reduces their commitment to the detriment of overall value creation.

The main purposes (and hoped-for benefits) and main contributions to value creation for each of the five major stakeholders are shown in Table 9–1.

Table 9–1   Stakeholder Purpose and Contribution

Stakeholder	Main Purpose (and Derived Benefits)	Main Contribution	Abbreviation
Customer	Satisfaction	Price paid	cus sat
Shareholder	Shareholder value improvement	Capital	shr val
Employee°	Benefits in terms of compensation, meaningful employment, personal growth	Work, motivation, followership	emp ben
Leadership°	Self-realization in terms of personal accomplishment, creativity, financial reward	Passion, commitment, leadership	ldr realz
Society (mankind, nation, region, and/or community)	Progress (at least not regress)	"Access" to society's legal, environmental, and educational infrastructures, and to the advantages (disadvantages) of a free (closed) economy	soc prog

°Many employees are also leaders, and vice versa. The distinction between employers and leaders is therefore prototypical only.

There is nothing in Table 9–1 to suggest that shareholder purpose has any particular supremacy over the purposes of other stakeholders. The truth of the matter is that each stakeholder is much more likely to pursue primarily his own purpose, and to see the other stakeholders as *means* to his ends rather than ends in their own right. We may therefore reasonably speculate the following.

- From the perspective of a shareholder, shareholder value creation is beyond doubt the ultimate end purpose of the enterprise, and customer satisfaction, motivated employees, committed leadership, and societal progress (at least compliance) are the means to achieve this end.
- From the vantage point of public policy, however, we could well imagine a different primacy; namely, that the ultimate end purpose of the enterprise is societal progress, and that adequate returns to shareholders, committed leadership, customer satisfaction, and motivated employees are the means.
- From the customer's point of view, outstanding products and services that exactly fit individual needs are the ultimate end. What happens at the level of the enterprise must be considered from the customer's standpoint mainly as a "black box" that provides the means to achieve his ends.
- From the leader's point of view, satisfied customers, motivated employees, societal progress, and value creation for shareholders may, in reality, simply be the means to satisfy personal creative passions and ambitions.
- And that if we ask employees what they really want, and why they dedicate themselves to their jobs and careers, the honest answer is much more likely to be their own personal growth, satisfaction, and compensation than the well-being of the shareholder.

Primacy of purpose obviously depends on which vantage point one looks from.

Consider Shareholder Value as the Result, not the Main Purpose, of Enterprise Value Creation

We can see from the aforementioned arguments that to ascribe singularity and centrality of enterprise *purpose* to shareholder value creation is plainly wrong and misleading. The confusion arises because shareholder value is the only meaningful measure of overall enterprise *success*. The present value of all future cash flows remains the best overall demonstration of whether stakeholders are working together to create value. We have already seen that to single-mindedly chase shareholder value at the expense of other stakeholders and their purposes could in fact put the achievement of shareholder value improvement at risk. On the contrary, to pursue simultaneously and in a balanced fashion the purposes of all shareholders is to raise the likelihood of shareholder value improvement.

One could of course argue that, theoretically, if shareholder value thinking is properly applied, it would already include proper attention to the purposes of all stakeholders. Alas, in practice this just does not happen. Enterprise management is usually neither far-sighted enough nor wise enough to build such considerations into their decision making. There is a natural tendency to the short term that arises both from management's own limited job horizons and because some investors look primarily for short-term gains; traders, for example, have different and shorter term purposes than long-term investors like pension funds, insurance funds, or owner-managers.

Therefore, it seems reasonable to conclude that while theoretically shareholder value *could* provide the central sense of purpose for all enterprise stakeholders and all activities, in practice it does not. We have only to observe the yawning gaps in many industries between stakeholder expectations and the real benefits accruing to these stakeholders to confirm this: Customer satisfaction with such products or services as air travel, fast food, the media, and government services (to name but a few) are currently at a low ebb; employee motivation in organizations where employees feel squeezed like lemons to support ever "leaner and meaner" strategies is in the basement; cleavages between rich and poor are widening; environmental sustainability remains a societal dream; and top management often seems more driven by handsome bonuses than by the passion to add value. Is it going too far to wonder whether September 11, 2001, and its aftermath is not an early warning sign at the macro level of many imbalances at the individual firm level? President George Bush intoned, soon after September 11, what many are hardly daring to imagine: that our very civilization may well be threatened.

We may summarize these interdependencies of purpose, and the effects on the end result of shareholder value improvement, in terms of whether shareholder value is viewed as the central purpose (I call this shareholder value "push"), or whether it is viewed as one of a number of other stakeholder purposes, all of which must be satisfied if shareholder value is to be maximized (I call this shareholder value "pull"; see Table 9–2).[3]

Table 9–2   Shareholder Value "Push" and "Pull"

Shareholder Value Push	Shareholder Value Pull
Shareholder value is viewed as the primary purpose of enterprise	Shareholder value is viewed as one of several stakeholder purposes to be satisfied
The fulfillment of other stakeholder purposes may be jeopardized	The fulfillment of other stakeholder purposes is also achieved
Vicious circles likely to result	Virtuous circles likely to result
End result: risk of lower shareholder value	End result: likelihood of higher shareholder value

Inherent Business Differences and Their Impact on Balance

Two factors describing the underlying nature of a business largely determine whether there is likely to be a tendency toward stakeholder balance or imbalance. The first factor is whether the product or service may be regarded as "noble" in its own right (noble here may be interpreted as a product or service that serves broad societal interests, as well as producing individual customer satisfaction). The second factor is the average level of profitability that prevails in the industry. Figure 9–1 shows four basic and

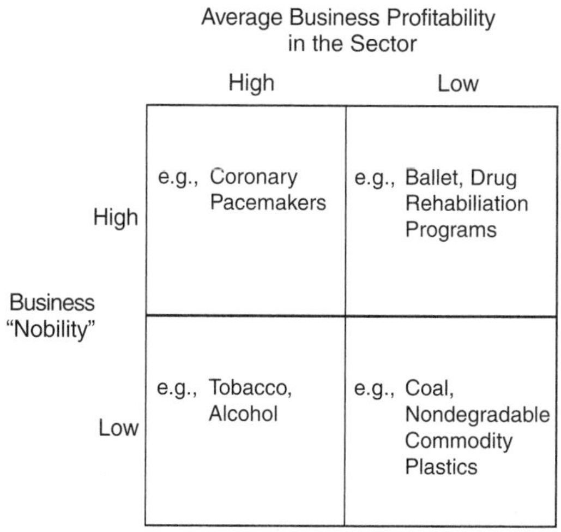

Figure 9–1   Nobility and profitability matrix.

contrasting conditions in which a company may be situated. It is also true that, in such a four-cell matrix, companies in the upper right-hand cell (i.e., with noble products or services but low profitability) often tend to be non-profit businesses. Companies in the remaining cells are usually in for-profit sectors.

Let us now describe each of the four underlying situations in more detail, and use a simple two-dimensional map of purpose and performance to depict these contrasting situations and approaches for each of the five stakeholders to better understand the possible interactions among each.

Products or Services with High Nobility and High Average Profitability

Examples would be health care products such as pacemakers, eye care devices, or implant hearing aids, represented respectively by companies such as Medtronic, Alcon, and Cochlear. In such businesses, stakeholder balance is not a given, but is certainly easier to achieve than in many other businesses (see Figure 9–2). The very fact of higher profitability provides at least the prospect of satisfying more than one stakeholder, and the noble nature of the business tends to inspire passionate leadership, motivated employees, and at least a promise of societal progress. In the long run, as Figure 9–2 also shows, high performance on each dimension and strong internal balance is likely to be maintained because the virtuous circles so created are self-reinforcing.

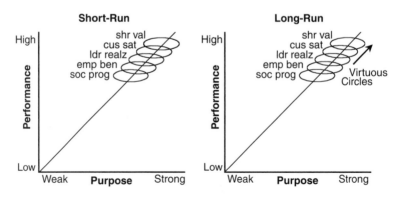

Figure 9–2   High-profit, high-nobility business.

Products or Services with Low Nobility and Low Average Profitability

Examples here would be old-technology coal mining, standard disposable plastic utensils, or nondegradable packages. Here, balance is difficult, if not impossible, to achieve (see Figure 9–3). Low profitability means that Peter has to be robbed to pay Paul, and shareholder value usually achieves primacy (often eventually undermining the long-term value creation process itself). Also, low nobility often means doubtful or disgruntled employees, dispassionate leadership, and the specter of societal regress. In the long run, as Figure 9–3 also shows, performance on all dimensions may fall even further as vicious circles are set up that further impair already fragile balances. A diminishing cake invites unhealthy internal competition for ever smaller slices of the shrinking benefits.

While companies in the top-left cell of the matrix (e.g., Medtronic, Alcon, and Cochlear) often exhibit natural balance and companies in the bottom-right (e.g., coal mines and disposable commodities) exhibit natural imbalance, companies in the other two cells may be more or less balanced or unbalanced and may be managed in two very distinct ways. When one dimension of performance is overly emphasized at the expense of others, vicious circles result, which only aggravate imbalances, often resulting in lower performance overall. When, however, management actively pursues strategies toward balanced performance, not only does each individual dimension improve, but interactions produce further positive effects overall. A virtuous circle results, in which performance on all five dimensions

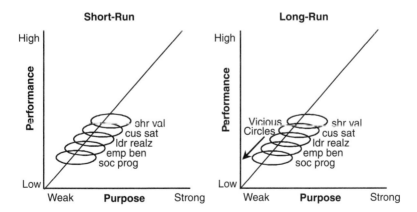

Figure 9–3   Low-profit, low-nobility business.

can increase. We may envision these interactions schematically by depicting the short- and long-term consequences of different primacies of purpose on maps similar to those used earlier.

Products or Services with High Nobility, but Relatively Low, or Even Negative, Average Profitability

Performing arts companies (even the Bolshoi has trouble making ends meet) or drug rehabilitation centers, such as San Patrignano near Rimini (which is nevertheless an outstanding example of getting near to financial sustainability, despite its underlying characteristics), are good examples. Balance here is an open question, depending very much on leadership and its priorities.

Vicious Circles Predominate

As Figure 9–4 shows, when high nobility is combined with low average profitability, the short run is often a mixed picture. Dedicated and passionate leadership can create value for the society and for customers, but employees sometimes get left behind (in financial compensation if not in motivation), and profitability, by definition, is low. In the long run, in the absence of any offsetting forces, vicious circles set in where funds shortages jeopardize the very accomplishment of the leader's vision. In turn, unless there is great stamina, personal leadership commitment is also undermined eventually, with falling performance all around.

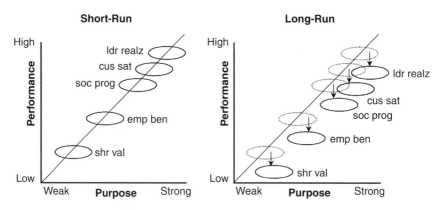

Figure 9–4   Low-profit, high-nobility, vicious circles.

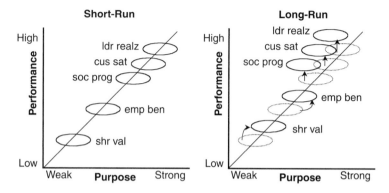

Figure 9–5   Low-profit, high-nobility business, virtuous circles.

Virtuous Circles Predominate

With the same underlying business characteristics, proper regard for the financial side of the activity can make all the difference. By taking this into account, as well as the people who work to actually create value for the customers, leadership passion is fully exercised, customers are satisfied, and society benefits. A classic example would be Diaghelev's success in taking the Ballets Russes[4] to France in the early 1900s. His passion and the dedication of his troupe were uncontestable. His talent to identify a totally new way of bringing together different art forms (each of which he mastered to a high degree himself) resulted in ecstatic Parisian audiences. Ballet literally took an upward leap. This success in turn provided an ever stronger case for funding, and Diaghelev himself always kept his eye on this financial side, tapping his allies in the Russian court to keep the Ballets Russes financially afloat, at every possible opportunity. This virtuous circle went on for 20 years, even surviving the World War I. It ended only with Diaghelev's death. Figure 9–5 shows a typical short-run imbalance for this kind of business, and how, in the long run, virtuous circles can lead to higher performance and better balance all around.

Products or Services with Low Nobility and High Profitability

Alcohol and tobacco companies come to mind here (e.g., Philip Morris or British American Tobacco). Again, balance is neither guaranteed nor excluded. It all depends on leadership's priorities.

Vicious Circles Predominate

A very analogous situation to what we have seen earlier is created. Here, however, profits start high but end lower in the long run because of lack of attention to leadership's own purposes, to people and their motivation, and to the ever open trap of societal regress. Conceptually, the result is similar: exacerbation of imbalances and falling performance all round. Profitability itself is undermined at the end. Lawsuits against the tobacco industry related to the health hazards of smoking are a good example of this downward spiral. Figure 9–6 attempts to capture these scenarios schematically for the short run and the long run.

Virtuous Circles Predominate

With the same starting conditions, strong leadership can make all the difference. We have seen this clearly demonstrated by leaders in the oil industry and in the chemical industry, where the potential for environmental damage is large. From a less glorious past, there are signs now that stronger leadership is paying much greater attention to performance, not only on the bottom line, but across all other dimensions of purpose, and particularly the environment. A marker point in this reversal was the attempted sinking of the Brent Spar by Shell. It became painfully obvious, as German drivers boycotted all Shell gas stations, that to ignore the society at large was an extremely perilous undertaking from a financial perspective. There was a substantial risk of profits landing in the basement, not only in Germany but all over Europe, as the boycott threatened to spread. Figure 9–7 shows scenarios for the short run and long run for these kinds of business.

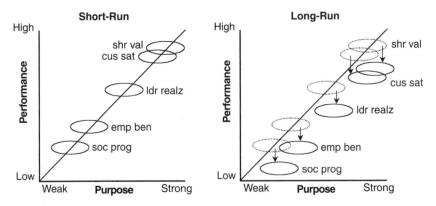

Figure 9–6   High-profit, low-nobility business, vicious circles.

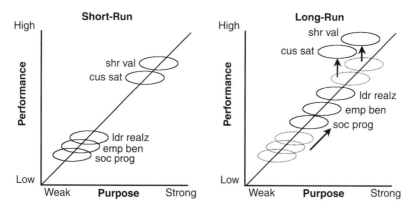

Figure 9–7   High-profit, low-nobility business, virtuous circles.

Leadership's Role in Promoting Balance and Thereby Improving Value Creation

We can now imagine two different processes that largely determine which stakeholders and which purposes are, in fact, given primacy.

The first, undoubtedly common in practice, results from the negotiating position, power, and communications advantage of one or other stakeholder. It is not surprising, therefore, that the phenomenon of global financial markets and the increasing transparency and immediacy of company financial data has led to the supremacy of shareholders and shareholder value in the current equation. This may or may not last, as other stakeholders are increasingly disaffected, and disenfranchised, but armed with the means to reverse the current balance. I speak here of everything from legislation and regulation on the part of public policy to buying embargoes on the part of unhappy customers, to radical unionization and worker disruption on the part of employees, to self-serving maneuvers like golden parachutes, and to extraordinary compensation packages on the part of management and entrepreneurs.

The second process is, however, of an entirely different nature. And it can lead to entirely different outcomes. It presumes the wisdom of leadership and the ability to foresee, articulate, and pursue combinations of purpose where multiple interests can be served, or even enhanced, in parallel. These virtuous circles stand in sharp contrast to what often tends to happen in practice, namely, vicious circles, where power and self-interest tip the balance in one direction or another. Leadership, and more than that, statesmanlike leadership, is the key to avoiding power-based outcomes, many of which turn into vicious circles in the longer term. The single-minded pursuit of shareholder value, even if it is ostensibly long-term in orientation, runs the risk, in the absence of statesmanlike leadership, of leading us down this unhappy road. Of course, balance and its preservation is one among many leadership roles. Leaders are also fundamentally responsible for enterprise direction and strategy (the "whats" of leadership) and enterprise functioning (the "hows" of leadership). But it is increasingly apparent that the "why" questions associated with balancing stakeholder purpose are central to long-term enterprise success—and maybe even to the future of our whole socioeconomic system.

"Corporate Citizenship" Is Not the Answer

Many companies are painfully aware of imbalances and want to either offset them or at least communicate to the world at large that they are aware and engaged in such issues. Therefore, these companies undertake various well-meaning corporate citizenship schemes. It cannot escape notice, for example, that major tobacco companies are also major sponsors of cultural and sports events. Many make large charitable contributions or engage with relatively low actual involvement in "good causes." This type of corporate citizenship is particularly prevalent in businesses with low nobility but high profitability. It is almost always done alongside the main business activity rather than inside the business itself. While it is an offset, or at least perceived as such, it falls far short of correcting the imbalances themselves. When 5,000 people showed up for a blues concert by B. B. King and Ray Charles sponsored by Philip Morris, it certainly did little to resolve the healthcare concerns or claims of smokers!

Also under the heading of corporate citizenship, management may claim to be dealing with imbalances from inside, when essentially what is happening is no more than legal compliance or grudging reactions to others' initiatives. While this is certainly more constructive than the window-dressing described earlier, it falls far short of what really needs to be done. Its reactive rather than proactive character is also its main shortcoming.

Figure 9–8 presents the story of "corporate citizenship" as it is often practiced today, in schematic form; it points to those real possibilities for proactive change that only statesmanlike leadership can produce. It is to this story that we now turn.

What Can Leaders Do?

Research at IMD is revealing pieces of a complex jigsaw puzzle, whose form still remains only in outline. The recent attention to shareholder value is prompting some leaders to put it at center stage in terms of enterprise purpose, notwithstanding evidence that value creation may be jeopardized;

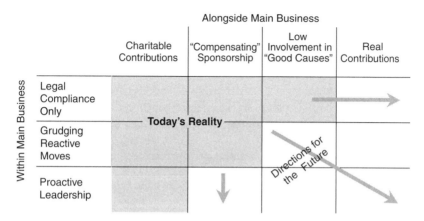

Figure 9-8 The limits of corporate citizenship.

others, more circumspect, are intuitively searching for ways to safeguard broader stakeholder interests. Few, if any, are systematically using all the avenues available to achieve balance. From the piecemeal evidence we do have, the following should certainly be considered.

With Respect to Purpose Itself

Hold the CEO Responsible

Recognize that it is the responsibility of the CEO, first and foremost, to balance stakeholder interests. Boards can help by focusing management attention on this issue when it is being overlooked or underestimated. Remember that the CEO wears two hats: the first as a stakeholder in his or her own right, with purposes related to self-realization and reward; the second, as the enterprise leader, with the responsibility to balance this self-interest with the interests of other stakeholders. When boards make CEO appointments, they must bear in mind the inherent predispositions of individuals in this respect and be sure to relate these predispositions to the underlying nature of the business and its inherent requirements for balance.

Enlarge Value Creation Ambitions

I have already intimated that leadership's responsibility is to "bake a big cake" in terms of value creation. The bigger the cake, as any child at a birthday party could tell us, the less squabbling there is likely to be about sharing it out; the smaller the cake, the harder it is to satisfy conflicting purposes. In fact, the smaller the cake, the more differences in purpose among diverse stakeholders are likely to become conflictual. The need in many companies is not just to modestly step up value creation ambitions, it is to massively redefine these upwards. Only then can we expect to achieve simultaneously the diverse, and sometimes divergent, demands of the different stakeholders.

Formally Recognize the Goals of All Stakeholders and Re-prioritize When these Are Not Being Met

It is usual, in fact nearly universal, to define financial targets for business. More and more, these are defined in shareholder value terms, and not just one- to three-year financial plans and budgets. Balanced scorecard approaches have resulted in improved measurement and control of customer satisfaction. These are steps in the right direction.

Unfortunately, it is rarer to find companies that set such clear goals for employee satisfaction. Shell, with its new three-part annual report dealing with economic, social, and environmental performance, is still an exception rather than the rule. It has apparently been a major step toward the achievement of their new balance.

When, as we have seen, the inherent nature of the business tends to favor some stakeholders at the expense of others, leadership's role is to provide counterbalance. In a performing arts company, this might mean paying greater attention to finance and financial stakeholders; in an energy company it might mean paying greater attention to the positive and negative impacts on society at large.

With Respect to Strategic Direction

Formulate a Dynamic and Engaging Mission Statement that Encourages Balance

Good mission statements are short and to the point. They should embrace purposes that spotlight stakeholder interests above and beyond shareholder value. Ball bearing manufacturer SKF's mission statement for its Bearing Services Division's "trouble-free operations" focuses on the customer stakeholder; Alcon, a world leader in the eye care business, has the mission statement "preserving and restoring sight." This implies benefits both for individual customers and for society at large. It reminds all involved that the company's fundamental purpose is to do good for customers and society, and that they expect that focus to lead to shareholder value. It does. Alcon is the fastest-growing and most profitable company in its industry and a high performer on all five dimensions of purpose. It can boast passionate leadership (its former CEO stayed nearly 40 years at the top and built the company from $20 million of sales to more than $2 billion). It can also boast highly motivated and engaged employees. The mission statement and the fundamental values it implies apparently play a major role in this.

Use Breakthrough Strategies to Achieve Enlarged Value Creation Ambitions

Experience tells us that the most effective way to achieve high levels of value creation is not to simply make incremental changes to what already exists, but to substantially redefine the business and possibly even the industry.

It is hard to imagine achieving balance among the five broad dimensions of purpose without such a breakthrough strategy. The ability to lead strategically towards the future (i.e., to be on the leading edge of new waves, rather than being on the back edge, or worse, submerged by change) is a vital ingredient. I have written extensively elsewhere about the need for all firms and their leaders to employ a dual approach; namely, to have a clear strategy to manage "today-for-today" and to spend equal time on "today-for-tomorrow."[5]

Remember that Balance is Only Achieved by Action, Not by Intent Alone

Words are not deeds. Statements of intent with respect to balance are necessary (as we shall see later) but not sufficient. This leadership intent has to be converted into action. In practice, the end result achieved is the sum total of many decisions made explicitly or implicitly by leaders at many different levels in the organization as they go about their daily business. Balance is achieved, or not achieved, because executives up and down the hierarchy put slightly more weight on one foot than the other as they go along. The CEO's foot, because it provides an example to all the rest, is infinitely heavier in showing the way than the feet of anyone else lower down. When, for example, Nestlé was confronted with a plant closing in Austria, the decision by top management to sell the plant to a competitor rather than closing it down was interpreted by the rank and file as a signal that Nestlé cared about its people.

With Respect to Implementation

Put in Place a Supportive Culture, Values, and Beliefs

All that has been recommended will be hard to implement unless the organizational ground for balance is fertile. In attempting to achieve balance, then, the CEO must be aware that his personal initiatives will fall flat unless this organizational context is attended to.

When shareholder value is held up as the central and sole purpose of the enterprise, it is quite possible that executives at levels below the top will interpret this too narrowly and make decisions that trigger vicious rather than virtuous circles. The CEO's job is to instill a clear set of values and beliefs that help the organization's members comprehend the real functioning of the value-creation system and to act accordingly. One such example is Canon corporation's philosophy of Kyosei. Ryuzaboro Kaku, Canon's president, described this as "a philosophy that would guide the company's future development and express its vision."[6] This philosophy was expressed as "the achievement of corporate growth and development, with the aim of contributing to global prosperity and the well-being of humankind."

Align People, Systems, and Processes

This recommendation is really an extension of the last one, but on a more operational level. Balance is not likely to be achieved, even when there is total commitment from the CEO, unless people, systems, and processes follow. When SKF developed the highly innovative approach to the bearings business by stressing service (under the slogan "trouble-free operations"), they went to enormous trouble to also create awareness among employees about the new strategy and its requirements, to train them to accomplish this, and to rely on them extensively for the detailed innovation that was required at the point of contact with the customer. Incentives were brought into line with the new service orientation and new measures of service quality. With this radical new strategy, SKF created substantial new value, dramatically improved customer satisfaction, convinced doubting employees and managers of its advantages, and raised profit margins and growth levels considerably.

Clearly Communicate the Broad Balance that Is Sought

Engraved into the stone above the entrance to the rector's palace in Dubrovnik (it was put there in the late 1500s, at the height of Dubrovnik's naval power in the Adriatic, Mediterranean, and beyond) is inscribed the following: "OBLITI PRIVATORV PVBLICA CURATE." Roughly translated, it means "to put aside private interests, and serve those of the public." Not only was it a constant reminder to the rector of the balance that he had to achieve, but because it was also read by all who entered the palace's main portal, it made everybody aware of the most fundamental purpose of this particular enterprise.

The point of this example is not to advocate that every leader should communicate the balance that Dubrovnik espoused; rather, it is to draw attention to the need for and power of communications. In some cases, communications must focus on the need for a new orientation to the customer (SKF's Bearing Services CEO spent huge amounts of time explaining the idea of "trouble-free operations" inside and outside SKF). In other cases communication must focus more attention on financial discipline and returns to shareholders, and in yet other circumstances it must underline that the company is deeply concerned about its employees. The point is that communication is an essential part of any attempt to achieve balance, promote virtuous circle thinking, and thereby create the best possible value result.

The concrete and specific actions that leaders may take may be summarized as shown in Table 9–3. Whatever the underlying nature of the business, they provide, when undertaken in concert, a powerful force for the creation of virtuous circles and for value creation improvement.

Table 9–3   What Leaders Can Do

	Purpose	Strategic Direction	Implementation
Policy level	Hold the CEO responsible	Formulate an engaging mission	Install a supportive culture, values, and beliefs
Strategic level	Enlarge value creation ambitions	Develop a breakthrough strategy	Align people, systems, and processes
Operational level	Recognize stakeholder goals	Follow-through/ action	Communicate broad sense of purpose

Conclusions

This chapter has raised questions not only about the validity, but also about the long-run efficacy of single-minded attention to shareholder value. While in theory such attention should lead to a proper consideration of other elements of purpose and accelerate shareholder value creation, in practice it is obvious that its application is often too narrow: Today's leadership often ignores the backlash of underestimation of other important elements of stakeholder purpose and/or the positive multiplier effect that proper attention to these factors could have.

We have concluded that in all businesses, long-term success requires attention to this balance, but in some businesses it is much more difficult to achieve than in others. In businesses that are naturally noble and profitable, water is already flowing in the right direction and leadership simply has to steer the ship into the stream. In other businesses, it is a continual struggle against the stream to correct natural imbalances. Most businesses fall somewhere between these two extremes.

Left to the market, as many believe it should be, there is a risk that relative stakeholder power tips the balance in one direction or another and self-interest wins out over long-term business health. It is here that leadership has to enter the picture. Leadership's role is a central one in determining whether a business, and possibly a whole industry, spirals downward in a vicious circle in which few, if any, stakeholder purposes can be satisfied, or whether virtuous circles can be created where the purposes espoused by each key stakeholder can be achieved together.

Corporate citizenship, as it is often currently defined, does not deal effectively with the problems of imbalance. Only statesmanlike leadership can do this. Although solid evidence is still skimpy, there are enough examples on the table to piece together at least a partial picture of what leaders can do to achieve balance and what such leadership might look like.

What is evident is the need for leadership initiative at the policy, strategic, and operational levels simultaneously, and attention to not only the "whats" and "hows" of balanced leadership, but even more importantly to the "whys." When any of these are ignored or only partially attended to, focusing on shareholder value improvement up front is like pushing on a string; when these are all used in a coordinated fashion, the resulting broad commitment has the combined effect of tautening the string and pulling shareholder value upward. The combination of satisfied customers, motivated employees, passionate leadership, societal progress, and returns that properly compensate shareholders for risk is an explosive mixture for value creation. Putting shareholder value creation too much in the forefront is, by contrast, to put the cart before the horse. As we move into the 21st century, leaders who ignore these truths do so at their own risk.

10

The Death and Rebirth of Organizational Development

Noel M. Tichy
Christopher DeRose

As a separate profession, organizational development (OD) is close to dead. Fortunately, as a set of practices and a way of applying learning from the behavioral sciences, it has been reborn as part of the mainstream methodology for running a world-class organization. Along the journey from near-death to rebirth, OD's metamorphosis has caused the demise of most internal OD staffs and professional positions labeled as OD consultants. But OD practices have never been more widespread in companies, thanks largely to Jack Welch and General Electric.

In 1978, Noel published a chapter in a book by Warner Burke, *The Cutting Edge*, which analyzed the history and probable future of OD, borrowing from Andrew Pettigrew's framework for analyzing new innovations. The chapter began with two quotes from OD practitioners that are as relevant today as they were in 1978.

OD Practitioner 1: Proactive, involved OD persons will be sought after. The accelerating pace of change demands people who are willing to make things happen even if it involves personal risk. (This will be a growing profession.)

OD Practitioner 2: Frankly, I don't see OD as a profession, and I think the movement in graduate schools and other places to make it a profession is doing more to foster an identity crisis than to build "change agents." The identity crisis is reflected in the following questions: Well, what the hell is OD anyway? Who really can do it? Where do you really learn it? (There will be a demise of OD.)[1]

This chapter assesses the transformation of OD over the more than two decades since these somewhat paradoxical views of OD were first advocated. Noel has been both a practitioner and scholar dealing with OD since the late 1960s, from his start as an internal OD consultant at Bankers Trust Company to the two years he spent on leave from the University of Michigan to lead the transformation of General Electric's Leadership Development Institute (Crotonville). This chapter reflects both authors' clinical and academic views, integrating a case study from Royal Dutch/Shell to highlight implications for future OD practitioners.

The Historical Phases of OD

Through the late 1970s, OD saw its most dramatic changes. The years since the late 1970s have been mostly marked by a search for role and identity within institutions.

Conception Phase (Late 1950s to 1963)

The roots of OD clearly draw on work from the late 1940s, when a group of Kurt Lewin's MIT researchers, led by Morton Duetsch, ran a workshop in New Britain, Connecticut, on race relations. In the process they discovered "experiential learning," or the examination of group and individual behavior in the "here-and-now" to draw conclusions about group dynamics and individual behaviors. This led to the launch of the National Training Lab (NTL) at Bethel, Maine, where T-groups ("T" for training) and sensitivity training started in 1948. By the end of the 1950s, a number of the NTL leaders focused increasingly on taking the applied behavioral sciences into organizational settings. Early efforts by Richard Beckhard and Herb Shepard at Esso Research and Engineering (as it was then known) laid the foundation for later developments in the field. Others at the time began calling their consultation work "organizational development"; most notably, Robert Blake and Jane Mouton. By the early 1960s, OD groups had emerged at major corporations such as Union Carbide, Bankers Trust Company, TRW, and Esso (now ExxonMobil).

Pioneering Phase (1964 to 1973)

By late 1964, leadership began to emerge in the field. Researchers and consultants such as Richard Beckhard, Warren Bennis, Edgar Schein, Matthew Miles, Ronald Lippitt, Robert Blake, Jane Mouton, and Herb Shepard conducted key training, consulting, and research projects under the banner of OD. There was a missionary zeal coupled with an esprit de corps. The mid to late 1960s witnessed the development of the NTL Institutes Program for Specialists in Organization Development as well as the creation of graduate programs at institutions such as Case Western Reserve, that provided formal training in the field. Additionally, by the late 1960s many corporations had developed separate internal OD staff and some had created dedicated OD departments. By 1969 there was sufficient work in the field to support a series of OD books by Addison-Wesley, marking the increased regard for OD among academics. These books, and the prominent work in the field, straddled two streams of practice. The source of both can be traced back to OD's conception phase in the 1950s. The first focused on interpersonal relations and humanistic psychology whereas the second focused on organizations as systems. The latter stream emphasized dynamics of the change process, work processes, and structural change. By the late 1960s, these streams became differentiated and OD became clearly identified with the second stream, even though it continued to draw heavily on humanistic psychology.

The mixture of these two streams in OD contributed to a phenomenon that Andrew Pettigrew identified as the "single most pervasive source of tension" in pioneering an innovation—the tension between the missionaries and the pragmatists. The pragmatists lined up behind system change while the missionaries associated their original cause with humanistic psychology. OD literature began ignoring more mainstream work in organizational psychology at the time as both streams became more absorbed in the struggle to advocate their positions. While many research projects were framed by theories associated with one of the streams, individual practitioners moved more fluidly between the two.

Self-Doubt Phase (1973 to Early 1980s)

Many factors undoubtedly contributed to this phase in OD's history. The general societal pessimism brought on by the Nixon era brought an end to federal support for large-scale liberal social change research. Social changes, coupled with an economic recession, led to a general loss of appetite for OD activities. The promise of OD practitioners at the time to forge a better, more meaningful organizational life had been discredited in the eyes of some. This created increased pressure on OD practitioners to justify their existence.

In 1978, Noel's interviews with OD practitioners demonstrated that the field was "largely tinkering at the margins." Implementation of OD projects within organizations was characterized by (a) a lack of involvement with strategic decision makers and (b) a follow-up role for OD practitioners in which they helped ease tensions created by strategic decision makers. The

1978 study concluded that OD would be increasingly marginalized unless it was revitalized into the mainstream of organizational effectiveness.

One example of mainstreaming OD was the U.S. Army's development of an Organizational Effectiveness School at Fort Ord in the early 1980s. The most promising officers rotated through the school before they were posted to two-year OD assignments. At the conclusion of these assignments, the officers rotated back to line positions. This had a profound impact on the U.S. Army, as colonels and lieutenant colonels were able to integrate OD practices into their operating roles. Although the military demonstrated a path for absorbing OD into mainstream management, most corporations were less deliberate in their efforts. As a result, by the early 1980s many organizations had eliminated OD specialists and departments. Only a few large companies such as Digital Equipment maintained such positions. At Digital, however, these positions became increasingly marginalized over time and were totally extinct by the time Compaq acquired the company in the 1990s.

Jack Welch Fathers the Rebirth of OD

Rebirth Phase (1980s to Present)

In the 1980s, Jack Welch, chairman and CEO of General Electric, fathered the rebirth of OD. How could this statement be true? After all, at the time Welch was known in the press by some as "Neutron Jack," after having laid off thousands of GE employees. He certainly had never read any OD books as a business leader and certainly not in the course of his PhD study in chemical engineering. Nonetheless, we argue that OD has finally found its place in the mainstream leadership of leading companies because of a series of steps Welch began in the 1980s, and that have since been emulated by other organizations around the world. Through a series of social innovations, Welch was able to expand upon the U.S. Army's model and demonstrate how to incorporate OD into the leadership repertoire of tens of thousands of GE workers.

Action Learning at GE's Crotonville Leadership Development Institute

In 1985, Welch was four years into his 20-year reign as GE's CEO. His transformation of the company's strategy and structure was well underway but Welch saw the threat of cultural inertia. Learning from history's great political revolutionaries, Welch knew that his transformation would fail if he could not use education as a platform for social change within the company. As a result, Welch identified Crotonville as his staging ground for cultural conversion and invited Noel to lead the overhaul of Crotonville's 50-acre campus and curriculum serving 10,000 GE professionals each year. The underpinning of Noel's efforts was a shift toward action learning that took GE's development efforts away from traditional study and case reviews. Instead, each course participant was forced to work on real business issues and undertake project work to drive technical and cultural change within his or her area. As Welch says,

> Tichy, who became head of Crotonville from 1985 to 1987, brought great passion to the job and introduced "action learning."…These classes became so action-oriented, they turned students into in-house consultants to top management. …In every case, there were real take-aways that led to action in a GE business. Not only did we get great consulting by our best insiders who really cared, but the classes built cross-business friendships that could last a lifetime.[2]

This movement toward action learning was predicated on a belief, shared by Welch, that meaningful cultural change would occur when people brought new work approaches back to their daily jobs. The Tichy Development Matrix[3] demonstrates the shift that Crotonville made (see Figure 10–1).

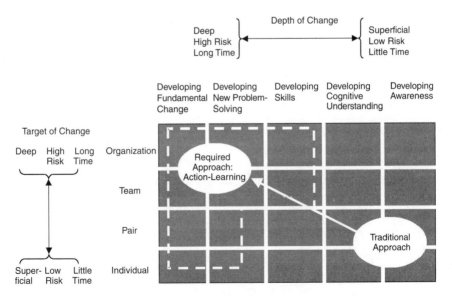

Figure 10–1   The Tichy Development Matrix.

Ultimately, Crotonville became a blend of traditional management development and OD. Real projects and team building were coupled with traditional education. The teams engaged in action learning at GE used contemporary OD technologies, such as organizational diagnostic frameworks, Beckhard's large system change methodology, team building, and coaching. The challenge that quickly became evident was ramping up the dissemination of these skill sets to tens of thousands so that they could have a meaningful impact on the GE culture.

Work-Out and the Development of Large-Scale OD Skills

By the end of 1987, Welch grew frustrated that cultural change at GE was not occurring fast enough. He had seen the impact Crotonville could have and he concluded that each of GE's 300,000 employees needed a similar experience. He wanted to liberate people from bureaucracy and empower them to work in an open and collaborative style. He knew the energy that would be created if people saw that their ideas were taken seriously and that they had the ability to break down hierarchy. Working with Jim Baughman (who replaced Noel as head of Crotonville), Noel and a team of consultants and key internal players created Work-Out, which Welch described in his 1990 annual report letter.

> Work-Out is a fluid and adaptable concept, not a "program." It generally starts as a series of regularly scheduled "town meetings" that bring together large cross sections of a business—people from manufacturing, engineering, customer service, hourly, salaried, high and lower levels—people who in their normal routines work within the boxes on the organizational chart and have few dealings with one another.
>
> The initial purpose of these meetings is simple—to remove the most egregious manifestations of bureaucracy: multiple approvals, unnecessary paperwork, excessive reports, routines, and rituals. Ideas and opinions are often, at first, voiced hesitantly by people who never before had a forum—other than the water cooler—to express them. We have found that after a short time, those ideas begin to come in a torrent—especially when people see action taken on the ones already advanced.
>
> With the desk largely cleared of bureaucratic impediments and distractions, the Work-Out sessions then begin to focus on the more challenging tasks: examining the myriad pro-

cesses that make up every business, identifying the crucial ones, discarding the rest, and then finding a faster, simpler, better way of doing things. Next, the teams raise the bar of excellence by testing their improved processes against the very best from around the company and from the best companies around the world.[4]

There is no question that Work-Out was designed to improve productivity. The equally important intervention, however, was creating a positive, high-energy process that forced managers to work collaboratively with employees to constructively change work routines. The managers who could not work this way and did not have basic inclusive, OD skills ultimately chose to leave GE or were asked to move on.

Work-Out was run by a team of external consultants that Welch funded to work with each of his 13 major businesses. In the late 1980s, there were over 25 consultants working with GE leaders to develop OD skills. Although GE did not label its work as OD, it advocated the large-scale adoption of OD principles and methodology at a time when many corporations had already jettisoned their OD practitioners.

Change Acceleration Makes OD a Mandatory Leadership Skill

By 1990, Welch and his team realized that Work-Out processes should be led and owned by line managers, not by consultants. Removing the consultants would ensure that managers had the necessary skills to sustain Work-Out efforts on a daily basis. In short, Welch wanted an internal army of change agents. GE launched the Change Acceleration Program (CAP) to give thousands of GE leaders change-agent skills, organizational diagnostic capability, skill in designing workgroup interventions, and basic team-facilitation skills. The three-workshop CAP process is outlined in Figure 10–2.[5]

CAP continues to run every year at GE, creating thousands of internal leaders equipped with change and OD skills.

Redefining Leaders as Teachers

By the mid 1990s the cultural transformation of GE was well established, but Welch was by no means done reinvigorating leadership and change skills. In 1995, he came across an article that we wrote for *Fortune* in which he described how Roger Enrico, former chairman and CEO of PepsiCo, was personally developing leadership talent.[6] Without staff, Enrico ran an action-learning leadership program for PepsiCo vice presidents. He personally taught a five-day off-site program to launch the group, coached

---

Workshop I
Facilitation Skills: Learn skills and techniques to assist
groups, manage group process, and be self-sufficient
- Group dynamics/group development
- Role of the process facilitator
- Range of facilitative interventions
- Facilitating Work-Out team meetings
- Facilitation lab

Workshop II
Process Leadership: Learn concepts, skills, and techniques
to take a leadership role in the integration of Work-Out within
their business; development of a focused, skilled, supportive
team of internal change agents
- Transformational leadership
- Work-Out and business process management
- Process consultation
- Role of the change agent
- Application planning

Workshop III
Organizational Systems: Learn skills and techniques to
grasp the "big picture" view of organizational change and
what it will take to reach Work-Out self-sufficiency and
organizational "boundarylessness"
- Systems view of organizational change
- Organizational analysis and diagnosis
- Intervening at an organizational level
- Managing conflict and increasing influence
- Leading in a boundaryless organization

Figure 10–2   Change Acceleration Program agenda.

each participant through a 60-day change project, and led a three-day follow-up workshop. Enrico's approach wove together many of the best practices from the individual, team, and organizational approaches utilized in
Crotonville and CAP: leadership feedback, group facilitation, organizational diagnostics, architecting systems intervention, and change processes.
The important improvement was Enrico's personal involvement, which he
described as a profound learning and development experience. It forced

Enrico to translate his experiences into simplified models and teaching points that could be vigorously debated, refined, and improved with the group. Enrico's story had a profound impact on Welch's thinking about who should lead the development of GE's future leaders. As he wrote in his book,

> I liked the Pepsi model and decided that every member of our leadership team should teach a session. Before, our senior staff and business leaders had done it only on a sporadic basis. The Pepsi model gave the classes a close look at our most successful role models, and it gave our leadership a broader pulse of the company. Today some 85% of the Crotonville faculty are GE leaders.[7]

The incorporation of GE leaders as teachers at Crotonville brought GE's OD efforts full circle. The action-learning projects at GE had launched an awareness of the need for line managers to utilize OD skills. Work-Out and CAP had developed those skills in thousands of GE leaders, eventually driving the replacement of OD staff and consultants with experienced teachers from the field. Embedding leaders as teachers at Crotonville was a natural next step for ensuring that line leadership was truly able to develop the people capabilities required for GE to maintain its success.

The final phase of moving GE to be the world's preeminent teaching organization was the launch of six sigma, the quality program aimed at producing fewer than three defects per million that was originally created at Motorola. Welch took the six sigma process, teaching organizational members statistical tools, process mapping, and problem-solving tools, to a new level by building the world's largest team of teachers. There are 12,000 full-time leader/teachers, called black belts, at GE spending two years teaching and running six sigma projects. No one will ever be promoted to upper management at GE without having been a black belt. These black belt teachers are engaging and teaching six sigma to all 300,000-plus GE associates. Their teaching also includes the soft skills of OD, the team process, individual dynamics, and systems change. One could argue that GE now has over 12,000 full-time OD consultants on two-year assignments, although GE never uses the term "OD" to describe them in any way.

The Dissemination of GE's Model

When Welch retired in 2001, GE was the most valuable organization in the world, as measured by its market capitalization. Over the course of Welch's 20-year reign as chairman and CEO, GE has been benchmarked by countless business and nonprofit organizations looking for the secrets of its success. The near total absorption of OD into the line leadership's daily responsibilities is certainly a key element of that story for it drove culture change and built an internal army of change leaders.

OD's rebirth is in the mainstream of how good leaders develop other leaders and their organizations. In *The Leadership Engine: How Wining Companies Build Leaders at Every Level,* the argument was made that organizations win by having more leaders at more levels than their competition, and that operational leaders—not consultants, staff, or professors— must develop leaders.[8] Leaders must teach. They must have a teachable point of view regarding how to develop a successful organization and how to energize its people.

We will demonstrate how to build a teaching organization that integrates OD into the mainstream by sharing the Royal/Dutch Shell case, one that we spent over three years helping to implement.

The Royal Dutch/Shell Story

Royal Dutch/Shell, the Anglo-Dutch energy and chemical company headquartered in London and The Hague, demonstrates how leaders who play a role as leader/teachers, who lead change and develop human capital, can transform a business at its core. The company engaged key leaders at all hierarchical levels as teachers to drive a global transformation of its business and workforce. In the process, an internal OD team called LEAP (Leadership and Performance), made up initially of less than a dozen high-potential line managers, was developed and later helped to drive the transformation effort. This group and the Royal Dutch/Shell case offer a compelling benchmark for OD practitioners everywhere for they have demonstrated solutions for helping leaders become teachers and scale this capability to thousands of people around the world, generating significant financial improvements estimated in the billions of dollars.

Step 1: Aligning the Point of View at the Top

When Cor Herkstroter took on the leadership of Royal Dutch/Shell as chairman of the Committee of Managing Directors (CMD), he recognized immediately that the organization had multiple, conflicting agendas. With its oil and quick service markets experiencing unprecedented competition from stronger global and regional players, Herkstroter knew that Royal Dutch/Shell would need to leverage its collective strength to maintain its industry leadership. This need contradicted the historical organization of

Royal Dutch/Shell that set up highly autonomous, powerful country leaders focused on creating conditions for local success. Herkstroter needed to unify these country leaders to drive learning across the group more rapidly. He also needed stronger centralized functions to leverage global cost and expertise without killing the creativity and competitive spirit of the country leaders.

Before Herkstroter could drive any of this, however, he needed his senior team aligned with him. The CMD, which served as the equivalent to Royal Dutch/Shell's office of the CEO, and was initially composed of four internal directors (Mark Moody-Stuart, John Jennings, Maartin van den Berg, and Cor Herkstroter), had a tradition of consensual management. Royal Dutch/Shell's decentralized structure also meant that there were relatively few decisions that the CMD would make that would directly affect each individual director's power. Herkstroter's change agenda threatened to fundamentally alter the balance of power at the senior level. Consequently, consensus would not work unless everyone had a shared view of the case for change. The CMD needed a shared point of view that would not only galvanize the rest of the organization but also align each individual's actions and teaching.

In 1995, Herkstroter and the senior team began work with a team of consultants to reinvent the organization. The initial consulting team included Noel; Michael Brimm, a professor from the Institute for European Business Administration (INSEAD) in Fontainebleau, France; and Patricia Stacey and Phil Mirvis, two independent consultants. The CMD first convened to try to develop a common view of the company and its future. With the consulting team's help, the CMD spent several days analyzing the company strategically, financially, and culturally. On the second afternoon, Noel gave each CMD member a mocked-up cover of *The Economist* dated four years in the future. Each person was asked to write his version of how and why Royal Dutch/Shell would change. At the end of an hour, the CMD members read their individual articles aloud. A clear picture of the case for change emerged and a fuzzy vision of the future started to show through. The CMD decided to engage other people in helping to sharpen this vision and develop a company-wide story of what Royal Dutch/Shell would be in the future. So, over the next several months, each CMD member met with several hundred other leaders to share the story and listen to others' responses.

Then, in October 1995, the CMD convened the top 50 Royal Dutch/Shell leaders. In an intensive three-day workshop, the leaders fleshed out the case for change, designed the "New Shell" vision and business strategy, defined shared values for the company, and identified how the company would drive large-scale change.

What emerged from these sessions was a common Teachable Point of View (TPOV).[9] For the leaders to ensure they were aligned and before they could teach thousands of people throughout the organization, the senior group needed to confirm that it shared the same point of view. In short, it needed to articulate

1. The ideas that will make the enterprise successful in the marketplace
2. The values and behaviors that are expected of people throughout the organization
3. Reasons the employees should be emotionally energized about the future
4. An explanation for how to handle difficult decisions that organizational members will face

This was critical during the months to come. Each of the senior leaders worked directly with some of the organization's highest potential leaders in a variety of forums. Although slight differences in nuance and style were revealed as each of the senior team members taught, their messages were consistent. They had a simple set of key themes that were grounded in the business reality and made a compelling case for individual and organizational change. This TPOV was summarized in a booklet that was distributed globally to tens of thousands of employees.

Step 2: Developing the Change Team

Although the CMD members were committed to personally teaching, the business case demanded rapid, large-scale change that senior management alone could not drive. Learning from benchmarking GE's Crotonville, Herkstroter created an internal change team. He first called on Mac McDonald, an American based in The Hague, who had been a long-time purchasing and operations manager and who exhibited both the straight-talking style and interpersonal skills to work with senior management.

From the ground up, McDonald built the infrastructure and team that would guide implementation of the leadership team's change agenda. McDonald recruited 10 high-potential line managers, without HR or OD backgrounds, who had successfully led major change efforts. The reasoning was simple: Those who had a track record of leading operational change from within the company knew how to avoid pitfalls of the change process. They could empathize with the leaders who they would coach and offer insight into effective change techniques.

In addition to setting stringent qualifying criteria, McDonald also put in place rigorous applicant screening. Each person was interviewed multiple times, put through team-building exercises to gauge interpersonal and team skills, and asked to demonstrate teaching skills.

The short-term imperative for McDonald's team members was preparing to teach others to be leaders and teachers. Utilizing change processes that we had designed for Royal Dutch/Shell enabled the team to focus on building coaching, teaching, and delivery capability. They achieved this through the equivalent of a modern-day, fast-cycle apprenticeship. Working with our team of outside consultants, they first observed how we taught the change processes and partnered with senior leaders. After documenting their learning from observation, they spent several sessions co-teaching with an experienced facilitator and senior leader. Once they demonstrated the necessary competency, usually within one to two months, they taught alone or with other team members and began working directly with Royal Dutch/Shell's senior leaders. Before they could be assured they had a full-time position on McDonald's team, however, their teaching and coaching was observed and evaluated, and they received written, video, and verbal feedback. This intense approach, coupled with several development workshops to foster better coaching, teaching, and teamwork gave McDonald the highly capable team he needed to drive large-scale change.

Step 3: Engaging the Organization

Herkstroter launched the initial phase of the Royal Dutch/Shell transformation in conjunction with developing the internal change team. The CMD used three processes to drive change. The first process, an action-learning program internally known as *Value Creation*, operated at the global strategy level. Pulling together the leaders with the highest potential from across the company, the CMD built cross-functional, global teams designed to tackle major strategic challenges. The process developed the participants' leadership capability through side-by-side work with the CMD members to understand, analyze, and fix global problems such as worldwide branding, employee satisfaction, and redefining the company's cost structure. Although the project outcomes had a dramatic impact on how Royal Dutch/Shell operates to this day, equally important was the effect on the senior management. Senior leaders personally taught each time the process was run, providing the opportunity for challenging dialogue from the highly thoughtful participants. The selection of strategic projects and the dialogue process utilized to review recommendations and make commitments also challenged the senior leaders' teachable point of view. The projects they selected had to match their TPOV on the future direction of the company. Additionally, the investment decisions they made—or did not make—as a result of participant recommendations had to align with the company's future vision.

In addition to Value Creation, the CMD, under the sponsorship of one member, Steve Miller, launched Business Framework Implementation (BFI). This process, designed in conjunction with Columbia Finance Professor Larry Selden and Yoko Selden, an independent consultant, brought in key operating managers from each of Royal Dutch/Shell's country operations with the goal of transforming Royal Dutch/Shell on both the "hard" and "soft" dimensions; that is, new business models were developed while simultaneously integrating new values, leadership behaviors, and change capacity. This three-workshop series began by engaging the participants in the Royal Dutch/Shell vision and case for change, often taught directly by a CMD member. The participants were also taught the Shell Business Framework, designed by the CMD with Selden's guidance, which outlined how Royal Dutch/Shell would drive future profitability. After learning new financial techniques and team building, organizational diagnostic skills, and leadership skills, participants were asked to build a business model for their country organizations that would achieve unprecedented operating returns on net assets and top-line growth. The teams operated under considerable pressure so, during the second workshop, much time was taken to not only review progress on the business model but also to improve teamwork and interpersonal dynamics. The last session involved senior leaders in a commitment process to review the country teams' business models, approve or reject them, and make supporting investment decisions as needed. Rather than formal presentations, the sessions were marked by a collegial, high-energy debate in which ideas prevailed over hierarchy. Throughout the BFI process, participants focused on developing financial and leadership skills that matched the company's future direction. They debated the Royal Dutch/Shell Mission and Values and Business Framework and determined the implications for their personal leadership. As a result, the company developed more capable teams that were aligned with the company's overall direction and had business plans that would contribute to Royal Dutch/Shell's bottom-line results. This enhanced the business acumen and leadership capability of thousands of Shell staff around the globe.

The two processes detailed so far extended Herkstroter's and the CMD's influence enormously. The first, Value Creation, engaged some of the brightest minds in the company to align global strategies with the Royal Dutch/Shell TPOV. The second provided penetration into key country networks and helped direct operational execution and investment to support Royal Dutch/Shell objectives. Although the impact from these programs was significant, Herkstroter and team needed a method to penetrate the organization at a large scale to build momentum and enthusiasm for the transformation.

Step 4: Developing Leaders at all Levels as Teachers

They achieved this through Focused Results Delivery (FRD). FRD, a two-workshop process, engaged each country's managing director (MD) and local leadership in teaching and developing their people. Our team designed a process that was kicked off by McDonald but transitioned to his replacement, Gary Steel. Steel, whose background included human resources, epitomized a pragmatic, no-nonsense approach to driving change and he continued to aggressively encourage local leaders to champion the change process by articulating their teachable points of view and teaching and leading projects.

In FRD, groups of 40 to 50 members of a country organization would attend together. The participants were organized in teams and asked to work on a project that would yield quantum improvement within the business. The projects were often defined or approved by the country MDs. This drove alignment in two ways. First, it enabled the country's senior leadership team to ensure that the process would help it meet its business objectives. The coaching of the country MD by Steel's team helped to align business and company goals in the process. Reviewing the recommended workshop content with Steel's team also helped the country leaders ensure that their understanding of the Royal Dutch/Shell mission and values and TPOV was current. The country leaders co-taught the sessions, so their preparation required them to reconcile their own TPOV with the company point of view. When dialogue with Steel's team revealed an inconsistency, they often sought guidance from a CMD member to clarify their own perspective or challenge the company's.

A Shell Best Practice: John Fletcher Transforms Shell New Zealand

Shell New Zealand offers insight into how this process cascaded throughout Royal Dutch/Shell. In 1997, when John Fletcher took over as managing director for Shell New Zealand, the company was facing new competitive entrants that planned to cherry-pick customers from Shell's most profitable territories. By learning from experiences in other markets, something that had improved as a result of Herkstroter's global restructuring, Fletcher knew what this would mean.

"Competitors were opening a few well-placed sites at our most profitable areas that could do enormous damage to our margins. This would be death by a thousand cuts as they slowly squeezed us into a cost competition that we couldn't win and that would leave us with a highly unprofitable margin mix."

Around this time, Fletcher happened to see a video created by Steel's group. The video showed the output of FRD in South Africa. As Fletcher said,

> I saw the energy and involvement of a big group of people making change happen. I had been thinking that the horsepower of most companies' people is so underutilized and we were no exception. I immediately rang the head of Shell Australia and said we have to do this together.

In February 1998, a group of 17 senior leaders from Shell New Zealand joined their colleagues in Australia for an FRD session. After crafting their TPOV and vision, the participants decided to take FRD mainstream when they returned to New Zealand. Twelve teams were organized and the leadership team held a series of meetings and town halls to teach everyone the basic principles covered in FRD. Fletcher and his finance director, Ed Johnson, openly told employees that headcount had to shrink by 30% to achieve the necessary cost structure. They also said that they had no concrete plan for where cuts would be made and that they wanted to work it out with participation from employees. Assuming the leadership team had a plan it was unwilling to share, "people just rolled their eyes when they heard that," Fletcher says.

Attitudes changed as Fletcher and his team utilized the FRD process to drive the organizational restructuring. One of the FRD teams was focused on organization, rewards, and employment contracts (ORE). Fletcher and the ORE team quickly agreed that the existing organizational structure was unsustainable.

Between the first and second month of the FRD process, one woman from the ORE team ran workshops that involved 70% of the New Zealand workforce. Although the young graduate's regular job was handling customer enquiries and orders in the customer service center, her FRD work yielded a clear set of Shell New Zealand values that were endorsed by the employees and consistent with Royal Dutch/Shell's overall mission and values. The ORE team recommended making the values part of every employee's performance contract and recruiting criteria. With the ORE team's support, every job within New Zealand was posted for placement. Reapplication interviews included the values and consequently some people with inconsistent values were beaten out for jobs they once held. As

Fletcher noted, the FRD process gained enormous credibility when "people started seeing new heads of teams and team members winning their positions, not the same old organization. Leadership followed [the new recruiting process] to the letter to build people's trust."

Three months after the FRD teams launched, the ORE team proposed a new organizational structure of 23 flat teams with no more than two layers between Fletcher and the front line. Staff members were invited to apply for up to five jobs in the new organization ranked in order of preference. "Whenever someone was unsuccessful with an application, they would get feedback so that they could learn and improve their chances for next time," Fletcher observed. As a result of ongoing coaching and dialogue with those who were unsuccessful, the company had only a handful of employees leave involuntarily. It achieved the 30% reduction and had done so in a process that actually generated employee commitment and belief in the organization's underlying values.

Meanwhile, other FRD teams focused on a range of commercial issues. A central group was created to reorganize customer contacts to free up sales people for growth activities and used process mapping to identify solutions for the customer service center. As a result, Shell customer representatives resolved over 90% of customer issues on the first call. In sum, Shell New Zealand reduced costs by more than 25%. "Margins did fall when competition came in," Fletcher said, "but [the competitors] got burned because they thought they were coming into a market with healthy margins. Of the three who had planned to enter, one turned around and never came, another is struggling, and the third has been acquired."

The process not only drove alignment within Shell New Zealand and with Royal Dutch/Shell's center, it also changed the lives of many who were involved. By engaging employees in a highly structured yet empowering process, it offered senior management unique insights into the participants' capabilities and values in ways that could not be revealed through day-to-day work. The young woman on the ORE team who had been a customer representative in the call center, for example, discovered a passion and great skill for working on organizational issues. Following FRD, she rotated through a position in which she helped Shell New Zealand win an award as the most family-friendly company in the country.

Learning From the Royal/Dutch Shell Experience

The results seen in Shell New Zealand are by no means unique. Gary Steel recalls an FRD project in Brazil that yielded five million dollars in 90 days and generated more than 80 million dollars in savings over five years. When the Brazilian management team asked why they had never identified the project before, Steel said "they responded that they had never been asked." Another program in Oman identified nearly two billion dollars in untapped reserves. Steel noted that at the end of the process the managing director said it was the most liberating experience he had ever had. "He learned three things. First, he didn't need to have all of the answers. Second, the best answers are within the organization. And third, if you build a plan with the involvement of 1,500 people, the organization will deliver." Stories like these abound within Royal Dutch/Shell.

The Royal Dutch/Shell experience demonstrates a few critical principles.

1. An aligned Teachable Point of View that is delivered with passion by senior leaders can motivate and engage an organization.
2. Leaders must personally teach and role model the new ways of thinking and behaving that they attempt to instill in their organizations.
3. Leaders need a structured process and support network to drive changes on a large scale.
4. Focus on developing the teaching and leadership capability at all organizational levels enables rapid, broad people development and organizational change.
5. When change occurs in the context of a common Teachable Point of View, change within pockets of the organization is more easily aligned with the overall organization's direction.
6. Those who are most capable of driving organizational change and identifying solutions to problems are those who work in key operating positions.

Implications and Conclusions

It is important to note that the Shell New Zealand story did not involve a single OD practitioner except the facilitator from Gary Steel's organization who ran the initial FRD session in Australia for 15 people. The rest of the change process was replicated and driven by the teaching of leaders throughout the organization. In fact, the entire Royal Dutch/Shell story has virtually no traditional OD influence. OD practices were embedded into the mainstream, just as they were at GE, and applying these practices were what all good leaders in the company had to do to succeed.

While this was undoubtedly a sobering lesson for the existing OD staff members within Royal Dutch/Shell, it effectively highlights the challenges facing OD practitioners today. The simple lesson is that OD is part of a skill set that all effective organizational leaders must possess and that they must be able to teach to others. This means that the role of OD practitioners essentially becomes one of skill transfer, coaching, and process design. In short, it is teaching leaders to be teachers.

Building teaching capability into an organization's leadership repertoire is no easy task. First, it requires a fundamental role reframing for leaders who rely on hierarchy and power relationships to influence others. Teaching requires a sincere openness to learning that is contradicted by the stifling air of the bureaucrat or power-monger. Second, some leaders appreciate the need for teaching but fail to make time to develop and align their TPOV with other organizational leaders. A multitude of teachers with different or conflicting messages can quickly create organizational confusion and lack of confidence in leadership. Third, the ability to scale the development of leaders as teachers is sorely missing in most organizations' leadership development processes. An organization simply cannot reach its potential if this capability is resident only in pockets of a business or contained to hierarchical echelons. Finally, leaders require the capability to drive large-scale processes that simultaneously implement and role model effective teaching while creating meaningful bottom-line results.

As Noel predicted in 1978, OD has been absorbed into other practices. Within scholarly work on the subject, OD theory and methodology has been folded into the fields of human resources, organizational behavior, operations management, and strategy. In a telephone poll of the admissions offices at the top 10 U.S. business schools (according to the most recent *BusinessWeek* survey), only two knew what we meant by the term and fewer than half offered courses. This is a simple reflection of how far removed OD has become from being a separate discipline.

The good news is that within world-class organizations, as GE and Royal Dutch/Shell have shown, OD has finally earned the respect it deserves and is increasingly practiced in the mainstream by organizational leaders. However, the challenge for any remaining traditional OD practitioners is that, faced with the absorption of OD into the daily role of operating leaders, they must learn new skills and ways of working with senior leaders or go the way of those who practiced at Digital Equipment Company and become extinct. Today, however, OD is by no means dead. Warner Burke captures the current state of the applied behavioral sciences in his book, *Organizational Change is Not a Linear Process*.[10] The theories and concepts in this book represent what all leaders in this millennium must master in order to be world class. The most interesting advances in OD in the future, we believe, will come from practitioners who are teaching leaders in their organizations to teach others.

PART 3
21C PEOPLE

What will be the corporate boardroom in the 21st century? Three professors from the Center for Effective Organizations in the Marshall School of Business at the University of Southern California—Jay A. Conger, Edward E. Lawler III, and David Finegold—open this part of the book and have outlined how boards and their governance practices must change if they are to truly play a greater leadership role in the future. There are five important changes that Conger, Lawler, and Finegold think need to be made to transform boards into effective governance structures: (a) the board must ensure their own independence from management; (b) they must hold themselves accountable for the performance of their boardrooms through rigorous annual evaluations; (c) they must more effectively build their knowledge capabilities especially in the areas of strategy, implementation, and globalization; (d) they must more successfully harness the power of information technology to ensure ready access to critical information; and (e) they must move their mandate from serving solely shareholders to serving a broader set of constituents.

In the 21st century, organizations will require people who are versatile and comfortable with themselves. They will have to be comfortable with exercising their tough and tender sides, with making tough decisions alone and with sharing power, with influencing and being open to influence, with passionately driving decisions and also being willing to admit that others may have better ideas or contributions that can shape the decisions, and with taking initiative in all directions. Distinguished professor of Babson College Allan R. Cohen and Stanford Business School professor David L. Bradford strongly believe that power and influence in the 21st century organization will be sophisticated and versatile. They've observed that too often managers are good at one or the other approach to getting things done, but that genuine lasting effectiveness requires both ways of functioning.

Framing has powerful consequences when it involves cleaving the world into *us* and *them*, an "in" group and one or more "out" groups; when others are included as part of *us*, their plight and delight are both felt almost as if they were our own, prompting effort on their behalf. When others are psychologically exiled to *them*, however, there is very little in the way of empathy, caring, or helping. Columbia University professor Harvey A. Hornstein's exciting findings are the scientific foundation for what has been labeled the *psychological golden rule of organizations*. His evidence invariably shows that when employees identify with their employing organization, experiencing it as *us* or *we*, rather than *them*, their work behavior is nudged by the golden rule's powerful psychological prescription: *Harming you becomes difficult for me because the two of us are part of we.*

People can develop emotional intelligence. Richard E. Boyatzis, chairman of the Department of Organizational Behavior at the Weatherhead School of Management at Case Western Reserve University, along with his doctoral student, Scott N. Taylor, confirmed this finding by their research with professionals and graduate students: Adults can develop the abilities that are vital to outstanding performance in management, leadership, and many other occupations and professions. As leaders and managers, we can only create environments in which others want to use their capabilities and emotional intelligence if we ourselves are authentic and consistent in our own demonstration of these behaviors. Through the self-directed learning process, we have the opportunity to truly make a difference by developing emotional intelligence in ourselves. And then, by extension, to help others develop them. Their research indicates that we can access and engage deep emotional commitment and psychic energy if we engage our passions and conceptually catch our dreams in our ideal self-image.

Why is the art of managing people such a challenge for us when we seem so much more advanced in our understanding of people than we were only a few generations ago? What makes people continue to be so parochial and tribal when business is becoming more global and networked? Renowned London Business School professor Nigel Nicholson finds that many features of human existence remain unaltered, and it is these that make us subject to the shortcomings. Human nature is what stays the same. He convincingly argues that if we persist in trying to squeeze the human foot into the badly designed organizational shoe, we'll continue to hobble, stumble, and complain our way into the future. So how can we shape the shoe to fit the foot? What strategies can we enact to accommodate what we know about the human animal? In the concluding chapter of Part 3, Nicholson finds those answers for us so that we can do better to design the shoe to fit the human foot.

11

The Boardroom of the Future

Jay A. Conger
Edward E. Lawler III
David Finegold

As we move into the 21st century, powerful forces are redefining the roles and activities of corporate boards. Chief among them are institutional investors who believe that a strong board can contribute to improved shareholder returns. No longer content to accept passive boards that tolerate mediocre corporate performance, major investors are demonstrating a heightened level of shareholder activism. They are demanding that boards assume a far greater leadership and oversight role than ever before.

A second force is the news media. More and more articles are appearing that closely examine boardroom performance—pushing directors into a very public spotlight. For example, periodicals including *BusinessWeek*, *The Financial Times*, and the *Wall Street Journal* now feature lists of the best and worst boards and in-depth coverage of decisions taken by boards. In part, this attention has been generated by the fact that boards themselves are generating more news. Their role in mergers and acquisitions, in determining often oversized executive and board pay packages, and in the firing and hiring of high-profile CEOs, has led the media to focus greater attention on the actions of directors. Boardrooms have also been the focus of numerous articles and investigations because of their actions and inactions in a number of high-profile corporate failures, most notably Sunbeam and Enron.

Watchdog groups dedicated to corporate governance are a third force. They now not only publicly target boards for poor governance but also publish best practice governance guidelines for boardrooms. These guides have set standards that many boards feel compelled to adopt.

In response to these forces, corporate boards in the United States began to experiment with some important new governance initiatives in the 1990s. A number of these initiatives have today become widespread practices among the largest U.S. companies. For example, many boards are now composed primarily of outside directors and have a profile that is more representative of society as a whole, they operate according to written guidelines, they meet regularly in executive sessions without inside directors, and they conduct formal appraisals of the CEO. Several of these practices have indeed improved boardroom effectiveness. We believe, however, that more important changes are needed in the way boards operate. Specifically, there are five important changes that we believe need to be made to transform boards into effective governance structures. An examination of each follows.

Shifting Leadership in the Boardroom: Truly Powerful Boards

Power plays a vital role in the overall effectiveness of a board, as it does in any working group. But boards face unique tensions in the kind of power they require and in how power is best distributed within the group. Many of today's new governance practices are aimed specifically at ensuring a greater balance of power between the CEO and the directors. In practice, however, this should be a balance that shifts depending on the issue that is being considered.

By design, a board's oversight role implies that it should have a strong role. Reality, however, often gets in the way. In the vast majority of American boards, our research and that of others suggests that power still remains largely vested in the CEO, in part because this individual is almost always the board chair. Some boards, however, are experimenting with non-executive chairpersons, lead directors, and outside board chairs as a counterbalance to the CEO's power. In addition, important increases have begun to occur in the power of boardroom committees. We believe these and other changes will lead to boards where more and more power is in the hands of the board members rather than being concentrated in the hands of CEOs.

As boards become more proactive and powerful, they must deal with a basic conflict between the two main roles board directors are being asked to play: Can they be a strategic partner with top management in formulating strategy and building the capabilities of the organization and still exercise independent oversight of management? In other words, can directors play a greater leadership role in addition to their current advisory role?

We believe the best way for a board to succeed simultaneously on its multiple, sometimes conflicting missions is to put in place structures and practices that provide the basis for a strong and independent board. A platform of independence is required for boards to exercise effective oversight and partnering. The following are characteristics that create truly independent boards.

1. Independent directors (with no formal business or family ties to the firm prior to joining the board) constitute a clear majority (at least two-thirds) of all board members.

2. Regular assessments of the knowledge and abilities of directors against the firm's changing market and technological demands to ensure that they have the skills necessary to effectively oversee the firm's actions and provide leadership.

3. Independent directors chair and control of all key committees—compensation, audit, and nominating/corporate governance. The compensation committee consists solely of outside directors.

4. The board has clearly established independent leadership—by separating the chairman and CEO roles, appointing a lead director, and/or having regular executive sessions where no inside directors are present.

5. Regular channels of information to the board that are independent of management are in place (e.g., direct communication links with employees, customers, suppliers, and investors).

6. The board has staff and/or resources so that it can conduct its own analysis of issues where it feels the need (e.g., in benchmarking executive compensation).

7. A regular executive succession planning process is conducted that reaches down several levels.

These practices can ensure the independence of the board from management and instill far greater leadership capability on the part of directors.

In this century, we are most likely to see the greatest emergence of board leadership in the committees. CEOs rarely have the time to be active members of all of a board's committees. As a byproduct, this is one of the board activities where CEOs play more of a consultative or advisory role rather than a leadership role. Often, they allow the committees to be led by independent board members. Reinforcing this is the fact that the board governance movement has discouraged their playing a more directive role in key committees (e.g., audit and compensation) and has placed a strong emphasis on outside directors assuming key leadership roles in board committees.

There are a number of steps that board members must undertake to ensure that they have strong leadership positions on committees. For example, for outsiders to take advantage of their majority position on committees, they need to develop action plans and positions of their own rather than be guided by those of the CEO. Since they may have few opportunities to get together independently of their board activities, it is important that their board activities provide them with such opportunities. Meetings held without company executives where directors can discuss sensitive issues concerning executive succession and corporate performance need to become a boardroom norm. These may also be the only opportunity a committee has to develop strong positions that are contrary to the stated preferences of senior management.

It is critical that committees have the ability to meet when they feel events call for it. They must be able to call meetings on short notice when they believe that a crisis or rapidly developing critical issue calls for it. It is also important that committees have a vehicle for placing issues that they identify on the board's agenda without significant advance notice. Board committees must be in a position to seek outside specialists who can make objective assessments about the company's operations, and they must be able to do this without management's prior permission.

One clear way that boards can exert leadership and gain power is through an annual review of the CEO's performance. An effective evaluation process is essentially an act of leadership on the board's part. CEO evaluations must include goals for the annual performance of the CEO as well as the systematic evaluation of whether current goals have been successfully accomplished. Goals need to take a balanced scorecard approach and include both personal development goals for the CEO as well as the organizational performance targets that the board deems as critical for the year. The results of this annual review should be tied to determining the CEO's total compensation level. The compensation committee should manage the evaluation process itself.

In conclusion, strong committee leadership is where the greatest progress can be made in terms of corporate governance practices that balance out the CEO's leadership and authority. It is important to recognize, however, the limits on the amount of leadership and power that committees can exercise. Committee leadership is splintered across a number of individuals. No single director has overall responsibility for the board and ensuring that its range of activities is both well coordinated and meets high standards of corporate governance. Given their more narrow focus, committees can at best only shape portions of the overall agenda. Under a system reliant upon committee leadership, there may be no central ombudsman to give the full board a collective voice.

The power limitations that are inherent in board committees suggest that committee leadership is only a partial solution to building truly effective board leadership. For this reason, even with strong committees it is important to separate the roles of board chairman and CEO. Ideally the board chair should be a nonexecutive director who is both highly respected and comfortable in challenging the standing CEO at critical junctures. The alternative is to appoint a lead director who can challenge the CEO.

Accountability for Performance: Formally Evaluating the Board and Its Directors

It is common practice for boards to evaluate their CEO (over 70% do it), but it is not common practice for boards to evaluate themselves and their members. This is simply no longer acceptable. It undermines the credibility of boards, not to mention ignoring what is known about creating effective groups and individual performance.

One solution is to utilize a formal, rigorous self-evaluation of the board. This can result in significant improvements, particularly when directors find they have common concerns that no one has raised publicly. But this approach can itself create problems given the desire of the board members to look and feel effective. A better alternative is to work with outsiders who conduct interviews with directors or carry out 360-degree feedback that involves vendors, customers, and investors. From this form of evaluation, boards can get more objective and in turn more valuable information about their own performance and the company's performance.

There is a growing consensus among board members that boards need to have regular evaluations. For example, a recent study by the National Association of Corporate Directors found that 91% of board members favor regular board evaluations. What should these evaluations cover? Clearly a balanced scorecard approach is called for. This means focusing on a wide range of factors including group process and decision making. Group process is an area that is often overlooked in board evaluations, to the detriment of an effective evaluation. Often large improvements can be made in board performance simply by paying attention to group process and meeting behaviors. In our research we found that simple changes in things such as meeting schedules can improve effectiveness. Evaluations can turn up issues having to do with how time is spent and dysfunctional personal relationships that get in the way of good decision making.

From the standpoint of individual board members, feedback about their performance can help them enhance their skills as directors and motivate them to be more effective board members. Evaluations can also provide an ongoing discipline for directors to reflect on and assess their performance.

In the absence of a formal review, all too often members are informally evaluated in a "hit or miss" fashion that provides neither good feedback nor valid data. Individual evaluations of directors need to be conducted on an annual basis and examine multiple dimensions of a board members' performance. In most cases, they should assess director contributions to group process, their technical knowledge, and their overall performance. Specific dimensions that should be measured would include knowledge of the business, personal initiative, adequate preparation, knowledge of senior management, commitment to attend meetings, candor, reasonable judgment, and integrity. Each director also brings a distinctive set of competencies to the boardroom. Therefore it is important that any assessment recognize the unique contributions of that individual. Finally, our research suggests that a board member's willingness to confront the CEO is very important, so the demonstration of this behavior should receive particular attention in any evaluation.

Today, individual board member appraisals are quite rare. However, a convincing case for change exists. In our research on boardroom appraisals, we have found that feedback on performance to individual board directors can help them to evaluate their own skills as directors and motivate them to be more effective contributors. Evaluations also provide a means for directors to assess their performance over time as the needs of a board shift. They can provide a basis for determining whether a director should be reappointed. They also demonstrate to investors that the board is holding *individual* directors accountable for their performance.

With the average size of boards decreasing and the demands and rewards for serving on boards increasing, companies need greater contributions from their directors. They have the right to ask for more from directors than simply attending and posing questions at regular meetings. Individual assessment is a good way of making performance expectations clear and improving director performance. Support for this view is provided by recent Korn/Ferry surveys of Fortune 1,000 board members which show that in companies where individual directors are evaluated, directors rate the board's overall effectiveness more positively.

Individual director evaluations are highly complementary to an evaluation of the board's performance. Certain key group effectiveness issues simply cannot be addressed without evaluating individuals; of these, membership is often the most important. Board members are typically replaced for performance reasons only in extreme circumstances (e.g., criminal misconduct, conflict of interest, active disruption, very poor attendance/participation record) or because they have reached a term or age limit. If directors are replaced for performance reasons, they are rarely given an early warning and a chance to improve. In most cases, boards wait for poorly performing directors to retire or fail to re-nominate them when they reach a term or age limit. While it appears from our research that underperforming directors are relatively rare, it is still a sound practice to identify such individuals through a formal assessment process so that timely corrective action can be initiated.

Finally, new directors often appreciate feedback on their contributions to a board. Board members are like other human beings. Although there is usually some anxiety associated with getting feedback, they realize it can be helpful and something they should receive. Rather than allowing feedback to take place in a happenstance manner, a formal appraisal process ensures more thoughtful and comprehensive feedback to new directors. In addition, appraisals can serve as one means of "on-boarding" new members.

Critical Knowledge for the Board: Strategy and Globalization

In our research on corporate boards, we discovered that directors are often asked to play an important role in a firm's overarching strategy. In addition, they are responsible for tracking the progress of implementing strategic initiatives. Given the fact that most directors are not directly involved in day-to-day management and are likely to be from outside the company's industry, it can be difficult for directors to possess sufficient relevant knowledge to be effective advisors with respect to strategy. Given the complexity of today's businesses and the rapid pace of change, it is critical that boards be structured and managed so that they will be able to effectively play a role in shaping their corporations' strategy. The following practices need to be adopted to accomplish this objective.

- Staff the board with directors who have a diverse, complementary set of expertise in many areas. This requires some directors who have in-depth expertise in the firm's sector(s) and key technologies and others who bring independent perspectives from outside the industry but possess knowledge of relevant organizational process (e.g., organizational change).
- Provide regular developmental experiences to increase directors' understanding of the firm's business, such as site visits, interviews with customers and suppliers, and exposure to market studies.
- Link directors directly into the firm's information systems, with a customized portal to provide the key metrics they wish to track.

- Minimize the time spent in meetings on discussion of operating and financial information that can be reviewed in advance. Focus discussions on real strategic issues.
- Conduct a special retreat each year devoted to a longer term strategy. Hold regular reviews of how the strategy is being implemented, and of the managers who are executing it and their progress, setbacks, and successes.

Our research on boardrooms suggests that certain knowledge required for effective strategy development and implementation is under-represented on boards. Foremost is an understanding of organizational design and transformational change. Key issues include assessing the organizational fit of key mergers and acquisitions, creating an internal context that is a fertile ground for new ventures and strategic innovation, and redesigning key processes or outsourcing others so that they can be delivered via the Web. Having other firms' chief executives serve as outside directors provides some of this knowledge, but these individuals are unlikely to have all of the expertise required to handle the broad array of change issues that boards routinely face.

The challenges facing firms in the rapidly evolving marketplace of the 21st century suggest boards need to add to their global perspective. While U.S. boards have become significantly more diverse in the last 25 years, only 13% of all the boards of Fortune 1,000 companies in 1998 had even a single director born outside the United States. One of the greatest obstacles to increasing the foreign membership on boards has been the travel requirement for directors to attend frequent meetings. The Internet and other advances in communication technology today make it easier for boards to enhance their global capabilities. While not a complete replacement for face-to-face meetings, videoconferences are of sufficient caliber to replace some in-person, full-board, and committee meetings, thus making it easier for firms to recruit directors from around the world.

Finally, to ensure that knowledge on the board is fresh and closely aligned with the firm's changing strategic needs, it is likely to be necessary to change the membership of boards more frequently than has been common among most firms. Cisco Systems, for example, has adopted a policy of regularly replacing one or two directors on its 10-member board.

Harnessing the Power of Information Technology: Information-Age Boardrooms

Most boards outside the information technology sector do not need to add individuals with in-depth knowledge of the technical workings of information technology or the Internet. Nor do they need to replace all of their senior directors with members of Generations X and Y. But they do need to ensure that several of their members have a clear understanding of how information technology and the Internet are changing the dynamics of their industry and the array of strategic options open to their firm.

Technology expertise can come from a director who is a CEO or senior manager at an information technology or Internet-enabled firm. These individuals can bring the rest of the board members up to speed on the latest developments and updates. Boards can also be kept updated through presentations from external experts, senior managers, visits to firms with leading-edge practices, and by ideally encouraging each member to spend time on information technology and Internet strategy as a routine part of their board responsibilities.

Just as boards can take advantage of the Internet's ability to improve communications among its members, they can also become more effective by tapping into the wealth of information contained on a firm's intranet and the Web. Motorola, for example, is enabling all its directors to access electronic courses through Motorola University, an inexpensive means of increasing their knowledge about the firm and its markets. However, because of the wide array of potentially relevant topics for the board and the limited time of its members, there is a very real danger of the Internet leading to information overload. Thus, it is vital that some means be put in place so that the intranet and Internet are deployed to distill the key data that directors require for financial and strategic oversight, without overwhelming them with the immense amounts of operational information that a corporation generates. Among the key kinds of information that boards need to gather and distribute electronically to its members are the following.

1. *Key performance indicators:* A growing number of firms use a balanced scorecard approach to monitor not just the short-term financial performance of the organization but also the extent to which the firm is building longer term capabilities and meeting the needs of key stakeholders (customers, suppliers, and employees). Rather than just gather these indicators in reports for each board meeting, organizations need to create an electronic dashboard that the directors and executives can consult on an ongoing basis.

2. *Internal communication:* Many boards have already attempted to improve their legal oversight and compliance function by establishing a toll-free number that concerned employees can use to raise any issue. The use of it will be supplemented in the future by creating a widely publicized e-mail

> address or Web site link where employees can send sugges-
> tions or voice concerns to an outside board member that they
> may be reluctant to share with management. For such a sys-
> tem to work, of course, employees must be assured that all
> such e-mail will be treated as strictly confidential. Thus, the
> board may want to contract with a trusted outside organization
> to act as an initial clearinghouse for such communications.

Employees are likely to be far more willing to share their thoughts with the board's directors if the board first takes advantage of the Internet's potential to build a two-way conversation with employees. Currently, most directors are invisible to employees. Company intranets, however, provide a low-cost and rapid way to share appropriate information—such as long-term strategy, celebration of key successes, rationales for major acquisitions or divestitures—with a firm's entire employee base. Some firms are already making good use of this capability, although more frequently it is the top managers rather than board directors who have taken the lead.

Broadening the Board's Mandate: From Shareholders to Stakeholders

Most of the major corporate governance initiatives in the 1990s had a singular aim: to create boards that were more responsive to *shareholders.* As a result, boards increasingly focused on shareholder value and shareholders prospered. But this perspective is too narrow for the 21st century. The decisions and actions of a board must be judged on criteria that go beyond financial performance to include their impact on employees, suppliers, customers, and communities. These stakeholders, after all, are investors of one kind or another in the success of a company.

The adoption of a stakeholder perspective is consistent with important trends that are unfolding in the global business environment, especially those concerned with knowledge workers and supplier relationships. If, as is often true, knowledge workers are a firm's primary capital, then companies and their boards need to have direct access to their thinking to be certain that they are getting a fair return on their human capital investments. In a networked world, the same view applies to suppliers and customers. If they are, indeed, an increasingly important determinant of a company's success, then putting their expertise on the board and attending to the returns they get on their investments in customer and supplier relationships ought to be a priority of boards.

In cases where companies are heavily regulated or subject to special interest group scrutiny, boards should consider adding directors from the government or interest groups. A good example of this is a decision made by the board at the petroleum company ARCO to put a leader of the Sierra Club, a prominent conservation organization, on their corporate board. Because of the company's oil exploration activities in Alaska, ARCO constantly found itself at odds with environmentalists. Adding a member of an environmental action group gave them an entirely different perspective on the board as to which issues were of greatest concern to environmentalists and how they could manage their operations in a way that would be less objectionable to environmental groups.

We believe the risks of pursuing today's shareholder-only vision for the board are twofold. First, for the companies themselves, there appears to be a growing tension between the increased role that employees, and in particular knowledge workers, are playing in the overall creation of a firm's value and an exclusive focus on the interests of shareholders. Unlike the traditional laborers of the past, an employee's stake in the company and its future may be extremely high today. As Margaret Blair has pointed out,

> In firms where highly specialized skills are important...employees may be as highly motivated as shareholders to see that the firm's resources are used efficiently. Moreover, employees of such enterprises exercise de facto control over many important decisions and, because of their inside knowledge of the business and their stake in its success, may be much better situated than distant and anonymous shareholders to act as monitors of management.[1]

Given the blurring of the traditional distinction between employees and owners, it makes less and less sense to focus on shareholders and owners as the only important stakeholders in a firm. In a growing percentage of large companies' workplaces, as well as high-tech start-ups, employees are typically given a high degree of control over their work, the financial and strategic information needed to make good business decisions, as well as rewards that entitle them to a share of the organization's success. Even residual control rights, the ability to deploy or sell a firm's assets after paying off firm's creditors, which have historically distinguished investors' privileges from those of managers and employees, are inevitably a shared right in knowledge-intensive organizations. While investors retain the right to sell off a firm's nonhuman assets, these are often worth only a small fraction of a knowledge-based firm's collective capabilities. By failing to recognize the important control that employees have, firms risk alienating their most valuable and mobile assets.

The second risk of pursuing a shareholder-only vision is to the wider society and, ultimately, to individual firms as well. The combined forces of global capital markets, the Internet, and free-trade agreements are shifting the balance of power from national governments to transnational corporations. The efficiencies and increased competition in these global markets have helped generate economic growth. But, if the firms that operate within these markets are held accountable by only one relatively small segment of society (the owners of capital), there is a danger that their actions may lead to greater inequality and failure to maximize the welfare and well-being of the population as a whole. The concern, as symbolized by the protests at the World Trade Organization (WTO) talks in Seattle in November 1999, is that global firms, responding to the constant pressure to maximize profits and the returns to global investors, will pursue strategies that sacrifice the environment, hold down wages, and call for low labor standards.

The ability of countries to regulate these firms, even if that is the desire of the majority of the electorate, is constrained by a collective action problem in the world marketplace. If one country pursues a governance regime that is less friendly to shareholders than that of other countries, then they risk losing the ability to attract the very investment from world capital markets needed to sustain employment and a growth in living standards. Conversely, governments that establish corporate governance regulations that are very favorable to managers or shareholders (or both) are likely to act as magnets for corporate headquarters. This has long been the case in Delaware in the United States, as it has been for The Netherlands in Europe. With governance laws that feature low corporate taxes and high tolerance for poison pills and other hostile takeover defenses, The Netherlands has attracted 57% of all multinational corporate headquarters in Europe.

One potential way to solve the problem of country-by-country regulation of corporations is to create a global code for the governance of corporations, one capable of regulating firms wherever they are headquartered. In place of the current de facto migration to the U.S. governance model, such a code could combine the best features of the shareholder and stakeholder perspectives. For example, it might feature the American emphasis on open, annually, and independently audited financial information, as well as the use of formal evaluations of management by independent directors to provide clear oversight of shareholders' interest. At the same time, it could include features from the European stakeholder model to recognize the investment in firm-specific human capital that employees have made and their accompanying ownership rights. These features might include an entitlement to employee voice in certain strategic decisions (sale of the firm, major relocation, or site closures), the protection of employee retirement and other benefits, and the right of fair compensation if an employee loses his or her job.

With respect to corporate governance, the 20th century was the American century. Although the victory is not nearly as clear-cut as on the battlefield, American-style capitalism and the shareholder model of governance appear to have triumphed over the stakeholder model of governance most closely associated with Japan and Europe. In the boardrooms of large U.S. corporations, two decades of governance reforms firmly entrenched the concept of "shareholder value," increased the independence of the board and management, and more closely aligned the interests of the board and the owners of the corporation.

We believe it is important, at this moment of "triumph" for the shareholder model of capitalism, to return to a question first posed by Karl Marx, the economic theorist most associated with the failed alternatives to a market economy: Does capitalism contain the seeds of its own destruction? Or, put more specifically in the language of corporate governance debates: Does focusing boards of directors on maximizing the returns to one group (shareholders) over the interests of other stakeholders in the corporation ultimately undermine the legitimacy of corporations' role in society?

We believe that the risk of corporations losing their legitimacy is real, and that the most effective way that corporations can retain their legitimacy is to balance the consideration to the interests of all of a corporation's important stakeholders. If corporations do not do this on a voluntary basis then it is likely that government regulations will increasingly insist that it happen. At this point in history we do not profess to know what form of regulation will appear or how it will be constituted and implemented. We are convinced, however, that to avoid mandated change corporations must voluntarily move toward a corporate governance model that gives greater attention to multiple stakeholders.

Concluding Thoughts

In the 21st century, boards will be held more accountable for their actions and for the performance outcomes of the companies they oversee. This will pose both dilemmas and opportunities for boards. Without adequate governance practices that both empower and assess overall performance, boardrooms are far more likely to fall prey to the dilemma side of the equation. In other words, they are likely to remain largely passive players in the governance process—best equipped to handle a few tasks such as succession planning and coaching. Their capacity to proactively address major crises will be akin to firemen who arrive at the scene long after the fire has started. In this chapter, we have outlined how boards and their governance practices must change if they are to truly play a greater leadership role in the future—in other words, if they are to successfully overcome the dilemmas they face. They must accomplish five outcomes: They must ensure their own independence from management. They must hold themselves accountable for the performance of their boardrooms through rigorous annual evaluations. They must build their knowledge capabilities more effectively, especially in the areas of strategy, implementation, and globalization. They must harness the power of information technology more successfully to ensure ready access to critical information. They must move their mandate from serving solely shareholders to serving a broader set of constituents. If boards are able to accomplish these five outcomes, we believe they will realize the role that society expects from them—real leadership.

12

Power and Influence

Allan R. Cohen
David L. Bradford

ittle could be more fitting in a book honoring Richard Beckhard than an attempt to come to grips with power and influence in organizational life. He was a master on this subject, though one had to watch closely to see just how clever he was. He could smell who possessed power in situations, instinctively knew how to figure out what it would take to gain their trust or, if necessary, nudge them aside. He could sense where the levers of power were and how to gain control of them, and was totally unambivalent about exercising power in the service of desirable ends.

The problem with this territory during the past century has been the difficulty many have had in gaining comfort with both the tough-minded, directive exercise of power and the more interpersonally engaging, collaborative practice of it. There have been skilled practitioners of directive organizational power who effectively moved organizations by demanding key changes at just the right time. But others have used bullying to move people and organizations, as exemplified by "Chainsaw" Al Dunlap, a turn-around specialist who delighted in firing executives, laying off hoards of employees, threatening salespeople, and using fear to drive earnings upward long enough to cash in and move on. As of this writing he has been accused by the securities and exchange commission of securities fraud for his actions at Sunbeam, where his reign fell apart—as often happens to those who operate exclusively from coercion. Although before that he had been successful at a number of companies, recently it has come to light that he got into trouble early in his career for questionable practices, but later hid those experiences by omitting them from his bio.[1] People like him have given directive power a bad name. But since power in organizations is the capacity to influence to get things done—requiring access to resources, information, and relationships[2]—it is inherently, absolutely necessary for leaders and managers to be powerful. The challenge is to exercise it directively when appropriate and collaboratively when it is needed—but in either case to exercise it to get work done.

Forceful and directive use of power is necessary when organizational members do not or cannot understand the need for, or pathways to, new directions, or do not have the relevant expertise to contribute to a decision. Exerting power this way, however, makes less sense when no one person has the answer, expertise is dispersed, and the cooperation of the influenced is needed. In those circumstances, a more collaborative exercise of power is required, in which all parties gain expanded influence rather than just the formal boss.

The "discovery" in the 1930s that how people are treated might make a difference in how they respond,[3] and that understanding and connecting with organizational members could gain their cooperation, spawned among academics, consultants, and then among leaders, a bevy of practices and movements encouraging some variation of being considerate. These included counseling (now coaching), participation, sensitivity training then team building, empowerment, and so on. These forms of power sharing were often effective, but sometimes overdone by those who do not like the directive exercise of power and confuse it with dominance or bullying.

We have observed that too often managers are good at one or the other approach to getting things done, but that genuine lasting effectiveness requires both ways of functioning. Effective leaders must be comfortable with listening *and* caring, with working from positive reciprocity as well as hard-nosed calculation, pushing, and assertion. Both directive and collaborative behavior are a requisite part of a manager's repertoire; overuse, underuse, or poor use of either can lead to dead ends, massive resistance, dissipation of effort, unproductive anger, and retaliation.[4] (This will be discussed more fully later and is summarized in Table 12–1.)

In addition, another useful distinction when examining the use of power is between power that directly changes individual behavior and power that alters structural elements that eventually change behavior. Each can be potent if used at the right time, but a waste of energy if not. The challenge is to become comfortable and skilled in the exercise of the full range of possibilities for moving people and organizations, and developing a sense of when to do what.

This challenge is not new; we want to address the question of whether the conditions for exercising power will be different in the 21st century, and how. That should be useful to managers trying to figure out how to be most effective in the future.

Table 12–1   Use and Abuse of Directive and Collaborative
Leadership

Too Directive	Directive	Collaborative	Too Collaborative
Takes over, doesn't give people enough rope.	Leads personally. Is personally involved in solving his or her unit's problems.	Enables subordinates to lead. Is able to let go and give individuals the same latitude to do their jobs.	Empowers to a fault. Gives people too much rope.
Other people don't speak out, aren't heard.	Lets people know clearly and with feeling where he or she stands on issues. Declares himself or herself.	Is interested in where other people stand on issues. Is receptive to their ideas.	People don't know where he or she stands.
Is insensitive, callous.	Makes difficult calls—including those with adverse effects on people.	Is compassionate. Is responsive to people's needs and feelings.	Is overly accommodating. Is nice to people at expense of work.
Is harshly judgmental. Dismisses the contributions of others. Is an unloving critic.	Makes judgments. Zeros in on what is substandard or is not working—in an individual's or unit's performance.	Shows appreciation. Makes other people feel good about their contributions. Helps people feel valued.	Gives false praise or praises indiscriminately. Is an uncritical fan.
Is parochial, a partisan, creates rivalries.	Is competitive. Is highly motivated to excel and have his or her unit excel.	Is a team player. Helps other units or the larger organization perform well.	Sacrifices sharp focus on own unit. Doesn't argue for legitimate interests.

Table 12-1   Use and Abuse of Directive and Collaborative
Leadership (continued)

Too Directive	Directive	Collaborative	Too Collaborative
Pushes too hard. Demands the impossible. Risks burnout.	Has an intense can-do attitude. Expects everyone to do whatever it takes to get the job done.	Is realistic about limits on people's capacity to perform or produce.	Is too understanding. Doesn't expect enough.
Is arrogant. Fails to recognize or acknowledge others' talents.	Is confident. Gives people the feeling that he or she believes in self and his or her abilities.	Is modest. Is aware that he or she does not know everything and can be wrong.	Is self-effacing or down on self. Is too quick to discount own views.
Sticks rigidly to a course of action, even in the face of strong evidence it's not working.	Is persistent. Stays the course—even in the face of adversity.	Is flexible. Is willing to change course if the plan doesn't seem to be working.	Is inconstant, changeable. Is too quick to change course.
Forces issues when finesse would work better.	Raises tough issues. Insists on working through to conclusion.	Fosters harmony, contains conflict, defuses tension.	Avoids or smoothes over tense issues that need attention.

°Adapted from Robert Kaplan, "The Dimensions of Forceful and Enabling
Leadership: Virtues and Vices," *Leadership in Action*, Vol. 19, No. 4 (1999).

Jack Welch: Master of Power

To begin the process of predicting what will change in the organizational
use of power and influence in the next century, let us look at a leader who
was named manager of the 20th century,[5] someone who was able not only
to get great results from a giant company, but be articulate about leadership and leave a (mostly) visible track record from which we can learn. Jack
Welch transformed General Electric, already considered a well-run company when he took over in 1981 but a rather sluggish agglomeration of hundreds of businesses, growing very slowly. His predecessor, Reginald Jones,
was a respected captain of industry, playing often on the national stage of

business leaders. Welch had been a dark horse candidate, only one of several well-groomed GE executives, not from a prominent business or professional family, and with a degree from the University of Massachusetts—distinctly not the Ivy League or Big Ten. He was relatively young, and had a reputation for being somewhat of a hothead who violated corporate hierarchy when he felt strongly about matters, which he often did.

Despite having a strong Massachusetts accent and a slight stutter, Welch was a compelling speaker, with intensity and conviction. Even when he was just a rookie CEO, he was already very sure of himself and charismatic.[6] Over the years, as his business success and reputation grew, he became more articulate, more visible, and even more charismatic, with an intensity that intimidated some and generated admiration in many others. His presence is so compelling that it would be easy to attribute his success to personal effectiveness, magnetism, and personal power. He has those in no small measure, but viewing his 20 years as CEO in retrospect, it is evident that he was also a master of identifying, capturing, and utilizing the organizational levers of power. These levers are not so readily grasped, and are often left out of treatises on power in organizations. But we can identify no one leading a very large company who combined personal style and structural command as successfully.

Within months of taking over, Welch decided that GE was too diverse, too unfocused, and too unable to grow rapidly as constituted. He declared that henceforth GE would buy and sell companies until it could be number one or two in every business it was in. That strategy became well known as he went into action, eliminating dozens of units, removing some 200,000 employees and adding back about 100,000, reducing the total number from 400,000 to 300,000. This earned him the nickname of "Neutron Jack," a person who took out the population while leaving the buildings standing. During this time some saw him as a hard-hearted destroyer, or assumed that all he cared about were profits. What has seldom been noted is that by reducing net payroll somewhere in the range of $3 billion, he took a company that was likely to have barely broken even and made it comparatively profitable, which provided the resources to grow and develop.

Another benefit from this imposition of discipline and will was that he earned considerable credibility with Wall Street and GE directors, a support base that would make it possible for him to introduce many radical organizational changes without opposition from above or outside. Others have played this game; Al Dunlap had a run as a radical cost cutter that for a while bought him credibility with number chasers, but slash and burn only goes so far. And without a growth strategy, it flames out, as it did for Chainsaw Al.

Structural Levers

Early on, Welch replaced many top executives and built a new team, and restructured to take out layers of management. He also opened up communication in all directions by visiting management training programs at Crotonville to create give-and-take sessions with managers, test new ideas, and preach his messages about what he expected. He introduced 360-degree feedback, and leveraged what he later called the GE "operating system," which included the planning and resource allocation processes, reviews of managerial talent (called Session C), and quarterly communication meetings to shape the company. Meanwhile, the vision as he articulated it was evolving toward "speed, simplicity, and self-confidence," toward making GE a great place to work, then to "boundaryless organization" to stretch goals, and recently to becoming a service organization. Numerous transformation programs were introduced, including "Work-Out," designed to eliminate unnecessary bureaucratic work (and open up hierarchical communication), and six sigma, using the Internet to reform processes ("Destroy your business.com"). Over time the programs and processes evolved as conditions changed and he learned, but from the beginning he was trying to create a company that would have the agility of a small organization combined with the strength of a large one.

At the same time, the vision of what it took to be successful at GE evolved, and Welch articulated the "social architecture," the need for managers to both make the numbers and operate according to GE values, including treating people "humanely." He insisted on focusing on "A" players and getting rid of "C" players, the bottom 10%, who were unlikely to improve—and he continued to raise the bar. For him there were no trade-offs between caring for people and demanding performance; in this as in many other actions, he demonstrated his comfort with the use of power in many dimensions.

From this brief review, it is possible to see that Welch used directive and collaborative forms of power, with both structural and personal focus. His charisma and intelligence allowed him to drive many structural decisions that were not popular, as well as directly influence many managers. He used some of these decisions to create more collaborative efforts at decision making, building his executive team, allowing ideas to come up from below, and making it possible for initiative to be taken at many levels. Part of his effectiveness was in using all forms of power toward corporate ends—and being willing to acknowledge and fix mistakes as they were discovered.

Situational and Personal Bases of Power

As should be increasingly clear, power is a complex result of organizational position *and* personal attributes. Some people have skills or characteristics that allow them to be influential with others; some people have organizational positions that allow them more access to resources, information, or relationships; and some, like Jack Welch, have both. No matter how many attempts are made to make organizations boundaryless, to eliminate arbitrary distinctions among members, or to enhance individual skills, differences in ability to influence will remain. Position and skills usually interact. Some personal attributes increase the chance of acquiring situational power, and having a powerful position can enhance the development of personal skills.

The way power works is that those who have it and use it effectively acquire more power (as we saw with Welch). Successful accomplishment of important tasks is the first critical component of acquiring power; doing one's job well may not be enough to assure sufficient power for accomplishing greater tasks, but it is usually the price of admission.

Power is about real differences in ability to control valuable assets, which lead to more ability to control the information, resources, or relationships. It is also about perceived differences in such control. If others think that someone is powerful, they behave in ways that reinforce actual power. The rich get richer, except when they abuse their actual or perceived power, and fail to act in ways that are perceived to be legitimate or organization-centered. In organizational life, power that is "socialized," as McClelland put it[7] (i.e., used in the service of organizational goals), is more effective than other forms of power. Because it is accepted and valued, it increases the power of the person who uses it. If, on the other hand, the use of power is seen as only aimed at personal glorification, it is likely to create a backlash, and sooner or later, others will find ways to undermine the abuser.

Nevertheless, differential amounts of power are an inevitable byproduct of position and skills. Further, to accomplish organizational ends, the behavior of some members will at times have to be influenced in directions they may not otherwise choose to go. The influence may be through positive attractive means such as articulation of an alluring vision, persuasiveness, and full collaboration in determining implementation if not direction. But at other times, it may require repetitive insistence, or even some form of coercion that uses rewards or induces fear, since there will be some members who will require steering toward organizational goals through the use of directive power.

Unfortunately, differences in hierarchical position and responsibilities can create attitudes among members of excessive fear or rigidity that get in the way of necessary upward communication. Thus, even the most egalitarian structures can inexorably erode into dysfunction, requiring considerable effort to maintain appropriate initiative, openness, and collaboration from those below.

There is another aspect to the exercise of power that is worth noting. Those who wish to make something happen can do it openly, making their attempts overt, or do it covertly, trying to keep their efforts out of sight or behind the scenes. Welch's style was relatively overt, whether pushing for changed behavior by an intense face-to-face encounter, or struggling to launch a program like Work-Out, designed to provide many opportunities for new behavior. As a consequence, Welch may have been feared by many, but—for most—he was trusted and perceived as genuine.

On the other hand, some powerful people have worked behind the scenes, in more manipulative ways, to shape behavior. Robert Caro has brilliantly documented the ways that Robert Moses and Lyndon Johnson covertly exercised power—and though both left office when it became clear they could not continue, both had many years of successful power plays.[8] Moses, for example, secretly wrote obscure clauses into bond legislation when he was a legislative assistant in New York that he later used to shield and give unusual powers to his position as parks commissioner. Both Moses and Johnson did illicit favors to create obligations that were collected when needed. This covert exercise of power is attractive to certain kinds of leaders, and has been used to shape organizations for better or worse. But sooner or later, such backroom operations are discovered, and the enemies accumulated along the way seek revenge.

Wider use of technology to make information available, a prying press, and a greater number of skillful employees and trained managers make it harder to conceal such actions and expectations of managerial transparency and accountability keep increasing. Certainly the current trend to give CEOs less and less time to make a difference before the board decides to remove a "poor performer" means that more scrutiny of how managers work is likely.

Nevertheless, our experience with managers over the last 30 years leads us to conclude that many still try to cover their tracks, fearing that if others know how they are trying to exercise influence these intended targets will be less controllable. The managers also fear that if the influence attempt does not work out, they will lose future influence. While successful use of power leads to more power, the opposite is also true; failed power attempts reduce power. Managers who are less than courageous often, therefore, try to disguise their intentions and actions. We have described this form of interaction as one version of "heroic leadership," manager-as-conductor, and it dies hard.[9] That it occasionally works only reinforces its survival, even though most of the time followers recognize the game, and either look to win it by direct counterattack, or apparently go along. But sabotage by tactics such as withholding critical information or failing to take desirable initiative is common.

What Will Not Change About Power and Influence

Many attempts like those at GE described earlier have been rightly made to mitigate the distancing and arbitrary effects of hierarchy, and there are organizational mechanisms such as open forums, (à la GE's Work-Out), electronic access (such as e-mail and Web sites), cross-cutting task forces, or 360-degree feedback that can help, but they are only ways of pushing against the hierarchical tide, not of permanently stopping it.

Similarly, there have been many training programs—some created by the authors of this chapter—aimed at reducing distance by teaching individual skills such as assertiveness, feedback, listening, confrontation, influencing, and "empowerment." No matter how good such programs may be, however, there will always be some people who don't have the ability or courage to use the skills when facing others who are more forceful, more verbally proficient, or in more potent organizational positions. As much as the desire for equality drives many Americans to look past natural differences among people, there are differing capacities inherent in biological beings. Just as with athletes, intensive development activities can raise the level of most, but there will remain inherent differences that neither training nor experience can eliminate.

Finally, it is unlikely that best efforts can eliminate all misuse of power. How people react to having power, or to those who have more or less than they do, is at least in part a function of their own personal experiences, both early in life with family and throughout their organizational experiences. Even deep psychoanalysis has no better a track record than chance at fundamentally changing personality, and basic attitudes about authority are deeply entrenched, despite the best intentions to be effective.

Furthermore, as the world becomes more complex and more difficult to predict or control, the longing for leaders who can provide certainty and direction is likely to increase, or at the least not diminish. We have written of the problems caused by heroic leadership assumptions, where leaders and followers alike think that leaders should be all knowing, have all the answers, and always be responsible for everything in their domain.[10] Although there has been an increase in numbers of managers who are trying to operate in a postheroic fashion, we do not believe that any foresee-able forces will soon eliminate these longings.

How Power and Influence Are Likely to Change

Two major forces will impact the use of power in organizations during the 21st century. There will be an ever increasing need for rapid, major changes, and requisite knowledge and expertise will be more widely disseminated throughout organizations. These forces will drive the use and forms of power in three ways:

1. The tension between the need for speed of action and the need to collect knowledge and expertise to make informed decisions will require increasing the total amount of power in organizations.
2. To ensure that there is both sufficient autonomy and speed, clear organizational vision must be articulated and committed to.
3. Further, mutual influence will become increasingly required as a way of assuring cooperation for organizational goals.

Increasing Need for Rapid Change

It isn't exactly late-breaking news that there is an increase in the requirements for organizational speed. With the rapid pace of technological change, increased global competition, changing workforce demographics and expectations, privatization, and so on, organizational survival will depend on the ability to rapidly adapt to change, make fast decisions, and then remake them in light of new information and results. In this sense, lack of speed kills, and therefore organizations will need to be able to rapidly make decisions and alter plans.

Technology alone is a central driver of the faster pace. One type of threat is from disruptive technologies, which look to be inferior to dominant technologies, but are much less expensive and therefore can open whole new markets, then increase in quality until they threaten the older markets.[11] Another threat comes from the commoditization of products once innovative, requiring shifts to new technologies that may call for skills not readily present in the firm. Intel's decision to get out of memory chips, its main business, was driven by this phenomenon. Polaroid and Kodak seem to have been unable to make the shift from chemical-based to electronic photography, despite many attempts.

Similarly, global competition can bring large, hungry competitors into markets where they previously were absent or minor players. The consolidation of companies makes competitors more able to bring scale to bear to drive down prices, buy into markets, or offer new benefits. Moving too slowly in response can lose market share that is very difficult to recapture.

All of this change of pace can make it imperative for leaders to be able to act rapidly and to mobilize their organizations, without being slowed by the need to consult with all stakeholders or build consensus. There are times when doing something, even the wrong thing, is better than inaction. In these circumstances, leaders must have the legitimacy and acceptance to be able to make the decisions, and to count on the organization's members to come through. Boldness, coupled with trusting support, become conditions for survival.

Knowledge and Expertise Throughout the Organization

Another force, related to the pace of change, is the rapid increase in the need for diverse expertise among employees, and the need to deploy them throughout the organization so that they can be close to the action. Education levels have risen, making it possible to ask more of employees (and raising their expectations that they will be used for more than routine execution). And as demands for rapid action have increased and information needs increase, it is increasingly necessary to have people at all levels who are empowered to act based on their first-hand knowledge of the issues and their capacities for exercising judgment and initiative. Information has to be accessible to many more than in the past, and they have to be able to use it quickly.

In addition, there is ample evidence that most innovation comes from the middle of organizations, not just from the top. Those who do the work, and have knowledge, are the most likely to see new opportunities and possibilities; they are not only the organizational Cassandras, as Intel chairman Andy Grove called them, warning of shifts in the markets, technologies, and industries, but also the developer of products and plans. Without their entrepreneurial energy and willingness to take initiative, organizations could not keep up. They cannot be stifled without serious consequences.

The Core Dilemmas

These two conditions set up contradictory needs that can make the exercise of power remarkably difficult. To respond rapidly, leaders must be decisive, and sometimes bold. Competing on speed[12] requires the willingness to move mountains if necessary. They have to be able to cut through organizational resistance and routine to dramatically shift course, or to make early bets before all the data are—or can be—in.

The danger with this kind of forcefulness, however, is that it may well kill the kind of upward information flow needed to make smart decisions in a complex changing world. Overriding opposition, or not even giving it a chance to be heard, can easily send the message that initiative is not welcome, pushback is dangerous, and that people are expected to go along to get along.

At the same time, leaders have to be able to rely on more and more people at all levels to be able to speak up, be decisive, and take action. It will seldom be the top person alone who has all the answers, sees all the trends, understands all of the customers, knows most about technology needs, or has all of the interpersonal skill and wisdom to deal with the aspirations and quirks of all stakeholders. It is difficult to make good decisions in isolation, since the input of so many different experts will be needed and must be somehow reconciled when the necessary trade-offs have to be made. It may not even be recognized experts who have the most useful information or ideas; anyone in a fast-moving and changing environment, regardless of formal position, may be at the forefront of the action at a given time, and may notice, sense, intuit, or stumble on critical intelligence. If they do not feel free to communicate their observations in any direction, including upward, and in turn if those with the formal power are not attuned to listening to people who are outside of the formal structure, the organization will be too slow to receive early signals that can make all the difference in discovering customer needs, generating new products, or reacting to competitors' moves.

Furthermore, to get the kind of individual investment needed to have people taking initiative at every level, it is necessary to give them not only access and voice, but considerable autonomy. When information rather than physical products is increasingly the basis for companies and their success, it is not possible to get excellent results through mere compliance. Members of the organization must be committed to the organization and its objectives, and ready to go beyond minimal requirements.

At the same time, this dispersion of skill and decision-making ability means that just when swift decisions are needed, the talent may decide to dig in and insist that they be heard—even when they do not agree with each other and are sure that their view of the world is the correct one. The greater the dispersion of power—an inevitability when employees are better educated, there are more experts, growth may be explosive, faster action is needed, and employees may be located far from headquarters—

the greater the number of people who can resist direction. *At just the times when decisiveness is needed, it becomes more difficult to gain support and acceptance for unpopular decisions.*

That responsible employees might resist or offer counter-suggestions, and make it harder to exercise direct power, can be frustrating to leaders, but it is not inherently bad. Resistance may be due to lack of understanding of urgency or business imperatives, which will necessitate clearer and more open communication from above. Resistance may be due to the general cultural changes around the world that result in less willingness of subordinates to blindly follow orders, which means that leaders will be obligated to explain their actions, and be more transparent about reasons for requests or directions. Or resistance may be due to the resisters having knowledge that was not available to the leader(s), but is necessary for informed decision making. In that case, the dispersion of power is beneficial, because it results in better decisions, with more relevant input from those who have the scattered or localized knowledge.

What a dilemma! Act fast, but don't squelch those below who know what you need to know, and don't get so bogged down in listening to them that the train has left while you are still trying to find the platform. Unfortunately, there are no simple guidelines for when to listen and when to charge ahead. Organizational members at all levels must learn to be comfortable both with making decisions on their own when they know what to do or there is a true emergency, and with seeking the many others who should be included to make good decisions. They must have a good sense of when to do which, and be comfortable in either mode. Neither simple mantras of empowerment nor rigid centralized control captures the sophisticated heuristics that will be needed.

Another dilemma arises from the speed and autonomy requirement. As we have said, to make timely decisions, leaders at all levels have to be able to use judgment and initiate appropriate action, or responses will be too slow. Measured action makes sense in stable environments, but not in rapidly moving ones. Yet if people have so much autonomy, there is the danger that they will make decisions that do not align with the organization's goals, miss important opportunities, or ignore critical implications for other parts of the organization. They can become wild ducks flying wherever they like, or even worse, loose cannons that could sink the ship (as happened with Nicholas Leeson, the bond trader in Singapore who sank his company, Barings, by unauthorized trading).

What makes this so difficult that it is not just leaders who have the dilemmas, it is also the people who report to them, leaders in their own right as we have explained, who have the dilemmas too. Leaders do not exercise leadership in a vacuum; they depend on the behavior of their subordinates, who are supposed to cooperate with the leader's directions and concerns, but also speak up when they believe the leader to be wrong or misinformed. Subordinates have to decide when it is appropriate to push back and when to go along, when it is critical to be heard and when it would truly be a career-limiting move, or just gratuitously irritating. For some it is all too easy to give away their power by hiding behind the subordinate role and acceding to the boss's right to make the decisions. Their concern about self-protection not only reduces the likelihood of the leader making the correct decision, but hampers their own potential for influence on future issues.

In addition, subordinates are also supposed to be leaders in finding problems, taking initiative to solve them, and leading others. Just as top leaders sometimes have to get things done when their subordinates are not quite ready or fully able, leaders below can't wait for the perfect leader above; they have to find ways to be effective whether or not their boss is providing the exact best conditions. Otherwise they are not taking the right kind of upward leadership initiative. Thus everyone has responsibilities in all directions, making the spread and use of power even more complex and challenging.

Power Use that Counters these Dilemmas

These dilemmas are real and will not go away in the foreseeable future, but there are three approaches that can help work through them and will therefore be increasingly common. The first is to increase the total amount of power in any system, so that all members are more effective. The second is to use and reinforce articulated vision as a uniting element. The third is to build skills of mutual influence, enhancing the quality of decision making.

Increasing the Total Amount of Power

Organizational power has often been conceived of as a limited, fixed commodity, subject to struggles for capture by competing players. In some circumstances that is an accurate description, and individuals who do not know how to (or do not care to do what is needed to) effectively compete for power end up relatively powerless, or even ejected from the organization. Tom Stallkamp, for example, president of Chrysler at the time of the merger with Daimler-Benz, discovered this to his dismay. Put in charge of "accelerating integration" of the merged companies, he tried to be collaborative but would not undercut Chrysler Chairman and CEO Bob Eaton in the way that Jurgen Schrempp, the chairman of the new DaimlerChrysler, wanted; so, he was increasingly cut out of the inner circle and was eventually fired.[13] Many executives in so-called mergers of equals have discovered too late that few managers from the weaker partner survive.[14]

Far more often, however, despite the belief by those who have only experienced competitive, cut-throat environments, power is expandable, with increases for all players possible. Helping subordinates become more powerful, for example, need not diminish the power of the leader; if they are more powerful and can get their work done better, the leader's power expands. Ability to deliver increases, credibility rises, and both leader and the whole group become more powerful. Furthermore, subordinates can take the initiative to expand the total amount of power by doing those things that make themselves and their colleagues more effective, and enhancing the power of the leader. For example, they can watch for new opportunities, provide helpful feedback or other forms of assistance to each other, anticipate the needs of the leader as he or she deals with the rest of the organization—in short, take ownership for the success of the unit and organization. Greater success leads to greater collective power.

Making Vision Real, Central

Another potent force that can overcome some of the insistence of highly autonomous people on getting their way is the use of organizational vision. Unfortunately, vision in many organizations is no more than an empty slogan. Yet when it is genuinely inspiring, clearly articulated, referred to often, a guideline for hiring, and used for decision making, vision can both help to free smart subordinates and keep them from completely digging in on any issue about which they have differing views. If there is a vision that most buy into, then the vision can serve as a broad constraint rather than the leader having to use personal or positional power to align people. When there is agreement about direction, then disputes focus on means rather than ultimate ends, and the nature of the conversation is different. The vision can be invoked to move discussions forward, and to in effect remind people that in some way their interests must be framed in terms of overall benefit to the organization and not just the specialty of the individual.

In rapidly moving situations, vision may not be as long lasting as it once was, but, as Collins and Porras have pointed out in *Built to Last*,[15] fundamental direction does not change with every technological shift, and fundamental values—a part of vision that matters a lot—can survive many product cycles.

Vision is in itself a powerful source of influence, moving people who would otherwise just keep their heads down and think only of their own function or projects. A high percentage of employees whose basic needs are satisfied very much want to feel that their work has meaning, making a difference to others and to the world. That desire can become a potent force when leaders throughout the organization are able to articulate a vision that makes vivid the impact of the work.

In addition, the existence of a clearly articulated and generally accepted vision works to provide direction for autonomous leaders throughout the organization, and prevents them from becoming loose cannons who shoot off in all directions at once. It isn't easy to get buy-in for vision, but repeated use of the vision for important organizational decisions like strategy, hiring, and investments; symbolic acts that vividly demonstrate the top leader's commitment to it; leader walking of the talk; and periodic discussions of the implications of the vision, can help to increase commitment.[16] Once there is buy-in, many unherdable cats can be headed roughly in the same direction, and therefore allowed considerable freedom. And again, subordinates can play a valuable role in enhancing the benefits of shared vision. They can reinforce its use by pointing out when it is not clear and asking for clarifying discussion, propose options for its articulation, or remind the boss and colleagues when struggling with current problematic issues that the vision could be helpful in resolution.

Using Mutual Influence

One of the best ways to influence smart, independent people is to allow them to have influence on the issues they care about. Since they usually know things that the leader does not, it only makes sense to be willing to explore together, using the expertise of anyone who has relevant information or ideas. When stated this way, it seems indisputable; why would any manager want to make a decision without using the most expert and relevant information? Although heroic assumptions die hard, the greater dispersion of talented people will make it ever more likely that leaders will use directive power only rarely.

The opposite of directive power is not exactly the same as what is often meant by "power sharing" or "empowerment," since those terms imply that the powerful person has to give up some of the power to make the others strong. Rather, it is about enhancing the power of all, making the others strong, and at the same time allowing the leader to be strong too. Few leaders will tolerate for long any philosophy or practice that means they have to be handcuffed, no matter how hard they try. It is in the nature of managerial work to want to be able to get things done, so giving up that capacity is not realistic. But creating the strength in others that guarantees they will not crumple when the leader pushes, nor resist just because the leader wants something, makes for better discussions, decisions, and implementation. Only when a leader can count on colleagues to push back when they have information that contradicts the leader can he or she use full strength in pursuing ideas.

At the same time, subordinates who know that they will be listened to, and will be encouraged to disagree, whether or not they ultimately prevail, do not act out the resistance of the powerless, digging in just to have some measure of control of a tiny piece of turf.[17] They are less likely to resist or sabotage. Since reciprocity is universal, those who feel that they are listened to develop at least some obligation to listen back in return. When there has been a continued pattern of mutual influence, the leader will be given some latitude at those rare times when directive action must be taken because of being at a strategic inflection point, emergency, or other causes discussed in the beginning of the paper. Having allowed upward influence, credit for being a manager who is not afraid of mutual influence will enable more latitude when it is needed. Abuse of this credit will generate widespread resistance, but occasional and proper use is generally granted those who are not perceived as arbitrary, closed, and unilateral.

In this way, leaders can be decisive when necessary without being seen and reacted to as coercive. Thus, the shared power of mutual influence needs to be coupled with more willingness to trust others in the organization when cooperation is needed. Over time that will start to build more open cultures where it is expected that people will disagree freely, but be willing to accept decisions with which they disagree. The Intel model of dissent and commit, which actually goes farther than acceptance of decisions to the obligation to commit to proving one's formerly dissenting position wrong, will become more common, helping to resolve the initiative dilemma.

Implicit in this model of spirited discussion and eventual commitment is the idea of mutual influence among colleagues, not just between leader and followers. Peers need to be willing to take one another on without being destructively competitive, and therefore must be skillful in both exercising influence and in being influenced when that will lead to better decisions. Enhancing the influence skills of all in the organization serves, along with the acceptance of a common vision, as another check on the inappropriate pursuit of autonomy. Interdependent colleagues will hold each other accountable, and confront any one of them who is disregarding the organization's direction or needs. And since mutuality goes in all directions, subordinates can add to their boss's effectiveness by being willing to enhance his or her influence when that is needed. Just pushing back is not the only way to ensure good decisions; sometimes propping up can be helpful, especially in difficult times. The initiative to increase organizational results can come from any direction.

Performance As an Increasingly Important Source of Power

Because of all this, there will be a shift in the sources of power in organizations. We mentioned earlier that power comes from both position and personal skills. During much of the 20th century organizational position was in part determined by having the right background, what sociologists call ascribed characteristics, such as class, gender, religion, and race.[18] In addition, certain factors that derive from such factors, like dress and school attended, were also important. People with the "right" background had a much greater chance of becoming high-level managers, and though competence at the job mattered, it mattered a lot less than these other factors. As we move more into the information age, where industries are more knowledge-based, what people know and can do will assume even greater importance.

Expertise has always been a source of power, but it will become proportionally more important—and easier to recognize—in organizations where power is more widely dispersed. There will be more peer judgment accessible, and therefore it will be ever harder to hide actual performance and capacities. Reputation, which derives from one's character, abilities, willingness to collaborate, and delivery on the job, along with ability to learn and be seen as open to learning, becomes ever more important. Since it will be harder to direct from above, more work will be accomplished by ad hoc teams and groupings, formal and informal, that will in effect choose their members. When important tasks are on the line, people will want to work with others who can actually deliver, and not just with those who look right and know which fork to use at a formal dinner. Another way of saying this is that power will increasingly accrue to those who can deliver, which is in keeping with organizational and democratic mythology, but hasn't always been the case in practice. One implication is that subordinates who deliver will accrue more power—which in turn can help their boss to utilize their talents more, and therefore deliver more and raise total unit performance.

In addition, remember that influence ultimately derives from reciprocity.[19] Whether the influencer has a good reputation for being able to deliver, organizational rewards and punishments to disburse, charisma that makes others feel confidence or attraction, or just the legitimacy of position, those who are influenced get something in return for allowing themselves to go along. What they get may be tangible or intangible—goods, services, or particular feelings—but they are in effect exchanging what is wanted for what they value. Thus, greater power goes to those who are skilled at building ways to generate reciprocity.

Since it is much easier to get others to reciprocate if they trust the person making the request, and have an existing relationship, the powerful will be good at understanding what is important to others, and at finding ways to deliver it, but also at making relationships before there is any business to transact. As the raw exercise of power by directiveness becomes less useful and less possible for a lot of work, there will be a premium on another kind of on-the-job performance: genuineness. Those who are only feared, or are widely mistrusted, will have less ability to get work done, and will lose power.

Conclusions

Power and influence in the 21st-century organization will be sophisticated and versatile. Those who cannot listen, utilize the expertise of many, articulate a uniting vision, or build mutual influence will create the very resistance that makes informed, concerted effort so difficult. If they cannot build a wide network of relationships and a reputation for being trustworthy as well as competent, they will find themselves unable to gain the cooperation needed for complex, challenging work. At the same time, those who can only be nice, and cannot exercise any of the more directive methods, are afraid to make anyone angry, afraid of causing conflict or hard feelings, will also be handicapped. When it is necessary to make the tough decisions, they will be paralyzed.

Thus organizations of the next century will require people who are versatile and comfortable with themselves. They will have to be comfortable with exercising their tough and tender sides, with making tough decisions alone and with sharing power, with influencing and being open to influence, with passionately driving decisions and also being willing to admit that others may have better ideas or contributions that can shape the decisions, and with taking initiative in all directions. They will need the capacity to do what will work in a given situation—including being so true to oneself that it is possible to choose not to do what is needed because it violates dearly held values or ethical standards.

This is a tall order, but we believe that we have shown that the future will demand no less than realistic and healthy people making informed choices. Dick Beckhard would be pleased.

13

Framing—It's Either
Us or *Them*

Harvey A. Hornstein

hree decades ago, Richard (Dick) Beckhard arranged for me to be part of a team of people consulting to Imperial Chemical Industries, a British firm. After finishing my first day of client meetings, I hurried to meet Dick for dinner in the restaurant of the hotel where we were staying—his favorite at the time—London's Sheraton Park Tower.

Drinks were ordered and menus were being studied while I fidgeted like a small child with abdominal discomfort because of an irrepressible desire to tell my mentor about my day. After only a few moments Dick peeked over his menu asking, "How did it go, Harv?" Freed at last, I proudly gushed a fountain of detail telling him what I had learned about who in the organization was doing what to whom, and why. It was a tour de force, I thought, patting myself on the back with a silent, "I really understand this one."

Dick listened patiently, and then overturned the pedestal on which I'd placed myself by saying simply, "Good Harv, that's how you see it. Now tell me about how the client sees it." Dick understood that how people framed the world was an important influence on how they behaved in it.

During the last three decades a series of articles published in psychology's scientific journals have also underscored the importance of framing by demonstrating that it affects whether ordinary citizens, going about their daily chores, choose to set aside self-interest to help strangers who are in need of their aid.[1] Research evidence showed that wide swings in the percentage of people anonymously helping strangers—as low as 20% in some cases to as high as 80% in others—depended on whether the potential helpers viewed the needy stranger as one of *us*, or as one of *them*.

Framing has powerful consequences when it involves cleaving the world into *us* and *them*, an in-group and one or more out-groups: When others are included as part of *us*, their plight and delight are both felt almost as if they were our own, prompting effort on their behalf. (Think of yourself in movie theaters when you weep, cringe, flinch, and feel relief because of what is happening to a character with whom you identify. Or, how either tears or cheers follow news about outcomes, positive or negative, being experienced by someone you love, your favorite sports team, or a preferred political party.) When others are psychologically exiled to *them*, however, there is very little in the way of empathy, caring, or helping.

These exciting findings are the scientific foundation for what has been labeled the *psychological golden rule of organizations.*[2] Call it loyalty, commitment, dedication, or emotional attachment, the evidence invariably shows that when employees identify with their employing organization—experiencing it as *us* or *we* rather than *them*—their work behavior is nudged by the golden rule's powerful psychological prescription: *Harming you becomes difficult for me because the two of us are part of we.*

A woman that I will call Joan Hoffman, who is actually a 32-year-old employee in a Massachusetts-based high-technology firm, told me of an experience she had that provides a clear example of how greatly work behavior is affected by the psychological golden rule of organizations and employees' sense of identification with their employers. She described an occasion when she was leaving the company after a long day's work.

> No one was around. I was the last person in my particular part of the site. No one was ever going to know that I was the last to leave. It was raining. I mean raining! I was dying to get home. My coat was zippered and Velcroed when I paused near the exit doors in order to put on my hat. It was then that I noticed that banks of lights were burning in several areas where they should have been off. It was across the shop, several glass partitions away, but there they were, plain as day. It's one of those things that's not a big deal, but is a big deal when you think about it—if you know what I mean. Somewhere, probably in the facility's lower whatever, a utility meter was happily ticking away the added costs.

> Now, to complicate things, I only vaguely knew where the switches were supposed to be. Even with that little bit of confusion, what was required should only cause me a three- or four-minute detour. Trotting across the empty space might take 30 seconds at most. Locating the controls could take a couple of minutes. But turning them off and getting out of there wasn't going to require more than another 30 seconds.

Of course, if my decision was to forget it, to go on to my warm, inviting home, leaving the lights burning and the meters running, who would know? And that would mean zero time and effort for me.

What to do?

Alone in the office on that rainy evening, Joan Hoffman turned her back and walked away, leaving the lights burning. Joan rarely experienced her organization's successes and failures as if they were her own. When discussing her organization she usually referred to it as *they,* not *we.* If others thought poorly of Joan's company it was not much of a bother for her. Praise of her employer was not interpreted as a personal compliment. Nor was criticism regarded as an insult.

Of course, framing employers as *they* or *we* does not merely apply to spur-of-the-moment decisions about light switches. Employees' sense of identification with employers has the power to advance business goals, if it is properly and carefully developed, or else thwart them if it is not. An explanation of what organizations can do to erect these vital ties follows a brief discussion of how current trends in business and society are associated with its erosion.

The Bottom Line

You'd think that organizations would work harder to earn their workers' allegiance; after all, no psychological force helps or hinders the achievement of organizational goals more than employee's identification with the organizations that they work for. Employee initiative, risk-taking, productivity, and creativity can all be linked to identification, and result in a more powerful company.[3] Cross-cultural evidence from nations as widely separated as the United Kingdom and Japan shows that employee turnover is diminished when their organizational identification is strong, resulting in major financial benefits to employers.[4]

The power of employees' organizational identification as a social adhesive with bottom-line consequences is also evident in *Fortune's* report of the 100 best companies to work for in America. Comparing the average annual return to stockholders generated by firms that were nominated for the list by their employees with that of firms that were not shows that investors were better off holding stock in companies that received employees' endorsements. Over a five-year period, these employee-approved companies returned 27.5% to investors, compared with only 17.3% for those not elected to the "Best 100." And over a 10-year period, those nominated returned 23.4% to investors, compared with only 14.8% among the unendorsed. This means that if $1,000 were invested in a firm boasting the emotional attachment of its employees, in eight years that money would have grown to $8,188. But if the same $1,000 were invested in a firm in which employees lacked such ties of allegiance, it would have grown to only $3,976 in the same amount of time.[5]

Rates of in-company theft and sabotage—a high eight-figure cost to corporations around the world—are also vivid illustrations of how employee behavior, devoid of organizational identification, is detrimental to the bottom line. The facts tell us that these crimes cannot be dismissed simply as economically motivated efforts to make up for deficient wages: Workers at all income levels steal, and what's commonly stolen tends to be petty and of little or no value to the thief; and sabotage, a common crime in organizations, never provides offenders with economic gain. Indeed, the most convincing evidence shows that employees tend not to steal from employers who treat them respectfully.[6] In short, workers are much more likely to give in to malevolent temptation if it means robbing or harming one of *them* rather than one of *us*.

When companies are relegated to *they*, there is no feeling of worker–employee oneness, no merging of personal and organizational goals, and no vicarious experience of organizations' ups and downs. And when it comes to making decisions at work, self-interest—instead of the psychological golden rule of organizations—is the most accurate predictor of employees' behavior.

Despite these bottom-line consequences, the data concerning organizations' efforts to earn the allegiance of their workers are not encouraging. Recently, the U.S. Department of Labor estimated that only 4% of American businesses are involved in employee inclusion-inducing activities.[7] Edward Lawler reports that although a study conducted by the University of Southern California's Center for Effective Organizations showed that 68% of *Fortune's* "Fortune 1,000" claimed that they used self-managed teams, additional evidence revealed that the activities touched a mere 10% of the employees.[8]

Discouraging data also come from managers surveyed by the Boston-based consulting company Rath and Strong. Eighty percent of these bosses asserted that employees should have a voice in mapping company change, but this positive assertion was quickly mitigated when 40% of them added that they did not believe that *their own employees* had anything valuable to contribute.[9]

Evidence from employee surveys supports the view that organizations' public pronouncements, boasting about their use of employee inclusion-inducing approaches, contain exaggeration. In 1997, an annual survey of 3,300 employees conducted by Towers Perrin showed increases in both employees' feelings of disenfranchisement and the number of workers—about one third—claiming that their bosses ignored their interests when making decisions.[10] Data from senior level managers also provide little reason to be cheery about organizations' efforts to gain their employees' allegiance. A survey of 196 executives of "40-something" age found that more than half of these senior-ranking workers felt less committed to their employers than they had five years earlier.[11]

Us in the Future

The intensity of tides that have been tugging at organizations for a while is gaining power, placing an even greater premium on building ties that bind. Organizations that fail to remedy their neglect of employee allegiance face growing peril.

Doing More With Less

Pressures requiring companies to do much more with fewer staff for greater numbers of customers show no signs of abating. Periods of protection from competitors' responses to product innovations are shorter today than they were yesterday, and they will be shorter still tomorrow. In response, companies are already seeking to shorten innovation cycles by organizing large sections of their workforces around temporary projects rather than permanent assignments. Personnel rosters are not only smaller, they are also constantly changing in composition in order to rapidly rearrange skill concentrations. These onrushing events are aggravated by the mounting use of part-timers, of "virtual" workers (who are physically separate from work sites), and of temporary workers (currently some 30% of the workforce and, significantly, labeled *disposable* and *throwaway* workers by economists). This increasingly common use of nontraditional job arrangements widens the psychological distance between workers and employers, thereby worsening the prospects for success in future efforts to build the ties that bind employees to their organizations.

Going Global

Globalization has resulted in the loosening of the hold that corporate headquarters have on affiliates, granting them greater freedom—but often breaking the bond between employers and employees in the process. In expanding worldwide, many companies have abandoned landmark sites that they believe are too narrowly identified with one nation, a plan that backfires when it cuts off the feelings of identification that workers may have for such traditional sites. In 1995, for example, Pharmacia AB, a Swedish company, acquired The Upjohn Company, an American firm based in Kalamazoo, Michigan. The headquarters for the new company that resulted, Pharmacia & Upjohn, were placed in London, a location that decision makers presumably hoped would prove more neutral ground. It was a reasonable ambition, but the move seems to have ended up as no more than a costly eradication of a corporate symbol to which employees felt attached. As the directors of Pharmacia learned the hard way, many bosses' *Field of Dreams* hope that a new corporate identity and faithful customers will magically emerge once balanced arrangements and neutral sites are constructed are destined for disappointment, having ignored the importance of workers' identification.

Outsourcing

Outsourcing has also made company success more dependent on the thorough development of employees' organizational identity. Originally conceived as a cost-cutting tool, outsourcing is increasingly seen as a means for more effectively producing products and for servicing internal and external customers. The idea is that by allotting certain tasks to firms outside the company, personnel resources can be focused on a narrower range of tasks, and specialized skills and economies of scale will be developed in place of sprawling efforts to cover all bases. If Peter F. Drucker is correct in guessing that within the next decade or two all organizations' support work will be outsourced, then someone had better begin paying attention to outsourcing's current afflictions. A 1996 PA Consulting Group survey of companies in France, Germany, Denmark, Hong Kong, Australia, England, and the United States showed that one third of the responding firms believed that outsourcing's disadvantages were greater than its advantages.[12]

Companies to which work and workers are outsourced face a different version of the common lack of emotional connection between employee and employer. Customers and clients, like some cousins, are "once removed." They are, in fact, part of *another* organization. This requires firms that *receive* outsourced work to build strong ties to their employees, so that their goal of servicing someone else's employees and customers become their own workers' goals as well.

Employing Generation X

Investigators and observers are nearly unanimous in pointing out that the group of adults currently moving into the labor force in America and elsewhere in the industrialized world lacks a pro-organizational orientation. In a Coopers Lybrand study of 1,200 business students, 45% identified a "rewarding life outside work" as one of their lives' leading priorities.[13] And 68% of nearly 1,800 MBA students at major American universities agreed that "the family will always be more important to me than career."[14] In 1995, three fourths of the respondents to a poll conducted by Penn, Schoen, and Berland supported the idea of giving workers a choice between overtime pay and compensatory time away from the job. They opted for the choice because in their list of priorities, time commonly comes ahead of money.[15] The effect of this trend is as evident in the professions as it is in corporate business. For example, a *Law Practice Management Journal* article titled "The Loyalty Crisis" complained about how young lawyers have less commitment and willingness to work the hours typically expected by law firms, preferring instead to focus on personal matters away from the office.[16]

Generation X represents an additional challenge in the new obstacle course of employee–employer relations, joining *doing-more-with-less, globalization,* and *outsourcing* as changes in business conditions to which organizations must swiftly adapt. Successfully employing Generation X necessitates policies of company management that create affiliation, not alienation, more effectively than ever before.

Affirming Employees: Moving to *Us* from *Them*

The bad news is that the problems created by human beings' ability to divide the world into *we* and *they* are worsened by their deep-seated inclination to behave in ways that boost the status of *we* at the expense of *they.*[17] The good news is that organizational arrangements do not have to enable these misbehaviors. Organizations create antidotes to bosses' *we-boosting* inclinations when they introduce unambiguously consistent policies and procedures that express their commitment to affirming the whole employee—*as a contributor to the firm's operations, as a worker who is part of the community's job market, as a member of groups outside of the firm that make legitimate demands (e.g., families, religious institutions, and civic associations), and as an individual with physical and psychological needs.* These affirming arrangements frame the perspectives of both bosses and subordinates by sending genuine messages of inclusion saying that the organization regards all of its employees as part of *we.* As a result, employees are invited to identify with the organization and bosses are inhibited from treating them as *they.*

Affirm Employees as Contributors

A new tool for organizational problem solving, *whole system intervention,* is also a powerful means of affirming employees as contributors. What distinguishes this approach from more traditional efforts is who gets invited to problem-solving discussions. Instead of having small, eight- or 10-person task forces secreted in some organizational cranny and concocting solutions, whole system interventions have scores of employees, from various levels and functions, as well as customers and vendors involved in analysis and action planning.[18]

In 1993, for example, Ford brought together 2,400 geographically related employees to plan the opening of a Mustang plant. And, when Boeing worked on developing the 777, meetings conducted under CEO Phil Condit's guidance included as many as 5,000 people.[19] Using some extraordinary logistical expertise, whole system interventions increase the opportunity for having the right information and ideas at the right place at the right time. They also make the transfer of agreed-upon actions back into the workplace easier because personnel involved in making the transition were also involved in developing what needs to be transferred. But, more than anything else, whole system intervention problem-solving procedures build connecting bonds of *we* by affirming the value of employees as contributors.

Affirm Employees as Workers

When employees believe that their employing organizations' loyalties to them depend largely on how those organizations' answer the question, *"What did you do for us today,"* their boundaries of *we* shrink until only *"I"* and self-serving behavior remain. The remedy is organizational effort communicating that *every employee's tomorrow is on this organization's list of today's responsibilities.* This does not mean that organizations are obliged to commit financial suicide by guaranteeing employment. The alternative to choosing between selfishly instrumental organizational decisions and guaranteed employment requires affirming employees as workers who have vocational lives that go beyond their immediate employment. One way to do that is by introducing efforts that result in employees' enhanced employability.

One example of these efforts is an AT&T project called Resource Link.[20] In one case, an "internal contingent workforce" staffed by displaced managers and professionals was temporarily "linked" (from three months to a year) to projects across the company. Reports indicate that Resource Link provided AT&T with greater staffing flexibility and employees with both stability and development.

A redeployment procedure used by Intel is another example of an effort at enhancing employability. This procedure has reportedly helped the firm diminish layoffs by successfully relocating between 80% and 90% of Intel employees who needed to find new jobs because their old ones disappeared. Intel employee development centers support redeployment by providing workers with opportunities for assessment, guidance, training, and Intel job listings. If all these opportunities fail to produce an internal placement, then outplacement assistance is also available.[21]

Other companies affirm employees as workers by providing them with college support, funded apprenticeships, and vouchers to use for retraining. Trustmark Insurance, for example, a Lake Forest, Illinois, company, recruited employees who volunteered to be trained as computer programmers. Trustmark then not only paid for the employees' college-level classes, but also provided them with mentors to help with material being presented in the classes. BGS Systems Inc., in Waltham, Massachusetts, and Hewlett-Packard also reportedly provide courses for software engineers who want to upgrade their skills.[22] These practices all reach for low-hanging fruit. They are nothing new but, shamefully, neither are they common practice.

In 1997, several companies (AT&T, DuPont, GTE, Johnson & Johnson, Lucent, TRW Unisys, and UPS) joined Talent Alliance, a system on the Web that provides employees with opportunities for vocational assessment, information regarding training at company expense, and job postings in the member companies.[23] Through their involvement in Talent Alliance these companies were sending a message: *We accept our responsibility to work with employees to help them enhance their employability.* The message says that although unwelcome decisions may have to be made, instrumentalism is out: Employees are part *we;* they are not commodities to be used and then uncaringly discarded because of an organization's immediate needs.

Affirm Employees as Members of Outside Groups

Events that began in a small clothing store, located in an Ohio shopping center, show how senior management's regard for employees' outside obligations can boost business success while becoming a powerful antidote to *we*-boosting. In only two decades, that small Ohio-based store grew into the Limited, Inc., a firm that included Express, Structure, Victoria's Secret, and Abercrombie & Fitch. But fortunes change and, by 1993, with Limited's growth stalling badly, its founder, Leslie Wexner, worked to restore its success by reconfiguring the organization's policies, procedures, and his own approach to management. His efforts were rewarded: Limited's growth resumed and its stock traded at peak values.

Leslie Wexner explained his success: In the reconfigured organization, "the nine retail brands are encouraged to work together, sharing information and holding monthly meetings of divisional heads who had been fierce sibling-rivals under the old structure." In addition, he confessed that his managerial style shifted to one that is broadly concerned about the workplace from one that was more narrowly concerned only about work: "When I talked with Calloway (that's Wayne Calloway, former CEO of PepsiCo, Inc.), I asked how he spent his time. And he said that he probably spent…40% or 50% of his time on people. To me it was startling. I like people, but I'm busy picking sweaters, visiting stores, doing things. How do you find that much time?"

Leslie Wexner found the time. Now, when he considers people for positions, he looks for three things: First, do they know their jobs? Second, are they whole people? (Do they have balanced lives? Do they care about community?) And, in Wexner's words, the third attribute that he assesses in selecting among job candidates is a person's "true sense of responsibility for the people that they are working with. That they not only say it, but they demonstrate that they really care about the people that they work with. You can't fake that."[24]

If these selection criteria are employed, and if they are one part of a company's consistent effort to affirm the whole employee, then they are capable of nourishing the growth of an anti-*we*-boosting culture by putting bosses on notice that they are not free to disregard legitimate outside obligations that employees bring into the workplace.

Affirm Employees as Individuals With Physical and Psychological Needs

Scientific evidence proves conclusively that a work area's aromas, temperature, noise levels, and air quality affect employees' feelings and behaviors.[25] When these environmental conditions are agreeable, conflicts are less frequent and positive performance appraisals are more frequent.

But simple bodily sensations are not the sole reason that these desirable work outcomes arise from favorable environmental conditions. Employees know that environmental improvements are the product of organizational decision making. It is easy to understand that employees decipher one message when they believe that their employing organization cares enough about their physical well being to provide them with pleasant aromas and sound levels, but an entirely different one when they believe that *they* (their employers) don't care if *we* work amidst noxious smells and sounds.

Deliberate efforts to improve employees' physical well being widen the boundaries of *we*. They say, *We're in this together. If it's not good for any one of us, then it's not good for any of us.* These efforts convey anti-*we*-boosting messages. In contrast, organizations' clear disregard of their workforces' physical experiences narrow the boundaries of *we*, inviting *we*-boosting by encouraging bosses to *forget about them!*

Organization attention to employees' psychological needs can have the same anti-*we*-boosting effects as attention to their physical needs. Offering employees free time to replenish personal batteries after a grueling patch of work provides them with opportunity for gaining mental health benefits while simultaneously sending them an anti-*we*-boosting message. Levi Strauss & Company can be applauded for providing employees replenishment opportunity and supporting its use. They have a Time Off with Pay Program (TOPP) that encourages employees to take time off for personal reasons. Jeff Friant, a Levi Strauss manager for staffing, explained why the time off program succeeds in this company while it so frequently fails in others: "People who thoughtfully utilize TOPP time are seen as working for balance in their professional and personal lives. People are admired for that."[26]

Of course, free time is only one way for firms to show their concern for employees' psychological needs. By providing employees with various, genuine demonstrations of caring—counselors of any sort, time off for personal reasons, or opportunities for creative expression and self-reflection—companies benefit because they are sending their workforces anti-*we*-boosting messages. *No elites here* is what is says. No members of this organization are free to treat any other members as if *their* needs are not *our* concern.

Although sending employees inclusive, affirming messages does not guarantee firms' financial success, users can safely expect that, if their efforts are genuine and consistent, they will enjoy greater employee commitment and initiative because the psychological golden rule of organizations will be guiding their workforces' behaviors.

An even stronger guarantee can be made to organizations whose bosses send employees disaffirming messages. There is no guesswork here. Scientific evidence and common sense prove that these companies might just as well hang a sign over their entryways reading:

WE INVITE ALIENATED WORKERS, NEGATIVE PUB-
LIC OPINION, AND POLITICAL INTERVENTION

because that is precisely what they are going to get.

The mass media loves a target, and bosses' constant stream of disaffirming messages to employees have given them a big, fat bull's eye. If the mass media's audiences were unwilling to accept the idea that businesspeople are uncaring about their employees or society, then it would be forced to find other villains. Unfortunately for business, the idea *is* credible to audiences. By constructing *we/they* barriers in their organizations, bosses have built a cadre of employees who enroll their families, friends, and political representatives in a protest organized around disillusionment with the business community. Their placards read: *They* do what's good for *them*.

But third-party responses to employees' pleas cannot rectify the real harm created by bosses' messages of exclusion. Restrictive legislation, tax incentives for responsible behavior, and tax disincentives for irresponsible behavior amount to coercion and bribery. If successful, they will compel the desired boss behavior without remedying deficiencies in organizational identification, because employees will easily recognize that their bosses' behaviors are attributable to external constraint, not genuine intent; *They* are being forced to include *us;* therefore, why should *we* choose to include *them?*

Employee commitment cannot be legislated any more than it can be bought. The framing is wrong. No one will interpret coerced or instrumental managerial efforts as messages of inclusion. These efforts will not erect bonds of *we* between employees and their employers. And, if no one is watching, they will never cause employees who are leaving their company's premises late at night to make even small detours in order to help by turning out the lights.

14

Developing Emotional Intelligence

Richard E. Boyatzis
Scott N. Taylor

lena was upset. She was snapping at people and felt out of sorts. She had not slept well the night before. Even though she was CFO of a large corporation in Moscow, something in the prior day's seminar bothered her. She had been considering how to improve her leadership style through developing more emotional intelligence. The instructor had explained that such efforts were short-lived if not anchored in a personal vision. Sometime after lunch, it dawned on Elena what was so troubling. She did not know what she wanted out of life. She does not dream about the future and so found it difficult if not impossible to conceive of a personal vision.

It certainly was not because she did not have a bright future. She was among the elite in her country. But she had trained and entered corporate life in Russia 20 years earlier, under a regime with different assumptions about possibilities in life and a career. Elena had trouble creating excitement about a future for the organization, which left her subordinates also frustrated. She had learned to not dream about the future, but react to things as they occurred. It had shaped her approach to leadership. This reactive style was not working well.

There are millions of Elenas working in organizations throughout the world. They want to be better managers and leaders, but are puzzled as to how to reach that elusive goal. With the best of intentions, they attend training programs, get MBAs, and hire consultants and coaches to help. And yet, the degree of change is often small. They feel compelled to throw more resources into training or slowly develop a belief that great managers and leaders are born not made. True, management of our organizations seems better than it was decades ago. But it is a sobering observation that the return on this massive investment in management and leadership development is small. If the outcomes were subjected to a rigorous utility analysis, a prudent businessperson would liquidate or divest the effort.

A growing body of research has helped us to discover a process that yields sustained behavioral change. These improvements provide hope and evidence that people can develop as managers and leaders. They can develop the abilities, or competencies, that matter the most to outstanding performance—the ones we call *emotional intelligence*. Although the process appears to be common sense, it is not common practice.

Can a Person Grow and Develop their Talent?

Decades of research on the effects of psychotherapy,[1] self-help programs,[2] cognitive behavior therapy,[3] training programs,[4] and education[5,6] have shown that people can change their behavior, moods, and self-image. But most of the studies focused on a single characteristic, like maintenance of sobriety, reduction in a specific anxiety, or a set of characteristics often determined by the assessment instrument, such as the scales of the Minnesota Multiphasic Personality Inventory. For example, the impact of Achievement Motivation Training was a dramatic increase in small business success, with people creating more new jobs, starting more new businesses, and paying more taxes than comparison groups.[7,8] The impact of Power Motivation Training was improved maintenance of sobriety.[9] But there are few studies showing sustained improvements in the sets of desirable behavior that lead to outstanding performance.

The "honeymoon effect" of typical training programs might start with improvement immediately following the program, but within months it drops precipitously.[10] Only 15 programs were found in a global search of the literature by the Consortium on Research on Emotional Intelligence in Organizations to improve emotional intelligence. Most of them showed impact on job outcomes, such as number of new businesses started, or life outcomes, such as finding a job or satisfaction,[11] which are the ultimate purpose of development efforts. But showing an impact on outcomes, while desired, may also blur *how* the change actually occurs. Furthermore, when a change has been noted, a question about the sustainability of the change is raised because of the relatively short time periods studied.

The few published studies examining improvement of more than one of these competencies show an overall improvement of about 10% in emotional intelligence abilities three to 18 months following training.[12,13,14,15,16] More recent meta-analytic studies and utility analyses confirm that significant changes can and do occur, but not with the impact that the level of investment would lead us to expect nor with many types of training.[17,18,19]

There are, undoubtedly, other studies that were not found and reviewed, or not available through journals and books and, therefore, overlooked. We do not claim this to be an exhaustive review, but suggestive of the percentage improvement as a rough approximation of the real impact. This approximation is offered to help in the comparison of relative impact of management training, management education, and self-directed learning.

The results appear no better from standard MBA programs, where there is no attempt to enhance emotional intelligence abilities. The best data here come from a research project by the American Assembly of Collegiate Schools of Business. They found that the behavior of graduating students from two highly ranked business schools, compared with their levels when they began their MBA training, showed only improvements of 2% in the skills of emotional intelligence.[20] In fact, when students from four other high-ranking MBA programs were assessed on a range of tests and direct behavioral measures, they showed a gain of 4% in self-awareness and self-management abilities, but a *decrease* of 3% in social awareness and relationship management.[21,22]

A series of longitudinal studies underway at the Weatherhead School of Management of Case Western Reserve University have shown that people can change on a complex set of competencies that we call emotional intelligence. These competencies distinguish outstanding performers in management and professions, and the improvement lasted for years. A visual comparison of the percentage improvement in behavioral measures of emotional intelligence from different samples is shown in Figure 14–1. MBA students, averaging 27 years old at entry into the program, showed dramatic changes on videotaped and audiotaped behavioral samples and questionnaire measures of these competencies, as summarized in Tables 14–1 and 14–2, as a result of the competency-based, outcome-oriented MBA program implemented in 1990.[23,24,25]

Four cadres of full-time MBA students graduating in 1992, 1993, 1994, and 1995 showed a 47% improvement on self-awareness competencies such as self-confidence, and on self-management competencies such as the drive to achieve and adaptability, in the one to two years to graduation compared with when they first entered. When it came to social awareness and relationship management skills, improvements were even greater: 75% on competencies such as empathy and team leadership.

Meanwhile, with the part-time MBA students graduating in 1994, 1995, and 1996, the dramatic improvement was found again, in these students who typically take three to five years to graduate. These groups showed 28% improvement in self-awareness and self-management competencies and 56% improvement in social awareness and social skills competencies by the end of their MBA program.

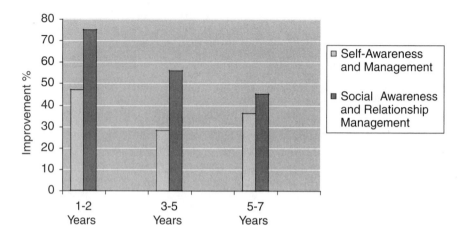

Figure 14–1   Percentage improvement of emotional intelligence competencies of different groups of MBA graduates taking the self-directed learning course.

That's not all. Jane Wheeler tracked down groups of these part-timers two years *after* they had graduated. Even after all that time, they still showed improvements in the same range: 36% on the self-awareness and self-management competencies and 45% on the social awareness and relationship management competencies. This is in contrast to MBA graduates of the Weatherhead School of Management of the 1988 and 1989 traditional full-time and part-time programs, who showed improvement in substantially fewer of the competencies.

The positive effects of this program were not limited to MBAs. In a longitudinal study of four classes completing the Professional Fellows Program (an executive education program at the Weatherhead School of Management) showed that these 45- to 55-year-old professionals and executives improved on self-confidence, leadership, helping, goal setting, and action skills. These were 67% of the emotional intelligence competencies assessed in this study.[26]

Self-Directed Learning

What these studies have shown is that adults learn what they want to learn. Other things, even if acquired temporarily (e.g., for a test), are soon forgotten.[27] Students, children, patients, clients, and subordinates may act as if they care about learning something, and go through the motions, but they

Table 14–1 Value Added to Full-Time Students from the Old versus the New MBA Programs

| | Old Program | | | New Program | | |
Evidence of Value Added	Self-Management	Social Awareness and Management	Analytic Reasoning	Self-Management	Social Awareness and Management	Analytic Reasoning
Strong	Self-confidence		Use of concepts Systems thinking Quantitative analysis Use of technology Written communication	Efficiency orientation Planning Initiative Flexibility Self-confidence	Social objectivity Networking Oral communication Empathy Group management	Use of concepts Systems thinking Pattern recognition Written communication Quantitative analysis Use of technology
Some	Efficiency orientation Initiative Flexibility	Empathy Networking Social objectivity		Self-control Attention to detail	Developing others Persuasiveness Negotiating	
None	Planning (attention to detail and self-control were not coded)	Persuasiveness Negotiating Group management Developing others Oral communication				
Negative			Pattern recognition (verbal)			

229

Table 14-2 Value Added to Part-Time Students from the Old versus the New MBA Programs

Evidence of Value Added	Old Program			New Program		
	Self-Management	Social Awareness and Management	Analytic Reasoning	Self-Management	Social Awareness and Management	Analytic Reasoning
Strong	Flexibility		Systems thinking Quantitative analysis	Efficiency orientation Initiative Flexibility Attention to detail Self-confidence	Group management Social objectivity Networking Oral communication Developing others Negotiating	Use of concepts Written communication Use of technology Pattern recognition Quantitative analysis Systems thinking
Some	Efficiency orientation	Negotiating Social objectivity	Written communication	Planning	Empathy Persuasiveness	
None	Self-confidence Planning Initiative (attention to detail and self-control were not coded)	Persuasiveness Oral communication Networking Group management Developing others	Use of concepts Pattern recognition	Self-control		
Negative		Empathy	Use of technology			

230

proceed to disregard it or forget it—unless, it is something that they want to learn. This does not include changes induced, willingly or not, by chemical or hormonal changes in one's body. But even in such situations, the interpretation of the changes and the behavioral comportment following it will be affected by the person's will, values, and motivations.

In this way, it appears that most, if not all, sustainable behavioral change is intentional. Self-directed change is an intentional change in an aspect of who you are (the real) or who you want to be (the ideal), or both. Self-directed learning is self-directed change in which you are aware of the change and understand the process of change.

The process of self-directed learning is shown graphically in Figure 14–2.[28,29,30] This is an enhancement of the earlier models developed by Kolb, Winter, Berlew, and Boyatzis between 1968 and 1971.[31,32,33,34,35]

The description and explanation of the process in this chapter is organized around five points of discontinuity. A person might begin self-directed learning at any point in the process, but it will often begin when the person experiences a discontinuity and the associated epiphany, or a moment of awareness and a sense of urgency.

This model describes the process as designed into a required course, and the elements of the MBA and executive programs implemented in

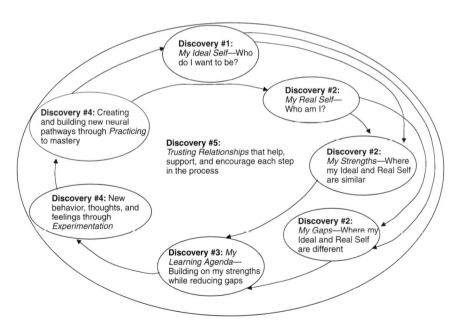

Figure 14–2 Boyatzis' theory of self-directed learning.

1990 at the Weatherhead School of Management. Experimentation and research into the various components have resulted in refinement of these components and the model as discussed in this chapter. For a detailed description of the course, read Boyatzis.[36,37]

The First Discontinuity: Catching Your Dreams, Engaging Your Passion

Franklin is wrestling with redirecting his career for an old reason. He has been executive director of a foundation for 10 years. Donors, program recipients, and policy makers consider him a distinctive success within the foundation world. His emotional intelligence is considered a model to be emulated by others, as is his incisive intellect. And yet he is restless. During a coaching session that was part of an assessment and development program, he identified two possible career paths for the future: He could leverage his expertise and join a larger, global foundation as executive director, or he could become an executive for a company. The attraction of corporate life would be higher compensation.

When asked if he was feeling pressure from his family about money, Franklin said, "Not at all." Asked why he considered leaving the arena he felt passionate about—with a deep sense of social mission—and if there were any challenges a company can give him that he did not feel in a foundation, he looked toward the ceiling and shook his head. He realized that he was reacting to the frustrations of his current situation. Once free of considering "doing time" or "paying his dues" in a company as a desirable option, he began to brainstorm ideas for adding to his personal income while leading foundations. He thought of expanding his writing to include books and giving speeches as ways to supplement his income.

Franklin was having trouble identifying his ideal work for the future. His deep, inner commitment to the nonprofit world was ignored in considering the attractiveness of the private sector. But these attractions were things others found desirable, not Franklin. The first discontinuity and potential starting point for the process of self-directed learning is the discovery of who you want to be. Our ideal self is an image of the person we want to be. It emerges from our ego ideal, dreams, and aspirations. The last 20 years has revealed literature supporting the power of positive imaging or visioning in sports psychology, meditation and biofeedback research, and other psycho-physiological research. It is believed that the potency of focusing one's thoughts on the desired end state of condition is driven by the emotional components of the brain.[38]

This research indicates that we can access and engage deep emotional commitment and psychic energy if we engage our passions and conceptually catch our dreams in our ideal self-image. It is an anomaly that we know the importance of consideration of the ideal self, and yet often, when engaged in a change or learning process, we skip over the clear formulation or articulation of our ideal self-image. If a parent, spouse, boss, or teacher tells us something that should be different, they are telling us about the person *they* want us to be. As adults, we often allow ourselves to be anesthetized to our dreams and lose sight of our deeply felt ideal self.

The Second Discontinuity: Am I a Boiling Frog?

Joe started a doctoral program to propel him into his new life. His friends and family thought he was crazy. He owned and ran three healthcare companies, a nursing home, a temporary service agency specializing in health workers, and a small consulting practice. The nursing home had some problems including cash flow and a quarrelsome partner. It was not clear who was the antagonist between the two partners, but the relationship felt like a bad marriage staying together "for the children." He began teaching management part-time at a local university and loved it. The university made him a full-time faculty member. He was pursuing an executive doctorate in management to refine his research and writing skills. This is a doctoral program designed for scholar-practitioners with typically 20 or more years of work experience, of which at least 10 are in management or leadership positions.

He loved the program but was running himself ragged with all of the responsibilities. When Richard Boyatzis asked him, "Joe, what do you most want to be doing in 5 to 10 years?," Joe did not hesitate, "I love teaching. I would like to contribute through writing. I can translate complex concepts into language that people understand. I would love to do some research and test my ideas. But mostly, I love teaching."

"Why are you keeping all these businesses?"

He turned with a questioning look, "What do you mean?"

Pointing to the draft of his essay on his desired future, Professor Boyatzis clarified, "You are a full-time faculty member. You want to be a full-time faculty member. You want to spend more time writing and doing some research. You are currently in a doctoral program. And yet, you are still involved in running three businesses. Don't you think this is too much? Haven't you made a choice already as to which you want? So why the ambivalence?"

He listed the contractual complications and financial implications lead-ing to his conclusion that he must continue all three businesses. But then he added, "I have considered handing the temporary services business to my son, and letting the consulting business drop away to nothing by just not taking any new projects." Once provoked in this way, he started to consider speeding the timeline. He brainstormed a few steps that would remove him from running the nursing home within a year, and from ownership of the nursing home within two years. Nodding his head with a growing smile, Joe said, "This could work. This could really work! Boy oh boy, do I look for-ward to two years from now!"

Joe had changed but was confusing his old self with the person he had become. Joe knew that he was not as exciting a leader in his businesses as he had been in the past; while in the classroom, he engaged students using his humor and playfulness. Facing his real self, looking in the mirror was difficult.

The awareness of the current self, the person whom others see and with whom they interact, is elusive. For normal reasons, the human psyche pro-tects itself from the automatic "intake" and conscious realization of all information about ourselves. These ego-defense mechanisms serve to pro-tect us. They also conspire to delude us into an image of who we are that feeds on itself, becomes self-perpetuating, and eventually may become dys-functional.[39]

The greatest challenge to an accurate current self-image (e.g., seeing yourself as others see you and consistent with other internal states, beliefs, emotions, etc.) is the boiling frog syndrome. It is said that dropping a frog into a pot of boiling water will result in it immediately jumping out. But place a frog in a pot of cool water, and gradually raise the temperature to boiling, and the frog will remain in the water until it is cooked.

Several factors contribute to us becoming boiling frogs. First, people around you may not let you see a change. They may not give you feedback or information about how they see it. Also, they may be victims of the boil-ing frog syndrome themselves, as they adjust their perception on a daily basis. Second, enablers—those forgiving the change, frightened of it, or who do not care—may allow it to pass unnoticed.

For a person to truly consider changing a part of himself or herself, you must have a sense of what you value and want to keep. These areas in which your real self and ideal self are consistent or congruent can be con-sidered *strengths*. Likewise, to consider what you want to preserve about yourself involves admitting aspects of yourself that you wish to change or adapt in some manner. Areas where your real self and ideal self are not con-sistent can be considered *gaps*.

All too often, people explore growth or development by focusing on the gaps or deficiencies. Organizational training programs and managers conducting annual reviews often make this mistake. There is an assumption that we can "leave well enough alone" and get to the areas that need work. It is no wonder that many of these programs or procedures intended to help a person develop result in the individual feeling battered, beleaguered, and bruised, not helped, encouraged, motivated, or guided.

There are four major "learning points" from the first two discontinuities in the self-directed learning process: (a) engage your passion and create your dreams; (b) know thyself; (c) identify or articulate both your strengths—those aspects of yourself you want to preserve—and your gaps or discrepancies of your real and ideal selves—those aspects of yourself you want to adapt or change; and (d) keep your attention on both characteristics, forces, or factors—do not let one become the preoccupation.

The fourth learning point—keeping a balanced attention on your strengths and gaps—ensures you are not becoming "weighed down" with your gaps or overly confident with your strengths. Further, it encourages you to leverage your strengths in an effort to minimize your gaps.

All of these learning points can be achieved by finding and using multiple sources for feedback about your ideal self, real self, strengths, and gaps. The sources of insight into your real self can include systematically collecting information from others, such as the 360-degree feedback currently considered fashionable in organizations. Other sources of insight into your real self, strengths, and gaps may come from behavioral feedback through videotaped or audiotaped interactions, such as collected in assessment centers. Various psychological tests can help you determine or make explicit inner aspects of your real self, such as values, philosophy, traits, motives, and such.

Sources for insight into your ideal self are more personal and more elusive than those for the real self. Various exercises and tests can help by making explicit various dreams or aspirations you have for the future. Talking with close friends or mentors can help. Allowing yourself to think about your desired future, not merely your prediction of your most likely future, is the biggest obstacle. These conversations and explorations must take place in psychologically safe surroundings because in such settings, you are less likely to be inhibited from really exploring your dreams and aspirations.

The Third Discontinuity: Mindfulness through a Learning Agenda

Karen was describing her career goals during an MBA class. At 27, she was energetic, poised, and ready to take on the world. She identified her long-term career goal to buy or open an art gallery in Chicago or in another big

Midwestern city. When asked why an art gallery, she admitted with embarrassment that she loved art but could not paint or sculpt.

Karen explained that she would approach her career goal by working for a large bank for a number of years to learn more about finance, not to mention make some money. Others in her class thought it made sense until the professor said, "So in order to learn to be an entrepreneur in the arts, you want to work in a large, bureaucratic organization that values conformity, where most people wear gray or blue suits with red ties or scarves, and managers demand adherence to policies, rules, and regulations? In this environment, you might extinguish the entrepreneurial spirit and confidence that you have and need to run an art gallery successfully."

Karen's original draft of her learning plan would not have led to her desired future. She had absorbed an image from her reference group of fellow students and her general image of business—she thought she needed to master finance to be an entrepreneur. MBA mythology has placed banks as one of the best places to work to master finance. So Karen had written her original plan to work in an organization that was not of interest to her. Later conversations with her professor resulted in a learning plan more directly aimed at a future toward which she had passionate commitment.

The third discontinuity in self-directed learning is development of an agenda and focusing on the desired future. While performance at work or happiness in life may be the eventual consequence of our efforts, a learning agenda focuses on development. A learning orientation arouses a positive belief in one's capability and the hope of improvement. This results in people setting personal standards of performance, rather than normative standards that merely mimic what others have done.[40] Meanwhile, a performance orientation evokes anxiety and doubts about whether or not we can change.[41]

As part of one of the longitudinal studies at the Weatherhead School of Management, Leonard showed that MBAs who set goals desiring to change on certain competencies changed significantly on those competencies as compared to other MBAs.[42] Previous goal-setting literature had shown how goals affected certain changes on specific competencies,[43] but had not established evidence of behavioral change on a comprehensive set of competencies that constitute emotional intelligence.

The major learning point from this section crucial in self-directed learning is: *Create your own, personal learning agenda.*

A major threat to effective goal setting and planning is that people are already busy and cannot add anything else to their lives. In such cases, the only success with self-directed change and learning occurs if people can determine what to say "no" to and stop some current activities in their lives to make room for new activities.

Another potential challenge or threat is the development of a plan that calls for a person to engage in activities different from their preferred learning style or learning flexibility.[44,45] In such cases, a person commits to activities, or action steps in a plan that require a learning style that is not their preference or not within their flexibility. When this occurs, a person becomes demotivated and often stops the activities, or becomes impatient and decides that the goals are not worth the effort.

The Fourth Discontinuity: Metamorphosis

Bob wanted to build a portfolio of manufacturing companies in which he would have significant ownership and meaningful involvement in the management. A passive approach to providing venture capital was not enough. But Bob knew he was often impatient and not as sensitive to others as he would like. He wanted to develop a style that was collaborative with others, not one focused on simply managing them. Too many companies acquired by venture capitalists languish from inattention or falter from too much "help." Bob said, "An owner will be reluctant to sell his or her business to someone with whom they have a poor rapport, and the envisioned 'advisory group' will become dysfunctional." So he wanted to build his empathy and patience with others as a stepping stone to a more collaborative leadership style.

To experiment with this enhanced or new talent in understanding others, he decided to start with an opportunity closer to home—actually, *at* home. Bob's relationship with two of his children, in particular his two daughters, should be more fun and supportive than it had been recently. He saw a way to work on his leadership style while rebuilding family relationships.

Bob declared a learning goal to "identify an activity of mutual interest that I can do with my daughters on a routine basis (i.e., two or three times a month)." He knew they had expressed interest in two sports: golf and horseback riding. Bob talked to his daughters; more important, he opened up the possibility and listened to their responses. They then set up a schedule to go riding and golfing on a monthly basis. He committed to watching movies with them that they wanted to see and even watching MTV with them.

The fourth discontinuity is to experiment and practice desired changes. Acting on the plan and toward the goals involves numerous activities. These are often made in the context of experimenting with new behaviors. Typically following a period of experimentation, the person practices the new behaviors in actual settings within which they wish to use them, such as at work or at home. During this part of the process, self-directed change and learning begins to look like a "continuous improvement" process.

To develop or learn new behavior, the person must find ways to learn more from current, or ongoing experiences. That is, the experimentation and practice does not always require attending courses or a new activity. It may involve trying something different in a current setting, reflecting on what occurs, and experimenting further in the same setting. Sometimes, this part of the process requires finding and using opportunities to learn and change. People may not even think they have changed until they have tried new behavior in a work or real-world setting.

Dreyfus studied managers of scientists and engineers who were considered superior performers.[46] Once she documented that they used considerably more of certain abilities than their less-effective counterparts, she pursued how they developed some of those abilities. One of the distinguishing abilities was group management, also called team building. She found that many of these middle-aged managers had first experimented with team-building skills in high school and college, in sports, clubs, and living groups. Later, when they became bench scientists and engineers working on problems in relative isolation, they still pursued using and practicing of this ability in activities outside of work. They practiced team building and group management in social and community organizations, such as 4-H Clubs, and professional associations in planning conferences and such.

The experimentation and practice are most effective when they occur in conditions in which the person feels safe.[47] This sense of psychological safety creates an atmosphere in which the person can try new behavior, perceptions, and thoughts with relatively less risk of shame, embarrassment, or serious consequences of failure.

The Fifth Discontinuity: Relationships that Enable Us to Learn

Our relationships are an essential part of our environment. The most crucial relationships are often a part of groups that have particular importance to us. These relationships and groups give us a sense of identity, guide us as to what is appropriate and "good" behavior, and provide feedback on our behavior. In sociology, they are called reference groups. These relationships create a context within which we interpret our progress on desired changes, assess the utility of new learning, and even contribute significant input to formulation of the ideal.[48]

In this sense, our relationships are mediators, moderators, interpreters and sources of feedback, support, and permission of change and learning. They may also be the most important source of protection from relapses or returning to our earlier forms of behavior. In 1999, Wheeler analyzed the extent to which Weatherhead MBA graduates worked on their goals in multiple "life spheres" (e.g., work, family, recreational groups, etc.).[49] In a two-year follow-up study of two of the graduating classes of part-time MBA students, she found those who worked on their goals and plans in multiple sets of relationships improved the most and more than those working on goals in only one setting, such as work or within one relationship.

In a study of the impact of the year-long executive development program for doctors, lawyers, professors, engineers, and other professionals mentioned earlier, Ballou et al. found that participants gained self-confidence during the program. Even at the beginning of the program, others would say these participants were very high in self-confidence. It was a curious finding. The best explanation came from follow-up questions to the graduates of the program. They explained the evident increase in self-confidence as an increase in the confidence to change. Their existing reference groups (e.g., family, groups at work, professional groups, community groups) all had an investment in them staying the same, but meanwhile the person wanted to change. The Professional Fellows Program allowed them to develop a new reference group that encouraged change.

Based on social identity, reference group, and now relational theories, our relationships both meditate and moderate our sense of who we are and who we want to be. We develop or elaborate our ideal self from these contexts. We label and interpret our real self from these contexts. We interpret and value strengths (i.e., aspects considered our core that we wish to preserve) from these contexts. We interpret and value gaps (i.e., aspects considered weaknesses or things we wish to change) from these contexts.

The major learning points from the fourth and fifth discontinuities critical in self-directed learning process are as follows: (a) experiment and practice and try to learn more from your experiences, (b) find settings in which you feel psychologically safe within which to experiment and practice, and (c) develop and use your relationships as part of your change and learning process.

Concluding Thought

Adults can develop emotional intelligence. Our research with professionals and graduate students has confirmed this finding. Adults can develop the abilities that are vital to outstanding performance in management, leadership, and many other occupations and professions. As leaders and managers, we can only create environments in which others want to use their capabilities and emotional intelligence if we ourselves are authentic and consistent in our own demonstration of these behaviors. Through the self-directed learning process, we have the opportunity to truly make a difference by developing emotional intelligence in ourselves. And then by extension, to help others develop them. Whether applied in universities or companies, government agencies or nonprofits, this process can help us coach each other to create the social environments we want and find so conducive to making a difference.

15

What Stays the Same

Nigel Nicholson

The Challenge—Managing the Human Animal in the 21st Century

- How is it that despite the work of Richard Beckhard and like-minded practitioner-scholars that brought such great sophistication to the practice, change management continues to be so difficult to achieve satisfactorily?
- Why is the art of managing people such a challenge for us when we seem so much more advanced in our understanding of people than we were only a few generations ago?
- How is it that our supply of good leaders is so thin when our education systems deliver us so much more talent than they used to?
- Why do disasters caused by human error keep occurring, even though our technological safeguards are ever more sophisticated?
- What makes people continue to be so parochial and tribal when business is becoming more global and networked?
- How is that even when we know what is right and rational and in everyone's collective shared interests, people persist in selfish, shortsighted, and irrational behaviors?

The bulk of this book is rightly concerned with the momentous challenges and changes we face at the dawn of a new century. My offering will only deviate from this theme in one respect—it sets against the whirlwind of change blowing through global business culture the idea that many features of human existence remain unaltered, and it is these that make us subject to the shortcomings I have just listed. For what stays the same is human nature. If we persist in trying to squeeze the human foot into the badly designed organizational shoe, we'll continue to hobble, stumble, and complain our way into the future. So let's look at the obvious alternative—how can we shape the shoe to fit the foot? The enormous challenges we face are also choices. What strategies can we enact to accommodate what we know about the human animal?

It has been my mission for the past six years or so to introduce to business the powerful new ideas of evolutionary psychology.[1] This is the collective name for the rapid advances in understanding brought to us by scholars revisiting, testing, and extending Charles Darwin's revolutionary insight of 150 years ago. It is true to say this presents nothing less than the most radical challenge to our ways of thinking about human existence and society since the time of Plato.

Human Nature, Culture, and Environment— Collision or Combination?

My concern in this chapter is the implications of the idea that there is potentially a collision between what stays the same—evolution's preprogrammed maturation and functioning of human brains—and what is changing with ever increasing rapidity—economy, demography, and ecology. Between the rock of our unchanging nature and the blizzard of social change lies the landscape we call culture. Culture is one of the most difficult concepts in our language—used to denote a mix of tangible and intangible differences between every kind of social unit. In groups it is used to denote the climate and norms. In organizations it is "the way we do things around here." In states and ethnic groups it is the predominant belief and value systems. At each level it embraces what lies on the surface— expressed values, rules of conduct, use of language—and what lies at deeper levels—implicit assumptions about the world, relationships, and the nature of reality itself.

Culture is the collective expression of human needs and actions, so it sits like a landscape over the bedrock of our psychology.[2] In geomorphology, the mainly invariant underlying substrata limit the types of landforms that can emerge, yet within these limitations landscapes adapt to local environmental conditions, such as climate, flora, and fauna. The relationship between culture and these local conditions is two-way, for landscape also affects climate and ecology. Deforest a country and the rains go away. The study of anthropology shows us a parallel relationship between the bedrock of human nature, the landforms of culture, and the local weather conditions of the economic environment. Cultural forms (e.g., marriage and inheritance laws) are adaptive to local circumstances, such as population pressures, war, famine, natural hazards, and life expectancy. This is why river peoples' and mountain peoples' cultures differ in quite patterned ways.[3] Moreover, the cultural solutions people have found to the adaptive demands they face also can mitigate and alter the demands. Mating systems and customs shape demography, for example.

So wondrous are the variations we have seen throughout history and across regions, it is easy to forget how many common features they share.[4] We are greatly impressed by cultural variations because they are "in your face," and because one of the prime sensitivities we have been equipped with is to be aware of them. Adapting to local cultures is one of the prime skills required by us as the most social of animals to survive and prosper. But actually, when you get used to a new culture, as any migrant will tell you, one finds the same things being done with a different accent, costume, and color, rather than a variation in substance.[5]

All cultures must ultimately follow the unswerving edict of genetically encoded human desires and demands. No society exists that does not provide opportunities for men and women to mate, for males to play competitive games, for women to engage in cooperative caring, for group projects and entertainments to be staged, and a host of other functions that have been observed and documented.[6] Some social experiments, such as the repressions of extreme forms of socialism, military dictatorship, and religious fundamentalism, can get by for a while, but in the end they cannot cohere or resist the persistence of human demands. The converse is true of idealistic communities such as the *kibbutzim*, where the model of total egalitarianism and communal childrearing proved to be unsustainable. For centuries our ancient impulses have been undermining our dream palaces. Our basic instincts erupt when we least want them to. We persist in all kinds of errors and idiocies despite our best intentions.

What has all this to do with business? A great deal. Many of the challenges of management and leadership lie in this domain. How can we tame the human animal so that he or she will perform according to the rigors and restraints of being disciplined, organized, predictable, consistent, and all the other things we need to make our trains run on time, our healthcare to be reliable, and our newly purchased automobiles to perform to specification? How we organize is critical, for organizations are cultural forms in the landscape of history; they are designed to be adaptive to the environmental demands—the business climate, stakeholders, competitive forces, economic trends, regulatory regimes, and technological innovations.[7] The field of strategic management is largely concerned with how to get these adaptations right, and how easy it is to get them wrong. This analysis is often rather one-sided, as it the human prerequisites can be taken for granted, or will readily adapt to whatever is needed. As we know, the best-laid strategies typically fall apart at the point where human judgement and action are required most intensively, usually at the point of implementation.[8] It is the irrational drivers of human nature that derail the rational engine of organization and economy.

Perhaps because of the supervening power of the old 19th- and 20th-century technologies, we have gotten used to man being the slave to the machine and expecting some psychological casualties from the march of progress. But we are now in a different world. Until recently there were few alternatives to the machine model of office or factory. Now our technologies are liberating us to think more openly about how we might organize, and it behooves us to be a bit more active, knowing, and wise about our choices, especially in light of what we now know about what stays the same: the major constraint of human nature. And this is a subject on which we can now truly claim we have a hard science-based perspective, with a powerful theory, a rapidly accumulating store of reliable knowledge, and experience of successful and failed applications of change.

The Scientific Foundations of the New Darwinism

So let us sketch out the field and the forces arrayed within it, and what this means for business leaders. In a nutshell, evolutionary psychology says three things.

- It reminds us that we are truly animals, clan dwelling hunter-gatherers who evolved to fill a new environmental niche that emerged during a global cooling period around five million years ago. We have a very refined genetic profile[9]—there is less difference between any two humans, say, an aboriginal and a Wall Street banker, than between any two chimpanzees. This is due to a cataclysmic narrowing of our gene pool caused by an environmentally triggered population collapse around 60,000 years ago (probably a short "nuclear" winter caused by a massive volcanic eruption).
- The cornerstone of much social philosophy and psychology of the last century is a big falsehood—the idea that the human capacity for learning means we can endlessly reinvent ourselves, socially engineer whatever we can imagine, and

shape the identity of our young as we please. We can only do these things to the extent that our nature will allow, for far from coming into the world with minds as naked as our bodies, we arrive with a well-stocked brain, brimming with biases, needs, routines, and skills. Many of these are programmed to emerge on a timed schedule—like language—when we most need them.[10] Evolution does not leave to chance or to the labor of learning what the survival of previous generations has shown each new member of species will need to survive and reproduce.

- For most of our existence this psychological design was in close congruence with our economy and lifestyle as hunter-gatherers, but then a short while ago—around 10,000 years—the world changed. A warming period at the end of the Ice Age created a new problem of population pressures through a rising sea level and loss of savanna, which agriculture and fixed settlements solved by feeding more mouths efficiently. The rapid march of what we call civilization followed this.[11] The incontrovertible key corollary to this is the fact that we stopped evolving long before we started building cities and organizations. There has been far too little time and no consistent pressure to change our basic psychology, forged over five million years, and fully formed 250,000 years ago. We may have taken ourselves out of the Stone Age, but we have not taken the Stone Age out of ourselves.

So what do we have to contend with as we move forward? Here's a short summary of what is on one side of the equation—the key features of our evolved psychological design.

The Nature of Human Nature

The "hardwiring" of human nature is a mixture of structures and capacities that emerge, more or less automatically, as we grow in and beyond the womb. Most basic needs and a bunch of cognitive capacities, such as face recognition and the production of language, fall into this category. Our toolkit also includes a series of biases for programmability—things that we will readily learn if given an appropriate environment. Many of our more social motives and potentialities, such as the capacity for loving relation-ships or our striving for status, develop in this way. Nature and nurture are not opposing forces. Nurture makes possible the expression of nature and gives it form.

Here is a brief overview of what we know about the evolved psychology of the human animal.

Drives

Many are concerned with what we can call self-regulation—getting what we want and what we need to survive and prosper. This gives our drives a strong "selfish" character—appetites for gratification and reward. Evolutionary theory shows us that one of the most important is status, for the benefits it brings are fundamental to the destiny of ourselves and our off-spring.[12] But greater than the desire for self-advancement is the power of fear. Fear of loss and failure will always trump other values when these devils are aroused, as they so easily are. As my colleagues and I have shown in our studies of finance traders, loss aversion has a major capacity to distort judgement and bias action.[13] In fact, it does so implicitly, even when not aroused—people's attitudes to change, for example, are full of fearful imaginings about downside risk.

Individual Differences

Advances in behavior genetics and neuroscience have confirmed what many people knew intuitively, but was a source of controversy because of its "political incorrectness": This is the idea that people are born different, with genetically encoded personality biases, cognitive skills, and physical attributes that seriously bias their life chances—in terms of achievement and partnership opportunities.[14] Moreover, men and women differ across the whole range of these because of their need for different life strategies to fulfill their personal and genetic destinies.[15]

Ways of Thinking

Our prodigious mental equipment makes us great at learning, adaptable, and quick-witted. But it is hopelessly inadequate at the most simple mathematical, logical, or reasoning tasks. We labor painfully to do sums, think straight, and avoid traps. We make huge errors in every sphere of business life—marketing, strategy, and finance especially—and rely extensively on technical systems to correct our inadequacies. Evolution—because it only looks back to what we have predictably needed, not what we might want in the future—gave us a quite different skill set to survive as hunter-gatherers: intuition, strategic imagination, and pattern recognition. These turn out to be immensely useful in every area of business life—giving us inspired leadership, inventive products and processes, and ingenious problem solving. It is in acts of implementation, where logic, control, cold reason, and detachment are needed, that we let ourselves down.

Social Instincts

It has long been recognized that the human animal is fundamentally social. Weak furless bipeds as we are, we can do almost nothing without the cooperation of others, but once we get together what wonders we can perform—from hunting massive woolly mammoths to building giant corporations. A huge amount of our mental capacity is devoted to the arts of making friends and influencing people, for the most important feature of the environment that humans have to deal with is other humans. We need to be able to attract people to be lovers, friends, and allies, and at the same time we need to be able to deal with those who might be enemies, out to trick and betray us for their own selfish ends. For this reason much of our social life revolves around soap opera politics—games and maneuvers to keep track of who is on our side and who might no longer be.[16]

Community Politics

Ego and reputation are vital to our survival in a social world and we expend a lot of energy gossiping to keep track of the network and our position within it. But our capacities here are limited in two important ways. One is that we were equipped mentally to survive in clans of an optimum size, around 150, corresponding to our cognitive capacities and cooperative needs. Much beyond this size and we can only relate meaningfully to subsets of no more than these dimensions. This is what produces corporate tribalism—the tendency for people to identify with known groups—usually the most local, tangible, and similar to themselves. This last point comes from the second important feature of our community instincts: to support and relate to those with whom we are genetically related—the "blood is thicker than water" phenomenon. In the absence of observable indicators, evolution programs us to prefer people we see as similar to ourselves. We were designed for a world where we could be guaranteed to be likely to interact with others on more than a single occasion—a community where you only enter via birth and exit via death, in which encounters with strangers would be rare events. Much of the flip-flopping we experience between high and low trust, and the way people persistently discriminate against others on the basis of superficial characteristics, springs from the fact that we are surrounded by strangers on whom, from time to time, we must depend.

Natural Magic and Mysticism

This is probably more a byproduct of other gifts—vision, language, self-awareness, emotional and cognitive biases, and so on—than an instinct in its own right, but it clearly has been a constant part of our approach to life since our first beginnings.[17] We respond to powerful symbols. We slip readily into superstitions. We are infatuated by magic. We yearn for charisma. We seek spiritual comfort. Even the most hardened rationalists—who arguably have had these things rigorously schooled out of them—continue to have dreams and impulses that betray these impulses, and respond to powerfully conjured images, despite whatever they say about what they say to the contrary.

Now let's look at the other side of the equation—what might be thrown at us and what we can do about it.

Future Shock? Implications for a 21st Century of Change

Soothsaying is a dangerous game, so I will not try to second-guess the future, but instead consider some of the areas of current speculation and imagination—considering how we might best direct our efforts to keep faith with who we are and minimize the risk of disasters.

Globalization

This is one area where we're already seeing marked effects on how we work and organize. It arouses a range of emotions from people who see the benefits of an ever widening range of possibilities for consumption, production, and exchange, and those who see the power of states being eroded and increased power for businesses to exploit undeveloped economies and the natural environment. These debates are a product of our infatuation with moral dramas and the demonization of each other, plus our dislike of inconsistency. If my position is all good, yours must be all bad. The simplifying of complex truths in an area like this is something that has to be continually countered. Beyond the debates the actual effects of globalization can be overstated. People's local adaptations are not going to be homogenized, for the reasons we have discussed. Local cultures and values—including patterns of production and consumption—will maintain their distinctiveness. Indeed, in a globalizing economy people's desire for local distinctive identity may become more rather than less emphatic, and be a source of political power.

Inequality and Conflict

This is a much greater source of risk. We have left behind a world of economic barriers and military brinksmanship between superpowers; instead, we have a new economic and political order around the global market economy. This has had one marked and highly dangerous consequence—rising wealth inequality within and between economies. These extreme status inequalities are quite new to humans—we are designed for communal clan living—and they weaken social cohesion by increasing levels of envy, mistrust, greed, and alienation. Depressive illness has already become one of the principal afflictions of developed societies.[18] The effects on business are quite direct. They include a general backwash of social stress among employees, and a lessening of loyalty and conscientiousness. People's commitments to their firms have become much more provisional and conditional. Workplace crime and deviance are increasing. One implication is that firms that place low emphasis on internal inequalities can create islands of communitarianism in our unequal societies. Certainly the companies most admired by employees exhibit all the characteristics one finds in true communities—emphasis upon recognition, inclusion, trust, empowerment, and egalitarianism.[19]

Environmental Costs and Catastrophes

Human loss aversion and awareness of the immediacy of effects on succeeding generations are providing a stimulus for action and change, somewhat belatedly in terms of the prolonged neglect of the causes. What economists call "the tragedy of the commons"—named after the self-defeating destruction of grazing land by herders not regulating the consumption of their own animals—is especially a product of societies where people see their interests as divided and mutually exclusive. One of the more hopeful aspects of the new economic order of the present age is a realization of the importance of networks. Not only via the Internet, but in all business dealings the importance of cooperative alliances is rising sharply as a way of gaining competitive advantage. It has become inefficient and costly to have vertically integrated systems and value chains locked within the boundaries of the single corporation. This spirit is one that can be pressed into the service of environmental risk reduction, though it will no doubt require a framework in which governments incentivize social goals. Within businesses there are also risks through the misjudged or mischievous acts of agents of the firm. A spate of high-profile cases in the 1990s showed how lone "rogue traders" can bring venerable and well-heeled businesses to the brink of destruction.[20] Many other catastrophes, such as Bhopal, Chernobyl, the Challenger disaster, plus a range of more everyday marketing or strategic blunders, are the product of the way the mind works, individually and in groups, where people reinforce each others' erroneous views. Human loss aversion has an unfortunate amplifying effect on such errors. It makes learning from failure very difficult because people are concerned about avoiding recurrences, so they draw hasty and wrong conclusions, often with recourse to "magical" wish-fulfillment thinking. Additionally, it leads people into denial and cover-ups to avoid getting blamed.[21] One important way of remedying these deficiencies is to try to improve the way we manage the aftermath of failure—substituting analysis for blame apportionment and trying to change the way in which people routinely treat errors.[22]

Demographic Time Bomb

We face a future in which by 2050, around a third of the population in the developed world will be over 60.[23] The implications stretch in several directions. Economists worry about the costs for benefit systems, but from an organizational point of view there are important challenges to how we manage. At the young end of the working age spectrum the war for talent will intensify, while at the older end there will be increasing redundancy. This will increase the importance of the role of human resources specialists, change the way we think about the concept of the career, and alter how we organize. The stakes will get higher still in the "transfer market" for talent, with headhunters becoming more aggressive in their executive search and deployment strategies. There will also be the challenge of incorporating greater diversity, since the developed economies will be increasingly dependent on immigrant labor to staff their businesses. All of these forces will increase the difficulty of maintaining a sense of community integration in firms, and leaders will need to make a conscious effort to develop policies that help to achieve that end.

Death of the Corporation

People proclaiming the death of the corporation do so prematurely. We should not forget that as long as people require commoditized supply—everything from automobiles to food items, and also in the delivery of services such as healthcare—corporate bureaucracies will be required to produce them to a standard of quality and promptness that cannot be secured by more informal methods of organizing. Yet corporations are changing radically, largely owing to major changes in how their essential elements are sourced. Rather than disappearing, the corporation may become more disassembled, through outsourcing and casualized labor supply.[24] This has major implications for how we reward and influence people. For example, for many it spells the death of the conventional one-company career, and increases the challenges on managers to find alternatives to promotions to incentivize success.[25] With new-form organizations—such as "modular," "hollow," and "virtual" ways of coordinating efforts—new skills are called into play and new ways have to be found to motivate people.[26] Selection and reward systems are going to have to find and encourage people with high tolerance for ambiguity, negotiation, and alliance-building skills, people with high general (rather than technical) intelligence plus verbal gifts; that is, quick-witted, fluent-talking relationship builders. Many more of these will be women, who possess better communications and relationship skills than many men.[27] At the same time, certain kinds of male entrepreneurialism—tough bargainers with flexible minds—will also become more valued. Old time "solid citizens" will still be needed for the "grunt" work of the reformed corporation, but in much fewer numbers. The net effect will be a further erosion of cohesion in the corporation and the need for management to find new ways of building a sense of common purpose.

Virtuality and the Networked Economy

These are overhyped, and increasingly people are recognizing that there are severe limits to what can be achieved through remote and virtual interaction. The boundary is being pushed back as the technology of telecommunications rushes forward, so that an increasingly large amount of business can be done very effectively by these means. A double-edged human gift is our ability to fill in the gaps that these media cannot reproduce. One hazard that has become common in everyday life is that people can be misled into disastrous liaisons with Web mates because the participants impute a breadth and depth to the relationship that reality falls short of. Similarly, almost all of us by now have experienced e-wars raging between correspondents who have read into each other's blunt expressions more ill-will than their authors intended. These effects are caused by the powerful gravitational tug of our instincts for relating and empathy. Improvements in virtual media will help us skirt the worst excesses of the quite crude state of current technologies, but never to the point of complete substitution for face-to-face communications. There are two barriers. One is the irreducibility of human intimacy—in touch, eye contact, bodily presence—which mean that it is not possible to completely virtualize any relationship requiring a handshake or a kiss for bread to be broken or wine to be shared together. The second is the more mundane restriction that where tools have to be shared or objects exchanged, physical presence is a prerequisite. It is for these reasons, more the first set than the last, interestingly, that virtual teams have to meet from time to time to keep up their cohesion and to keep their feet on the same road.[28]

Transformed Roles in the Knowledge Economy

This too has been over-egged as a vision of a future where even jobs as we know them will cease to exist.[29] Increasing numbers of people may be sitting tapping keys at terminals but let us not forget that a hundred years from now people will still be tending plants, herding livestock, handling raw materials, cutting each others' hair, making meals, playing music, traveling, and a host of activities either that cannot be removed by technological innovation or that people will not allow to disappear *because they enjoy them*. It is quite a different kind of truth, however, to assert that knowledge workers will become more powerful as the elite members of our changing society, pushing mere technologists and others into the background. People with intellectual skills have always had advantages in our society but the increasing demand for them will further increase the divisions between the haves and have-nots. In businesses, we can expect to see a microcosm of this, intensifying the separation of the core from the periphery of temporary and casualized routine workers. It will only be by organizations seeing the advantages of building cohesive cultures by embracing all their members as equal in corporate citizenship that the benefits will be claimed.

New Forms of Governance and Leadership

As I have argued elsewhere,[30] we seldom get much better leaders than the ones we deserve, and the supply of quality leaders is so thin because the process of leadership accession is fundamentally "selectionist." This means that not just consciously, but implicitly and unconsciously, people are selected and deselected—and they also select and deselect themselves through their motives to join, stay, and compete—for all the rungs on the ladders leading to leadership. It is the practices and values inherent in the way organizations are structured and run that thins the supply of leadership talent. Qualities needed at the top—like integrity—are all too easily screened out in the middle strata, where qualities like thrusting ambition and political nous are recognized and rewarded. Women, especially, are casualties of the biases in these systems, and of their own lack of interest in submitting to the machismo rituals of leadership politics.[31] And it is because the personal biases relevant to leadership are biogenetically encoded differently not just for men and women but for all of us as individuals that we cannot just pump resources into people on the Pygmalion principle that we can manufacture leaders at will. Similar problems beset us in the area of governance where corporate boards exist mainly for two purposes: as structures for political brokering (to represent and balance different interests) and for decisional prudence (to protect against abuse of power or gross folly). The failures of governance systems to perform these tasks are a function of the infusion of "natural" hot political behaviors into the cool world of institutional decision making. These are well documented as (a) collisions between local and collective identifications, (b) "groupthink" and other failures of interpersonal influence in group decision making, and (c) what Chris Argyris calls "defensive routines" to cover up or avoid confronting contradictions and failures.[32]

Ways Forward to Change

As we enter a new century, how are the risks we have described to be avoided? How can we build systems that are more free from myopia, moral hazard, conflict, and incompetence?

The general theme of the answer is the same as I have been giving throughout this chapter—a mixture of structural and process solutions, guided by the insights of evolutionary psychology. The *structural* solutions are whatever bring us closer to the kinds of communities for which we evolved.

- Small-sized or decentralized units.
- Flexible division of labor according to fitness and motivation.
- Fluid status hierarchies, with low power distance between levels.
- Multiple paths to positions of eminence and leadership.
- Adaptive reward systems that stress collective achievements while providing individual recognition.

The process measures we will need to sustain such systems are those that promote our best instincts while guarding against our impulses and biases that could lead us into danger and difficulty in a fast-moving and sophisticated, changeful world.

- High-involvement, high-trust practices in decision making.
- Continual informal coaching for excellence and changing contribution over the life span.
- Methods for critical examination of decisions made under uncertainty and complexity and where there are high negative costs for the actor(s).

- Encouraging teamwork between people with differing skills, values, and approaches (i.e., avoiding "cloning").
- Recognizing and developing people with the qualities needed for visionary and integrative leadership.

Change Management and Hard-Wired Resistance

It is often and wrongly said that we humans possess an inbuilt and "natural" resistance to change. This is not true. As Richard Beckhard and others have recognized, people willingly accept change if they see it as in their interests and feel they can retain some control over the means of implementation. The problem of change management is that people possess a bunch of illusory beliefs about self and society that derail the process at any of its stages, from conception to implementation. These same beliefs also mean that the insights of evolutionary psychology are often dismissed out of hand, and cannot be readily deployed to help evade the traps we repeatedly fall into. They include the following.

- Rationalism—the sense that with powers of reason we can tame or master the natural world, including our own impulses.
- Utopianism—the idea that we are building generation upon generation toward a world that is not just better materially, but happier.
- Perfectibility—the idea that through social engineering we can eliminate the ills that beset us, such as deviance, crime, drug addiction, and so forth.
- Optimism—the inclination for hope to triumph over experience, as we forget the past and forge on in the belief that the grass will be greener wherever we're headed.
- Overconfidence—the tendency to engage in risky projects, fueled by a belief that we can deal with whatever circumstances may throw at us.
- Pygmalionism—the belief that we can mold any human raw material, if we can get people early enough, into whatever social characters we wish.
- Hubris—the belief that the ego, self, or soul has some mystical transcendent quality, implying that we alone among creatures are immune to the laws of nature by virtue of "free" will.

Let us not forget that this belief set is what is also most noble and wonderful about the human spirit. Possession of these beliefs enables people to triumph over seemingly insuperable odds, to endure trauma and great hardship, and to engage in behaviors that are generous and self-abnegating for the benefit of kith and kin. Yet they underlie our greatest follies. Can we have one without the other? Most of what I have described comes from the gift that humans possess more than any other species—the ability to self-reflect. It is self-reflection that gives us our most grandiose illusions and at the same time allows us to make the widest array of choices.

Armed with insights about what stays the same—our true nature and the limits to change, the tug of the gravitational forces of our psychology, even when we are not aware of them—we can do better to design the shoe to fit the human foot. The self-reflexive gifts that lead us to these delusions are also potentially the means of our liberation. A true view of human nature does not release us from its grip, but it does forewarn and forearm, so we can build organizations fit for humans and school ourselves in practices that can steer us around our own most besetting difficulties.

PART 4
21C ORGANIZATION

O rganizational performance, rather than job security and work satisfaction, became the central thrust of corporate change agents. Dexter Dunphy, distinguished professor at the University of Technology—Sydney, Australia, opens the final part of the book by arguing that the new challenge for change agents is to provide corporate leaders with a blueprint for the way forward as we redesign organizations for the 21st century. He explores the potential of sustainable practices for improving organizational performance, building human capability, contributing to community development, and renewing the biosphere. This is the new task for change agents—to help reshape the organization to achieve outstanding performance that actually contributes to the fulfillment of human needs on a healthy planet. Corporate human sustainability is the contribution of the corporation to developing the capabilities of its workforce members, creating a just, equitable, and healthy workplace, and contributing to the welfare of the external community, particularly those community members who have some stake in the future of the organization.

An organization's culture is the single most sustainable source of competitive advantage. London Business School professor Rob Goffee and visiting professor at INSEAD, France, Gareth Jones explains the importance of the organizational culture that likely to grow as the "hard" integrators in organizations—systems, structures, and careers—decline in significance. They have provided a framework for its analysis, and suggest typical patterns of cultural change. Leadership has a critical role to play as exemplar of culture. But there is more; questions about organizational culture entail a set of moral questions. How are we to live in an age characterized by the pursuit of self-interest? How much will we compromise as individuals to fit in with our organizations? What does work really mean for us? It is naïve to think that any cultural change program or organizational development intervention can avoid these moral questions. For social ties are complex, fragile, and carry meaning for individuals. Changing them, and change we may have to, needs care. Organizational life is not just about how well a company does but how well we live our lives.

Does leadership really matter? W. Warner Burke, professor at Teachers College of Columbia University, addresses this critical question and concludes that leadership *does* matter, particularly in times of significant organizational change. He considers some important characteristics of leadership, such as leadership being a reciprocal relationship between leader and follower, leadership being personal, and leadership being an interaction of leader, follower, and context. Burke devotes most of his chapter to leading organizational change. He uniquely suggests that organizational change is planned linearly but actually occurs in a nonlinear fashion. Even so, it is useful to plan and implement large-scale change according to four broad phases—pre-launch, launch, post-launch, and sustaining the change.

It seems quite clear that a wide array of firms do not possess the capacity to learn and change, what Harvard Business School professor Michael Beer calls *organizational fitness*. Nor do their leaders possess the capacity to develop this capability. What organizational and leadership characteristics reduce organizational fitness? More importantly, what can be done to build organizational fitness? In the final chapter of the book, Beer describes an approach to building organizational fitness, called Organizational Fitness Profiling (OFP), that has its roots in the work of Richard Beckhard, to whom this book is dedicated. Research into the application of OFP at the corporate and business unit level has revealed that senior managers must embrace a number of paradoxes if they are to ensure high performance and survival of their institutions and reputation.

16

The Sustainability of Organizations

Dexter Dunphy

This book is dedicated to the memory of Richard (Dick) Beckhard—a creative contributor to a social movement that has had a significant impact on the nature of modern organizations. Practitioners such as Dick referred to the body of theory they were developing, and their practice, as organization development (OD). However, OD was but one phase in a wider social movement that, in the second half of the 20th century, aimed to change the fundamental character of traditional bureaucratic organizations. My colleague Andrew Griffiths and I have called this broader movement the organizational renewal movement (ORM).[1]

In our book, *The Sustainable Corporation,*[2] we trace the historical genesis and growing influence of ORM. The ORM began in the United States with the emergence of the human relations and OD movements. There was a parallel development in Europe of socio-technical systems (STS) theory and practice, which was closely related to the industrial democracy movement (ID). STS and ID emerged and had the greatest influence in the United Kingdom, Scandinavia, Germany, Holland, and Australia. Both the American and European streams of theory and intervention were a form of incremental humanism; that is, they were informed by liberal humanistic values and designed to make incremental, ameliorative changes in the nature of the prevailing rigid, hierarchical bureaucracies of the time.

However, the ORM underwent a controversial and major reorientation in the late 1970s. This was a time of major political, social, and economic change, and led into world recession. During this time the humanistic values of the movement were challenged. The Japanese, leading the first wave of Asian industrialization, developed very distinctive management strategies and techniques that focused on productivity, quality, and continuous improvement rather than on a humanized workplace. At the same time the globalization of business intensified market competition and dramatically sped up the pace of corporate change.

Some OD practitioners began to realize that the kind of incremental, participative strategies they had been advocating were inadequate to meet these challenges; these strategies were too slow and often did not address the fundamental issues standing in the way of creating flexible, proactive organizations that could deploy resources with speed and agility. There was consequently an increasing advocacy of transformative change strategies (organizational transformation—rather than OD),[3] and of charismatic or even directive leadership. But the critical transformation of the ORM philosophy and methodology came from the increasing link made to corporate strategy. Organizational performance, rather than job security and work satisfaction, became the central thrust of corporate change agents. At the time this was a controversial move for OD practitioners to make and was seen by some as selling out on humanistic values. It had the consequence, however, of making people issues central to the agenda of strategic change and of creating a new profession of human resource managers increasingly represented on senior executive teams. Thanks to this link to strategy, by the end of the 20th century, the ORM and many of its practitioners had come from being heretics outside the corporate walls to occupying a central and influential place in the corporate boardroom and strategic change practice of a variety of organizations.

Partly as a result of this shift, in most leading organizations the old bureaucratic structures were stripped down—hierarchies shortened or turned to networks, decision-making processes sped up, flexible team working was set in place, enlightened human resource processes with high levels of employee involvement were introduced. While remnants of the old organizational order linger on, the world of work is substantially different from how it was around the middle of the past century. The value drivers, however, were more instrumental than humanistic.

This raises the question of whether the work of the OD movement and the wider organizational renewal movement is complete. Perhaps we can look back with satisfaction, praise those such as Richard Beckhard who achieved so much, and declare that the mission has been accomplished. If so, is it time to sit back and relax?

My own answer to this is "no." The challenges organizations are facing in this new century are greater and the need for corporate transformation more critical. The future of humanity and other species on this planet depends on it. And the considerable knowledge and skill acquired by change practitioners will be even more essential to the transformation of our organizational world. The corporation is a relatively new phenomenon in historical terms; in its short history it has been significantly modified several times and is currently undergoing further change. Around the world active thought is going into considering the shape of tomorrow's organizations. Some key groups involved in the re-examination are The Center for Tomorrow's Company, The Prince of Wales Business Leaders Forum, and the New Academy of Business in the United Kingdom and Business for Social Responsibility and the Council on Economic Priorities in the United States.

What is the Nature of the Re-examination and Renewal We Must Undertake Now? And What is the Future Role of the Change Practitioner?

Each century has a central focus—a core-defining issue around which much of the debate, human effort, and conflict swirls. The central focus of last century was economic growth—all major social ideologies favored it—capitalism, communism, and fascism all supported economic growth from industrialization; what they disagreed about was how to distribute the resulting wealth. By the end of last century the issue was resolved in favor of the capitalist solution. The central focus of this century will be sustainability; that is, how to redesign the industrial system—the triumph of the 20th century—to support a just and equitable social order and to sustain rather than damage the biosphere.[4] This is not just the idea of a handful of prophets crying in the wilderness. The authors of a worldwide survey commissioned by the Millennium Project concluded, "Never before has world opinion been so united on a single goal as it is on achieving sustainable development."[5]

There is not space here to review the evidence of the crisis of modern capitalism and its industrial base. However, it is increasingly clear that we cannot continue to plunder and pollute the planet without jeopardizing the future of generations to come. The events of September 11, 2001, emphasized that we live in an interdependent world and that there is no secure fortress for the wealthy to hide from the envy and anger of the starving millions of the world. To survive and thrive on this planet we must create both a viable social fabric for a global society and technologies of wealth creation that enhance the fragile ecology on which life depends. Corporations have played a large part in creating the current problems and so corporations must be part of the solution. The concept around which the new solutions are emerging is sustainability.

What is Sustainability?

Sustainability is a contestable concept—it is more a symbol, a rallying point for a challenge to the dominance of neoliberal economics than a clearly specifiable philosophy. The conflicts in this century, as with economic progress in the last, will be to shape it and to work out its implications for social organization. Nevertheless we can attempt a definition.

Sustainability results from activities that

- Enhance the planet's ability to maintain and renew the viability of the biosphere and protect all living species.
- Enhance society's ability to maintain itself and to solve its major problems.
- Maintain a decent level of welfare for present and future generations of humanity.
- Extend the socially useful life of organizations so that they can contribute resources needed to achieve the aforementioned.

Sustainable organizations engage in these kinds of activities. We can no longer act as if the economy is a separable, independent entity from society and the ecology. Organizations are fundamental cells of the society and the ecology as well as the economy. The growing realization that this is so is leading to a change in the way business does business.[6] Part of this redefinition is coming from social pressures for business to take more responsibility for its impact on the world and partly from new technologies that are already dematerializing production processes and reducing energy consumption. Whatever the causes, business leaders themselves are now providing much of the momentum for the change.

Economic liberalism has been the prevailing philosophy in Western economies in the last 20 years. It is, however, increasingly under challenge for its emphasis on short-term returns and lack of concern for long-term consequences; for its philosophy of "greed is good," which emphasizes material wealth rather than fulfillment and spirituality; for its pursuit of shareholder wealth and neglect of the firm's other important stakeholders; for its penchant for externalizing to the general community the social and ecological costs of business decisions; and for its neglect of the collective good for private gain. A recent trenchant criticism of the exclusive obsession with shareholder interests as against stakeholder interests has been made, for example, by Kennedy in *The End of Shareholder Value*.[7]

So I am arguing here that the new challenge for change agents is to provide corporate leaders with a blueprint for the way forward as we redesign organizations for the 21st century. The OD movement attempted this with some success in the last century; this century demands the development of new strategies to meet the emerging new problems.

Is it Possible to Create Sustainable Enterprises?

To begin the answer to this question, I will briefly outline some of the achievements of a relatively small but important operation in Australia that is part of the worldwide Fuji Xerox Corporation—the Fuji Xerox Eco Manufacturing Center, located in Zetland, Sydney.

As part of instituting a worldwide philosophy of sustainability, Fuji Xerox Corporation moved from selling to leasing office equipment and made a commitment to recycle component parts of their products. Management in Australia saw this as an opportunity and established a new plant, the Eco Manufacturing Center, in 1999. The Eco Manufacturing Center takes used products and reprocesses them and their componentry ready for later reuse in supporting their customers' machines. This is not as simple as it seems because new manufacturing processes are needed to rebuild used equipment that has been subjected to such factors as heat and vibration.

The plant developed the required manufacturing processes and also new technology for diagnosing faults in returned components. As a result of diagnosing faults in parts returned for reprocessing, designs of components are continually improved so that secondhand, reconditioned machines show improved performance over the original new machines. Rather than remanufacturing costing more than manufacturing, the plant has shown substantial savings. The savings in 2000, the first year of operation, were $14 million and in 2001, $16.5 million. How could this be? In the past, for example, a circuit board that was inoperative would simply be thrown away; it might be worth $5,500. However, only two small components may have been malfunctioning. The new equipment developed at the plant can now identify these specific components that may, for example, be worth $140. By replacing the components rather than the entire board, massive savings are achieved.

But it was not only valuable equipment that was being trashed in the past; throwing away whole machines or complex components was also throwing away valuable information about the reasons for equipment failure (i.e., data that could help the manufacturer redesign the equipment for better long-term performance). This data has now become a major input to research and development on product design. Newly designed products are now sent from other Fuji Xerox operations around the world to be tested on the equipment developed in this plant—a major R&D payoff. The parent company regards the plant as best practice in eco-manufacturing worldwide and teams from Japan and the United States have visited the plant to help diffuse the innovative practices throughout the company.

There are also significant contributions to the community. As all parts are re-used or recycled, there is zero waste to landfill. What is waste from the company's viewpoint has become a resource for other companies; for example, the plant has developed a CO_2 dry-cleaning process to draw off carbon deposits in used equipment. The waste carbon is taken by steel maker BHP Steel and used in the process of steel manufacture.

Communities will increasingly deny business the right to dump waste to landfill. In Japan, for example, it is now illegal to dump white goods and computer equipment into landfill. Those companies that develop technologies ahead of this demand will have a significant strategic advantage worldwide as this trend extends.

Developing this plant has also brought about a transformation of workforce culture. The workforce had a history of adversarial trade unionism. There is an entirely different culture of voluntarism and commitment now. The plants of the future require a new culture to operate effectively, new levels of professional skill, and new approaches to participative problem solving. To achieve ecological sustainability, the social system of the plant must also be sustainable in human terms.

There are many managers who believe that in a competitive situation it is too costly to pay attention to issues of sustainability. In reality, the traditional industrial process is extremely wasteful of resources—reclaiming and recycling those resources can be a source of wealth, lay the foundation for a learning organization, provide satisfying work with meaning, and contribute to a more healthy community and natural environment.

Now, I want to explore the potential of sustainable practices for improving organizational performance, building human capability, contributing to community development, and renewing the biosphere. This is the new task for change agents—to help reshape the organization to achieve outstanding performance that actually contributes to the fulfillment of human needs on a healthy planet.

The nature of organizational performance is changing and to improve performance, we must first establish what kinds of performance will matter as this century unfolds. The era of "slash and burn" in the 1980s and 1990s placed an overwhelming emphasis on cost reduction as the measure of performance. Many companies taking that path found that it led, paradoxically, to financial collapse, takeover, and/or demise.[8]

One reason was that the dismantling of the iron and bamboo curtains brought one billion low-wage workers into the world labor market. Given this new level of cost competition, playing the cost reduction game alone was not enough to save the firms in developed countries. They had to compete to some extent on price, of course, but had to justify a higher price by adding value and, more recently, maximizing speed, flexibility, and innovation as they introduce new products and, from time to time, reinvent their basic business concept.[9] Part of the key to achieving this is a skilled, innovative workforce using advanced technologies.[10]

This brings us to the first element of corporate sustainability, what we call human sustainability. Corporate human sustainability is the contribution of the corporation to developing the capabilities of its workforce members; creating a just, equitable, and healthy workplace; and contributing to the welfare of the external community, particularly those community members who have some stake in the future of the organization.

The internal part of this agenda involves adopting a strategic perspective to workplace development. This can be vital for business success. For example, BP launched a major internal culture change program in the 1990s that was designed to transform the inflexible, hierarchical, and rigid structure of a traditional oil company into a much more flexible, strategic culture with the capacity to react quickly to emerging events. As a result, within two hours of the events of September 11, 2001, the company had used its globally distributed crisis centers and nonhierarchical networking capacity to gauge the reaction in different cultural contexts worldwide. Senior executives were then able to move quickly to generate their response. There was no way that they could have achieved this without the investment they had made in developing a new kind of organization based on significantly different human resource strategies.[11]

The internal agenda for human sustainability also involves systematically building the corporate knowledge and skill base, fostering productive diversity in the workplace, organizing work for high performance and satisfaction, giving employees an increased role in decision making, and developing the capacity for continuing corporate reshaping and renewal. This is what Gratton refers to as "living strategy" and Stace and Dunphy as "the new flexible work order."[12] The capacity for continually reshaping the organization involves distributing leadership throughout the organization—ultimately, every individual becomes a leader.

This agenda has implications for senior managers. They spend more of their time leading than managing ongoing operations,[13] give priority to leading-edge human resource practices, and spend effectively half their time in people management. Leaders of this kind create highly engaged employees and a strong, value-based culture. In Pfeffer's words,

> Success comes from successfully implementing strategy, not just from having one. This implementation capability derives,

in large measure, from the organization's people, how they are treated, their skills and competencies, and their efforts on behalf of the organization. Fixing an organization's management practices may be more difficult than readjusting the strategy, but the payoff is often much greater.[14]

The external agenda for human sustainability requires real time from senior executives. The traditional firm simply managed shareholders' interests, as interpreted by the market. This is still necessary but in the new world of sustainability, strategy must be reinterpreted around other stakeholders as well. This means identifying who the critical stakeholders are—the list usually includes investors, employees, suppliers, customers, the natural environment, community groups, and future generations. Then, cooperative relationships are developed with these groups and a business strategy developed that adds, rather than subtracts, value for these groups. (I am using the concept of value here to mean delivering desired outcomes.) This involves establishing an ongoing dialogue with key stakeholders to define key elements of social responsibility and to set priorities. After goals are set and agreed upon, action plans are developed to reach these goals, key performance indicators (KPIs) against which performance will be measured are agreed upon, and a system of monitoring against the KPIs is developed. By making this process transparent, the organization wins, by responsible and informed action, widespread stakeholder support. This creates a "trust bank" that preserves the organization's license to operate and supports its continued growth. Hirsh and Sheldrake refer to this as "inclusive leadership."[15]

Many major global corporations such as Shell, Nike, BP-Amoco, and Renault now produce comprehensive annual social reports, and social auditing has become a boom business in the United Kingdom and Europe. The result of the internal human sustainability agenda is a progressive build up of the intellectual capital of the organization; similarly, the result of the external human sustainability agenda is an increase in the relationship capital of the organization. Success in the business world is increasingly dependent as much on collaboration (alliances, joint ventures, networking, etc.) as it is on competition.

I have outlined the nature of human sustainability, both internal and external. The other major aspect of sustainability is ecological sustainability. This involves creating organizations linked in an industrial ecology that ensures we live within our means as creatures dependent on the thin film of organic material and life-giving gases that surround the surface of the earth. This is ecological sustainability.

Economic affluence has been achieved in part by using global resources at a rate unsustainable into the future, particularly with rising aspirations and population growth. Continuing economic success and a sustained quality of life depend on developing a different relationship with the natural environment. We have been living as if there is no tomorrow and, unless we change the way we use resources, there may be no tomorrow we would wish to contemplate. Tim Flannery refers to the human race as "the future eaters," and our future-eating behavior threatens the livelihood and quality of life of the generations to whom we will bequeath the world.[16] We have discovered the secret of creating wealth on a large scale, but, like Midas, we are finding that we cannot live on gold alone.

As we move into this century our success in developing efficient technologies for gathering and processing the world's natural resources is threatening the planetary life-support system we have taken for granted in the past. We are depleting the seas of fish, logging the forests out of existence, changing the world's climate, and polluting and degrading the soil and water. Our profligate waste of nonrenewable resources is creating a looming environmental crisis. Nature cannot forever absorb the massive and expanding impact of traditional production and consumption processes. A planet under threat means the end of business as usual. So we must rethink our approach to wealth creation, in particular moving from an exploitative to a regenerative mode, reducing resource use, recycling products, and eliminating waste.

Von Weizacker and others have provided many examples of businesses that have more than quadrupled their productivity while halving their resource use.[17] Far from reducing productivity and profits, these companies found that introducing ecologically sustainable practices provides sustainable success.

How is Ecological Sustainability Achieved?

First, we need to understand that the only truly sustainable production processes are those that make production integral to the ecological system. Like an earthworm, an ecologically sustainable factory processes materials so that anything superfluous to the production process ends up in the natural world either environmentally neutral or actually helping sustain a healthy ecology. For example, effluent becomes clean water. This demands (a) a new emphasis on life cycle assessment of products and stewardship of resources and (b) the elimination of waste and pollution, particularly by product redesign and developing an industrial ecology where the "waste" from one firm's production process is a resource to another's. (For example, in beer production the spent hops become cattle feed.) It demands active monitoring of the firm's environmental "footprint," a process of environmental auditing preferably carried out by an external party. There are also active partnerships with "green" and other environmentally concerned community groups. In addition, the strategic action on ecological sustainability must be linked with strategic action on human sustainability to create a seamless, integrated approach to corporate sustainability as a whole.

My colleagues and I are currently working on a research project designed to identify organizational change strategies that corporations can use to advance on the path to sustainability. As part of this project, we have identified a series of phases through which many organizations move—these phases define a broad path that can be followed in moving to a fully sustainable economy.

The path to corporate sustainability includes:

- Rejection of Sustainability—active opposition
- Nonresponsiveness—indifference and apathy
- Compliance—risk reduction to avoid potential problems
- Efficiency—improving organizational processes to capture the benefits to be gained from eliminating waste, and so on
- Strategic Sustainability—profiting from sustainability by making it central to strategy
- Ideological Commitment—moving beyond the business case to work actively for a fully sustainable world[18]

We have made a detailed study of the characteristics of each of these phases and of the change strategies that can help corporations to move incrementally or transformationally through them.[19] There is not space here to treat this in detail but I will make some key points about the phases.

Phase 1, Rejection of Sustainability, and Phase 2, Nonresponsiveness, are increasingly dangerous places for organizations to be. For example, in the United States, Honda has had to pay $267 million to settle claims that it disconnected pollution-monitoring equipment on 1.6 million automobiles. Honda contravened the Clean Air Act and this was the reminder that the U.S. government is now taking air pollution seriously. In Australia, Esso (Exxon) has been fined $1.1 million after governmental safety regulator Workcover laid 45 charges at the end of its investigation of an explosion and fire in Esso's gas processing plant in Longford, Victoria. Esso is facing an additional class action suit seeking damages of $720 million.

Risk avoidance is not simply a matter of compliance to governmental regulations; it is possible to comply with all governmental regulations and still fail to meet community expectations, with damaging results for corporate reputation. Nike met governmental regulations but that did not prevent a punishing boycott from consumers who objected strongly to the poor labor conditions, particularly for children, in the manufacturing plants of subcontractors in less developed countries. Similarly, Greenpeace targeted Ford in the United Kingdom because they had not installed, in European models, the catalytic converters that were standard equipment in their U.S. autos. Ford countered that the converters were not required under EU legislation, but Greenpeace argued publicly that nothing but best practice was acceptable regardless of the legislative requirements. The thousands of postcards mailed by Greenpeace supporters to Ford dealers read F U G B (_ _ _ _ You, Great Britain) to emphasize Greenpeace's reading of Ford's attitude.

Further pressure to develop sustainable policies can be expected from socially responsible investment funds. SRI funds have grown at 30% per annum for the last 15 years in the United States and are now 13% of all funds under management. (Figures for other developed economies are comparable.) As these funds have yielded consistently higher returns to date than other funds, they are expected to continue to grow even faster. Similarly, governments are increasingly demanding environmental and social reporting and auditing. A company in touch with its stakeholders, who include financial institutions and green activist groups, will seldom be surprised at their expectations and will go beyond compliance with base level legislative requirements to "compliance plus," as represented by our Phases 3–6. Compliance is vital to reduce risk and provide the baseline for further steps down the path of sustainability—it is not the end of the journey.

Phases 4, Efficiency, and 5, Strategic Sustainability, represent the business case for sustainability. They create a new mindset that transforms traditional business approaches. The well-known case of Interface, a U.S. multinational manufacturer of commercial carpets operating in over 100 countries, illustrates this. Interface, like Fuji Xerox, decided to lease rather than sell, and to service the carpets and carpet tiles they delivered to clients for environmental reasons. This resulted in millions of dollars of savings in waste—the carpets could largely be recycled—and it also created a profitable service business, an interesting case of business concept redefinition.

In the Efficiency phase, companies typically engage in sociotechnical systems analysis of their own operations; examine supply chain and delivery systems; undertake life-cycle analysis, energy and waste audits, and materials analysis; and establish ISO 14000 systems to enable continuous improvement.

Making positive business gains by improving efficiency normally encourages firms to begin to make sustainability more central to business strategy; that is, to move it into Phase 5. There is a growing perception that a strategy centering around sustainability can be used to help reposition the firm (e.g., in emerging markets). A classic case of this is BP-Amoco's redefinition of BP (originally standing for British Petroleum) as Beyond Petroleum, illustrating that the company had become an energy company rather than a petroleum company. The new business definition has been accompanied by increasing investment in alternative energy technologies. Another example is Heinz, an international food producer, which has adopted a policy of making Australia and New Zealand "an environmental oasis for Heinz." It is committed to growing clean food for global export; Heinz is already exporting organically produced food from New Zealand to Japan, where it attracts a premium price.

Finally, the move to Phase 6, Ideological Commitment, represents a realization within the organization that, while successful businesses make profits, great businesses are driven by strong values and are committed to supporting quality of life and a healthy environment. Businesses at this stage exert leadership locally, nationally, and/or in the international arena. They develop an advocacy role, lobbying governments against subsidies for nonsustainable products and services and for "favored supplier" status for clean, green, regenerative companies. They work toward an industrial ecology by building alliances with other socially and environmentally responsible companies and promote the principles of human and ecological sustainability in the workplace, industry, and society. The Body Shop and Ben and Jerry's are well-publicized examples of ideologically committed companies. This returns us to the original humanistic values of the OD movement, but writ larger to include care for the planet as well as people.

One day all companies will be led this way:

- They will manage to a variety of stakeholders as well as shareholders
- They will develop a new social and ecological contract with their stakeholders, including future generations
- They will lock in place systems to ensure compliance to regulatory requirements covering health and safety, product safety, and environmental safety
- They will produce wealth but go beyond financial returns to add value through active collaborative relationships with a range of community groups
- They will build cultures of efficiency, effectiveness, and caring and involve themselves in the development, renewal, and regeneration of the natural world

Corporate sustainability is one vital aspect of the creation of a sustainable world. We need corporations that are sustainable themselves, but that also sustain the natural world—organizations that are sustainable and sustaining. The new task to be taken up by change agents of the future is to apply what we know of how to manage organizational change to moving organizations along the path to sustainability. The children of the future deserve nothing less than to inherit from us a regenerative society working in harmony with a healthy planet. Our leadership will be critical to creating sustainable corporations that create value for all stakeholders, including future generations.

17

Organizational Culture

Rob Goffee
Gareth Jones

Organizations are in trouble. As the pace of change accelerates, old certainties are under threat. We used to believe that when business enterprises reached a certain size with extensive global reach they became market makers, not market takers. Nothing could be farther from the truth. Consider the following: not long ago we expected DEC to dominate the IT sector—it has since been swallowed up by Compaq—the combined group merged with Hewlett-Packard; Daimler-Benz has merged with Chrysler; the United Kingdom's leading clearing bank, NatWest, had been acquired by RBS. Never has the churn among the Fortune 500 been higher.

In response to this, organizations are focused ever more closely on sources of competitive advantage. The strategy gurus used to tell us that this could be achieved by technology, global reach, supply chain management, and market segmentation techniques. We now know that important as these are, they can all be copied and exceeded by the competition. They are not sustainable sources of competitive advantage.

Let's conduct the following thought experiment. Think of your two favorite organizations in the world—organizations that, in your view, can continue to be successful. Now imagine that you are an organizational spy. What do you want to know about them? While it would be useful to know of their next technology, or new products under development, the most important information would answer "how?" questions. How do they innovate? How do they attract and retain the best? How do they stay close to customers? Questions, in other words, to do with their cultures. Those habitual, taken-for-granted assumptions about how things get done around the place. It is our proposition that an organization's culture is the single most sustainable source of competitive advantage.[1]

However, we need to enter at least one substantial caveat here. The recent history of the analysis of organizational culture has been beset with a "one best way" fallacy. Peters and Waterman's classic, *In Search of Excellence,* comes close to arguing that if only organizations could develop certain cultural characteristics then their success would be assured.[2] In our view, this is based on a misconception. There are no right cultures; only appropriate cultures. That is to say there can be no generically correct culture, only ones that are suited to the particular environment of a business and to the complexity of its value chain. Producing, bottling, and selling beer, for example, is fundamentally different from developing, testing, manufacturing, and selling innovative pharmaceutical products. The value chains are different, as are the external environments. Later on in this chapter we will describe and explain a contingency model of culture that addresses these issues.

We need, however, to briefly explore the role of leadership in all of this. First, our view is that leadership is a nonhierarchical concept—leaders can and should be found all over organizations.[3] Indeed, one of the most pervasive organizational trends of the last 50 years has been based on the recognition of the importance of encouraging leadership behaviors at all levels of an organization. Second, because our view of culture is based on a contingency model, it follows that a key leadership task is the maintenance and modification of culture to an organization's changing environment. For example, when we interviewed executives at Hewlett-Packard about their jobs they frequently cited the constant adjustment of the culture as a critical success factor, taking all that was essential to the traditions of HP and applying them in new and changing circumstances. Finally, therefore, the role of leaders is as the embodiment of culture. Their behaviors will be closely observed to see if they merely mouth the key values of the culture or whether they practice them. It is one of the most admirable human qualities that people can identify the gap between what others preach and what they practice. It becomes clear that the role of the leader is as an exemplar of the culture, crucial to both the continuance of appropriate elements of the culture and equally significant in the process of constant adjustment in response to a changing external environment.

Clearly, culture is a complex concept, sometimes too elusive for the pressured employee to grasp, even though they may somehow recognize its importance. Because of this we have developed a framework for the analysis of organizational culture. It is based on the view that shared values, attitudes, behaviors, and assumptions are shaped by different sets of organizational relationships. Therefore, it draws largely from the classical sociological literature that emerged as a response to the widespread division of labor associated with the emergence of modern societies. The key concepts are those of sociability and solidarity.

Analyzing Corporate Culture

Sociability refers primarily to affective relations between individuals who are likely to see one another as friends. As such, they tend to share certain ideas, attitudes, interests, and values and to be inclined to associate on equal terms. In essence, sociability represents a type of social interaction that is valued for its own sake. It is typically maintained through ongoing, face-to-face relations characterized by high levels of implicit reciprocity; there are no "deals" prearranged. Individuals help each other "with no strings attached."

Solidarity, by contrast, describes task-focused cooperation between individuals and groups. It does not necessarily depend upon close friendship or even personal acquaintance, nor is it necessarily sustained by continuous social relations. Solidarity is displayed instrumentally and discontinuously—as when a perceived need arises. In contrast to sociability, then, its expression is both intermittent and contingent.

To cooperate in the instrumental pursuit of common goals it is not necessary for individuals to like one another. In fact, solidarity may often be exhibited among those who strongly dislike each other. Equally, intimate forms of sociability may actually be less likely among those who feel constrained to act solidaristically as work colleagues.

The intensity of sociability may vary directly, independently, or inversely with the intensity of solidarity. We have found it useful to distinguish organizations as exhibiting high or low levels of sociability and solidarity. This suggests four distinctive corporate forms: networked, mercenary, fragmented, and communal.[4] We have also distinguished, as shown in Figure 17–1, between positive and negative aspects of each form.

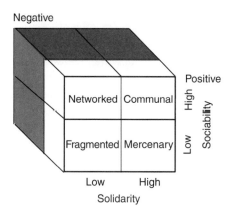

Figure 17–1   The Double S Cube: solidarity versus sociability.

Networked Cultures

Networked organizations exhibit high levels of sociability but relatively low levels of solidarity. They are often characterized by loyalty, a "family" ethos, and important work-related social events and rituals of one kind or another. These serve to sustain a strong sense of intimacy and friendship. Patterns of sociability within the workplace often extend beyond it, via leisure and sporting clubs and informal social contacts among families.

Levels of solidarity, however, are low. In fact, although social networks are characterized by well-established friendships, the culture of networked organizations can become gossipy and political. Members of network cultures sometimes make the mistake of assuming that well-established patterns of sociability will form the basis for solidaristic cooperation. In fact, the reverse may be true. Close friendships, for example, may constrain open expression of difference. This, in turn, may be a necessary condition for developing and maintaining a shared sense of purpose.

Networked cultures tend to emerge in organizations where

- Knowledge of local markets is a critical success factor.
- Corporate success is an aggregate of local success (interdependencies are minimal).
- There are few opportunities for transfer of learning between divisions or units.
- Strategies are long-term (sociability maintains strategic intent when short-term calculations of interest would not).

Business organizations with *networked* cultures often benefit from informal social relations that, in turn, facilitate flexible responses to problems, fast communication between members, and a preparedness to help. Those drawn to such cultures report satisfaction with the friendship and empathy of work colleagues and the relaxed, easygoing atmosphere.

But, as we have suggested, networked cultures can also suffer from negative politics. To some extent, this may be inevitable—at least in large-scale organizations. Networks can degenerate into cliques. Similarly, informal information exchange can easily become malicious gossip; meetings between friendly people may produce much talk but little action. More than other cultures, it is the informality of the *networked* culture that sanctions political game playing: for example, manipulation of communication, high rates of job mobility to avoid performance measures, and advanced impression management—particularly in senior managers. The defining characteristics of this type, both positive and negative, are summarized in Table 17–1, along with some suggestions for preventing slippage into the negative form, as shown in Table 17–2.

Table 17–1 Networked Cultures

Positive Networked	Negative Networked
Informality	Gossip, rumor
Flexibility	Negative politics
Rapid exchange of information	Endless debate about measures
Willingness to help	Long meetings with no action
High trust	Manipulation of communication (e.g., copying e-mails)
Ease of communication—no hidden agendas	CYA management style
Fun, laughter	Risk aversion—Keep your head down
Loyalty	Change jobs in the organization frequently (this builds networks and minimizes performance measurement)
Empathy	Concentrate more on managing upward than managing outcomes
Caring for others	
Compatible people	
Less defensiveness	
Relaxed	

Table 17–2 Preventing a Networked Organization from Slipping into the Negative Form

Symptom	Solution
Extensive gossip, rumor, and intrigue	Control it by confronting rumor mongers, getting to the grapevine first, making more information public
Exclusive cliques	Move people around—change their jobs, move their location
Long meetings without commitment to action	Introduce more structure to meetings; limit time, conclude with action points and clear accountabilities
Cynicism about the products	Celebrate quality, invite employees to use products and make constructive suggestions for improvement

Mercenary Cultures

In *mercenary* organizations, a heightened sense of competition and a strong desire to win—or at least survive—is often a central feature of corporate culture. Values are often built around competitive individualism and personal achievement but these do not preclude cooperative activity where this appears to produce measurable benefits. Solidarity, then, does not depend upon close friendships or ties of affection. Good teamwork may be described by members of such cultures as "eagles flying in formation." Day-to-day relationships in such organizations are rarely characterized by high levels of collective cooperation—quite the reverse may be true. As we have pointed out, solidarity may be both intermittent and contingent.

The mercenary culture occurs where

- Capacity to act swiftly in a highly coordinated way is a critical source of competitive advantage.
- Economies of scale and competitive advantage can be gained from creating corporate centers of excellence that can impose processes and procedures on operating units.
- The nature of the competition is clear—external enemies help to build internal solidarity.
- Corporate goals are clear and measurable and there is little need for consensus building.

Organizations that have a predominantly mercenary culture often benefit from a clear understanding of purpose and the ability to mobilize resources swiftly to achieve ends. Members of these cultures are attracted by their intolerance of poor performance, the preparedness to openly address conflict, and the relentless drive to measurably improve standards.

The benefits of a mercenary culture for business organizations operating within competitive market economies are clear.[5] But there can be a dark side to the mercenary culture. The tendency to focus upon measurable performance may ignore the unmeasurable. Because cooperative behavior is not always easily assessed, these cultures can easily become internally competitive. The predominance of means–ends relationships also implies that the management of uncertain and ambiguous circumstances is often difficult. Finally, low levels of sociability can reduce emotional involvement and result in a relatively brittle psychological contract. Even a brief perceived misalignment of individual and organizational interests can be enough to result in the loss of organizational members. In knowledge-based businesses, in particular, this can prove extremely expensive. Positive and negative features are summarized in Table 17–3, along with guidelines for managerial actions to prevent the drift to negative characteristics, as shown in Table 17–4.

Table 17–3   Mercenary Cultures

Positive Mercenary	Negative Mercenary
Focused	Internally competitive—no time for cooperation
High energy, task oriented	Only does what is measured
Energy	Poor at alliance management (because alliances always require the management of ambiguity and mercenary cultures are bad at this)
High levels of competition awareness	Fails to explore synergy opportunities (good at exploiting them once they are clear)
Recognition of shared interests	Fragile psychological contract (this is a real problem in business where knowledge management is critical; e.g., pharmaceutical industry)
Quick response rate	"Quick suicide"; will march over the cliff in step—intolerance of dissent
Intolerance of poor performance	
Conflicts openly addressed	
Relentless pursuit of improving measured outcomes and standards	

Table 17–4   Preventing a Mercenary Organization from Slipping into the Negative Form

Symptom	Solution
Factions fighting (unit A vs. unit B, business against corporate, etc.)	Repeat collective purpose and common enemies through company videos, newsletters, speeches, etc.; create opportunities to link activities; publicly reward common purpose goals
No time to think—always diving straight into action	Initiate strategic review focused on the future; use "away days" to help people step back and gain perspective
Important things don't get done because they are not measured	Refocus measurement systems, include some items that require cooperation
Ego clashes and people seeking revenge	Train people in conflict resolution skills

Fragmented Cultures

But what of cultures that exhibit low levels of both sociability and solidarity? Can these *fragmented* organizations survive or succeed? Although it seems at first unlikely, there is evidence that, at least in some contexts, these "disintegrated" corporate cultures can survive and grow. For example, organizations that rely heavily on outsourcing or home-based work or those dependent upon the contribution of individual, noninterdependent experts and professionals may be predominantly fragmented.

Thus, fragmented cultures are typical where:

- Innovation is produced mainly by individuals.
- Standards are achieved primarily through input (e.g., professional qualifications) rather than process controls.
- There are few learning opportunities between individuals.
- There are low levels of work interdependence.

Organizations with predominantly fragmented cultures can derive substantial benefits from the autonomy and freedom granted to its members. University professors or partners in a law firm, for example, possess considerable discretion to set their own work agendas and develop their professional talents without external "interference." Under such conditions individual creativity can flourish and resources are distributed to those with proven track records.

But fragmented cultures can sometimes become so individualized that they fall apart. Freedoms are abused by selfish and secretive behavior, organizational commitment is nonexistent, and simple attempts at cooperation—meetings, for example—are disrupted or ignored. Contrasting negative and positive features are described in Table 17–5, and some tips for addressing negative symptoms are outlined in Table 17–6.

Communal Cultures

Despite the viability of the fragmented culture in some contexts, it is perhaps not surprising that the *communal* organization is sometimes seen as the ideal. Solidarity alone may produce an excessively instrumental organizational orientation; cooperation may be withdrawn the moment that it is not possible for members to identify shared advantage. By contrast, organizations that are characterized primarily by sociability may lose their sense of purpose. Critics claim that such organizations tend to be overly tolerant of poor performance and possibly complacent.

Table 17-5   Fragmented Cultures

Positive Fragmented	Negative Fragmented
Freedom from organizational interference	Selfish
Focus on individual excellence	No knowledge sharing (secretive)
Set out own agenda	Low identification with organization
Define your own goals	Very fragile psychological contract
Scope for individual creativity	Cannot manage meetings or any collective events
Work with whom you choose (either inside or outside; therefore good opportunities to network)	Bad-mouth colleagues (excessive critique can degenerate into inaction)
Can steal ideas and practices from anywhere	All ideas get savaged
Resources follow stars (i.e., those who can deliver get what they need)	
Space to explore ideas without either sociability or solidarity getting in the way	

Table 17-6   Preventing a Fragmented Organization from Slipping into the Negative Form

Symptom	Solution
Good people leaving	Tie in your stars; rewards must be highly competitive and relate to their desires for self-fulfilment
Lying about outputs or exaggerating their significance	Repeated market testing to check that you *have* stars. Use search consultants to find out who wants your people. Collect objective data about the reputations of your stars from clients and respected authorities
Immediately savaging all ideas that are not your own	Create contexts that reduce risk—brainstorming, train in feedback skills, recognize good work
Failure to see interdependencies where they exist	Light-touch leadership that makes connections between people (too heavy and it will be resisted)

Certainly, the communal organization has much appeal. Indeed, this form shapes much of the literature on innovative, high-performance business organizations.[6] However, it may be an inappropriate and unattainable ideal in many corporate contexts. Those businesses that are able to achieve the communal form frequently find it difficult to sustain. There are a number of possible explanations. High levels of sociability and solidarity are often formed around owner-founders or leaders whose departure may weaken either or both forms of social relationship. Similarly, the communal culture may be difficult to sustain in the context of growth, diversification, and internationalization. More profoundly, there may be a basic tension between relationships of sociability and solidarity that makes the communal corporation inherently unstable. In effect, friendships can undermine collective interests or vice versa.

The communal form is often seen where

- Innovation requires extensive and complex teamworking across functions and locations.
- There are measurable synergies and opportunities for teamworking across organizational sub-units.
- Strategies are long-term and emergent rather than the sum of measurable stages.
- The business environment is dynamic and complex, requiring multiple interfaces with the environment and an advanced capacity for internal organizational information processing.

Organizations with communal cultures can become "cult-like." Members are often passionate about the "cause" and so are able to expend high levels of energy in the pursuit of their case—or "converting" others. Communal cultures can often sustain complex teams apparently divided by geography, nationality, and function, for example, but united in a common purpose and close ties between espoused values and embedded practices.

As we discuss next, many successful business start-ups and fast-growth enterprises have been built around a communal culture. But such cultures can be prone to what has become known as the "paradox of success"; the tendency to persist with behaviors even when they have ceased to be appropriate to context.[7] Successful communal cultures often develop an inappropriate sense of invulnerability. Competitors may be too easily dismissed and customers seen to be in need of education. New ideas are rejected because of an uncritical adherence to values or principles that may have ceased to serve their purpose. Look at, for example, the way in which IBM—a communal culture—was undermined by new entrant Apple, who then paradoxically were undermined by the same collective sense of invulnerability as their original target. Differences between the positive and negative characteristics are summarized in Table 17–7 and in Figures 17–2 to 17–5, along with possible solutions to prevent the drift to the negative form, as shown in Table 17–8.

Table 17–7   Communal Cultures

Positive Communal	Negative Communal
Passionate	Sense of invulnerability
Committed	Inability to see strengths of competitors
High energy	No leadership development, only disciples
Creative	Excessive reliance on charismatic founder figures
Able to sustain teams over long periods	Willingness to "carry" underachieving colleagues, as long as they continue to believe in the values (i.e., confusing beliefs with performance)
Loyal	Unwillingness to change (e.g., IBM)
Equitable, fair, just	
Close tie between espoused values and embedded practices	
Stimulating (rather more than fun—almost obsessive)	

Table 17–8   Preventing a Communal Organization from Slipping into the Negative Form

Symptom	Solution
Complacency—undervaluing the competition	Regularly benchmark; compare yourself with radically different kinds of organizations
Believing your own propaganda	Build opportunities to discuss and critique credo
Talking the values but not practicing them	Ensure values and associated behaviors are built into appraisals and reward systems
Not learning from other organizations	Exposure to others (alliances; consultants bring in new people)

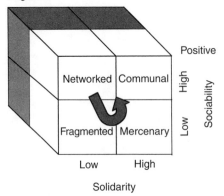

Figure 17–2 Preventing return to networked culture.

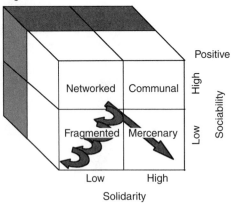

Figure 17–3 Preventing descent into fragmentation.

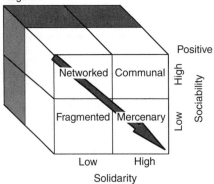

Figure 17–4 Preventing dive into mercenary.

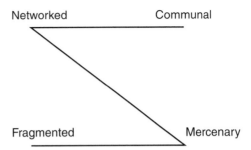

Figure 17–5   The reversed zed form.

Culture and Change

How, then, can this framework be used to map patterns of organizational change? Clearly, there is a need to distinguish planned, programmatic change interventions from more evolutionary patterns that may reflect, for example, stages of firm growth or industry sector patterns. It is equally important to distinguish changes across the front of the Double S Cube from those involving a shift from negative to positive cultural types. Bringing these two distinctions together it would appear that although it is possible, for example, for a positive networked or mercenary culture to evolve gradually into a more negative form, the reverse process of change is almost certainly impossible. In other words, we know of no cases where negative cultures (networked, mercenary, communal, or fragmented) have been able to recapture positive attributes without planned, consciously managed interventions. Organizations can slide into the negative form of the culture but can only climb out of it.

But what of movements that may be mapped across the front of the Double S Cube? In much of our consulting work over recent years we have seen many companies launch change initiatives designed to shift the culture from networked to mercenary. This is a move we should expect during periods of intensified market competition where swift, coordinated action and a piercing focus on goal achievement is at a premium— even if this is at the expense of carefully built and longstanding social relationships. It is perhaps no surprise that the "strategic intent" model that gained popular currency during the 1990s—largely through the work of Hamel and Prahalad—is, in many respects, a celebration of the positive mercenary culture.

But the journey from networked to mercenary culture is hazardous. Although the failure rate of planned organizational change is typically high in most circumstances, we suspect that the success rate of this particular move may be extremely limited. Why is this? To some extent, it may result from a failure by those involved in such projects to grasp the fundamental shift in cultural assumptions that such a journey involves. These are summarized in Table 17–9.

Table 17–9   Contrasts between Networked and Mercenary Cultures

Networked	Mercenary
Implicit goals	Explicit goals
Acceptance of ambiguity	Need for clarity
Obsession with analysis	Bias to action
Comfortable with complexity	Drive for simplicity
Personal agendas	Corporate goals

Even if the scale of the change is appreciated, there remains the problem of the unintended consequences created by planned interventions. Three patterns are common. First, there is the tendency for networked cultures to "pull back" change efforts.

Here is a familiar story. Executives at negatively networked companies respond to market threats by attempting to be more mercenary. They realize that to become more ruthless toward competitors, employees need to be less friendly with each other. Thus executives will specify clearer goals, identify competitors with greater exactitude, and install processes that measure performance and milestones on the way to results. As the organization approaches the mercenary form and people realize the implications of the change, they rebel against the loss of social ties, and the organization returns "home," as it were. In other cases, the sociability of networked organizations hijacks the effort to become more mercenary and undermines the attempt at change. Employees may look as if they understand and embrace the calls for more solidaristic behaviors, but once they are out of earshot of the change proponents, they criticize their efforts, accusing them of oversimplifying market challenges and organizational dynamics. In still other cases, organizations in the N–M–N migration simply run out of steam. It situations like these, the train of change has returned to the station before some of the last cars have even left.

So, what can be done to prevent it?

- Keep up the pressure for change using external events and internal change champions. This is a push factor.
- Paint a vivid and attractive picture of your destination. This is a pull factor.
- Make change appear practical by focusing on clear and prioritized action items.
- Redesign your reward system to encourage the new behaviors.
- Celebrate achievements along the way.
- Act swiftly to correct those who falter. Help them with the new behaviors.

A second pattern sees the drive to more mercenary behaviors undermining long-established ties of sociability in such a way that there is a rapid descent to the fragmented form. In a sense, the social ties that held the networked culture together fall apart. Typical symptoms include increased turnover, often of the best people; lower levels of trust; and reduced patterns of social interaction as individuals become increasingly concerned with "looking after themselves."

What can be done to prevent this?

- Keep talking to people. This will help you detect the warning signs of an uncontrolled descent into fragmentation (e.g., increased absenteeism, poor attendance at meetings, antisocial behaviors).
- If you must release people, let them exit humanely, generously, and with their dignity intact.
- Make sure you keep your stars.

A third pattern involves a change program that inadvertently produces an exaggerated dive into mainly negative aspects of the mercenary culture.

Under these circumstances, executives may be so anxious to move rapidly to more solidaristic behaviors—and to resist the "pull back" effect—that they overcompensate and effectively drive the culture into an exaggerated mercenary form. Worried about insufficient pressure on the accelerator, they press too hard. As a result, the positive aspects of both networked and mercenary cultures may be simultaneously lost. Behaviors may change, but largely through reluctant compliance rather then commitment. Pressure to perform produces a fear of mistakes that, in turn, drives out creativity and innovation. Work ceases to be fun. Insofar as solidarity emerges, it is patchy and destructively competitive between different parts of the organization (e.g., functions, business units, or territories).

There are several steps that can be taken to limit the dangers of this particular syndrome.

- *Explain* change
- *Agree* on new measures
- Keep a longer term vision
- Watch out for silos—measure cooperation, repeat collective purpose
- Tolerate mistakes, but not poor performance
- Don't grind down—retain fun

The shift from networked to mercenary is one that we expect to continue in the near future—particularly within larger, well-established businesses. But which other patterns may become particularly pronounced in the 21st century? Given the resilience—and, in some cases, powerful resurgence—of smaller and medium-sized enterprises in various industries, it is worth exploring two further patterns of organizational change.

Both patterns begin in the communal quadrant. This is because many start-ups and small- and medium-sized enterprises (SMEs) develop a tightly knit family-like culture where bonds of sociability and solidarity are simultaneously high. Such cultures are often strongly shaped by powerful founder-owners who have a clear sense of purpose (which builds solidarity) and who are able—because of their relatively small scale—to maintain the "little and often" face-to-face contacts with colleagues that are the lifeblood of sociability.

We refer to the first pattern as the "reversed zed form" because organizations move across the face of the Double S Cube in a backward letter Z.

Communal cultures can become networked for different reasons. At a fundamental level it is the case that the behaviors of sociability tend to undermine the relations of sociability. Another reason is that as communal companies do well, they can get somewhat lazy. They lose their focus on the external enemy—Goliath has been slain—which had been the source of their solidarity. Time passes, and eventually management comes to realize that the now-networked company has lost the energizing and productive competitive spirit it once had in its more communal form. They begin, often quite fervently, to encourage and compensate behaviors that move the organization toward the mercenary, such as explicit targets and financial objectives. They may be trying to move back to the communal, but their zealousness about solidaristic behaviors undermines the effort. In the process, social ties have come undone. Feelings get hurt. Mistrust often develops. The initiatives toward solidaristic behaviors fail to take hold, and bit by bit, the culture slips into the fragmented.

We suspect that the history of many smaller scale companies can be described in these terms, and the bursting of the dotcom bubble should not deflect our interest in small, dynamic companies. So what can be done to prevent the slide to fragmentation? We have already discussed the pitfalls in managing changes from networked to mercenary and fragmented cultures. The key initial challenge for smaller organizations in the reversed zed move is to retain the spirit of the communal culture and to prevent the drift to networked cultures. From our consulting experience, useful advice includes the following.

- Resist the temptation to let friendship get in the way of business decisions.
- Make sure your appraisal system focuses on objective measures.
- Fight complacency by reminding everyone of the power of existing and potential competition.
- Make the mission *live;* don't let it become a tablet of stone that can't be revisited.

But there is a second pattern of change associated with smaller businesses that develop communal cultures. This is where the communal culture—often with unexpected speed—fragments. As we have already suggested, the communal form is enormously fragile because of the inherent incompatibility between high sociability and high solidarity. And so, when the charismatic leader leaves, or the company is purchased, or any disruptive event occurs, the culture implodes, or in many cases, collapses. Indeed, this is where many promising entrepreneurial start-ups meet their end.

We must recognize that this change path is hard to resist, so what can be done?

- Develop successors. Entrepreneurs, in particular, are guilty of never having enough time for this. The urgent drives out the important.
- Use consultants. They will help you to objectively assess your needs (in the excitement of the communal culture you are the least well-equipped to know).

Conclusions

In this chapter we have attempted to show that culture is a major sustainable source of competitive advantage. Further, culture is likely to grow in importance as the hard integrators in organizations—systems, structures, and careers—decline in significance. We have provided a framework for its analysis and suggested typical patterns of cultural change. Finally, we have argued that leadership has a critical role to play as exemplar of culture. But there is more: Questions about organizational culture entail a set of moral questions. How are we to live in an age characterized by the pursuit of self-interest? How much will we compromise as individuals to fit in with our organizations? What does work really mean for us? It is naïve to think that any cultural change program or organizational development intervention can avoid these moral questions. Social ties are complex, are fragile, and carry meaning for individuals. Changing them, and change we may have to, needs care. Organizational life is not just about how well a company does, but about how well we live our lives.

18

Leading Organizational Change

W. Warner Burke

ccepted wisdom today is that there is sufficient difference between leadership and management, between a leader and a manager, that the two concepts or forms of influence should not be used interchangeably. In addition, leadership is more often associated with change and management with stability and daily operations. We can, of course, carry this distinction too far. In times of significant organizational change, both leadership and management are required. For our purpose of focusing on organizational change, in this chapter we will emphasize leadership more than management, bearing in mind the caveat just mentioned. More specifically, our emphasis will be on the leader's role for initiating, implementing, and sustaining organizational change. Furthermore, our stance is that without leadership, organizational change will never be achieved.

With such a strong statement, let us first raise the underlying question regarding this premise: Does leadership really matter? Following our response to this question, we will briefly review a number of ideas that are based on sound research and theory as well as accepted wisdom about the nature of leadership, that is, tenets that help to define leadership, and then we will cover the main theme of this paper—phases of organizational change and the leader's role. Finally, we will address change leadership today and in the future.

Does Leadership Matter?

There is a school of thought that questions the importance of organizational leadership. The argument is that many variables influence organizational outcomes—the external environment, an organization's culture, the sales force, and rapid technological changes, to name a few—and leaders are simply responding to these variables.[1,2,3,4] Others in this school of thought have argued that precedence plays a critical role—that previous organizational decisions and actions affect final strategic decisions more than leaders do.[5,6]

These positions that question the importance of leaders, however, are quite dependent on how leadership is defined, the methods used in research studies, and the types of statistical analyses used. The point is that some of these conclusions can be traced directly to the methods used; as a consequence, other interpretations of research results are possible. It is clear, in any case, that leaders' actions do not account for all or even most of organizational outcomes. Leaders do make a difference nevertheless. And this difference is especially true in times of organizational change.

We do not have to rely solely on research results to answer this question of whether leaders make a difference. Historical events provide evidence. President Lincoln's army during the Civil War was failing. The president replaced one general after another. It was not until U.S. Grant took over that the tide began to shift. Grant, who later became president himself of the Union that Lincoln had been so instrumental in saving, clearly made a difference with respect to the outcome of the war.

On the other side of the coin, individuals in positions of leadership can have a negative, harmful effect. Hitler and Stalin come immediately to mind, not to mention the more recent Osama bin Laden. As Hogan, Curphy, and Hogan have pointed out,

> Conversely, reactions to inept leadership include turnover, insubordination, industrial sabotage, and malingering. Organizational climate studies from the mid-1950s to the present routinely show that 60 to 75% of the employees in the organization—no matter when or where the survey was completed and no matter what occupational group was involved—report that the worst or most stressful aspect of their job is their immediate supervisor.[7] Good leaders may put pressure on their people, but abusive and incompetent management create billions of dollars of lost productivity each year.[8]

Zaccaro has also provided convincing evidence that leaders make a difference.[9] He cited, for example, the research by Weiner and Mahoney, who studied 193 companies over a 19-year period.[10] Their results demonstrated that leadership accounted for approximately 44% of the variance in profits and 47% in stock price. As noted earlier, these leadership study results do not account for all performance indices but do account for a significant amount nevertheless. Zaccaro cites other evidence as well.[11,12,13] What is not clear, however, is the degree of impact of leadership during times of organizational change. There is some anecdotal evidence but little that is scientifically based.[14] It seems reasonable to proceed, however, with the hypothesis that leaders do influence organizational performance and even more likely have considerable impact on organizational change.

Important Characteristics of Leadership

When beginning a presentation on leadership I usually show on the screen a headline for an article from the *New York Times* (May 1, 1992) that caught my eye a few years ago. The headline stated, "Afghan Leader Lacks Followers." Then I ask my audience to tell me what is wrong with this picture. They quickly get the point and laugh. (As it happened, this headline and story was well before September 11, 2001.) The point is that *first* and foremost, leadership is a relationship. It does not matter what a person's self-concept may be; in the case of leadership, without a follower there is no leader. This is the first of three important characteristics of leadership.

Second, leadership is personal. A leader can hold a legitimate position in an organization, of course, but his or her authority as a leader (in contrast to a manager) is not vested in the position. Rather, the leader's authority comes from content expertise and knowing how to persuade and influence, and how to be persuaded and influenced by others. Leadership is not about position but about how one uses oneself.

Third, leadership cannot be adequately understood unless three variables are considered and assessed:

1. The leader with his or her values, beliefs, dimensions of personality, and general behavior
2. The followers with their values; beliefs; needs such as achievement, affiliation, and power; and general behavior.
3. The situation.

More specifically, the person as leader concerns self-awareness—the degree to which the leader has insight about how he or she affects others, about how well self-control is exercised and feelings managed, and about insight into how others affect him or her. Two additional personal variables of importance are ambition and content of leadership. With respect to the former, O'Toole quite candidly states:[15]

> In fact, I believe only one inherent character trait is essential for effective leadership, and that is ambition. …Granted, it is not necessarily an attractive personal trait, that desire for power, distinction and public approval…[but] even the saintly Mohandas K. Gandhi had ambition.

The point O'Toole makes is that to be an effective leader one needs to have a desire about influencing others. Without such a motive, one would simply not have the drive, the energy required (and it takes considerable energy) to succeed as a leader. We know that too much ambition leads to failure, but having an above-average level is no doubt necessary.

Regarding the content of leadership, the successful leader is one who has a vision about the future and can communicate a long story that incorporates the vision. This story emphasizes identity—who we are as a group, an organization, and who we want to be in the future. Gardner's *Leading Minds* is particularly useful for understanding the importance of conveying a story by the leader.[16]

With respect to the followers, it should be noted first that most people prefer this role or choose not to be involved at all when it comes to having organizational responsibility or being responsible to someone else. As followers, however, the primary responsibilities are to interact and be engaged with the leader regarding goal accomplishment, and always to tell the leader the truth, whether the news is good or bad, and not to tell the leader what they think he or she wants to hear. When Warren Bennis was in a leader role as president of the University of Cincinnati, he put it this way:[17]

> The one thing a president—whether of the United States, a corporation, or a university—needs above all is the truth, all of it, all the time, and it is the one thing a president is least likely to get from his assistants. ...[As] president for six years...I had to endlessly struggle for the whole truth. ...When I finally pried whatever it was I needed to know out of them, they would say things like "Well, I didn't want to bother you" or "I didn't want to call you wrong in front of other people"...or "I thought you were making a mistake, but I didn't want to argue with you."...I believed...that the buck indeed stopped in my office, but I was lucky to be able to find the buck, much less learn where it had stopped outside my office and why.

And one final point about followers: If you want to know what a leader is really like, ask the #2 person.

The third variable in the important trilogy of understanding leadership is the context or situation. What is important to understand regarding leadership is the setting, the environment within which the leader must lead, and the resources at hand. Some specific examples of what is meant by context or situation are (a) the way performance for the leader is determined—this in turn affects directly his or her behavior; (b) the nature of the organization's culture especially in terms of expectations (what is expected of a leader in this particular culture) and norms and values regarding such things as leader-follower relations, the degree to which hierarchy is respected, how accountability and decision making are structured, etc.; and (c) how the kind of organization—whether a corporation, family-owned business, nonprofit organization, or government agency—influences leader behavior. For example, the title "department head" may be used in any one of these different kinds of organizations, but the role and expectations will be different. In a university a department head is not the same as a department head in a corporation or nonprofit organization (I should know—I've been one in both a university and nonprofit organization). In a corporation, a department head "runs things"; has formal authority; and expects followers to behave like subordinates. In a university, a department head serves the members, not the other way around; has no formal authority; and expects followers to behave like cats, that is, not to be herded.

Back to the lead statement for this *third* section—the point that leadership cannot be fully understood without accounting for three primary variables. Leadership, then, can best be understood as an interaction between and among the leader (behavior, expertise, personality, and motivation); the followers, with their motives, personality, and behavior; and the situation or context, the environmental specifics that influence both leader and followers. This interaction is intricate and complex but must be analyzed as completely as possible to understand the important characteristics and nature of leadership.[18]

In the final section of this chapter, we will return to further important characteristics of leadership, but we now need to explore the role of the leader in another context—organizational change. This exploration will set the stage more thoroughly for our return to leadership at the end of the chapter.

Leading Organizational Change

A paradox of organization change is that we plan in a linear fashion—step 1, 2, 3 or stage A, B, followed by C, etc.—but in the implementation of the change we discover that the process is anything but linear. As I have stated elsewhere, organization change in reality is a nonlinear process.[19] The change never occurs quite the way it was planned. As interventions are made, organizational members react in ways that are not entirely predictable. In other words, unanticipated consequences arise from the planned initiatives and interventions that then have to be addressed and managed. Resistance to the change is what we usually call these consequences, but organization change is not resisted by everyone. And resistance that does occur rarely takes the same form in different people.[20] In any case, most of leading and managing organization change is a process of dealing with unanticipated, unpredictable consequences.

But we do need to plan. We also need to be clear, however, that things will not go precisely according to the plan. So, how do we proceed?

Imperative is having a vision for the future that generates clear goals. With goal clarity and a broad phased way of planning the change process we can deal with and manage unanticipated consequences.

With the aforementioned caveat stated, we will now proceed with a phased way of thinking about organizational change that emphasizes the change leader's role within each phase. The broad phases of organizational change can be considered in terms of (a) prelaunch, (b) launch, (c) post-launch or further implementation, and (d) sustaining the change effort.

Prelaunch Phase

As stated earlier, leadership is personal. It is about the use of oneself to be influential, be persuasive, and embody the organizational vision. During the prelaunch, the leader works more alone than with others, although from time to time he or she will want to seek guidance and opinions from trusted others. There are at least four elements that comprise the pre-launch phase—self-examination, assessing the organization's external environment, establishing the need for change, and providing clarity of vision and direction.

1. *Self-examination:* This element consists of three parts (self-awareness, motives, and values) and is the loneliest aspect of leadership. It requires introspection to (a) be aware of one's strengths and limitations as a leader; (b) examine one's motives, especially regarding the desire to bring about change that will be disruptive and affect organizational members' (and their families') lives, particularly their emotional lives; and (c) be clear about one's values and how congruent they are with the desired culture of the organization.

    • *Self-awareness*—Arguing that this self-examination is an important early step in the organizational change process is grounded in recent research findings that increased self-awareness is significantly related to performance. For example, high-performing executives and managers tend to have greater congruence between how they view themselves and how others perceive them than do moderate- and low-performing executives and managers.[21,22]

- *Motives*—As noted earlier, O'Toole believes that ambition is *the* motive of importance for leadership. To elaborate on O'Toole's argument, let us briefly examine the work of David McClelland.[23,24] O'Toole's point and McClelland's research together suggest that ambition and need for power are not necessarily deplorable motives. The three primary needs that McClelland studied were need for achievement, need for affiliation, and need for power. Need for achievement is critical to task accomplishment, but a need too high militates against effective leadership. High achievers "can't find good help." They tend to want to do the job(s) themselves to make sure that it's done right. In other words, delegation is practically impossible for high achievers. Having a high need for affiliation does not foster effective leadership either. In positions of leadership, having a need for affiliation means that decisions are often made impulsively owing primarily to a desire to please the last person to whom the leader talked and to assure a relationship rather than to decide according to more objective criteria. That leaves high need for power, which is the one most relevant for effective leadership. The important question here is something like, "having a need for power to do what?" The classic study by McClelland and Burnham provides an answer to this question.[25] These researchers used subordinates' ratings of their organizational unit's degree of clarity and amount of team spirit as measures of effective management and leadership. Their study results showed that if a manager/leader had an above-average need for power, had a low need for affiliation, and was high in inhibition—that is, his or her need for power was mature, socialized, under control, and not for the purpose of self-aggrandizement—the organizational unit's degree of clarity was higher (subordinates were clear about what was expected of them and what the unit's goals were) and the team spirit was also higher. In summary, the change leader would do well to examine his or her motives to make sure one's ambition is sufficient to serve the organization's change goals, that is, to have the necessary energy to accomplish all four of the phases for organizational change that are required for success. Furthermore, the change leader should be certain that he or she has a power need that is strong enough yet under control—clearly in the service of the greater cause, and not for self-glory.

- *Values*—The greater the alignment of individual needs and values with the organization's culture (norms and values), the more likely motivation and performance will be high.[26] All the more important is that change leaders, especially the CEO, have alignment of their personal values with those of the organization. Achieving this alignment is, of course, imperative for successful organizational change, particularly regarding the culture. In the merger of SmithKline Beecham (which joined two pharmaceutical firms, the American SmithKline and the British Beecham Group), values were developed to help establish the newly merged culture. Robert P. Bauman, CEO and president of the new company at the time, described the value generation this way:

> So the executive committee and I went away again, this time to define the values that would make up that culture. Obviously, there were certain values that were critical to our company. *Innovation*, for example, was critical. We didn't have much trouble getting people to agree on that. ...There was no disagreement that *customers* were critical and that our customer base was changing. ...HMOs were coming in, which brought up the question, "Who's the buyer now, the HMO or the doctor?" and "How do we bridge this gap?" So we had to start thinking more about customers and had to do a better job—not just in providing good drugs but also in how we managed and serviced our customers.

> We extended our discussion of customers incidentally to include not just the outside world but also our own organization. Because we thought it important to say that everyone in the company has a customer. ...Another value we believed in was winning. We wanted to create a winning attitude inside the company, so we thought *performance* was important. And there was some feeling in our early discussions that we weren't driving as hard in the area of performance as we needed to. ...We agreed we wanted to be winners and perform better than our competitors. ...Another value that was clearly agreed to but harder to articulate was *people*. We knew we had to have the best people we could find and that they were key to our competitive advantage. So as part of articulat-

> ing this value, we emphasized that people needed to contribute to the goals of the organization; we wanted to give everyone a chance to influence and participate in how work was done and how it got measured. And we wanted people to feel ownership for continuously improving the ways they worked on the job.
>
> Finally we agreed to the value of *integrity*. It's something we felt we possessed and that was important to the nature of our industry.
>
> We felt five values was the right number. We believed that if we got too many it would be very hard to drive them all through the organization.[27]

This quote provides an example of how one change leader of a highly significant corporate merger dealt with the element of values with his top team. For more about the successful SmithKline Beecham merger, see Bauman, Jackson, and Lawrence.[28]

2. *External environment:* This element of the prelaunch phase concerns monitoring the organization's external environment; in particular, for the purpose of change, to gather as much data as possible about current and future trends. It is the change leader's responsibility to see that this data gathering occurs. Moreover, the need for this element of the prelaunch phase is based on open-system theory, that is, the reality that an organization's survival is dependent on its external environment. How well an organization assesses and analyzes its environment has a direct bearing on its degree of success and ultimately its survival. With respect to organizational change, the content and process of such change is typically a reaction to change in the external environment—the entry of some new technology, changing customer desires, new competitors, or perhaps change in government regulations. For example, in the case of the SmithKline Beecham merger, a transformational level of change for these two companies, the decision to merge made jointly by the respective CEOs was the desire to compete on a global level and to counter a shrinking market share problem for both organizations. In other words, within their industry it was clear that competition was becoming more global and that acquisition and merger were likely to be a major form of responding. This judgment by the two CEOs in 1988–1989 has been supported unequivocally since that time. The pur-

poses of the prelaunch activity, therefore, are to ensure that the change effort will be directly in response to changing environmental factors, to establish the groundwork for making the case for change during the launch phase, and to gather relevant change content to incorporate into the vision and into a clear change direction.

3. *Establishing the need for change:* Richard Beckhard used to say, "No pain, no change." What he meant was that if people in the organization feel no need for change they are not likely to embrace it. So a case has to be made. This is a change leader's responsibility during the prelaunch phase. Beginning with information about changing trends in the external environment, the change leader creates a scenario about how the organization is going to be affected by these environmental factors. Whether the CEO delivers the message or someone he or she designates, the case must be made—and convincingly. A case example is provided by the recent large-scale change of British Aerospace (BAe). CEO Richard Evans (now Sir Richard) saw the need for organizational change, but could not seem to convince his top 100 executives. Part of the reason was the fact that Evans rose to the top via sales and marketing and was not an engineer, like most of his top 100. He lacked a certain amount of technical credibility. In his own words, here is what he did:

> In the eyes of many of BAe's top managers, the lack of a "burning platform" weakened my argument that change was urgently needed. How could I make them see that the present good times were not symptomatic of the way things would be five years hence? The easier way was to present them with scenarios of likely futures. For this job I turned to one of our top line executives, John Weston (an engineer), then managing director of military aircraft, now my successor as chief executive. I seconded him from his regular duties and gave him carte blanche to analyze the company from end to end and then report his findings.

> With characteristic thoroughness, John documented "The Case for Change." His report probed every single part of the business, its macroeconomic environment, its competitive structure, the state of technology, and so forth. Time and again he documented a stark conclusion: Our business units' rate of progress and future prospects of performance gains were inadequate, given the emer-

gent threats in the external environment. What's more, even if we took a whip to them to urge them to improve sales and profits and squeeze the cash flow, any conceivable improvement would not change the analysis substantially. At the end of the day BAe would be trailing and not setting the industry tempo.

Because John Weston was the divisional head of our largest and most profitable business unit, his call to action could not easily be dismissed. If he saw the writing on the wall, so might everyone else. "We wanted to give them the macroeconomic and geopolitical picture right between the eyes. The paradigm for defense and aerospace markets was changing dramatically, and we had to learn superior skills and way of reacting," says Weston.[29]

The top 100 executives were convinced and the culture change proceeded forthwith. Establishing the need and preparing the case, the message is the third element in the prelaunch phase.

4. *Providing clarity of vision and direction:* Preferably the vision and directional goals should be delivered by the CEO or the head of the unit targeted for significant change. Since he has provided an excellent statement of what a vision and its purpose are, we return once again to O'Toole:

A robust vision mobilizes appropriate behavior. It uses memorable, simple concepts that make clear what needs to be different about tomorrow. It describes the distinctive competencies needed to deliver on the desired end state (for example, "Here's what we have to do differently in order to succeed"). Often, a vision will make choices clear by making the case for change as either an opportunity or a burning platform (for example, "If we don't change in this way, the company won't survive"). That's not asking much, is it?

Leaders don't even have to create visions themselves (although many do). But, at a minimum, they must initiate a process for developing a vision and then engage themselves fully in generating buy-in. Shared commitment to a vision can be built either through wide-scale participation in the act of its creation or through involvement immediately thereafter in its dissemination.

...We're not talking quantum mechanics here. This is simple stuff—so simple that many leaders gloss over the basics. For example, by definition, vision has to do with "seeing, sight, and sensing with the eyes." Recognizing that simple fact, effective leaders make their visions, well, *visual*. Remember Ronald Reagan's budget message when he explained that a trillion dollars amounts to a stack of dough as high as the Empire State Building? By using that visual reference he got Americans to see that federal spending amounts to real money! In doing so, he changed the terms of the national debate and, for the first time, created a majority in support of lower taxes. It was his most effective moment as a leader.[30]

As O'Toole noted, the CEO may not personally craft the vision, but the responsibility to see that it gets done is definitely the head person's job. Without clear direction about the future, and the organization's place and role in that future, the desired organizational change simply does not occur.

Launch Phase

The launch phase has three elements—communicating the need, initial activities, and dealing with resistance. The primary purpose of this phase is to begin the process of organizational change.

Communicating the Need

The case for change that was developed in the prelaunch phase is now communicated. Careful attention needs to be paid to both the content of the need and how it is communicated. As stated earlier regarding the content of leadership, providing a vision and communicating this vision and the new direction in the form of a story that incorporates the notion of identity—who we are as an organization and who we want to be in the future—is highly useful for getting the message across.[31] With respect to how the message is communicated, by far the best way is face to face. Sending out a video of the CEO as a "talking head" is not likely to be effective regardless of how professionally done. Organizational members want a chance to ask questions and have a dialog about the significance of the change. As a part of launching their merger, Robert Bauman and Henry Wendt (CEO and chairman of the board, respectively) traveled around the world meeting with groups at each SmithKline Beecham location to deliver the change message.[32]

Initial Activities

Starting the change effort in earnest can take a variety of forms. The primary purpose, regardless of form, is to launch an activity—an event that will provide focus, capture attention, and create the reality that the change effort is not just an exercise or yet another initiative that will soon pass. Change was launched at the British Broadcasting Corporation during the early 1990s with John Birt, the director general, authorizing a one-day workshop on "Extending Choice"—a label for the change that focused on the new vision and mission for the organization. The workshop, for 100 organizational members at a time, was conducted again and again over many months to ensure that most everyone had a chance to participate in the launch. Another example from the United Kingdom was the launch of change at British Airways (BA) by the CEO, Colin Marshall (now Lord Colin). BA in the 1980s began the transition from a government-sponsored organization to a private enterprise. The following quote from CEO Marshall provides his rationale for the change, followed by an example of the initial activity for change at BA:

> But to get people to work in new ways, we needed a major change in the company's culture. That meant refocusing everyone on the customer, on the marketplace, and away from the exclusively engineering and operations focus we'd had. That had to be done, of course, without sacrificing safety, technical, or maintenance standards. And that proved tricky. People had difficulty understanding why I kept hammering away at the need to focus on customers while also saying, "We've got to fly these aircraft at a very high technical standard too." The focus before had always been on the technical side alone, but I made the point repeatedly that we had to do both. It was at this point that we saw the explicit need for a culture-change program. ...The first thing we did was to launch a program called "Putting People First," ...a two-day seminar. We took roughly 150 employees at a time and drew people from various departments within BA and from various geographical areas. The program focused on how one creates better relationships with people, with one's fellow employees, with customers, even with members of one's own family.[33]

Dealing with Resistance

The most important point to remember is that organizational members do not always resist change. What they are more likely to resist is the *imposition* of change. Imposing change tends to cause people to feel a loss of control. The prudent change leader will therefore work hard to find ways to involve organizational members in the change process. The change leader can more easily be directive about the change goals than be directive regarding the ways to reach the goals. For every given goal there are myriad ways to reach the goal, thus in the implementation process there are many more opportunities for disagreement and consequent resistance. The change leader needs to be as participative as possible in the ways to achieve change goals. In a sense the change leader should care far more about the goal per se than the way to accomplish the goal.

Postlaunch: Further Implementation

Once the launch has occurred and the change is underway, the change leader begins to realize that he or she cannot control much of the process. The feeling is analogous to launching children into the world by parents. As a parent you hope that the life directions you have suggested will be followed, at least to some extent, and that the values you have espoused and lived will have been noticed by your children, but once they leave the nest you as a parent have no control. In fact, during the teen years you didn't have much control either. Launching organizational change is much the same. You as change leader hope that the direction remains clear and that the values are beginning to be adopted and lived, but now it is largely up to others to make the change work.

But there are things to consider and to do. While not exhaustive, the following five actions will help the change leader to continue to lead. These five are (a) multiple leverage, (b) taking the heat, (c) consistency, (d) perseverance, and (e) repeating the message.

Multiple Leverage

To rely on one intervention or one lever to implement organizational change, especially large-scale change, is doomed to failure.[34] Coverage of seven different case studies that represented successful organizational change revealed that multiple leverage was key. Two relevant summary points regarding these cases are as follows:

- Time and again, these cases illustrate the absolute necessity of strong leadership for change to occur. We see change leaders in living color here. There is no substitute for visionary leadership in times of change. By definition, if there is leadership there are followers.
- In addition to demonstrating how the phases of organizational change work, all these cases show the deployment of multiple interventions. True organizational change is too complicated for one intervention. Multiple sources of influence are required.[35]

Examples of interventions from these case studies included crafting mission statements, process engineering, training and development, crafting corporate values and new leadership behaviors, developing a new process of supply chain management, installing a new pay-for-performance system, team building, and establishing self-directed work groups.

Taking the Heat

Organizational change unleashes all kinds of feelings. Some people didn't want the change in the first place; others bought the idea, tried to make things work out, but ran into one roadblock or another; and, in general, having to deal with unanticipated consequences of change interventions can be frustrating. The change leader(s) is the likely target to blame regarding the aforementioned. The change leader must take the heat. Richard Evans of BAe described the process this way:

> I got a lot of pushback from people. People asked, "Why do we need to do this? We're operating perfectly well. We all have big change programs to deal with in our own businesses. Why the hell do we need to do all this other stuff?" Many seriously thought and believed that I had some sort of hidden agenda and simply wanted to be told what to do so they could go away and do it.

Taking the heat means that the change leader must use considerable self-control and work hard to listen, not to show defensiveness, and to be as patient as possible.

Consistency

Now a cliché, "walking the talk" is nevertheless what is meant here. During times of significant change the leader's behavior is watched like a hawk. Looking for inconsistencies in the leader's behavior seems to be everyone's job. Do these guys at the top really mean it? Will this initiative fall by the wayside like all the rest? Of course these questions are all about trust, and trust is not only built on openness and telling the truth, but on consistency between what one says and what one actually does as well.

Perseverance

When things get tough as they inevitably will during the implementation of a transformation, it is imperative that the change leader "stay the course." When all may look bleak and the change does not seem to be working, organizational members look to the change leader to see if he or she is still

306 Chapter 18 Leading Organizational Change

holding on to the vision and is remaining at the helm. Perhaps the premier example of perseverance was Colin Marshall of BA. In his own words, perseverance is obvious:

> I made a particular point of attending every one of these "Managing People First" sessions. I spent two to three hours with each group. I talked with people about our goals, our thoughts for the future. I got people's input about what we needed to do to improve our services and operations. The whole thing proved to be a very useful and productive dialogue. We found it so valuable in fact, that in cases when I was away, we offered people the opportunity to come back and have a follow-up session with me. So I really did talk to all 110 groups in the five-year period.

Repeating the Message

As a coach to change leaders, I have heard their frustration many times about "the troops not seeming to get the message." The change leader will say something like, "But I told them as clearly as I knew how!" My question is always, "How many times have you told them?" It's hard to repeat the vision, new mission, and our story too many times. As noted in the previous section, repeating the message demonstrates perseverance. The most important point here is that during the chaos of change, organizational members need to be constantly reminded of not only the goal itself but *why* we are taking this journey as well.

As stated at the outset of this section on the postlaunch phase, these five actions are not the only things the change leader needs to pay attention to during the chaotic process of trying to make the change work but they do represent perhaps the primary activities of the change leader.

Sustaining the Change

Concluding an article about the successful organizational changes at BA, the authors stated:

> It may be that BA's biggest problem now is not so much to manage further change as it is to manage the change that has already occurred. In other words, the people of BA have achieved significant change and success; now they must maintain what has been achieved while concentrating on continuing to be adaptable to changes in their external environment—the further deregulation of Europe, for example. Managing momentum may be more difficult than managing change.[36]

Sustaining the change is the most difficult of the four phases of leading organizational change. The following four thoughts and suggestions may help: countering equilibrium, dealing with unanticipated consequences, choosing successors, and launching yet again new initiatives.

Countering Equilibrium

Seeking equilibrium is the natural process of organizational behavior. Countering this natural process is key to sustaining the change effort. Pascale and his colleagues have addressed this quandary by relying on complexity theory and the life sciences. They consider the application of what they call "four bedrock principles" to be key:

1. *Equilibrium* is a precursor to *death*. When a living system is in a state of equilibrium, it is less responsive to changes occurring around it. This places it at maximum risk.
2. In the face of threat, or when galvanized by a compelling opportunity, living things move toward the *edge of chaos*. This condition evokes higher levels of mutation and experimentation and fresh new solutions are more likely to be found.
3. When this excitation takes place, the components of living *systems self-organize* and new forms and repertoires emerge from the turmoil.
4. Living systems cannot be *directed* along a linear path. Unforeseen consequences are inevitable. The challenge is to *disturb* them in a manner that approximates the desired outcome.[37]

The point that Pascale et al. made was that since equilibrium seeking is such a natural process, actively managing events ("disturbing unforeseen consequences") to counter the trend is absolutely necessary to sustain change. But so is having patience, which may sound paradoxical. Patience is required on the part of change leaders during chaotic times to allow creativity and innovation to emerge.

Dealing with Unanticipated Consequences

What is meant by unanticipated consequences? Examples are (a) expecting that certain people will resist change and they actually embrace it, and the negative, expecting others to "buy in" but in the end do not; (b) different organizational units interpreting the overall organization's change goals differently and therefore causing a lack of concerted effort; and (c) expecting a certain intervention like a new software package to work but it doesn't.

So-called change management, which in this context is almost an oxymoron, is therefore the process of reacting to and attempting to correct actions that work against the change effort.

Choosing Successors

Another way to counter equilibrium is to infuse "new blood" into certain units of the organization—to recompose an ongoing task force or to choose new leaders for units that are critical to the change effort, but for some reason have bogged down. Choosing a successor for an important change leader position is a complex process. At the CEO level especially it is best not to select "a clone" so that new thinking and energy will be brought to sustaining the change effort. Colin Marshall's successor at BA failed at sustaining the change. It will be interesting to see how Immelt works out as Welch's successor at General Electric. For more about these succession issues, see Levinson's article.[38]

Launching Yet Again New Initiatives

Rarely does any initiative continue to work for many years. The external environment continues to change and new responses are required. Moreover, new initiatives can engender new energy, generate innovative thinking, and help to propel the organization continuously toward its vision. This latter point is highly important, that is, new initiatives must be in the service of the original change goals. Examples of new initiatives include (a) starting a different program to help improve quality and reduce costs, (b) acquiring another organization, (c) establishing a new joint venture or strategic alliance, and (d) creating a new business line based on different products or services.

Conclusion

We began this chapter by addressing the question of whether leadership actually matters and concluded that it does matter, particularly in times of significant organizational change. We then considered some important characteristics of leadership, such as leadership being a reciprocal relationship between leader and follower; leadership being personal; and leadership being an interaction of leader, follower, and context. Then the bulk of the chapter was devoted to leading organizational change. The point made at the outset of this section was that organizational change is planned linearly but actually occurs in a nonlinear fashion. Even so, it is useful to plan and implement large-scale change according to four broad phases—prelaunch, launch, postlaunch, and sustaining the change. Table 18–1 is a summary of these four phases.

Table 18–1   Summary of Leader's Role in the Four Phases of Organizational Change

Organizational Change Phase	Leader Actions for Sub-Phases of Organizational Change
Prelaunch	Self-examination
	Self-awareness
	Motives
	Values
	External environment
	Establishing the need for change
	Providing clarity of vision and direction
Launch	Communicating the need
	Initial activities
	Dealing with resistance
Postlaunch	Multiple levers
Further implementation	Taking the heat
	Consistency
	Perseverance
	Repeating the message
Sustaining the change	Countering equilibrium
	Dealing with resistance
	Choosing successors
	Launching yet again new initiatives

Leadership today and for the foreseeable future requires that leaders have the abilities and the motivation to deal with four primary values:

1. Ambiguity—the complexity of external environments, organizations as open systems, and the growing diversity of organizational members means that leaders rarely face a situation that is clear-cut and obvious. Tolerance for ambiguity is a must.
2. Unanticipated consequences—As noted in this chapter, things, especially organizational change, never go as planned.

Human beings are simply not that predictable. Thus, leaders must have a plan, a set of values to which they adhere, yet at the same time be adaptable and modify their behavior as changing situations demand. As long as leaders follow the vision and stick with their values yet adjust their behavior, they can still come across to others as consistent.

3. Avoiding impulsive behavior—Spontaneity can be fun and admired by others, but for leaders impulsive acts, particularly with decision making, can confuse followers. Moreover, impulsive people in leadership usually spend most of their time controlling the damage they have caused with this form of behavior.

4. Dealing with tension and paradoxes—As an academic department chair for many years I have learned firsthand about the concept of servant leadership and about the necessity of dealing with extraordinary demands and values. Here are some examples of what followers simultaneously demand:

- To buffer them from the bureaucracy and the vagaries of higher administration *yet* keep them fully informed as to what is going on

- To provide them with feedback regarding their performance *yet* leave them alone to conduct their work as they see fit

- To avoid telling them what to do *yet* provide direction for the department and for the future

- To be open and always tell them the truth *yet* remain optimistic and upbeat regardless of circumstances

So what is a poor leader to do? One or the other of these contradictions? Leaders, of course, are expected to do both. Dealing with paradox, with tensions, and with contradictions is the core of leadership today—and will be for quite some time to come. The previous examples come from my personal experience, but these conclusions are not idiosyncratic. As Zaccaro has summarized, there is a theory of executive leadership—behavioral complexity theory—that covers these ideas. The theory concerns the multiple roles that leaders are expected to perform and explains that a number of these roles have conflicting values and contradictory demands.

Finally, an irony: Being an effective leader is more complex and difficult than ever before, yet we need effective leadership more than ever before.

19

Building Organizational Fitness

Michael Beer

he 21st century promises to be characterized by rapid change in technology and relentless competition spurred by globalization. It is hardly news that in this environment firms will have to possess the capacity to adapt or suffer the consequences—low performance and ultimately death and destruction.

Unfortunately, firms do not seem to be adaptive. Consider these startling findings by Foster and Kaplan regarding the survival rate and performance of U.S. firms.[1] Of those firms in the original "Forbes 100" list published in 1917, 61 ceased to exist by 1987. Of the remaining 39, only 18 stayed in the top 100. These firms (which included Kodak, DuPont, General Electric, Ford, General Motors, Procter & Gamble) survived momentous events such as the Great Depression and World War II, but, with the exception of General Electric and Kodak, underperformed the overall market by 20%. Recently, Kodak's performance has suffered as it struggles to respond to challenges by foreign competitors. Similarly, of 500 companies in Standard & Poor's original S&P 500 list in 1957, only 74 remained on the list in 1997 and of these only 12 outperformed the S&P 500. In a Darwinian economic environment, *unfit* organizations—those that *do not adapt to fit new circumstances*—do not survive.

Failure to perform not only hurts investors. There are human costs involved in all these corporate failures. Employees of Polaroid Corporation, a firm that had been failing for years and declared bankruptcy in 2001, found that out recently.[2] Not only did they lose their jobs and attachment to an organization about which they cared deeply, promised and critical healthcare and retirement benefits have disappeared. Leaders themselves are hurt by their inability to change their organizations and their leadership behavior. CEO tenure has declined from 10.5 years in 1990 to 4.2 years in

2000. Leaving a proud legacy, something most CEOs strive for, is much harder in a business environment that demands rapid change.

It seems quite clear that a wide array of firms do not possess the capacity to learn and change, what I call *organizational fitness*. Nor do their leaders possess the capacity to develop this capability. What organizational and leadership characteristics reduce organizational fitness? More importantly, what can be done to build organizational fitness? I will describe an approach to building organizational fitness, called Organizational Fitness Profiling (OFP), that has its roots in the work of Richard Beckhard, to whom this book is dedicated. Research into the application of OFP at the corporate and business unit level has revealed that senior managers must embrace a number of paradoxes if they are to ensure high performance and survival of their institutions and reputation.

The Dynamics of Organizational Fit and Fitness

Research over the past 40 years has shown clearly that organizations naturally evolve their design—work systems (structure), management processes, human-resource system, principles and values, and leadership behavior—to "fit" their business environment and their chosen strategy within that environment (see Figure 19–1).[3] It is this alignment that enables the business to develop the organizational capabilities/culture (attitudes, skills, and behavior) needed to compete successfully. As firms meet challenges in their environments, they respond by developing management and business practices. These "habits of the business" become institutionalized through the process of recruitment, selection, promotion, and attrition that sorts people in and out of the firm based on their fit. Schneider has shown that firms tend to attract, select, promote, and attrite people based on their likeness to the dominant coalition of the firm.[4] Over time, a culture is developed (a pattern of beliefs and values) that reinforces historically successful business and administrative practices. Not surprisingly, the leaders of the organization reflect the core beliefs embedded in the culture and use their power to sustain that culture.[5]

The fit associated with past high performance seems to lead to long-term rigidity, however. When the environment shifts and new business habits are required, the strengths that led to success become weaknesses and lead to failure. Danny Miller has called this phenomenon the Icarus paradox.[6] Icarus, a boy from Greek mythology, flew on wings of feathers and wax. Ignoring his father's warning, he became distracted by his power and the thrill of flying—and flew too close to the sun, whereupon his wings melted and he fell into the sea. Likewise, highly successful firms can be blinded by

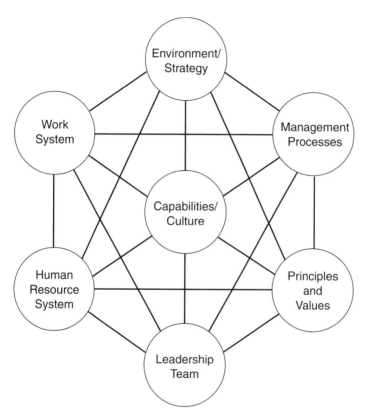

Figure 19–1   Organizational fitness model.

their own success, not realizing that the patterns that worked before are now leading to their downfall.

Nowhere is the cycle of corporate rise and decline clearer than in the economy's technology sector. Consider the case of Xerox Corporation. Its technological innovations in the reprographic industry made it one of the most admired American firms in the 1970s. However, failure to commercialize breakthroughs in computer and related technologies from its Palo Alto Research Center (PARC) in the 1970s and 1980s prevented it from adapting its business to market changes. Digital Equipment Corporation, the second-largest computer company in the world next to IBM in the 1980s, failed to capitalize on personal computing technology it possessed and was ultimately acquired by Compaq. Apple Computer, a firm that founded the personal computer industry in the mid 1970s and later introduced a new generation of computers that utilized innovations first made at Xerox's PARC, was unable to respond to the threat that lower-priced computers posed to its dominance.[7] Looking for a professional marketing executive to run the company, founder Steve Jobs recruited PepsiCo president John Sculley. Unfortunately, Sculley was unable to forge a top team that could listen to those in the company who recognized the need for lower-cost computers. One product manager related his unsuccessful attempts to introduce a low-cost Macintosh in 1988, when Apple still had the time to respond to the threat of Microsoft's much lower-cost Windows solution: "For two and a half years I wanted to do low-cost Macintoshes. I was always yelled at by senior managers that this was wrong."[8] Sculley himself was ultimately fired in 1993. Once a leader in market share, Apple's 2001 share of the fragmented computer market was 2%, trailing 2001 market share leader Dell's 13.3% share.[9]

Failure of corporations to survive and prosper in the long term is not caused by a lack of innovative ideas. Xerox, Digital Equipment Corporation, and Apple possessed the ideas that could have saved them. What existing and new CEOs often fail to do is to redesign their organization (its work systems, processes, human resource systems, culture, and leadership behavior) to enable new ideas and technologies to emerge. In effect, top management needs to take a "helicopter view" of the firm's organizational arrangements. It must reexamine all the organizational levers in Figure 19–1 and redesign them to create organizational capabilities (at the center of the figure) the firm needs to evolve its business model. Apple lacked the capability to develop effective teamwork between talented engineers in the research and development function and the sales and marketing people who understood the need for lower-cost products. It lacked a work system of cross-functional product development teams to achieve needed coordination and the business-oriented managers with leadership skills to lead them. It also needed a leadership team that could agree on this new business and organizational direction, and lead the organization through the changes needed with commitment.

The challenges for each firm are different but they have to be met with the same *total systems approach* to organizational transformation. In effect, firms must be able to develop strategy from the inside out.[10] Management must be able to discover how the firm's existing organizational capabilities can be augmented with new capabilities to meet new challenges. What is clear is that organizational fitness—the capacity to adapt organizational design, behavior, and culture to fit new circumstances—depends on the capacity of leaders and organizations to confront and learn from internal tensions.[11]

The Silent Killers: Undiscussible Barriers to Organizational Fitness

Recent research by Russell Eisenstat and myself sheds light on the specific organizational dynamics that block organizations from learning about their internal functioning.[12] Using an intervention I will describe later, we found that top teams and key lower-level managers in a dozen underperforming organizations had very similar and consistent perceptions of barriers to organizational effectiveness. These barriers had not been communicated to top management by lower levels nor had top management taken action to confront them until the intervention we designed to help them do so made it possible. The barriers identified were as follows:

- Unclear strategy and/or conflicting priorities
- An ineffective top team
- A top-down or laissez-faire style of the CEO or general manager
- Poor vertical communication
- Poor coordination across functions, businesses, or geographic regions
- Insufficient leadership skills and development of down the line leaders

These barriers typically appear together as a syndrome. The dynamic relationship between these barriers is depicted in Figure 19–2 and is based on our in-depth understanding of how these organizations worked. Everyone knew about these barriers. They were discussed behind closed doors, but not confronted in a way that enabled the open, public conversation needed to overcome them. We call them "silent killers." Like cholesterol and high blood pressure they can cause death—in this case, organizational death. These barriers block the senior management teams from learning whether the organization's strategy makes sense and whether the organization's design and behavior as well as their own leadership "fit" and support strategy implementation.

The first three barriers at the top of Figure 19–2 (an ineffective team, unclear strategy and conflicting priorities, and the CEO's leadership style that is too top down or laissez-faire) are interdependent and mutually reinforcing. They are key to the *quality of direction* management provides the rest of the organization. Ineffective top teams (teams that cannot develop agreement about where the business is going or how to organize) lead lower levels to perceive unclear strategies and conflicting priorities. Inef-

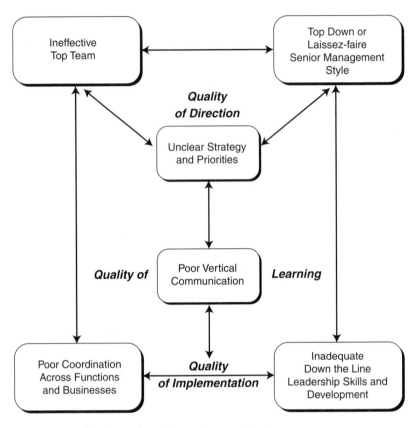

Figure 19-2   The dynamics of an unfit organization.

fective top teams result when leaders go around the team to micromanage the business or when they do not engage the top in developing agreement about strategic and organizational matters and/or replace those who will not or cannot come to agreement after a fact-based discussion. Both styles avoid confronting and resolving conflict in the top team regarding direction, priorities, and organizational arrangements.

All three of these silent killers were present at Apple.[13] Employees at all levels were unsure about the company's strategic direction and saw conflicting priorities between a powerful R&D function and the sales and marketing organization. This lack of clarity stemmed from a leadership team that did not agree on what direction the company should take or how to organize to do it. As late as 1988 a new head of Apple Products, the company's product development function, was an engineer who believed the company should design high-end computers when the market and CEO

John Sculley saw it going the other way. Sculley's conflict-averse leadership style prevented him from engaging his team in a constructive discussion that would have resolved differences or cause needed replacements. According to the vice president of human resources, 50% of his time was spent in efforts to resolve conflict between warring members of the team.[14]

Poor coordination and inadequate leadership and leadership development at lower levels (the bottom two barriers in Figure 19–2) affects the quality of implementation. Coordination across functions, business units or regions is essential for a strategy to be well implemented. The requisite coordination links differ from business to business but are those that connect key activities that comprise the value chain, activities that create economic value.[15] This often involves creating semi-autonomous teams across functions, regions, or businesses, and designating an effective leader with general management orientation to lead the teams.

Concerned about potential loss of power, top teams in the companies we studied were usually slow to confront these design questions. To do so meant they would have to consider shifting power and decision rights or give up resources. At Apple, the creation of cross-functional business or product development teams with authority over functional resources would have meant a dramatic shift in power from functional managers to team leaders. It would have meant diminished decision rights for these managers. It is because these are wrenching changes that organizational fitness requires an effective leadership team, one that is able to confront needed changes in roles and responsibilities for the good of the enterprise.

The second barrier to strategy implementation, inadequate down-the-line-leaders and leadership development, also prevents an organization from forming needed innovation teams. Faced with the need to form teams, top management does not see sufficient leadership resources to lead them. Already reluctant to shift power to leaders of these teams, the lack of talent becomes a convenient excuse not to redesign the organization. My research and experience suggest that the formation of teams with young inexperienced leaders is much preferred to delaying.[16] With coaching, some of these managers develop into effective team leaders and the rest are replaced over time, but the organization has begun the organizational learning process. Apple certainly had a shortage of managers who had the breadth of business and functional experience to lead cross-functional teams. Many of their managers were engineers with little management experience.

Of the six silent killers, poor vertical communication is the silent killer that affected the quality and speed of learning in the organizations we studied. Middle-level managers who perceived problems with the strategy or experienced difficulties in coordination did not take the risk to communicate concerns to top teams. Yet, they knew better than anyone else what was working and not working. To communicate honestly up the line meant that they would be exposing the six silent killers and raise questions about power, politics, and leadership at the top. To do so in a productive manner an organization needs a forum that brings the top team and lower levels together to discuss problems in a public yet safe manner. Only a conversation that involves all key members of the community, as John Dewey noted, can lead to organizational learning and break the norm of silence.[17]

Apple did not have effective vertical communication. An employee survey in 1990 showed that there was a big gap in trust and communication between top management and lower levels. As described earlier, "yelling" at a product manager that low-cost Macintoshes are wrong does not produce a fact-based conversation enabling a top team and lower levels to explore a strategic problem in a fact-based manner. It was not until 1991 that Sculley took the top 70 managers to an offsite meeting where problems of coordination were honestly aired for the first time; by then it was too late to respond to the threat of Microsoft's Windows and low-cost PCs.

The six barriers I have described are not only interconnected but deeply rooted in organizations. As I have shown, they defeated John Sculley's efforts to change Apple's strategy and organization despite the fact that he was unencumbered by the Apple culture and had the marketing expertise Apple needed. Rick Thoman, a new CEO recruited from IBM in 1999, was Xerox's hope for a turnaround. He and former CEO Paul Allaire agreed that Xerox needed to reinvent itself to succeed in a digital age. Only 13 months after he was brought in to lead the reinvention process, Allaire fired Thoman because "his colleagues had lost confidence in him."[18]

The conventional wisdom is that replacing the leader will ensure strategic and organizational issues are confronted. After all, these leaders command the heights and have the authority to change the organization. Forming an effective new team is certainly an essential first step. But, as the Apple and Xerox stories suggest, without engaging key managers in an honest conversation that reveals the "unvarnished truth" about strategic and organizational issues, they cannot discover and come to understand the real problems and solve them.[19] More importantly, without involving lower-level managers, a commitment to solve problems cannot be developed. This is what organizational fitness is about. Unfortunately, it is all too rare in organizations. Norms of silence about how the organization works or doesn't work prevent the honesty needed to move leaders and key managers to a shared understanding of what must be changed. How can such conversations be enabled?

Enabling an Honest Organizational Conversation That Will Produce Fit and Fitness

Looking at the "whole truth" about the silent killers and their consequences is essential for companies to avoid decline. Yet, years of research by Chris Argyris have shown that defensive routines are deeply embedded in organizations and their leaders.[20] Fearful of threatening or embarrassing higher ups, peers, subordinates, and themselves, the whole truth is rarely communicated. We learned about the silent killers from task forces composed of eight high-potential individuals appointed by top teams to interview 100 key managers about the organizations' strengths and weaknesses as part of an intervention I describe below. These task forces often displayed great anxiety about this assignment. When they were confronted with telling top management about the silent killers they became even more anxious, often starting the feedback process with a plea not to "shoot the messenger."

Two factors prevent employees from speaking up, according to research by James Detert.[21] The first is psychological safety. Employees are afraid that telling the truth will affect their acceptance and their careers. They also, undoubtedly, protect themselves from the anxiety associated with upward feedback. The second is a concern about the utility of honest feedback. Their experience tells them that speaking up does not lead to change. To establish this link, organizations need to establish forums for open, safe conversation and then do something about what they learn. The link between the conversation and their decisions must be explained to the employees. By open I mean that the whole organization (all relevant participants in the conversation) know the conversation is going on, there are clear signals from the leadership team that it wants candid feedback, and there are well-understood mechanisms for upward feedback and for everyone to learn about the actions management plans so they can be discussed and modified if needed. By safe I mean people believe their status in the organization will not be affected. Only if management is clear that they want feedback and demonstrate that bad news does not get punished can a climate of good vertical communication be established. Organizations are rather poor at doing this well, as the barrier of poor vertical communication we found indicates.

How organizations might be helped to confront organizational and leadership problems has occupied the field of organization development for several decades. A pioneer in the field, Richard Beckhard developed "The Confrontation Meeting."[22] In this meeting several levels of the organization are brought together to identify problems and solve them in a supportive atmosphere that encourages risk taking. In the past two decades other large system interventions based on Beckhard's model have followed.[23] Underlying the use of these methods is the acknowledgement that organizations are generally poor at confronting difficult issues and that a disciplined method—a social technology—that creates the condition for a public, open and safe conversation is needed.

While methods for confronting hidden issues safely have been largely effective in surfacing the unvarnished truth about what is going in the organization, they have not been based on a comprehensive theory of business and organizational effectiveness. Nor have they incorporated the latest research on organizational change. The underlying theory has been that hierarchy prevents open communication and that open communication will help solve problems. In short, these methods have been focused on changing the human condition in organizations, making them less hierarchical and more democratic. They have failed to populate psychologically safe processes for feedback with means by which leadership teams could actually redesign their organization to *fit* the firm's objectives and strategy. That is because existing methods have failed to embrace the following paradoxes essential for successful business transformations:

- **Embrace both the objective economic value creation and organization development.**[24] Many of the methods for confronting internal organizational problems do not focus the inquiry sufficiently on task/business objectives and strategy. Successful corporate change efforts, research has shown, are motivated by task/business issues as opposed to programs focused solely on changing the human condition in organizations.[25] That is because many managers see human resource and organization development programs as important for the long term but irrelevant for solving urgent business problems. Moreover, clarity of direction is an essential first step for beginning a dialogue about the organization's fit with its competitive environment.
- **Embrace the paradox of top-down direction and bottom-up participation.**[26] Effective change efforts are a partnership between leaders and led. Current methods for enabling honesty focus on empowering lower levels to speak but in the process of doing so may actually unempower top teams to lead change. In effect the methods developed assume that for organizations to be more effective they must become more democratic. While excessive hierarchy will undermine organizational effectiveness, so can indecisive

leadership teams at the top. Along with other researchers, we have found that effective top teams are essential to a successful corporate transformation.[27] Methods for organizational change must, therefore, enable leadership teams to get stronger and develop greater effectiveness as a team, to learn how to lead while leading learning and change.

- **Embrace the paradox of "hard" and "soft."**[28]
  Organization change efforts tend to split "hard" structure and systems changes from interventions aimed at changing "soft" emotional, behavioral, and cultural factors. Management consulting firms recommend changes in structure and systems while organization development consultants focus on surfacing valid data—what people perceive and feel are problems. The former result in valid solutions that run into implementation problems. The latter often fail to result in the structure or systems that are required for a fundamental transformation in the business. The coordination problems surfaced in the companies we studied had their roots in organizational structures and processes, not just leadership behavior. Top teams needed a framework for analyzing and changing organizational design to create a long-term solution to problems they were experiencing while also targeting for change their behaviors as leadership teams.

- **Embrace the paradox of advocacy and inquiry.**[29] The methods for confronting hidden problems are often used to cope with crisis. A meeting that surfaces problems leads management to plan and advocate change. Too frequently, however, leaders do not then re-engage the organization to inquire about the efficacy of the organizational changes they have made. They particularly avoid inquiring into whether they have been successful in adopting the leadership behaviors required to support organizational changes. When inevitable inconsistencies between what leaders advocate and their actual decisions and behavior are not addressed publicly, cynicism emerges, trust is reduced, commitment diminishes, and momentum is lost. Leaders' capacity to elicit commitment to changes in the future is also reduced. If organizations are to be adaptive, their leaders will have to adopt a disciplined organizational learning process that "enforces" a continuous cycle of advocacy and inquiry throughout the life of the organization.

Convinced that the barriers to creating an honest conversation about the state of the organization as a total system is essential but very difficult for managers to orchestrate, Russell Eisenstat and I developed a strategic change process called Organizational Fitness Profiling (OFP).[30] OFP creates an honest organizational conversation about the *fit* of the organization and its leadership with objectives and strategy advocated by the top management team. It guides top management through a diagnosis of the organization as a system (see Figure 19–3), the development of a plan to redesign and change the organizational levers in the model, and then further inquiry into the success of the change over time. Fitness Profiling embraces the paradoxes discussed earlier, thus allowing it to be a systemic change process—to change structure and systems as well as leadership and organizational behavior, to make change in the top team and in the coordination at lower levels, and to create broad change across several organizational levers while also creating deep cultural change. It has been applied in over 150 organizational units within 18 corporations operating in several different national cultures with quite different work values. Below I describe OFP through the lens of its application at the Santa Rosa Systems Division of Hewlett-Packard.[31]

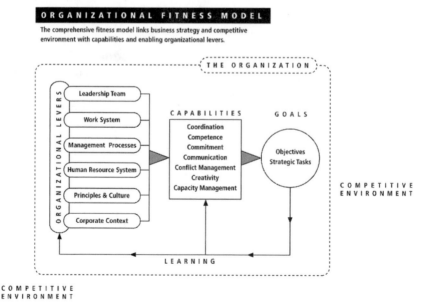

Figure 19–3   Organizationa fitness mode .

Organizational Fitness Profiling

The Santa Rosa Systems Division of Hewlett-Packard (SRSD) was created in 1992 to target new systems integration opportunities in the growing communication business sector. By 1994 SRSD faced fundamental challenges that threatened its success and that of its leadership team. Organizational members perceived the following organizational issues.

- Two competing strategies that were threatening to "tear the organization apart."
- Coordination—"a cold war"—problems between two functions competing for common engineering resources. These problems were caused by a functional structure with very poorly designed cross-functional business teams.
- Cross-functional teams that were not effectively led or managed and did not produce needed coordination.
- A top team that was not effective—spent too little time on strategic issues.
- A general manager who was not confronting and resolving key strategic and organizational issues.
- Low trust that prevented organizational problems, known to everyone, from being discussed and managed.
- Underperformance in rate of growth and profitability as well as low morale and turnover of key technical people.

OFP enabled SRSD's leadership team to surface these problems and make changes that allowed the business unit to capitalize on the market opportunities it was chartered to exploit. The leadership team and many of the key managers in the division had grown up in Hewlett-Packard's traditional instrument business. Not surprisingly, SRSD's organizational design and management behavior reflected this experience and did not fit the new systems business strategy Hewlett-Packard was pursuing. Fitness profiling enabled the leadership team to have an honest organizational conversation about the silent killers and diagnose root causes. Using the organizational systems model in Figure 19–3 they were able to take a helicopter view of the organization and clarify their strategy for themselves and the organization as well as change a number the organizational design levers in the model needed to implement the strategy. These changes in turn affected the key capabilities needed to compete (middle box in Figure 19–3), particularly coordination, commitment, communication, conflict management, and capacity management (allocation of resources).

Following is a description of each of the four stages in OFP that unfold over an eight- to 10-week time frame as well a brief description of the organizational and leadership changes at SRSD that occurred at each stage. A third party outside of the organizational unit (an external consultant for corporate profiles or internal HR/OD professionals for organizational units below the corporate level) facilitates the process, leads the top team through the analysis of their organization using research-based heuristics and tools embedded in the process, and acts as a thought partner in developing plans for organization change.

Stage 1: Develop a Statement of Business and Organizational Direction (1–2 Weeks)

Description

The first major event in a Fitness Profile is a one- to two-day meeting with the senior management team to craft a statement of direction. It articulates the links between the competitive context, performance goals, business strategy, and needed business and organizational changes. Each member of the team prepares answers to questions designed to help the top team crystallize its strategy and test for agreement.

Outcomes at SRSD

The meeting surfaced a number of differences in interpretation of the strategy and the role of business teams. It helped crystallize the strategy and organizational capabilities needed for the business to succeed. As in most profiles, the process began to develop better communication and trust. It started a process of learning for the general manager that gave him new insights about his top team and his own leadership. Finally the meeting produced a document that was used throughout the process as the basis of the inquiry into the fit of the organization with its environment and strategy.

Stage 2: Complete a Broadly Validated Assessment of the Current State of the Enterprise (3–5 Weeks)

Description

The CEO and his or her management team select a task force of eight highly regarded managers from various parts of the firm. The task force conducts in-depth interviews with approximately 100 managers in pivotal roles throughout the corporation. They ask about key organizational strengths to be preserved and barriers to be overcome if objectives and strategy are to be achieved. In one day the task force organizes its data using the rigorous analytic framework shown in Figure 19–3. The consultant interviews the top team using the same questions as the task force and also asks about the leadership teams effectiveness.

On the following day the task force feeds its findings back to the senior team using a process we have found reveals the "whole truth" about the firm's problems. The task force sits in a "fishbowl" in the middle of the room, facing one another, while the top team sits at tables in the shape of a U surrounding the task force. Psychological safety is bolstered by several factors. The task force is seated facing each other signaling that they are speaking as a group. As they discuss their findings they remind the top team that they are reporters. These arrangements provide the psychological safety needed for the task force and enable a rich conversation between the top team and the task force. Top team feedback to the task force's findings follows the "fishbowl."

Outcomes at SRSD

The top team received an unvarnished and comprehensive assessment of the organization's current capabilities and effectiveness. It revealed the business's "core DNA" (a strong tradition of engineering) as well as its core weaknesses—inadequate linkages between engineering, marketing, and the custom systems function. The root cause was the functional organization, a legacy of the traditional instrument business and the way the top team managed this organization. The top team was not functioning is a way that enabled effective cross-functional and cross-business decisions. The general manager's style prevented the top team from dealing with critical strategic issues.

The honest feedback had a powerful emotional impact, something that is not possible through more traditional one-on-one discussions or consultant presentations. It built a shared commitment to change SRSD and reduced the silo mentality that caused poor performance and resistance to change.

Because they heard about problems from their own people and in their own language, the top team felt a strong obligation to lead change. Task force members shifted allegiance from their own functional unit to the division as a whole. They become deeply knowledgeable about, and committed to, the transformation of the business as a whole.

Stage 3: Create an Integrated Agenda for Action (2–4 Weeks)

Description

After a day of receiving feedback about the current state of the organization, the task force departs and calls those who they interviewed about how the feedback was received. The senior team spends the next two days using the Fitness Model in Figure 19–3 to perform a root cause diagnosis of the organization's fit with its strategy and develops a plan to realign the organization.

Outcomes at SRSD

An integrated organizational change plan was developed. The top team

- Combined warring engineering groups into one department
- Created a matrix organization with a business team leader responsible for profitability and authority to run four key businesses, an organizational form unpopular at Hewlett-Packard
- Redefined the role for the top team and rules for engaging conflict and making decisions

The profiling meeting did not only change formal (hard) organizational arrangements. Its powerful emotional impact enabled the leadership team to develop trust and commitment to a new organizational vision. It began to reduce cynicism and built a partnership among the top team, the task force, and the "top 100" who were interviewed.

The top team also developed a structure and process by which change was to be managed in the next year.

Stage 4: Develop and Mobilize the Commitment of Key Managers and Stakeholders Behind the Transformation Plan (1–3 Weeks)

Description

Shortly following the three-day profiling meeting, the top management team meets with the task force a second time to share what they heard, their diagnosis, and their plans for change. After caucusing separately, the task force critiques the proposed change plan. Does it address the key issues identified in their interviews? Will it meet resistance in the organization? Has the leadership team identified the changes in their own decision-making process and behavior essential to the success of the new organizational arrangements?

Following the meeting with the task force, the leadership team takes their vision of change to the larger organization. They meet with the "top 100" people for further discussion and to enlist their support. Changes are then communicated widely, often with the help of the task force.

Outcomes at SRSD

The task force was quite vehement in its critique of the change plan the leadership team created. They had some specific concerns about the organization's design but they were also concerned about the "soft stuff," the leadership team's ability to change their behavior. The general manager, to explore alternative organizational designs, formed sub-groups. Within a week a slightly modified organizational design emerged, to which the leadership team and task force were committed. It was communicated to the whole organization. Trust and openness in SRSD improved as a result of the process. Within less than four months SRSD had simultaneously transformed the fit of its organization with strategy; taken significant first steps in the development of an effective leadership team; and established a climate of hope, trust, and commitment to the new organizational arrangements.

Building Organizational Fitness: Results and Implications

What were the effects on SRSD's performance? In the first year alone sales doubled and profitability quadrupled. SRSD continued to employ OFP as a core strategic management process over the next five years. During that period organizational effectiveness and performance increased steadily. Five years after OFP was introduced, the CEO of the company stated that the division had progressed from the worst to one of the best in the company.[32] Employees saw it as a listening division in which the leadership team was now exerting effective strategic direction of the business. Moreover, members of the senior team and task force saw the experience of going through OFP as a powerful management and leadership development experience.

Research on the application of OFP in over a dozen organizations has shown that a disciplined process like OFP can produce an honest organizational conversation that reveals the unvarnished truth about the organization's fit with its business environment and its fitness to adapt. The discipline of the process helps general managers embrace the paradox inherent to building fit and fitness. The analytic frameworks embedded in

OFP have produced dramatic changes in organizational design, leadership, and performance in a variety of corporate settings and national cultures.

I began this chapter by presenting evidence that corporations and their leaders fail to adapt, endangering their performance and even survival. Our program of action research, using Organizational Fitness Profiling, has shown that sustaining high performance depends heavily on the willingness of top managers to confront the fit of their organization with the demands of the competitive environment and the fit of their assumptions and leadership behavior with the needs of the organization. Managers, like those at the Santa Rosa Systems Division of Hewlett-Packard, who are willing to confront the unvarnished truth can evolve their organization and management systems to changing circumstance. But it requires humility and courage. We have, however, met just as many managers who prefer to avoid the truth about their business, organization, and leadership behavior. Courage to learn seems to be what limits organizational fitness.

Given that not all managers are ready to embrace the truth and learn, what might firms do that want to develop the organizational fitness required in the 21st century? A strong case can be made for institutionalizing a strategic change process like OFP in corporations so that CEOs and business unit managers can be held accountable for continuous learning about the fit and fitness of their organization and leadership. Candid review by the CEO with the board of directors and by business unit managers with the CEO about what they have learned about their organization, their top team, and themselves would develop a corporate learning culture that embraces paradox. It would create accountability for fit and fitness—the crucial ingredients for sustained corporate performance and survival.

What I Learned from Richard Beckhard: A Personal Retrospective

Edgar H. Schein

In this tribute I want to share with the readers some of the reasons why I have always considered Richard (Dick) Beckhard my primary mentor. I have had many mentors and am grateful to all of them. They include my PhD thesis advisors Gordon Allport and Richard Solomon at the Harvard Graduate School of Social Relations; Alex Bavelas, a teacher at MIT; David Rioch, a brilliant psychiatrist who was my boss at the Walter Reed Institute of Research; and Douglas McGregor, who brought me to MIT—where I have spent my entire academic career. But none had such an immediate and profound influence on me—directly, through his advice and through the role model that he was—as Dick Beckhard.

I met Dick in 1956 during my first year at MIT and worked closely with him until his death. And I have to conclude as I look over my own 50-year career that Dick influenced what I do and how I do it more than all of the others I named above. This influence covered primarily how I view my relationship to organizations and clients, secondarily what and how to teach, and last, but not least, how to deal with the ordinary vicissitudes and frustrations of life. How is it possible for one man to be so influential? What magic touch did Dick have that made him so profoundly influential? I want to put this into a series of stories, each of which makes a central learning point. These stories are organized somewhat chronologically going back to 1956.

Dick's First Intervention

Doug McGregor decided to build the Organization Studies Department of MIT's School of Industrial Management (now the Sloan School of Management) by hiring psychologists from the discipline even if they had no experience with business or industry. My assistant professor colleagues were a social psychologist, Marvin Shaw, and a brilliant psychological statistician and scale builder, Warren Torgerson. I think Doug sensed that we were not particularly skilled in collaboration and teamwork and decided to use an outside resource to catalyze this process. So one day, when we walked into Doug's office, he said he had a visitor who was interested in what we were doing, so could we all sit together and tell him a bit about ourselves. The visitor was, of course, Dick Beckhard, and I am sure that he had been briefed to help us to become more of a group.

What I learned from the next hour or two is the power of the outsider catalyst. Dick was brilliant in asking each of us to talk about ourselves. After all, we had to be polite to the outsider. He asked us innocent but potent questions about how our work connected, which reminded me vividly of something that I had learned from David Rioch. If you are inquiring about something that may be socially sensitive, do not ask about it. You will only elicit answers that the respondent considers "safe." Instead, the outsider can ask "dumb" questions that elicit the desire to tell the friendly outsider what they *really* think.

I learned a great deal that day about what my colleagues thought and how we could work together better but only realized years later that this result was the product of the skillful interventions that Dick had made in his role as visitor. I also learned, in retrospect, that we are always intervening, not just when we are in official consultant roles. I learned from Dick to think like an interventionist and to seize whatever opportunities presented themselves to intervene constructively.

At that time we were all stuck in the incorrect model that one should or could make a diagnosis before intervening. I now understand much better by having watched Dick over the years that "everything we do is an intervention," and that everything we observe in response to it is diagnostic data. The two processes are completely intertwined.

Dick's Practical Wisdom and Emphasis on "Process"

In the summer of 1957 I went to the National Training Labs (NTL) three-week human relations workshop. Doug had recommended this highly, no doubt based on observing in me some personal rigidities that would eventually undermine my ability to teach executives and do consulting. Dick was a regular attendee on the NTL staff, so I observed him first as a lecturer and later as a designer of labs and a co-trainer.

In his brief "lecturettes," a regular daily feature of the NTL workshops, I learned from Dick how much could be gotten across in 20 minutes if you made it vivid, simple, and descriptive. The goal was not to impart heavy academic knowledge about communication, groups, and organizations, but to give the participants simple models for thinking about things. To this day I remember and use Dick's model of the "circular process"—how our expectations of another person make us hear him or hear in that way, and, thereby, create in that other person responses that eventually confirm our initial expectation. The "quiet" person does not get heard when he or she occasionally speaks and concludes therefore that his or her comments are of little value and decides to speak less, thus confirming our initial impression. This lecturette was delivered in the late 1950s, when research on self-fulfilling prophecies and the Pygmalion effect were still to be published. Dick had an intuitive wisdom about how things worked that was way ahead of what the academic fields understood.

When and how things are presented was viewed by Dick as an "educational intervention," and I came to learn later that such interventions were often the only way to get into a client system. If you did them well, if you stimulated the client with ideas and possibilities, then the next steps in a consulting project might result. Of special importance were educational interventions that an OD person might generate to get senior line executives involved in situations where they would not attend anything that might be more directly personally involving or where high degrees of skepticism were evident at the outset. On many occasions I watched Dick present material to skeptical CEOs and executive VPs that got them very curious to learn more, and thus launch what might become a major consulting project.

Dick's Brilliance as a "Designer of Social/Organizational Process"

When I became a staff intern and later staff member at NTL, I had many occasions to work with Dick in planning the labs. Of all the staff members with whom I worked, none could hold a candle to Dick when it came to inventing exercises and designing the flow of a day or a week in terms of the arrangement and pacing of training groups, lecturettes, larger group exercises, free time, and various other kinds of assignments that made the labs powerful learning experiences. I now realize 40 years later that this skill of designing social and organizational process is a critical management skill and that, in fact, most managers are woefully lacking in it. Particularly weak is our ability to design meetings, so I find myself in both my professional and personal life often being the only person who has a sense of when to do what, how to arrange a room, how to get a meeting or some other event started, how much time to allot to different parts of the event, and how to ensure that learning and results are achieved.

I have vivid recollections of working with Dick in later years. We were usually working in hotel conference rooms that were not well-suited to the kinds of processes that we wanted to stimulate, so our first job was always to "rearrange the furniture." I find myself doing exactly the same thing today and always think of Dick as I am trying to make long tables more circular or whatever.

It has always puzzled me why the physical and social design of social and organizational events is so obvious to OD people and so consistently ignored by most managers I have worked with. They will call a meeting and hold it in a room that is absolutely impossible to work in without ever considering the possibility of changing the layout of the room or moving to another room. They will start off the meeting of a group of strangers with a difficult task and be completely oblivious of the psychological dynamics that are operating in the group, and then wonder later why the group was not more productive.

If it is true that Dick's great sense of design and process came from his background as a stage manager in the theater, then perhaps a stint in drama and stage management should be a part of all management training. There have been efforts recently at the Academy of Management meetings to bring in improvisational theater actors and have them tell how they manage their interactions. It is high time because it strikes me that the essence of management, if not all of life, is improvisation. We are constantly facing unpredictable events and having to improvise in dealing with them.

Designing for Involvement in the Management of Change

It has been known ever since Lewin's classic studies that if you want to produce change you must involve the participants in the change process. But with this knowledge there was precious little design skill to implement it until Dick's classic confrontation meeting design. Consider the audacity of it— bring virtually your entire organization into the meeting and design an upward cascade to bring the ideas and knowledge of the entire organization to the attention of top management within a single day. It is bold and it works.

In the mid 1960s the management of change became a major issue. Under NTL auspices Dick and I designed a one-year change management program that taught me the secret of motivation. The managers who signed up for this program met quarterly for three-day segments. Before arrival at the first segment they were instructed to choose an organizational change problem that they were actually working on and that could be substantially impacted in a one-year time frame. It had to be real, meaningful, and something that they felt they could personally impact. The message was that this one-year program would not just teach *how* to produce change, but would actually *produce* change. The measure of success would be the actual changes produced and the learning would, therefore, be experiential, not academic.

In the first three-day workshop we taught some models of change theory, gave the participants some diagnostic tools like force-field analysis, and had them present their change problems to each other to develop the data that would allow them to form some natural teams that would work together throughout the year. Once they were in teams of three or four they diagnosed each problem and made specific plans for what to do in the next three months, knowing that they would be reporting back to each other at the next quarterly meeting. At the same time they made plans to stay in touch with each other so that if things came up back in the organization that had not been anticipated they could telephone each other or meet to think about what to do next.

Dick and I served as sounding boards, designers, and audiences. At each quarterly meeting of two or three days, each person would review their change project, tell what was accomplished, where further help was needed, and make new plans. Motivation was always very high because each participant was working on a real problem in his or her own organization and had an audience to whom to report progress and problems.

I used this design concept many years later in a one-semester MBA course at the Sloan School. Each student had to identify a change goal in the university or the greater Boston area that he or she, with one or two others, would actually accomplish. At the same time each student had to pick a personal change problem, something that he or she wanted to change by the end of the semester. My role was to teach some change theory, give the students diagnostic tools, and help them get organized into teams, but, most important, not get involved in the choice of change goal.

Each week each student had to report goals and progress so I could provide feedback. I was always careful not to influence the *content* of what the person wanted to work on, although I might challenge the realism, the timetable, or the choice of how to go about it. I learned over many years of doing this class that the key to the students' motivation was their ownership of their own change goals. And this lesson was first learned in Dick's and my NTL change workshop.

Keeping Your Cool, Working the Problem

I first learned to manage my own emotions and stay focused on solving the problem in the NTL staff meetings when we were designing the workshops. In the tense confrontations between strong-minded staff members with different ideas about how to design the lab, frustration and anger would run high. I watched Dick and learned from him that the best way to deal with such tension is to try to stay focused on the problem that needs to be solved. Calmly but firmly Dick would focus us on the schedule and ask calmly what would be best to do next rather than letting us get into academic arguments about philosophy of design.

The best example actually came from watching Dick deal with an airline ticket agent when Dick was told that his flight to Chicago had been peremptorily canceled. The agent was not particularly helpful and Dick faced the possibility of missing an important meeting. What was most noticeable to me was that Dick did not show any sign of anger. Instead, he stated clearly and articulately, "I need to get to Chicago this evening, can you help me?" The agent replied that the airline did not have any other flights that evening, to which Dick replied, "I need to get to Chicago tonight, what can you do for me?"

What I and, no doubt, the agent observed was that this person had a need and that he would not back off from the need. It had nothing to do with upset or anger, it was focused on how to get to Chicago. At that point the agent said, "Well, I could check the other airlines," to which Dick said, "Please do." It developed, of course, that there were alternatives, that the ticket could be signed over to another airline and Dick got to Chicago. I always try to remember this set of events when I lose my temper at an airport or store when things thwart what I want. Stay focused on what you want and keep making your need known until you get the help you need.

The Consummate Consultant

Consulting is usually a lonely activity. One does not typically attend a session where a consultant is one-on-one with the client. Yet that is where some of the more subtle interventions occur. Dick always made an effort to make his style visible by bringing clients into the classroom and by modeling his style on his ordinary interactions with colleagues. When I observed Dick in this role over many years I learned some critical lessons that I want to pass on.

1. Know who your client is. In a complex organizational situation it is often confusing to determine on whose behalf what is being done. Thinking clearly, asking questions, and taking a broad view all have to be done to sort out who is a contact client, who is a primary client (usually the one who is footing the bills), and who is an ultimate client (who will be affected

but may not know it). I learned from Dick how important it is to consider the possible ultimate clients of any given project.

2. Know when to remain in a process consultant role and when to become an expert. I learned from Dick and from my own experience that the best kind of help is to help the client to help him or herself (what I later came to call *process consultation*). However, clients often want to be dependent, they want to have an expert to lean on and to tell them what to do. Dick had a wonderful prescription for the situation where you want to keep the client on the hook but the client wants a recommendation. Dick said, "If the client insists on a recommendation, always give him (or her) at least two. That way they still have to make a choice and be actively involved."

I also observed Dick becoming quite directive, and that used to puzzle me. We often co-trained in the NTL workshops and Dick would direct the group in ways that often made me uncomfortable. What I learned eventually is that if one has a basically trusting relationship with a client group, direction is acceptable, especially if the consultant is more experienced and really does know what kind of expertise will be helpful. It is essential to stay in the process consultant mode until that trust is established, but I have learned in my own experience that once there is a sense that the client trusts you—that you are working with the client in a team context trying to solve the client's problem together—almost any kind of intervention and confrontation can work.

3. Be prepared for anything. The most striking thing about Dick was that nothing ever seemed to upset him. Whatever happened, that was the reality to be dealt with. Dick could invent designs to cover virtually any situation that could come up and be a role model for how to handle adversity with calm flexibility—often the most important lesson the client learned.

Co-editing the Addison-Wesley Series on Organizational Development

One of my greatest pleasures of the last four decades was to work with Dick in the creation of the Addison-Wesley OD Series. Warren Bennis, Dick, and I knew that the field was not ready for a single textbook, so we decided to let practitioners speak for themselves. We had a great division of labor. We would each look at the submitted manuscript and if we all agreed, no problem. If we had a difference of opinion we either met or phoned each other and made our points of view known. In every case these short discussions resolved immediately whether we should reject, send back for editing, or accept the manuscript. Eventually, Warren Bennis went on to university administration, which made it impossible for him to devote time to this editing so Dick and I carried on.

Having learned a bit about this editing game, we also edited each other's work to great mutual profit. Dick had an uncanny knack for spotting good ideas and representing them in a clear fashion. I usually supplied a more academic view, looking for theoretical inconsistencies or connections to other work. We both benefited greatly from the different way in which we each approached our work.

Knowing Oneself

So much more could be said about Dick and my relationship to him. Perhaps the most important residue of that relationship is a commitment to knowing oneself, to honest self-confrontation, and to a practical kind of wisdom based on "working the problem." Dick never seemed to get flustered, no matter how fouled up a situation might be. His direct cutting through to the essence of the problem and his calm handling of it will remain with me forever as a model of how to conduct oneself in an increasingly turbulent world. Thanks for that, Dick.

Notes

Chapter 1

[1]J. Welch and J.A. Byrne, *Jack: Straight from the Guts* (New York: Warner Books, 2001).

[2]S. Redstone, *A Passion to Win* (New York: Simon & Schuster, 2000).

[3]S. Chowdhury, *The Talent Era: Achieving a High Return on Talent* (Upper Saddle River, NJ: Financial Times Prentice Hall, 2002).

[4]S. Chowdhury, ed., *Management 21C: Someday We'll All Manage this Way* (London: Financial Times Prentice Hall, 2000).

Chapter 2

[1]Our database concerning global leadership and the global organization is twofold. First, we obtained field data in the course of a large number of consultations and action research projects in global companies interested in corporate transformation or acquisitions (mindset or attitudinal change among executives being one of the desired outcomes). Second, we gathered much of our material from interviews with over 300 senior executives. A large number of the individuals interviewed were presidents or members of the board of their respective companies. Many of them participated in Manfred Kets de Vries' leadership program at INSEAD, titled "The Challenge of Leadership: Developing Your Emotional Intelligence"—a seminar whose major objective is to provide participants with a better understanding of their leadership style, deepen their awareness of the cross-cultural dimensions of leadership, and help them develop their emotional intelligence. Because participants were self-selected (they approached us for intervention and advice) and highly motivated by a desire to change their leadership style and/or their organizations, we were able to conduct in-depth and quite personal interviews. These open-ended, exploratory interviews were conducted in a semi-structured fashion. Each respondent was asked open-ended questions pertaining to global leadership and organizational practices. Depending on the responses, revisions were made to the questions. Observational data consisted of notes taken while studying the various executives in meetings and during informal discussions, and in many cases by repeated visits to the organizations in question (British Petroleum, Virgin, Nokia, ABB, etc.). In engaging in this kind of fieldwork, we

used "grounded theory" to arrive at a set of hypotheses about global leadership practices; in other words, while engaged in the process of hypothesis formulation, we delineated connections, patterns, and themes, continuously modifying the hypothesis depending on emerging material. Through this ethnographic and clinical orientation, ideas were developed and a "thick" description emerged.

[2]J. Rost, *Leadership for the 21st Century* (New York: Praeger, 1991).

[3]P. Dorfman, ed., *International and Cross-Cultural Leadership* (Cambridge, UK: Blackwell, 1996).

[4]G. Hofstede and M. Bond, "The Confucius Connection: From Cultural Roots to Economic Growth," *Organizational Dynamics* (Spring, 1988), 5–21.

[5]M. Kets de Vries, "The Leadership Mystique," *Academy of Management Executive* (Vol. 8, No. 3, 1994), 73–89.

[6]D. Goleman, *Working with Emotional Intelligence* (New York: Bantam Books, 1998); R. Hogan, G.J. Curphy, and J. Hogan, "What Do We Know About Leadership?," *American Psychologist* (Vol. 49, No. 6, 1994), 493–504.

[7]M. Kets de Vries, *Struggling with the Demon: Essays in Individual and Organizational Irrationality* (Madison, CT: Psychosocial Press, 2000).

[8]See S.R. Kobassa, "Stress Life Events, Personality, and Health: An Inquiry into Hardiness," *Journal of Personality and Social Psychology* (Vol. 37, 1979), 1–11.

[9]M. Kets de Vries and C. Mead, "The Development of the Global Leader within the Multinational Corporation," in V. Pucik, N. Tichy, and C. Barnett, eds., *Globalizing Management* (New York: John Wiley & Sons, 1992), 187–205; M. Kets de Vries and E. Florent-Treacy, *The New Global Leaders* (San Francisco: Jossey-Bass, 1999).

[10]Y. Doz, "Strategic Management in Multinational Companies," *Sloan Management Review* (Vol. 21, No. 2, 1980), 27–46.

[11]M. Porter, "Competition in Global Industries: A Conceptual Framework," paper presented at the Prince Bertil Symposium on Strategies for Global Competition, Stockholm School of Economics, November 7–9, 1984.

[12]D. Heenan and H. Perlmutter, *Multinational Organizational Development: A Social Architecture Perspective* (Reading, MA: Addison-Wesley, 1979).

[13]C. Bartlett and S. Ghoshal, "Managing across Borders: New Organizational Responses," *Sloan Management Review* (Fall, 1987), 43–53.

[14]B. Chakravarthy and H. Perlmutter, "Strategic Planning for a Global Business," in F. Root and K. Visudtibhan, eds., *International Strategic Management* (New York: Taylor & Francis, 1992), 29–41.

[15]M. Kets de Vries and E. Florent-Treacy, "British Petroleum: Transformational Leadership in a Transnational Organization," INSEAD case study, 1997.

[16]B. McKay, "New Coke Chief Tries to See through Eyes of the World," *Wall Street Journal Europe*, June 23–23, 2000, 1, 10.

[17]N.J. Adler, *International Dimensions of Organizational Behavior* (Cincinnati, OH: Southwestern College Publishing, 1997); N.J. Adler and S. Bartolomew, "Managing Globally Competent People," *Academy of Management Executive* (Vol. 6, No. 3, 1992), 52–65.

[18]J. Kahn, "The World's Most Admired Companies," *Fortune* (October 26, 1998), 76–94.

[19]S. Branch, "The Hundred Best Companies to Work for in America," *Fortune* (January 11, 1999), 58.

[20]W. Safire, ed., *Lend Me Your Ears: Great Speeches in History* (New York: W.W. Norton, 1992), 688–689.

Chapter 3

[1]Paul Evans and Tom Murtha contributed heavily in developing many of the ideas presented in this chapter.

[2]Cited in K. Barham and C. Heimer, *ABB: The Dancing Giant* (London: Financial Times, 1998), X.

[3]The integration/responsiveness framework is most closely associated with C.K. Prahalad and Y. Doz, *The Multinational Mission: Balancing Local Demands and Global Vision* (New York: Free Press, 1987); C.A. Bartlett and S. Ghoshal, *Managing across Borders: The Transnational Solution* (Cambridge, MA: Harvard Business School Press, 1989).

[4]For early arguments on the mindset implications of international decision making, see Aharoni (1966); Kindleberger (1969); C.K. Prahalad and R.A. Betis, "The Dominant Logic: A New Linkage between Diversity and Performance," *Strategic Management Journal* (Vol. 7, 1986), 485–501.

[5]H.V. Perlmutter, "The Tortuous Evolution of the Multinational Corporation," *Columbia Journal of World Business* (Vol. 4, 1969), 9–18.

[6]H.V. Perlmutter, "The Tortuous Evolution of the Multinational Corporation," *Columbia Journal of World Business* (Vol. 4, 1969), 13.

[7]For this perspective on global mindset, see S.H. Rhinesmith, *A Manager's Guide to Globalization: Six Keys to Success in a Changing World* (Homewood, IL: ASTD & Business One Irwin, 1993); N.M. Tichy et al., "Leadership Development as a Lever for Global Transformation," in *Globalizing Management: Creating and Leading the Competitive Organization,* V. Pucik, N. M. Tichy, and C. K. Barnett, eds., (New York: Wiley, 1992); R. Ashkenas et al., *The Boundaryless Organization: Breaking the Chains of Organizational Structure* (San Francisco: Jossey-Bass, 1995).

[8]V. Govindarajan and A. Gupta, "Success Is all in the Mindset," *Financial Times*, February 27, 1998. Similarly, R.M. Kanter, *World Class: Thriving Locally in the Global Economy* (New York: Simon & Schuster, 1995) sees this as a difference between new "cosmopolitans" and "locals"—to use terms developed earlier by the sociologist Gouldner to describe the difference between people who identified with the wider profession as opposed to those who identified with the "local" interests of the firm.

[9]K. Barham and D. Oates, *The International Manager* (London: Economist Books, 1991).

[10]O.S. Levy, S. Beechler, and N. Boyacigiller, "What We Talk About When We Talk About 'Global Mindset': Managerial Cognition in MNCs." Paper presented at the 1999 annual meeting, Academy of Management, Toronto.

[11]The importance of balanced cognitive orientation was emphasized by Prahalad and Doz; G. Hedlund, "The Hypermodern MNC: A Heterarchy?," *Human Resource Management* (Spring, 1986), 9–35; C.A. Bartlett and S. Ghoshal, *Managing across Borders: The Transnational Solution* (Cambridge, MA: Harvard Business School Press, 1989).

[12]C.A. Bartlett and S. Ghoshal, *Managing across Borders: The Transnational Solution* (Cambridge, MA: Harvard Business School Press, 1989), 212.

[13]For further elaboration, see T.P. Murtha, S.A. Lenway, and R.P. Bagozzi, "Global Mindsets and Cognitive Shift in a Complex Multinational Corporation," *Strategic Management Journal* (Vol. 19, 1998), 97–114.

[14]V. Pucik and T. Saba, "Selecting and Developing the Global versus the Expatriate Manager: A Review of the State-of-the-Art," *Human Resource Planning* (Vol. 21, No. 4, 1998), 40–54.

[15]See the discussion and references on expatriate issues in Evans, Pucik, and Barsoux, Chapter 3.

[16] T.P. Murtha, S.A. Lenway, and R.P. Bagozzi, "Global Mindsets and Cognitive Shift in a Complex Multinational Corporation," *Strategic Management Journal* (Vol. 19, 1998), 97–114.

[17]The initial study (Company A) was reported in Murtha.

[18]A. Edström, and J.R. Galbraith, "Transfer of Managers as a Coordination and Control Strategy in Multinational Organizations," *Administrative Science Quarterly* (Vol. 22, 1977), 248–263.

[19]N.M. Tichy et al., "Leadership Development as a Lever for Global Transformation," in *Globalizing Management: Creating and Leading the Competitive Organization*, V. Pucik, N.M. Tichy, and C.K., ed., (New York: Wiley, 1992).

[20]For an analysis of the roles of global business, country, function, and corporate managers, see C.A. Bartlett and S. Ghoshal, "What is a Global Manager?," *Harvard Business Review* (September–October 1992), 124–132.

[21]For a detailed discussion of various coordination mechanisms in global firms see Chapter 7 in Evans, Pucik, and Barsoux.

[22]R.M. Kanter, *World Class: Thriving Locally in the Global Economy* (New York: Simon & Schuster, 1995), 60.

[23]The Japanese firm Sony first coined this now well-known aphorism, later adopted by ABB and other firms as their corporate slogan.

Chapter 7

[1]Some of the material presented in this chapter is adapted from S.A. Culbert and J.B. Ullmen, *Don't Kill the Bosses!* (New York: Berrett-Koehler, 2001).

[2]P. Freire, *The Pedagogy of the Oppressed* (New York: Continuum, 1992).

[3]The socialization process is described in S.A. Culbert, *The Organization Trap* (New York: Basic Books, 1974).

[4]For deeper views please refer to Culbert 2001 and S.A. Culbert, *Mind-Set Management* (New York: Oxford University Press, 1996).

[5]First stated in S.A. Culbert and J.J. McDonough, *Radical Management* (New York: Free Press, 1985).

[6]S.A. Culbert, *Mind-Set Management* (New York: Oxford University Press, 1996).

[7]One such system is detailed in Culbert 2001, Chapter 8.

Chapter 8

[1]See G.T. Milkovich and J.M. Newman, *Compensation, 7th ed.* (Boston: McGraw-Hill/Irwin, 2002) for a review of basic reward principles. The first compensation book was D.F. Schloss, *Industrial Remuneration* (London: Williams and Norgate, 1892).

[2]D.G. Jenkins, Jr. et al., "Are Financial Incentives Related to Performance? A Meta-Analysis Review of Empirical Research," *Journal of Applied Psychology* (Vol. 83, 1998), 777–787.

[3]D.G. Jenkins, Jr. et al., *Skill-Based Pay: Practices, Payoffs, Pitfalls, and Prescriptions* (Scottsdale, AZ: American Compensation Association, 1987); J.L. McAdams and E.J. Hawk, *Organizational Performance and Rewards* (Scottsdale, AZ: American Compensation Association, 1995).

[4]R.L. Heneman, *Business-Driven Compensation Policies: Integrating Compensation Systems with Corporate Strategies* (New York: AMACOM, 2001); R.L. Heneman, *Strategic Reward Management: Design, Implementation, and Evaluation* (Greenwich, CT: Information Age Press, in press).

[5]R.L. Heneman, "Job and Work Evaluation: A Literature Review," *Public Personnel Management* (in press).

[6]R.L. Heneman, G.E. Ledford, and M. Gresham, "The Changing Nature of Work and Its Effects on Compensation Design and Delivery," in S.L. Rynes and B. Gerhart, eds., *Compensation in Organizations: Current Research and Practice*, Society for Industrial and Organizational Psychology Frontiers of Industrial and Organizational Psychology Series (San Francisco: Jossey-Bass, 2000), 195–240.

[7]J.R. Hackman and E.E. Lawler, III, "Employee Reactions to Job Characteristics," *Journal of Applied Psychology* (Vol. 55, 1971), 259–286.

[8]E.E. Lawler, III, S.A. Mohrman, and G.E. Ledford, Jr., *Strategies for High Performance Organizations* (San Francisco: Jossey-Bass, 1998).

[9]D. Ulrich, M.R. Losey, and G. Lake, eds., *Tomorrow's HR Management* (New York: John Wiley & Sons, 1997).

[10]R. Heneman and D. Greenberger, *Human Resource Management in Virtual Organizations* (Greenwich, CT: Information Age Press, in press).

[11]P. Drucker, "The Next Society: A Survey of the Near Future," *The Economist* (November 3, 2001), special insert.

[12]R.L. Heneman and K.E. Dixon, "Rewards and Organizational Systems Alignment: An Expert System," *Compensation and Benefits Review* (in press).

[13]J. Greenberg, "A Taxonomy of Organizational Justice Theories," *Academy of Management Review* (Vol. 12, 1987), 9–22.

[14]R. Folger and M.A. Konovsky, "Effects of Procedural and Distributive Justice on Reactions to Pay Raise Decisions," *Academy of Management Journal* (1989), 270–272.

[15]R.L. Heneman et al., "Alternative Rewards in Unionized Environments," *American Compensation Association Journal* (Summer, 1997), 42–55.

[16]B. Alge et al., "Measuring Customer Service Orientation Using a Measure of Interpersonal Skills: A Test in a Public Sector Organization," *Journal of Business and Psychology* (in press).

Chapter 9

[1]This chapter proposes a framework for understanding the underlying stakeholder purposes that influence organizational performance, and the leader's role in balancing these purposes and interests to achieve long-term sustainable success. This framework is the basis of an ongoing research project at IMD, which will develop these concepts further and move from the tentative recommendations with which this chapter ends to more extensive empirically based conclusions.

[2]See P. Rosenzweig, "Crisis at Renault (A) and (B). The Vilvoorde Plant Closing," IMD case (1997).

[3]The metaphor of push and pull was suggested to me during informal discussions on this text. When we "push" on shareholder value, it may or may not result; when we pay balanced attention to all shareholders and their purposes, value creation will be "pulled" up as a result.

[4]See D.F. Abell and N. Karpova, "Diaghelev and the Ballets Russes," IMD case (2001).

[5]See D.F. Abell, *Managing with Dual Strategies: Mastering the Present; Preempting the Future* (New York: Free Press, 1993).

[6]See Harvard Business Review, July–August, 1997.

Chapter 10

[1]W.W. Burke, *The Cutting Edge: Current Theory and Practice in Organization Development* (La Jolla, CA: University Associates, 1978), 70–87.

[2]J. Welch and J.A. Byrne, *Straight from the Gut* (New York: Warner Books, 2001), 173–174.

[3]V. Pucik, N.M. Tichy, and C.K. Barnett, eds., *Globalizing Management: Creating and Leading the Competitive Organization* (New York: John Wiley & Sons, 1992), 207.

[4]Letter to Shareholders, GE Annual Report, 1990.

[5]N.M. Tichy and S. Sherman, *Control Your Destiny or Someone Else Will* (New York: Doubleday, 1993), 359–361.

[6]N.M. Tichy and C. DeRose, "Roger Enrico's Master Class," *Fortune* (Nov. 27, 1995), 58.

[7]J. Welch and J.A. Byrne, *Straight from the Gut* (New York: Warner Books, 2001), 175.

[8]N.M. Tichy with E. Cohen, *The Leadership Engine: How Winning Companies Build Leaders at Every Level* (New York: HarperCollins, 1997).

[9]W.W. Burke, *Organizational Change is Not a Linear Process* (New York: Sage, in press).

[10]Teachable Point of View and TPOV are registered trademarks of Tichy Cohen Associates.

Chapter 11

[1]M. Blair, *Ownership and Control: Rethinking Corporate Governance for the Twenty-First Century* (Washington, DC: Brookings Institution, 1995), 239.

Chapter 12

[1]For a good summary of his history, see "Albert Dunlap and Corporate Transformation, (A) and (B)," *Babson College Case Series* (1999). His recently revealed early disputes with employers were reported in F. Norris, "The Incomplete Resume: A Special Report. An Executive's Missing Years: Papering Over Past Problems," *New York Times*, July 16, 2001.

[2]R.M. Kanter, "Power Failure in Management Circuits," *Harvard Business Review* (July–August, 1979).

[3]See, for example, E. Mayo, *The Human Problems of an Industrial Civilization* (New York: Macmillan, 1933); F.J. Roethlisberger and W.J. Dickson, *Management and the Worker* (Cambridge, MA: Harvard University Press, 1939); D. McGregor, *The Human Side of Enterprise* (New York: McGraw-Hill, 1960), etc.

[4]R. Kaplan, "The Dimensions of Forceful and Enabling Leadership," *Leadership in Action* (Vol. 4, 1999). We have chosen the terms "directive" and "collaborative" because we find them more descriptive of the phenomena.

[5]*Fortune*, November 22, 1999.

[6]See *GE Compilation: Jack Welch 1981–1999*, Harvard Business Publishing Corporation videotape 300–511, where he spoke to an MBA class just months after taking over as CEO.

[7]D. McClelland and D.H. Burnham, "Power is the Great Motivator," *Harvard Business Review* (March–April, 1976), 100–110; D. McClelland, *Power: The Inner Experience* (New York: Irvington Publishers, 1975).

[8]R.A. Caro, *The Power Broker: Robert Moses and the Fall of New York* (New York: Knopf, 1974); R.A. Caro, *The Years of Lyndon Johnson* (New York: Knopf, 1982, 1990), 2 vols.

[9]D.L. Bradford and A.R. Cohen, *Power Up: Transforming Organizations Through Shared Leadership* (New York: Wiley, 1998); D.L. Bradford and A.R. Cohen, *Managing for Excellence* (New York: Wiley, 1984).

[10]D.L. Bradford and A.R. Cohen, *Power Up: Transforming Organizations Through Shared Leadership* (New York: Wiley, 1998).

[11]C.M. Christensen, *The Innovator's Dilemma: When New Technologies Cause Great Firms to Fail* (Harvard Business School Press, 1997).

[12]S. Davis and C. Meyer, *Blur: The Speed of Change in the Connected Economy* (Reading, MA: Addison-Wesley, 1998); B. Capodagli and L. Jackson, *Leading at the Speed of Change: Using New Economy Rules to Invigorate Old Economy Companies* (New York: McGraw-Hill, 2001).

[13]D. St. Jean and A.R. Cohen, "DaimlerChrysler Merger: The Quest to Create One Company," *Babson College Case Series*, 103–C01 A, 2000.

[14]For a vivid example, see C. Gasparino and A. Raghavan, "How Dean Witter Boss Got the Upper Hand in Merger with Morgan; Phillip Purcell Edged Out John Mack, a Dealmaker Famed on Wall Street," *Wall Street Journal*, March 22, 2001, A1.

[15]J.C. Collins and J.I. Porras, *Built to Last: Successful Habits of Visionary Companies* (New York: HarperBusiness, 1994).

[16]See Bradford (1998), Chapter 7, "Creating Commitment to a Tangible Vision."

[17]R.M. Kanter, "Power Failure in Management Circuits," *Harvard Business Review* (July–August, 1979).

[18]T. Parsons, *The Social System* (New York: Free Press, 1965).

[19]See A.R. Cohen and D.L. Bradford, *Influence without Authority* (New York: Wiley, 1990). The traditional way of categorizing sources of power is in J.R.P. French, Jr., and B. Raven, "The Bases of Social Power," in D. Cartwright and A. Zander, eds., *Group Dynamics: Research and Theory* (New York: Harper & Row, 1960), 607–23.

Chapter 13

[1]H.A. Hornstein, *Cruelty and Kindness: A New Look at Aggression and Altruism* (Engle-wood Cliffs, NJ: Prentice Hall, 1976); H.A. Hornstein, "Promotive Tension: The Basis of Prosocial Behavior from a Lewinian Perspective," *Journal of Social Issues* (Vol. 28, 1976), 191–218; H.A. Hornstein, "Promotive Tension Theory and Research," in V.S. Der-lega and J. Grzelak, eds., *Cooperation and Helping Behavior: Theory and Research* (New York: Academic, 1982), 229–248; H.A. Hornstein et al., "Effects of Sentiment and Com-pletion of a Helping Act on Observer Helping: A Case for Socially Mediated Zeigarnik Effects," *Journal of Personality and Social Psychology* (Vol. 17, 1971), 107–112; S.A. Hodgson, H.A. Hornstein, and E. LaKind, "Socially Mediated Zeigarnik Effects as a Function of Sentiment, Valance, and Desire for Goal Attainment," *Journal of Experimen-tal Social Psychology* (Vol. 8, 1972), 446–456.

[2]H.A. Hornstein, *The Haves and the Have Nots: The Abuse of Power and Privilege in the Workplace and How to Control It* (Upper Saddle River, NJ: Financial Times Prentice Hall, 2003). This chapter is also based on this forthcoming book.

[3]D. Hemlock, "I.P.O.s: When Employee-Friendly = Investor-Friendly, *New York Times* (February 25, 1996), sec. F4; L. Grant, "Happy Workers, High Returns," *Fortune* (January 12, 1998), 81; E.D. Morrison, "Role Definitions and Organization Citizenship Behavior: The Importance of the Employee's Perspective," *Academy of Management Journal* (Vol. 37, 1994), 1543–1567; D.L. Altheide et al., "The Social Meanings of Employee Theft," in J.M. Johnson and J.D. Douglas, eds., *Crime at the Top: Deviance in Business and the Pro-fessions* (Philadelphia: J.B. Lippincott, 1978), 90–124.

[4]D. Abrams, K. Ando, and S. Hinkle, "Psychological Attachments to the Group: Cross-Cultural Differences in Organization Identification and Subjective Norms as Predictors of Workers' Turnover Intentions," *Personality and Social Psychology Bulletin* (Vol. 24, 1998), 1027–1039.

[5]L. Grant, "Happy Workers, High Returns," *Fortune* (January 12, 1998), 81.

[6]Altheide, 90–124.

[7]F. Swaboda, "Conference Tries to Define 'High-Performance' Jobs," *Washington Post* (July 27, 1993), D1, D5.

[8]B. Dumaine, "The Trouble with Teams," *Fortune* (September 5, 1994), 86–92.

[9]B.P. Noble, "On Bosses, Barriers, and Beliefs," *New York Times* (March 6, 1994), Bu25.

[10]S. Shellenbarger, "Investors Seem Attached to Firms with Happy Employees," *Wall Street Journal* (March 19, 1997), B1.

[11]G. Burkins, "Work Week," *Wall Street Journal* (May 20, 1997), A1.

[12]N. Moran, "Look to Corporate Federations," *The Daily Telegraph* (May 28, 1997), 2.

[13]"Work Week," *Wall Street Journal* (June 3, 1997), A1.

[14]"What the New Generation Really Wants," *Fortune* (April 14, 1997), 157.

[15]C. Alston, "Comp Time's Time has Come," *Wall Street Journal* (May 15, 1997), A22.

[16]J.W. Zinober, "The Loyalty Crisis: Today's Employee is Quite a Different Breed from Yesterday's," *Law Practice Management* (Vol. 18, April, 1992), 26–32.

[17]H. Tajfel, ed., *Differentiation between Social Groups: Studies in the Social Psychology of Intergroup Relations* (London: Academic, 1978); J.C. Turner et al., eds., *Rediscovering the Social Group: A Self-Categorization Theory* (Oxford, UK: Blackwell, 1987); N. Elle-mers, R. Spears, and B. Doosje, eds., *Social Identity: Context, Commitment, Content* (Oxford, UK: Blackwell, 1999).

[18]B.A. Bunker and B.T. Alban, *Large Group Interventions* (San Francisco: Jossey-Bass, 1997).

[19]B. Filipczak, "Critical Mass: Putting Whole Systems Thinking into Practice," *Training* (September 1995), 33–41.

[20]M. London, "Redeployment and Continuous Learning in the 21st Century: Hard Lessons and Positive Examples from the Downsizing Era," *Academy of Management Executive* (Vol. 10, 1996), 67–79.

[21]W.F. Casio, *Guide to Responsible Restructuring* (Washington, DC: U.S. Department of Labor, Office of the American Workplace, 1995).

[22]R. Rose, "Work Week," *Wall Street Journal* (January 30, 1996), A1.

[23]H. Lancaster, "Companies Promise to Help Employees Plot Their Careers," *Wall Street Journal* (March 11, 1997), B1.

[24]R. Quick, "A Makeover that Began at the Top," *Wall Street Journal* (May 25, 2000), B1, B4.

[25]R.A. Baron, "Affect and Organization Behavior: When and Why Feeling (Good or Bad) Matters," in J.K. Murnighan, ed., *Social Psychology in Organizations: Advances in Theory and Research* (Englewood Cliffs, NJ: Prentice Hall, 1993).

[26]M. Chase, "Weighing the Benefits of Mental-Health Days Against Guilt Feelings," *Wall Street Journal* (September 9, 1996), B1.

Chapter 14

[1]M.A. Hubble, B.L. Duncan, and S.D. Miller, eds., *The Heart and Soul of Change: What Works in Therapy* (Washington, DC: American Psychological Association, 1999).

[2]F.H. Kanfer, and A.P. Goldstein, eds., *Helping People Change: A Textbook of Methods 4th Edition* (Boston: Allyn & Bacon, 1991).

[3]D.H. Barlow, *Anxiety and Disorders: The Nature and Treatment of Anxiety and Panic* (New York: Guilford, 1988).

[4]C.C. Morrow, M.Q. Jarrett, and M.T. Rupinski, "An Investigation of the Effect and Economic Utility of Corporate-Wide Training," *Personnel Psychology* (Vol. 50, 1997), 91–119.

[5]E.T. Pascarella and P.T. Terenzini, *How College Affects Students: Findings and Insights from Twenty Years of Research* (San Francisco: Jossey-Bass, 1991).

[6]D.G. Winter, D.C. McClelland, and A.J. Stewart, *A New Case for the Liberal Arts: Assessing Institutional Goals and Student Development* (San Francisco: Jossey-Bass, 1981).

[7]D.C. McClelland and D.G. Winter, *Motivating Economic Achievement* (New York: Free Press, 1969).

[8]D. Miron and D.C. McClelland, "The Impact of Achievement Motivation Training on Small Business," *California Management Review* (Vol. 21, 1979), 13–28.

[9]H. Cutter, R.E. Boyatzis, and D. Clancy, "The Effectiveness of Power Motivation Training for Rehabilitating Alcoholics," *Journal of Studies on Alcohol* (Vol. 38, 1977).

[10]J.P. Campbell et al., *Managerial Behavior, Performance, and Effectiveness* (New York: McGraw Hill, 1970).

[11]C. Cherniss and M. Adler, *Promoting Emotional Intelligence in Organizations: Make Training in Emotional Intelligence Effective* (Washington, DC: American Society of Training and Development, 2000).

[12]R.A. Noe and N. Schmitt, "The Influence of Trainee Attitudes on Training Effectiveness: Test of a Model," *Personnel Psychology* (Vol. 39, 1986), 497–523.

[13]H.H. Hand, M.D. Richards, and J.W. Slocum, Jr., "Organizational Climate and the Effectiveness of a Human Relations Training Program," *Academy of Management Journal* (Vol. 16, 1973), 185–246.

[14]K.N. Wexley and W.F. Memeroff, "Effectiveness of Positive Reinforcement and Goal Setting as Methods of Management Development," *Journal of Applied Psychology* (Vol. 60, 1975), 446–450.

[15]G.P. Latham and L.M. Saari, "Application of Social-Learning Theory to Training Supervisors through Behavioral Modeling," *Journal of Applied Psychology* (Vol. 64, 1979), 239–246.

[16]D.P. Young and N.M. Dixon, *Helping Leaders Take Effective Action: A Program Evaluation* (Greensboro, NC: Center for Creative Leadership, 1996).

[17]C.C. Morrow, M.Q. Jarrett, and M.T. Rupinski, "An Investigation of the Effect and Economic Utility of Corporate-Wide Training," *Personnel Psychology* (Vol. 50, 1997), 91–119.

[18]T. Baldwin and J.K. Ford, "Transfer of Training: A Review and Directions for Future Research," *Personnel Psychology* (Vol. 41, 1988), 63–105.

[19]M.J. Burke and R.R. Day, "A Cumulative Study of the Effectiveness of Managerial Training," *Journal of Applied Psychology* (Vol. 71, 1986), 232–245.

[20]Development Dimensions International (DDI), *Final Report: Phase III.* Report to the AACSB (St. Louis, MO: 1985).

[21]R.E. Boyatzis and M. Sokol, *A Pilot Project to Assess the Feasibility of Assessing Skills and Personal Characteristics of Students in Collegiate Business Programs.* Report to the AACSB (St. Louis, MO, 1982).

[22]R.E. Boyatzis, A. Renio-McKee, and L. Thompson, "Past Accomplishments: Establishing the Impact and Baseline of Earlier Programs," in R.E. Boyatzis, S.S. Cowen, and D.A. Kolb, eds., *Innovation in Professional Education: Steps on a Journey from Teaching to Learning* (San Francisco: Jossey-Bass, 1995).

[23]R.E. Boyatzis et al., "Will it Make a Difference? Assessing a Value-Based, Outcome-Oriented, Competency-Based Professional Program," in R.E. Boyatzis, S.S. Cowen, and D.A. Kolb, eds., *Innovating in Professional Education: Steps on a Journey from Teaching to Learning* (San Francisco: Jossey-Bass, 1995).

[24]R.E. Boyatzis et al., "Competencies Can Be Developed, but Not the Way We Thought," *Capability* (Vol. 2, 1996), 25–41.

[25]R.E. Boyatzis, J. Wheeler, and R. Wright, "Competency Development in Graduate Education: A Longitudinal Perspective," *Proceedings of the First World Conference on Self-Directed Learning* (Montreal, GIRAT, in press).

[26]R. Ballou et al., "Fellowship in Lifelong Learning: An Executive Development Program for Advanced Professionals," *Journal of Management Education* (Vol. 23, 1999), 338–354.

[27]L. Specht and P. Sandlin, "The Differential Effects of Experiential Learning Activities and Traditional Lecture Classes in Accounting," *Simulations and Gaming* (Vol. 22, 1991), 196–210.

[28]R.E. Boyatzis, "Self-Directed Change and Learning as a Necessary Meta-Competency for Success and Effectiveness in the 21st Century," in R. Sims and J.G. Veres, eds., *Keys to Employee Success in the Coming Decades* (Westport, CT: Greenwood Publishing, 1999).

[29]R.E. Boyatzis, "Developing Emotional Intelligence," in D. Goleman and C. Cherniss, eds., *Research and Theoretical Advances in Emotional Intelligence: Volume 1* (San Francisco: Jossey-Bass, 2001).

[30]D. Goleman, R.E. Boyatzis, and A. McKee, *Primal Leadership: Realizing the Power of Emotional Intelligence* (Boston: Harvard Business School Press, 2002).

[31]D.A. Kolb, S.K. Winter, and D.E. Berlew, "Self-Directed Change: Two Studies," *Journal of Applied Behavioral Science* (Vol. 6, 1968), 453–471.

[32]R.E. Boyatzis and D.A. Kolb, *Feedback and Self-Directed Behavior Change,* Unpublished Working Paper #394–69 (Sloan School of Management, MIT, 1969).

[33]D.A. Kolb and R.E. Boyatzis, "On the Dynamics of the Helping Relationship," *Journal of Applied Behavioral Science* (Vol. 6, 1970a), 267–289.

[34]D.A. Kolb and R.E. Boyatzis, "Goal-Setting and Self-Directed Behavior Change," *Human Relations* (Vol. 23, 1970b), 439–457.

[35]D.A. Kolb, *A Cybernetic Model of Human Change and Growth,* Unpublished Working Paper #526–71. (Sloan School of Management, MIT, 1971).

[36]R.E. Boyatzis, "Cornerstones of Change: Building a Path for Self-Directed Learning," in R.E. Boyatzis, S.C. Cowen, and D.A. Kolb, eds., *Innovation in Professional Education: Steps on a Journey from Teaching to Learning* (San Francisco: Jossey-Bass, 1995), 50–94.

[37]R.E. Boyatzis, "Stimulating Self-Directed Change: A Required MBA Course Called Managerial Assessment and Development," *Journal of Management Education* (Vol. 18, 1994), 304–323.

[38]D. Goleman, *Emotional Intelligence* (New York: Bantam Books, 1995).

[39]D. Goleman, *Vital Lies, Simple Truths: The Psychology of Self-Deception* (New York: Simon & Schuster, 1985).

[40]J.M. Beaubien and S.C. Payne, "Individual Goal Orientation as a Predictor of Job and Academic Performance: A Meta-Analytic Review and Integration," Paper presented at the Meeting of the Society for Industrial and Organizational Psychology, Atlanta, GA, April, 1999.

[41]G. Chen et al., "Examination of Relationships Among Trait-Like Individual Differences, State-Like Individual Differences, and Learning Performance," *Journal of Applied Psychology* (Vol. 85, 2000), 835–847.

[42]D. Leonard, "The Impact of Learning Goals on Self-Directed Change in Management Development and Education," doctoral dissertation, Case Western Reserve University, 1996.

[43]E.A. Locke and G.P. Latham, *A Theory of Goal Setting and Task Performance* (Englewood Cliffs, NJ: Prentice Hall, 1990).

[44]D.A. Kolb, *Experiential Learning: Experience as the Source of Learning and Development* (Englewood Cliffs, NJ: Prentice Hall, 1984).

[45]R.E. Boyatzis, "Stimulating Self-Directed Change: A Required MBA Course Called Managerial Assessment and Development," *Journal of Management Education* (Vol. 18, 1994), 304–323.

[46]C. Dreyfus, "The Characteristics of High-Performing Managers of Scientists and Engineers," unpublished doctoral dissertation, Case Western Reserve University, 1990.

[47]D.A. Kolb and R.E. Boyatzis, "Goal-Setting and Self-Directed Behavior Change," *Human Relations* (Vol. 23, 1970b), 439–457.

[48]K.E. Kram, "A Relational Approach to Careers," in D.T. Hall, ed., *The Career is Dead: Long Live the Career* (San Francisco: Jossey-Bass Publishers, 1996), 132–157.

[49]J.V. Wheeler, "The Impact of Social Environments on Self-Directed Change and Learning," unpublished doctoral dissertation, Case Western Reserve University, 1999.

Chapter 15

[1]See N. Nicholson, "How Hardwired is Human Behavior?" *Harvard Business Review* (July–August, 1998), 134–147; N. Nicholson, *Executive Instinct: Managing the Human Animal in the Information Age* (New York: Crown Business, 2000). Also published in the UK as *Managing the Human Animal* (Texere).

[2]See D. Sperber, *Explaining Culture* (Oxford, UK: Blackwell, 1996).

[3]See M. Harris, *Cannibals and Kings: The Origins of Cultures* (Glasgow: William Collins, 1977); T. Megarry, *Society in Prehistory: The Origins of Human Culture* (London: Macmillan, 1995).

[4]G.P. Murdock, "The Common Denominator of Cultures," (1945, reprinted in G.P. Murdock, ed., *Culture and Society;* Pittsburgh, PA: University of Pittsburgh Press, 1965). See also D. Brown, *Cultural Universals* (New York: McGraw-Hill, 1991).

[5]S. Fisher and C.L. Cooper, eds., *On the Move: The Psychological Effects of Change and Transition* (Chichester, UK: John Wiley, 1991).

[6]See D. Brown, *Cultural Universals* (New York: McGraw-Hill, 1991).

[7]See T.E. Teal and A. A. Kennedy, *Corporate Cultures: The Rites and Rituals of Corporate Life* (Reading, MA: Addison-Wesley, 1982).

[8]C. Markides, *All the Right Moves* (Boston: Harvard Business School Press, 1999).

[9]M. Ridley, *Genome: The Autobiography of a Species in 23 Chapters* (London: Fourth Estate, 1999).

[10]S. Pinker, *How the Mind Works* (New York: Norton, 1997).

[11]See C. Tudge, *Neanderthals, Bandits, and Farmers* (London: Weidenfeld and Nicolson, 1998).

[12]See D.A. Waldron, "Status in Organizations: Where Evolutionary Theory Ranks," *Journal of Managerial Economics* (Vol. 19, 1998), 505–520.

[13]See E. Soane and N. Nicholson, "Are Traders Rational?," *Foreign Exchange and Money Markets* (July 2000), 17–20.

[14]R. Plomin, *Genetics and Experience: The Interplay between Nature and Nurture* (Beverly Hills, CA: Sage, 1994); T.J. Bouchard, "Genetic Influence on Mental Abilities, Personality, Vocational Interests, and Work Attitudes," in C.L. Cooper and I.T. Robertson, eds., *International Review of Industrial and Organizational Psychology* (Vol. 12, 1997), 373–396.

[15]See G. Miller, *The Mating Mind* (London: Heinemann, 2000).

[16]A. Whiten and R.W. Byrne, eds., *Machiavellian Intelligence* (Oxford, UK: Clarendon, 1988); A. Whiten and R.W. Byrne, eds., *Machiavellian Intelligence II* (Cambridge, UK: Cambridge University Press, 1997).

[17]A. Glucklich, *The End of Magic* (Oxford, UK: Oxford University Press, 1997). See also Robert Hinde, *Why Gods Persist: A Scientific Approach to Religion* (London: Routledge, 1999).

[18]See R.M. Nesse and G.C. Williams, *Why We Get Sick: The New Science of Darwinian Medicine* (New York: Vintage Books, 1996).

[19]Annual surveys based on what employees rate as the best company to work are published each year by *Fortune* in the United States and *The Sunday Times* in the United Kingdom. The top-rated companies are usually highly successful in business terms, and deploy strategies embodying these values.

[20]N. Nicholson and P. Willman, "Folly, Fantasy, and Roguery—A Social Psychology of Finance Risk Disasters," in J. Pickford, ed., *Mastering Risk: Volume 1: Concepts* (Upper Saddle River, NJ: Financial Times Prentice Hall, 2001).

[21]See D. Cannon, "Cause or Control? The Temporal Dimension in Failure Sense-Making," *Journal of Applied Behavioral Science* (Vol. 35, 1999), 416–438; C. Argyris, *Organizational Learning* (Oxford, UK: Blackwell, 1994).

[22]See M. Frese, "Error Management in Training," in S. Bagnara et al., eds., *Organizational Learning and Technical Change* (Frankfurt, Germany: Springer-Verlag, 1996).

[23]See P.F. Drucker, "The Next Society," *The Economist* (November 3, 2001).

[24]G.D. Dees et al., "The New Corporate Architecture," *Academy of Management Executive* (Vol. 9, 1995), 7–18.

[25]M. Peiperl et al., eds., *Career Frontiers: New Concepts of Working Life* (Oxford, UK: Oxford University Press, 2000).

[26]N. Anand, "Sound Organisation: Radical Organisation Design the Nashville Way," Working Paper (London Business School, 1999).

[27]D.C. Geary, *Male, Female* (Washington, DC: American Psychological Association, 1998).

[28]See H.W. Chesbrough and D.J. Teece, "When is Virtual Virtuous? Organizing for Innovation," *Harvard Business Review* (January–February, 1996), 65–73.

[29]W. Bridges, *Jobshift: How to Prosper in a Workplace Without Jobs* (Reading, MA: Addison-Wesley, 1994).

[30]N. Nicholson, "Gene Politics and the Natural Selection of Leadership," *Leader to Leader* (Vol. 20, Spring 2001), 46–52.

[31]See D. Moore, *Women Entrepreneurs: Moving Beyond the Glass Ceiling* (Beverly Hills, CA: Sage, 1997).

[32]C. Argyris, *Organizational Learning* (Oxford, UK: Blackwell, 1994).

Chapter 16

[1]D. Dunphy and A. Griffiths, *The Sustainable Corporation: Organizational Renewal in Australia* (Sydney, Australia: Allen and Unwin, 1998).

[2]D. Dunphy and A. Griffiths, *The Sustainable Corporation: Organizational Renewal in Australia* (Sydney, Australia: Allen and Unwin, 1998).

[3]R. Harrison, "Strategies for A New Age," *Human Resource Management* (Vol. 22, 1983), 209–235; J. Porras and P. Robertson, "Organization Development Theory: A Typology and Evaluation," in R. Woodman and W. Passmore, eds., *Research in Organization Change and Development* (Greenwich, CT: JAI, 1987), 1–57.

[4]Dunphy et al., eds., *Sustainability: The Corporate Challenge of the 21st Century* (Sydney, Australia: Allen and Unwin, 2000).

[5]J.R. Glenn and T.J. Gordon, *State of the Future: Issues and Opportunities* (Washington, DC: American Council for the United Nations University: The Millennium Project, 1998).

[6]M. McIntosh et al., *Corporate Citizenship: Successful Strategies for Responsible Companies* (London: Financial Times Pitman, 1998).

[7]A.A. Kennedy, *The End of Shareholder Value: Corporations at the Crossroads* (London: Orion Business, 2000).

[8]D. Dunphy and A. Griffiths, *The Sustainable Corporation: Organizational Renewal in Australia* (Sydney, Australia: Allen and Unwin, 1998).

[9]G. Hamel, *Leading the Revolution* (Boston: Harvard Business School Press, 2000).

[10]J.C. Collins and J.I. Porras, *Built to Last: Successful Habits of Visionary Companies* (New York: HarperCollins, 1994); D. Dunphy and A. Griffiths, *The Sustainable Corporation: Organizational Renewal in Australia* (Sydney: Allen and Unwin, 1998), 151–152; J. Pfeffer, *The Human Equation: Building Profits by Putting People First* (Boston: Harvard Business School Press, 1998).

[11]Personal communication, G. Bourne, regional president, BP Australasia.

[12]L. Gratton, *Living Strategy: Putting People at the Heart of Corporate Purpose* (Harlow, UK: Pearson Education, 2000); D. Stace and D. Dunphy, *Beyond the Boundaries: Leading and Re-Creating the Successful Enterprise, Second Edition* (Sydney, Australia: McGraw Hill, 2001).

[13]J. Kotter, *A Force for Change* (London: Free Press, 1990).

[14]J.E. Elkington, *Cannibals with Forks: The Triple Bottom Line of 21st Century Business* (Oxford, UK: Capstone, 1999).

[15]B. Hirsh and P. Sheldrake, *Inclusive Leadership: Rethinking the World of Business to Generate the Dynamics of Lasting Success* (Melbourne: Information Australia, 2000).

[16]T. Flannery, *The Future Eaters* (Sydney, Australia: Reed Books, 1994).

[17]E. von Weizacker, A.B. Lovins, and L.H. Lovins, *Factor 4: Doubling Wealth—Halving Resource Use* (Sydney, Australia: Allen and Unwin, 1997).

[18]For a more detailed description of these phases, see Dunphy et al. (2000), Appendix 1, 15–18.

[19]Dunphy et al., eds., *Sustainability: The Corporate Challenge of the 21st Century* (Sydney, Australia: Allen and Unwin, 2000).

Chapter 17

[1]R. Goffee and G. Jones, *The Character of a Corporation* (New York: Harper Business, 1998).

[2]T.J. Peters and R.H. Waterman, *In Search of Excellence: Lessons from America's Best-Run Companies* (New York: Harper & Row, 1982).

[3]R. Goffee and G. Jones, "Why Should Anyone Be Led by You?," *Harvard Business Review* (September/October, 2000).

[4]R. Goffee and G. Jones, "What Holds the Modern Company Together?," *Harvard Business Review* (November 1996). Reprinted in *Harvard Business Review on Managing People* (1999).

[5]G. Hamel and C.K. Prahalad, *Competing for the Future* (Boston: Harvard Business School Press, 1995).

[6]R.M. Kanter, *When Giants Learn to Dance* (London: Unwin, 1990).

[7]P.G. Audia, E.A. Locke, and K.G. Smith, "The Paradox of Success: An Archival and a Laboratory Study of Strategic Persistence Following a Radical Environmental Change," *Academy of Management Journal* (Vol. 5, 2000), 837–853.

Chapter 18

[1]H.E. Aldrich, *Organizations and Environments* (Englewood Cliffs, NJ: Prentice Hall, 1979).

[2]L.J. Bourgeois, III, "Strategic Goals, Perceived Uncertainty, and Economic Performance in Volatile Environments," *Academy of Management Journal*, (Vol. 28, 1985), 548–573.

[3]P. Lawrence and J. Lorsch, *Organization and Environment* (Boston: Harvard University Business School, Division of Research, 1967).

[4]E. Romanelli and M.L. Tushman, "Inertia, Environments, and Strategic Choice: A Quasi-Experimental Design for Comparative Longitudinal Research," *Management Science* (Vol. 32, 1986), 608–621.

[5]R.E. Miles and C.C. Snow, *Organizational Strategy, Structure, and Process* (New York: McGraw-Hill, 1978).

[6]W.H. Starbuck, "Organizations as Action Generators," *American Sociological Review* (Vol. 48, 1983), 91–102.

[7]R. Hogan, R. Raskin, and D. Fazzini, "The Dark Side of Charisma," in K.E. Clark and M.B. Clark, eds., *Measures of Leadership* (West Orange, NJ: Leadership Library of America, 1990), 343–354.

[8]R. Hogan, G.J. Curphy, and J. Hogan, "What We Know About Leadership," *American Psychologist* (Vol. 52, 1994), 130–139.

[9]S.J. Zaccaro, *The Nature of Executive Leadership: A Conceptual and Empirical Analysis of Success* (Washington, DC: American Psychological Association, 2001).

[10]N. Weiner and T.A. Mahoney, "A Model of Corporate Performance as a Function of Environmental, Organizational, and Leadership Influences," *Academy of Management Journal* (Vol. 24, 1981), 453–470.

[11]M.R. Barrick et al., "Assessing the Utility of Executive Leadership," *Leadership Quarterly* (Vol. 2, 1991), 9–22.

[12]D.C. Hambrick, Guest editor's introduction: "Putting Top Managers Back in the Strategy Picture," *Strategic Management Journal* (Vol. 10, 1989), 5–15.

[13]M.A. Hitt and B.B. Tyler, "Strategic Decision Models: Integrating Different Perspectives," *Strategic Management Journal* (Vol. 12, 1991), 327–351.

[14]W.W. Burke and B. Trahant, *Business Climate Shifts: Profiles of Change Makers* (Boston: Butterworth Heineman, 2000).

[15]J. O'Toole, *Leadership A to Z: A Guide for the Appropriately Ambitious* (San Francisco: Jossey-Bass, 1999).

[16]H. Gardner, *Leading Minds: An Anatomy of Leadership* (New York: Basic Books, 1995).

[17]W. Bennis, *Why Leaders Can't Lead: The Unconscious Conspiracy Continues* (San Francisco: Jossey-Bass, 1989).

[18]W.W. Burke, "Leadership Behavior as a Function of the Leader, the Follower, and the Situation," *Journal of Personality* (Vol. 33, 1965), 60–81.

[19]W.W. Burke, *Theory and Practice of Organization Change: A Nonlinear Process* (Thousand Oaks, CA: Sage, in press).

[20]D.C. Hambrick and A.A. Cannella, Jr., "Strategy Implementation as Substance and Selling," *Academy of Management Executive* (Vol. 3, 1989), 278–285.

[21]L. Atwater and F. Yammarino, "Does Self–Other Agreement on Leadership Perceptions Moderate the Validity of Leadership Predictions?," *Personnel Psychology* (Vol. 45, 1992), 141–164.

[22]A.H. Church, "Managerial Self-Awareness in High-Performing Individuals in Organizations," *Journal of Applied Psychology* (Vol. 82, 1997), 281–292.

[23]D.C. McClelland, *Power: The Inner Experience* (New York: Irvington, 1975).

[24]D.C. McClelland, "N Achievement and Entrepreneurship: A Longitudinal Study," *Journal of Personality and Social Psychology* (Vol. 1, 1965), 389–392.

[25]D.C. McClelland and D.H. Burnham, "Power Is the Great Motivator," *Harvard Business Review* (Vol. 54, 1976), 100–110.

[26]W.W. Burke and G.H. Litwin, "A Causal Model of Organizational Performance and Change," *Journal of Management* (Vol. 18, 1992), 532–545.

[27]W.W. Burke and B. Trahant, *Business Climate Shifts: Profiles of Change Makers* (Boston: Butterworth Heineman, 2000).

[28]R.P. Bauman, P. Jackson, and J.T. Lawrence, *From Promise to Performance: A Journey of Transformation at SmithKline Beecham* (Boston: Harvard Business School Press, 1997).

[29]R. Evans and C. Price, *Vertical Take-Off: The Inside Story of British Aerospace's Comeback from Crisis to World Class* (London: Nicholas Brealey Publishing, 1999).

[30]J. O'Toole, *Leadership A to Z: A Guide for the Appropriately Ambitious* (San Francisco: Jossey-Bass, 1999), 302–303.

[31]H. Gardner, *Leading Minds: An Anatomy of Leadership* (New York: Basic Books, 1995).

[32]R.P. Bauman, P. Jackson, and J.T. Lawrence, *From Promise to Performance: A Journey of Transformation at SmithKline Beecham* (Boston: Harvard Business School Press, 1997).

[33]W.W. Burke and B. Trahant, *Business Climate Shifts: Profiles of Change Makers* (Boston: Butterworth Heineman, 2000), 95.

[34]W.W. Burke, L.P. Clark, and C. Koopman, "Improve Your OD Project's Chances for Success," *Training and Development Journal* (Vol. 38, 1984), 62–68.

[35]W.W. Burke, "The Broad Band of Organization Development and Change: An Introduction," in D. Giver, L. Carter, and M. Goldsmith, eds., *Best Practices in Organization and Human Resources Development Handbook* (Lexington, MA: Linkage, Inc., 2000), 5–10.

[36]L.D. Goodstein and W.W. Burke, "Creating Successful Organizational Change," *Organizational Dynamics* (Vol. 19, 1991), 5–17.

[37]R.T. Pascale, M. Milleman, and L. Gioja, *Surfing the Edge of Chaos: The Laws of Nature and the New Laws of Business* (New York: Crown Business, 2000).

[38]H. Levinson, "Beyond the Selection Failure," *Consulting Psychology Journal: Practice and Research* (Vol. 46, 1994), 3–8.

Chapter 19

[1]R. Foster and S. Kaplan, *Creative Destruction: Why Companies that Are Built to Last Under-Perform the Market—and How to Successfully Transform Them* (New York: Currency, 2001).

[2]E. McNamara, "Retirees Ask for Justice at Polaroid," *The Boston Globe* (December 9, 2001).

[3]P.R. Lawrence and J.W. Lorsch, *Organization and Environment* (Boston: Division of Research, Graduate School of Business Administration, Harvard University, 1967).

[4]B. Schneider, "The People Make the Place," *Personnel Psychology* (Vol. 40, 1987), 437–453.

[5]E.H. Schein, *Organizational Culture and Leadership, Second Edition* (San Francisco: Jossey-Bass, 1992).

[6]D. Miller, *The Icarus Paradox: How Exceptional Companies Bring About Their Own Downfall* (New York: Harper Business, 1990).

[7]M. Beer, *Apple Computer: Corporate Strategy and Culture (Abridged): Case (A)* (Boston: Harvard Business School 1991).

[8]M. Beer, *Apple Computer: Corporate Strategy and Culture (Abridged): Case (A)* (Boston: Harvard Business School 1991).

[9]Gartner Dataquest, cited in M. Kanellos and D. Becker, "PC Shipments Shrink; Dell Keeps Growing," *CNET* (Jan 17, 2002), http://news.com.com/2100–1040–817659.html

[10]D. Miller, R.E. Eisenstat, and N. Foote, "Strategy from the Insider Out: Building Capability-Creating Organizations," Unpublished Paper (August, 2001).

[11]C.K. Prahalad and R.A. Bettis, "The Dominant Logic: A New Linkage between Diversity and Performance," *Strategic Management Journal* (1986).

[12]M. Beer and R.E. Eisenstat, "The Silent Killers of Strategy Implementation and Learning," *Sloan Management Review* (Vol. 41, Summer 2000a), 29–40.

[13]M. Beer, *Apple Computer: Corporate Strategy and Culture (Abridged): Case (A)* (Boston: Harvard Business School 1991).

[14]Personal communication with Kevin Sullivan, vice president of human resources at the time.

[15]M. Porter, *Competitive Advantage* (New York: Free Press, 1985).

[16]S. Davis and P.R. Lawrence, *Matrix* (Reading, MA: Addison-Wesley, 1977), chapter 4; M. Beer, *Corning Glass Works, The Electronic Products Division Case (A–C)* (Boston: Harvard Business School, 1977).

[17]J. Dewey, *Logic: The Theory of Inquiry* (New York: Holt, Rinehart and Winston, 1938).

[18]"Xerox: The Downfall, the Insider Story of the Management Fiasco at Xerox," *Hoover's Online*, www.hoovers.com.

[19]J. Collins, *Good to Great: Why Some Companies Make the Leap and Others Don't* (New York: Harper Business, 2001).

[20]C. Argyris, *Overcoming Organizational Defenses* (Boston: Allyn & Bacon, 1990).

[21]J. Detert, "Speaking up in Hi Co," Unpublished Paper, 2001; A. Edmondson, "Psychological Safety and Learning Behavior in Work Teams," *Administrative Science Quarterly* (Vol. 44, 1999), 350–383.

[22]R. Beckhard, "The Confrontation Meeting," *Harvard Business Review* (Vol. 45, 1967), 149–156.

[23]M.R. Weisbord, *Productive Workplaces: Organizing and Managing for Dignity, Meaning, and Community* (San Francisco: Jossey-Bass, 1991); B. Bunker and B.T. Alban, *Large Group Interventions: Engaging the Whole System for Rapid Change* (San Francisco: Jossey-Bass, 1997).

[24]M. Beer and N. Nohria, "Cracking the Code of Change," *Harvard Business Review* (2000b); M. Beer, "Developing an Organization Capable of Sustained High Performance: Embrace the Paradox of Results and Organization Capability Driven Change," *Organizational Dynamics* (Summer, 2001).

[25]M. Beer, R. Eisenstat, and B. Spector, *The Critical Path to Corporate Renewal* (Boston: Harvard Business School Press, 1990).

[26]D. Dunphy, "Embracing Paradox: Top Down versus Participative Management of Organizational Change," in M. Beer and N. Nohria, eds., *Breaking the Code of Change* (Boston: Harvard Business School Press, 2000c).

[27]Beer (1990); M. Tushman and C. O'Reilly, *Winning through Innovation* (Boston: Harvard Business School Press, 1997).

[28]M. Beer and N. Nohria, "Cracking the Code of Change," *Harvard Business Review* (2000b); M. Beer and N. Nohria, eds., *Breaking the Code of Change* (Boston: Harvard Business School Press, 2000d).

[29]M. Beer and N. Nohria, "Cracking the Code of Change," *Harvard Business Review* (2000b); M. Beer and N. Nohria, eds., *Breaking the Code of Change* (Boston: Harvard Business School Press, 2000d).

[30]R.A. Eisenstat and M. Beer, *Organizational Development Profiling Manual* (Waltham, MA Center for Organizational Fitness, 1977); R.A. Eisenstat and M. Beer, "The Organizational Fitness Profiling Process," Unpublished Paper (Cambridge, MA: Harvard Business School); M. Beer and R.A. Eisenstat, "Developing an Organization Capable of Implementing Strategy and Learning," *Human Relations* (1996). See also Web site of Center for Organizational Fitness (*www.orgfitness.com*).

[31]M. Beer, *Hewlett-Packard's Santa Rosa Systems Division: Cases A–A4* (Boston: Harvard Business School, 1996). This sector of Hewlett-Packard was spun out as Agilent Technologies in 1999.

[32]M. Beer, *Hewlett-Packard's Santa Rosa Systems Division Case B3* (Boston: Harvard Business School, 1999).

For Further Reading

Abell, Derek F. *Managing with Dual Strategies: Mastering the Present, Preempting the Future.* New York: Free Press, 1993.

Ashhenas, Ron, Dave Ulrich, Todd Jick, and Steve Kerr. *The Boundaryless Organization: Breaking the Chains of Organizational Structure.* San Francisco: Jossey-Bass, 1995.

Bartlett, Christopher A., and Sumantra Ghoshal. *The Individualized Corporation: A Fundamentally New Approach to Management.* New York: Harper Business, 1997.

Bartlett, Christopher A., and Sumantra Ghoshal. *Managing across Borders: The Transnational Solution.* Boston: Harvard Business School Press, 1989.

Beatty, Jack. *The World According To Peter Drucker.* New York: Broadway Books, 1998.

Beer, Michael, and Nitin Nohria, eds., *Breaking the Code of Change.* Boston: Harvard Business School Press, 2000.

Bennis, Warren. *On Becoming a Leader.* New York: Perseus Press, 1994.

Bennis, Warren, and Burt Nanus. *Leaders: Strategies for Taking Charge.* New York: Harper Business, 1985.

Bradford, David L., and Allan R. Cohen. *Power Up: Transforming Organizations through Shared Leadership.* New York: Wiley, 1998.

Bradford, David L., and Allan R. Cohen. *Managing for Excellence.* New York: Wiley, 1984.

Burke, W. Warner. *Organizational Change is Not a Linear Process.* New York: Sage, 2002.

Chowdhury, Subir. *The Talent Era: Achieving a High Return On Talent.* New Jersey: Financial Times Prentice Hall, 2002.

Chowdhury, Subir, ed. *Management 21C: Someday We'll All Manage This Way.* London: Financial Times Prentice Hall, 2000.

Collins, James C. *Good to Great. Why Some Companies Make the Leap and Others Don't.* New York: Harper Business, 2001.

Collins, James C., and Jerry I. Porras. *Built to Last: Successful Habits of Visionary Companies.* New York: Harper Business, 1994.

Conger, J. A., E.E.Lawler, and D.L.Finegold.*Corporate Boards: New Strategies for Adding Value at the Top.* San Francisco: Jossey-Bass Publishers, 2001.

Conger, J. A., D.L. Finegold, and E.E. Lawler. "Appraising Boardroom Performance," *Harvard Business Review* (Vol. 76, No. 1, 1998), 136–148.

Conger, J. A., D.L. Finegold, and E.E. Lawler. "CEO Appraisals: Holding Corporate Leadership Accountable," *Organizational Dynamics* (Vol. 7, No. 1, 1998), 6–20.

Conklin, David W. *Comparative Economic Systems: Objectives, Decision Modes, and the Process of Choice.* London: Cambridge University Press, 1991.

Dale Carnegie and Associates Inc, with Stuart R. Levine and Michael A. Crom. *The Leader In You: How to Win Friends, Influence People, and Succeed in a Changing World.* New York: Simon & Schuster, 1993.

Davis, Stan, and Christopher Meyer. *Blur: The Speed of Change in the Connected Economy.* New York: Warner Books, 1998.

Dell, Michael, with Catherine Fredman. *Direct from Dell: Strategies that Revolutionized an Industry.* New York: Harper Business, 1999.

Drucker, Peter F. *Managing in a Time of Great Change.* New York: Penguin Group, 1985.

Drucker, Peter F. *Managing for the Future: The 1990s and Beyond.* New York: Dutton, 1992.

Drucker, Peter F. *The Executive in Action.* New York: Harper Business, 1996.

Drucker, Peter F. *The Frontiers of Management.* New York: Penguin Group, 1999.

Dunphy, Dexter, and Andrew Griffiths. *The Sustainable Corporation: Organizational Renewal in Australia.* Sydney: Allen and Unwin, 1998.

Gates, Bill, with Collins Hemingway. *Business @ the Speed of Thought: Using a Digital Nervous System.* New York: Warner Books, 1999.

Gibson, Rowan. *Rethinking the Future.* London: Nicholas Brealey Publishing Limited, 1997.

Goffee, Robert, and Gareth Jones. *The Character of a Corporation.* New York: Harper Business, 1998.

Grove, Andrew S. *Only the Paranoid Survive: How to Exploit the Crisis Points that Challenge Every Company.* New York: Currency Doubleday, 1996.

Hamel, Gary, and C.K. Prahalad. *Competing for the Future.* Boston: Harvard Business School Press, 1994.

Handy, Charles. *The Hungry Spirit Beyond Capitalism: A Quest for Purpose in the Modern World.* New York: Broadway Books, 1998.

Heenan, David A., and Warren G. Bennis. *Co-Leaders: The Power of Great Partnerships.* New York: John Wiley & Sons, 1999.

Hesselbein, Frances, Marshall Goldsmith, and Richard Beckhard. *Leader of the Future.* San Francisco: Jossey-Bass, 1996.

Hesselbein, Frances, Marshall Goldsmith, and Richard Beckhard. *Organization of the Future.* San Francisco: Jossey-Bass, 1997.

Hornstein, Harvey A. *Arrogant Bosses, Alienated Employees.* (Forthcoming).

Kanter, Rosabeth Moss. *When Giants Learn to Dance: Mastering the Challenges of Strategy, Management, and Careers in the 1990s.* New York: Simon & Schuster, 1989.

Kanter, Rosabeth Moss. *World Class: Thriving Locally in the Global Economy.* New York: Simon & Schuster, 1995.

Katz, Donald. *Just Do It: The Nike Spirit in the Corporate World.* Holbrook, MA: Adams Media Corporation, 1995.

Kelley, Tom, with Jonathan Littman. *The Art of Innovation.* New York: Currency Doubleday, 2001.

Kets de Vries, Manfred F.R., and Elizabeth Florent-Treacy. *The New Global Leaders*. San Francisco: Jossey-Bass, 1999.

Kotter, John P. *Leading Change*. Boston: Harvard Business School Press, 1996.

Kotter, John P. *On What Leaders Really Do*. Boston: Harvard Business School Press, 1999.

Kouzes, James M., and Barry Z. Posner. *The Leadership Challenge*. San Francisco: Jossey-Bass, 1995.

Lorsch, J. W., and E.A. MacIver. *Pawns or Potentates: The Reality of America's Corporate Boards*. Boston: Harvard Business School Press, 1989.

Mintzberg, Henry. *The Rise and Fall of Strategic Planning: Reconceiving Roles for Planning, Plans, Planners*. New York: Free Press, 1994.

Moore, James F. *The Death of Competition: Leadership and Strategy in the Age of Business Ecosystems*. New York: Harper Business, 1996.

Nicholson, Nigel. *Executive Instinct*. New York: Crown Business, 2000.

Peters, Thomas, and Robert H. Waterman. *In Search of Excellence: Lessons from America's Best-Run Companies*. New York: Warner Books, 1990.

Pfeffer, Jeffrey. *The Human Equation: Building Profits by Putting People First*. Boston: Harvard Business School Press, 1998.

Porter, Michael E. *Competitive Advantage: Creating and Sustaining Superior Performance*. New York: Free Press, 1980.

Pucik, Vladimir, Noel M. Tichy, and Carole K. Barnett, eds., *Globalizing Management: Creating and Leading the Competitive Organization*. New York: John Wiley & Sons, 1992.

Redstone, Sumner. *A Passion to Win*. New York: Simon & Schuster, 2000.

Roddick, Anita. *Business as Unusual*. London: Thorsons, 2000.

Rubin, Harriet. *Soloing: Realizing Your Life's Ambition*. New York: Harper Business, 1999.

Senge, Peter M. *The Fifth Discipline: The Art and Practice of the Learning Organization*. New York: Currency/Doubleday, 1990.

Senge, Peter M., Art Kleiner, Charlotte Roberts, Richard Ross, George Roth, and Bryan Smith. *The Dance of Change: The Challenges to Sustaining Momentum in Learning Organizations*. New York: Doubleday, 1999.

Sloan, Alfred P., Jr. *My Years with General Motors*. New York: Doubleday, 1996.

Stewart, Thomas A. *Intellectual Capital: The Wealth of Organizations*. New York: Doubleday/Currency, 1997.

Tichy, Noel M., and Stratford Sherman. *Control Your Destiny or Someone Else Will: How Jack Welch is Making General Electric the World's Most Competitive Company*. New York: Doubleday, 1993.

Tichy, Noel M., with Eli Cohen. *The Leadership Engine: How Winning Companies Build Leaders at Every Level*. New York: Harper Collins, 1997.

Useem, M. *Executive Defense: Shareholder Power and Corporate Reorganization*. Cambridge, MA: Harvard University Press, 1993.

Welch, Jack, with John A. Byrne. *Straight from the Gut*. New York: Warner Books, 2001.

About the Thinkers

DEREK F. ABELL is professor of strategy and marketing at IMD Switzerland. He also is professor of technology and management at the two Swiss Institutes of Technology, in Zürich and Lausanne. He is program director of the jointly offered program Mastering Technology Enterprise and IMD's International Program for Board Members. His primary teaching and research interests are in strategic marketing, general management, and leadership in technology-based industry. He joined IMD (then IMEDE) as dean in 1981. Prior to that, he was a professor at the Harvard Business School for 12 years. He has also served as a member of the faculty at INSEAD while on leave from Harvard in 1971 and 1972. He has served as a consultant to governments in Eastern and Central Europe, as well as to many multinational corporations. He is a board member of a number of public and private organizations, as well as IMD itself. He has published five books and numerous articles. His most recent book, published in August 1993 by Free Press, is titled, *Managing with Dual Strategies: Mastering the Present, Preempting the Future*. It was based on original research undertaken with 12 large multinationals including such companies as Nestlé, Heineken, Caterpillar, Sulzer, and Schering AG.

MICHAEL BEER is Cahners-Rabb professor of business administration at the Harvard Business School, where his research and teaching have been in the areas of organization effectiveness, human resource management, and organization change. He is the author or co-author of several books, including *Organization Change and Development: A Systems View*, *Managing Human Assets*, and *The Critical Path to Corporate Renewal*. The latter received the Johnson Smith & Knisely award for the best book on executive leadership in 1990 and was a finalist for the Academy of Management Terry Book Award in 1991. His most recent book is *Breaking the Code of Change*, edited with Nitin Nohria. He has served on the editorial boards of several academic journals, was chairman of the Organization Development and Change Division, and served on the board of governors of the Academy of Management. Beer has also consulted with many Fortune 500 companies, served on the board of GTECH Corporation, and is chairman and co-founder of the Center for Organizational Fitness, which guides top teams of companies through an organizational learning process for diagnosing the organization's fit with its strategy and its fitness to learn and change.

RICHARD E. BOYATZIS is professor and chair of the department of organizational behavior at the Weatherhead School of Management at Case Western Reserve University. Prior to joining the faculty at Case Western, he was president and CEO of McBer & Co. from 1976–1987 and chief operating officer of Yankelovich, Skelly, & White from 1983–1985. Professor Boyatzis has consulted to many Fortune 500 companies, government agencies, and companies in Europe. He is the author of numerous articles and books, including a new book called *Primal Leadership: Realizing the Power of Emotional Intelligence* with co-authors Dan Goleman and Annie McKee, published by Harvard Business School Press. Professor Boyatzis has a PhD and MA in social psychology from Harvard University and a BS in aeronautics and astronautics from MIT.

DAVID L. BRADFORD is a senior lecturer in organizational behavior at the Graduate School of Business at Stanford University. He is co-author of the best-selling books *Managing for Excellence: The Guide to Developing High Performance in Contemporary Organizations* (1984), *Influence without Authority* (1990), and *Power Up: Transforming Organizations through Shared Leadership* (1998). All three were co-authored with Allan R. Cohen and published by John Wiley & Sons. He has helped develop three executive training programs in conjunction with Wilson Learning Corporation, ODI, and Ninth House. In addition, Bradford has been a leader in the field of innovative approaches to the teaching of management and organizational behavior. He is the founder of the Organizational Behavior Teaching Society and the first editor of its journal, *EXCHANGE*. He received the Exemplar of Excellence in Education award in 1998 from the University of Phoenix. Bradford has lectured at and consulted for a range of organizations in the private sector, including Frito-Lay, Hewlett-Packard, IBM, Levi Strauss & Co., McKinsey & Co., Raychem, Dow Chemical, and NetLedger, as well as in such nonprofit organizations as The Asian Art Museum of San Francisco, The Art Gallery of Ontario, The Detroit Institute of Art, and The Whitney Museum of American Art.

W. WARNER BURKE is professor of psychology and education at Teachers College of Columbia University. His consulting experience has been with a variety of organizations in business and industry, education, government, religion, medical systems, and professional services firms, including British Airways, SmithKline Beecham, National Westminster Bancorp, British Broadcasting Corporation, Business Consultants, Inc. of Japan, PriceWaterhouseCoopers, the National Aeronautics and Space Administration, Dime Savings Bank, and the Miller and Chevalier law firm. Beginning in 1967, for eight years he served as the executive director of the Organization Development Network. Burke is a Fellow of the Academy of Management, the American Psychological Society, and the Society of Industrial and Organizational Psychology. He has served on the board of governors of the Academy of Management and the American Society for Training and Development, and he is a diplomate in industrial/organizational psychology, American Board of Professional Psychology. From 1979 to 1985 he was editor of the American Management Association's quarterly, *Organizational Dynamics*, and from 1986 to 1989 he started and served as editor of the *Academy of Management Executive*. Burke is the author of more than 100 articles and book chapters on organization development, and author, co-author, editor, and co-editor of 14 books. His latest book, co-authored with William Trahant, is *Business Climate Shifts: Profiles of Change Makers*. In 1989 he received the Public Service Medal from the National Aeronautics and Space Administration, in 1990 the Distinguished Contribution to Human Resource Development Award, and in 1993 the Organization Development Professional Practice Area Award for Excellence—The Lippitt Memorial Award—from the American Society for Training and Development. Burke has also served on the Committee on Techniques for the Enhancement of Human Performance, National Research Council of the National Academy of Sciences.

JAMES A. CHAMPY is chairman of Perot Systems' consulting practice and is also head of strategy for the company. He is responsible for providing strategic direction and guidance to the company's team of business and management consultants. He consults extensively with senior-level executives of multinational companies seeking to improve business performance. Prior to joining Perot Systems, he was chairman and chief executive officer of CSC Index, the management consulting arm of Computer Science Corporation. He was one of the original founders of Index, a $200 million consulting practice that was acquired by CSC in 1988. Under Champy's aegis, the company's consulting practice grew at a rate of 25% per year. He is recognized worldwide for his reengineering and change management insight. He is co-author of *Reengineering the Corporation*, a bestseller that sold more than two million copies and was on the *New York Times* best-seller list for more than a year; it has been translated into 17 languages. His follow-up book, *Reengineering Management*, is also a bestseller and was recognized by

BusinessWeek as one of the best business books of 1995. His newest book, co-authored with Harvard Business School Professor Nitin Nohria, is *The Arc of Ambition*. Champy also collaborated with Nohria for the book *Fast Forward*, which is a compilation of significant *Harvard Business Review* articles on change; it was published in March 1996. Champy's latest work, *X-engineering the Corporation: Reinventing Your Business for the Digital Age*, was published in early 2002. His columns on management have appeared in *ComputerWorld*, *Sales & Marketing Management*, and *Forbes*.

SUBIR CHOWDHURY is the executive vice president of the ASI—American Supplier Institute—an international consulting firm headquartered in Livonia, Michigan. Prior to joining ASI, he served as a quality management consultant at General Motors Corporation. Hailed by the *New York Times* as a leading quality expert, Chowdhury was also recognized by Quality Progress of the American Society for Quality as one of the voices of quality in the 21st century. Author of seven books, Chowdhury's most recent international best-selling books include *Design for Six Sigma* (2002) and *The Power of Six Sigma* (2001), both from Dearborn, and *The Talent Era: Achieving High Return on Talent* (2002) and *Management 21C: Someday We'll All Manage This Way* (2000), both from Financial Times Prentice Hall. His books have been translated into more than 15 languages. He is frequently cited in the national and international media. Chowdhury has received numerous international awards for his leadership in quality management and major contributions to the automotive industry. Chowdhury was honored by the Automotive Hall of Fame, and the Society of Automotive Engineers awarded him its most prestigious recognition, the Henry Ford II Distinguished Award for Excellence in automotive engineering. He also received the honorable U.S. Congressional Recognition. In 1999–2000, he served as chairman of the American Society for Quality's Automotive Division. A leading authority in the Six Sigma management strategy, he consults for Global Fortune 500 companies.

ALLAN R. COHEN is the Edward A. Madden distinguished professor of global leadership at Babson College. Cohen recently completed seven years as chief academic officer, leading major curriculum and organizational changes, and has returned to the faculty to teach leadership, change, and negotiations. Cohen is the co-author of the bestseller, *Managing for Excellence* (recently re-issued by Wiley as a Management Classic), and *Influence Without Authority*. His latest book with David Bradford, *Power Up: Transforming Organizations through Shared Leadership*, was published in March 1998, and selected as one of the best leadership books of 1998 by the Management General Web site. Among his many publications is a co-authored textbook, *Effective Behavior in Organizations* (McGraw-

Hill/Irwin, 7 editions, latest 2000), which has had a major impact on the teaching of organizational behavior. He also co-authored the award-winning *Alternative Work Schedules: Integrating Individual and Organizational Needs*. Cohen edited *The Portable MBA in Management* (Wiley, 1993). Cohen's consulting clients for a variety of change projects have included General Electric (Work-Out), Rohm and Haas, The Hartford, Polaroid, Home Depot, Reebok, Pfizer, Decision Resources, General Scanning, General Mills, Chubb Life, SmithKline Beecham, Digital Equipment Corporation, DSM, and Sulzer Infra. He is a member of the Sulzer Infra Academy Advisory Board.

JAY A. CONGER is professor of organizational behavior at the London Business School and senior research scientist at the Center for Effective Organizations at the University of Southern California, Los Angeles. Formerly the executive director of the Leadership Institute at the University of Southern California, Conger is one of the world's experts on leadership. He has been selected by *BusinessWeek* as the best business school professor to teach leadership to executives. In 2001, *BusinessWeek* named him the number five management guru in the world. *The Financial Times* named him one of the world's top educators. Author of over 80 articles and book chapters and nine books, he researches leadership, innovation, influence skills, boards of directors, organizational change, and the training and development of leaders and managers. His articles have appeared in the *Harvard Business Review*, *Organizational Dynamics*, *Business & Strategy*, the *Leadership Quarterly*, the *Academy of Management Review*, and the *Journal of Organizational Behavior*. He is currently the associate editor of the *Leadership Quarterly*. One of his books, *Learning to Lead*, has been described by *Fortune* as "the source" for understanding leadership development. A recent book, *Building Leaders* (1999), explores how corporations can most effectively develop future generations of leadership talent. Other book titles by Conger include *The Leader's Change Handbook* (1999), *Charismatic Leadership in Organizations* (1999), *Winning 'Em Over* (1998), and *The Charismatic Leader* (1989).

SAMUEL A. CULBERT has developed a blunt yet sensitive way of framing situations so that all forces driving people's opinions and actions, including the subjective, self-interested, and political, can be matter-of-factly considered and explicitly discussed. Throughout his career he has creatively welded three activities: consulting, teaching, and writing. For more than 30 years, Culbert's base of operations has been UCLA's Anderson graduate school of management, where he holds the title Professor of Management. Prior to assuming his UCLA post he was Program Director for Organization Studies at The NTL Institute of Applied Behavioral Sciences and an adjunct Professor at The George Washington University. Culbert has achieved wide-scale recognition as an expert and theoretician in the management field, and his books and articles continue to receive recognition. He received a McKinsey award for a Harvard Business Review article, and has contributed chapters in many leading management-related books. His own books include *The Organization Trap* (1974); *The Invisible War: Pursuing Self-Interests at Work* (1980, written with John J. McDonough), which won the AAP award as the best business and management book published that year; *Radical Management: Power, Politics, and The Pursuit of Trust* (1985, also with John J. McDonough); *Mind-Set Management: The Heart of Leadership* (1996); and *Don't Kill the Bosses!* (2001, with John Ullmen).

CHRISTOPHER DeROSE is an active researcher and consultant in the area of organizational change and leadership. He assists business leaders to improve their organizations' growth and profitability while concurrently developing the next generation of leadership. He has been an associate of the University of Michigan Business School's Global Business Partnership, a consortium of leading multinational corporations, since 1989. He also teaches executive education at the University of Michigan Business School. Additionally, DeRose is a senior partner with Action Learning Associates, a consulting firm engaged in developing and delivering CEO-driven, large-scale transformation. He has consulted and taught around the world with companies such as Ameritech, Intel, Hewlett-Packard, Chrysler, Royal Dutch/Shell, and Ford Motor Company. DeRose has also worked in the financial services industry and led a sales organization in Japan. His research in the areas of leadership, organizational change, and growth has taken place in the automotive, telecommunications, financial services, and beverages industries. DeRose has co-authored articles for *Fortune, Training & Development*, and *Australian Human Resources Journal*.

DEXTER DUNPHY is a distinguished professor at the University of Technology, Sydney, Australia. His main research and consulting interests are in corporate sustainability, the management of organizational change, and human resource management. He also has a special interest in comparative management, particularly in East Asia where he has traveled widely. His research is published in over 60 articles and 15 books, including the Australian bestsellers *Under New Management: Australian Organizations in Transition* (McGraw Hill, 1990; with Doug Stace) and *Beyond the Boundaries: Leading and Re-creating the Successful Enterprise* (McGraw Hill, 1994, revised edition 2001; with Doug Stace), *The Sustainable Corporation: Organizational Renewal in Australia* (Allen and Unwin, 1998; co-authored with Andrew Griffiths) and *Sustainability: The Corporate Challenge of the 21st Century* (Allen and Unwin, 2000; co-edited with others). Dunphy has consulted to over 150 private- and public-sector organizations in Australia and abroad. In 1998 he was awarded the Australian Human Resources Institute's Mike Pontifex Award for Outstanding Contribution to the Human Resources Profession and The Australian and New Zealand Academy of Management's Distinguished Member Award for contributions to management research, scholarship, education, and leadership. In 2001 he was elected a Fellow of the Academy of Social Sciences in Australia.

DAVID FINEGOLD is a professor at the Claremont School and an associate research professor at the Center for Effective Organizations at the Marshall School of Business at the University of Southern California, Los Angeles. He has also been a social scientist at RAND in Santa Monica, California. Finegold has conducted research on the changing employment relationship and successful talent strategies for attracting, developing, and retaining employees. His work has focused on the key role of employee development in improving a firm's performance. His current research includes work in the following areas: the impact of the Internet on organizational design and human resources, psychological contracts and career paths of temporary workers, design of corporate boards, and managing technical excellence. He is the author of more than 25 journal articles and book chapters and has written or edited four books, most recently *Are Skills the Answer?* (1999) and *The German Skills Machine* (1999).

ELIZABETH FLORENT-TREACY is a research affiliate in leadership, entrepreneurship, and family business at INSEAD. She has co-authored articles and a recent book on global leadership, *The New Global Leaders: Richard Branson, Percy Barnevik, and David Simon* (1999, with Manfred F. R. Kets de Vries), as well as eight case studies, two of which won the ECCH European Case Award for best case of the year.

ROB GOFFEE is professor of organizational behavior at London Business School. He also serves as deputy dean for executive education, director of the Innovation Exchange, and as a member of the governing body. He was director of the Accelerated Development Program from 1989–1991 and chair of the Organizational Behavior Group from 1995–1998 and from 2000–2001. Goffee has led significant executive development initiatives in Europe, North America, and Asia. His work has covered a range of industries with a focus on leadership, change, and corporate performance. His clients have included Heineken, Roche, Sonae, KPMG, Unilever, and MLIM. Rob has published nine books and over 50 articles in the areas of entrepreneurship, managerial careers, organization design, and corporate culture. These include *Entrepreneurship in Europe* (1987), *Reluctant Managers* (1989), *Corporate Realities* (1995), and *The Character of a Corpora-*

tion: How Your Company's Culture Can Make or Break Your Business (1998, with G. Jones). His recent lead article in the *Harvard Business Review*, "Why Should Anyone Be Led by You?," written with Gareth Jones, won the *HBR*'s McKinsey Award for best article published in 2000. He is a founding partner of Creative Management Associates, which consults to major international companies around the world in the areas of change management, top teams, and organizational development.

ROBERT L. HENEMAN is a professor of management and human resources, and director of graduate programs in labor and human resources at the Max M. Fisher College of Business at Ohio State University. His primary areas of research, teaching, and consulting are in performance management, compensation, staffing, and work design. He has received over $1 million in funds for his research from the Work in America Institute, AT&T Foundation, Ford Motor Company, WorldatWork, the state of Ohio, Society for Human Resource Management, and the Kauffman Center for Entrepreneurial Leadership. He has been awarded the Outstanding Teacher Award in the Masters in Labor and Human Resources Program numerous times by the students at Ohio State University, and is recipient of the WorldatWork Distinguished Total Rewards Educator Award. He has over 50 publications to his credit. He has written seven books including, *Merit Pay: Linking Pay Increases to Performance Ratings; Staffing Organizations (third ed.); Business-Driven Compensation Policies: Integrating Compensation Systems With Corporate Business Strategies; Human Resource Management in Virtual Organizations;* and *Strategic Reward Management: Design, Implementation, and Evaluation.* He has consulted with over 60 public and private sector organizations including IBM, Owens-Corning, BancOne, Time Warner, American Electric Power, Whirlpool, Quantum, AFL-CIO, Nationwide Insurance, The Limited, Borden, ABB, POSCO, U.S. Government Office of Personnel Management, and the states of Ohio and Michigan. His work has been reported in *The Wall Street Journal, USA Today, Money Magazine,* and *ABCNEWS.com,* and he is listed in *Who's Who in the World, Who's Who in America,* and *Outstanding People in the 20th Century.*

HARVEY A. HORNSTEIN has been a professor in the department of social and organizational psychology for more than 30 years, and for nine years chaired the graduate training program in psychology at Teachers College, Columbia University. Hornstein operates a private consulting practice and has been a consultant to senior management groups in more than 15 countries and four dozen firms in businesses ranging from communication, banking, life insurance, and air travel, to chemicals, agriculture, entertainment, petrochemicals, and computers. As a management educator he has worked with thousands of men and women from scores of organizations. He was director of the NTL Institute of Applied Behavioral Science's Division of Professional Development and is director of Columbia University's Principles and Practices of Organizational Development and Organization Development and Human Resources Management programs. Hornstein is a licensed psychologist and, for 15 years, practiced psychotherapy in New York City. His publications include over 80 articles and eight books, including *Social Intervention: A Behavioral Science Analysis, The Social Technology of Organization Development, Applying Social Psychology, Cruelty and Kindness, Managing Human Forces in Organizations, Managerial Courage: Revitalizing Your Organization Without Sacrificing Yourself, A Knight in Shining Armor,* and *Brutal Bosses and Their Prey.* He is currently completing a book that he calls *Arrogant Bosses, Alienated Employees.*

GARETH JONES is a visiting professor of organizational behavior at INSEAD, France. His career has spanned both the academic and business worlds. He began as a university academic in economic and social studies at the University of East Anglia before moving to the London Business School where he joined the organizational behavior faculty. During this period he directed the school's Accelerated Development Program. As senior vice president for Polygram's global human resources, his responsibilities covered more than 80 countries. In 1996 he returned to academia when he became the BT Professor of Organizational Development at Henley Management College, where he was also on the board of governors. His most recent business job was as director of human resources and internal communications at the BBC. His research interests are in organizational design, culture, leadership, and change. He has published several books, most recently *The Character of a Corporation: How Your Company's Culture Can Make or Break Your Business* (1998, with R. Goffee). His articles have appeared in the *European Management Journal, Human Relations,* and the *Harvard Business Review.* He has recently won the prestigious McKinsey Award for the best article in *HBR,* titled "Why Should Anyone Be Led by You?," written with Robert Goffee. In addition, he is a founding partner of Creative Management Associates, a consultancy focused on organizations where creativity is a source of competitive strength.

ANDREW KAKABADSE is a professor of management development and deputy director of the School of Management and chairman of the management development board at Cranfield University. He is ACT visiting professor at the Australian National University, Canberra, visiting professor at Hangzhou University, China, visiting fellow at Babson College, Boston, and was honorary professorial fellow, Curtin University of Technology, Perth. He is a fellow of the International Academy of Management,

368	About the Thinkers

fellow of the British Psychology Society, and fellow of the British Academy of Management. He has consulted and lectured in the United Kingdom, Europe, the United States, Southeast Asia, China, Japan, Russia, Georgia, the Gulf states, and Australia. He was also vice chancellor of the International Academy of Management and was named chairman of the Division of Occupational Psychology, British Psychological Society, in 2001. His current areas of interest focus on improving the performance of top executives and top executive teams, excellence in consultancy practice, corporate governance, conflict resolution, and international relations. His top team database covers 14 nations and over 10,000 private- and public-sector organizations. The study of the strategic skills of top teams has now extended into Japan, China, Hong Kong, and the United States. He has published 21 books, over 132 articles, and 14 monographs, including the best-selling books *Essence of Leadership, Politics of Management, Working in Organizations,* and *The Wealth Creators.* He holds positions on the boards of a number of companies. He is editor of the *Journal of Management Development* and sits on the editorial board of the *Journal of Managerial Psychology* and the *Leadership and Organization Development Journal.* He has also been adviser to a Channel 4 business series in the United Kingdom.

MANFRED F. R. KETS DE VRIES is a clinical professor of leadership development and holds the Raoul de Vitry d'Avaucourt Chair of Human Resource Management at INSEAD, Fontainebleau, France. He is program director of INSEAD's top management program, "The Challenge of Leadership: Developing Your Emotional Intelligence" and co-program director of the joint master/diploma program "Coaching and Consulting for Change" and has been awarded INSEAD's distinguished teacher award five times. *The Financial Times, Le Capital, Wirtschaftswoche,* and *The Economist* have judged Manfred Kets de Vries one of Europe's leading management thinkers. Kets de Vries is the author, co-author, or editor of 17 books, including the prize-winning *Life and Death in the Executive Fast Lane: Essays on Organizations and Leadership* (1995, the Critics' Choice Award 1995–1996), *Family Business: Human Dilemmas in the Family Firm* (1996), *The New Global Leaders: Richard Branson, Percy Barnevik, and David Simon* (1999, with Elizabeth Florent-Treacy), *Struggling with the Demon: Perspectives on Individual and Organizational Irrationality* (2001), *Meditations on Happiness* (forthcoming), and *The Leadership Mystique* (2001). His books and articles have been translated into 15 languages. He is a member of 10 editorial boards. Kets de Vries is a consultant on organizational design/transformation and strategic human resource management to leading U.S., Canadian, European, African, and Asian companies. As a global consultant in executive development his clients have included ABB, Aegon, Air Liquide, Alcan, Alcatel, Accenture, Bain Consulting, Bang & Olufsen, Bonnier, BP, L. M. Ericsson, GE Capital, Goldman Sachs, Heineken, HypoVereinsbank, Investec, KPMG, Lego, Lufthansa, Novartis, Nokia, NovoNordisk, Rank Xerox, Shell, SHV, Standard Bank of South Africa, Unilever, and Volvo Cars. As an educator and consultant he has worked in more than 30 countries. The Dutch government has made him an Officer in the Order of Oranje Nassau.

EDWARD E. LAWLER III is the director of the Center for Effective Organizations and a distinguished professor of business at the University of Southern California's Marshall School of Business. Founded by Lawler, the Center for Effective Organizations is one of the nation's pre-eminent institutes for cutting-edge research on important leadership and human resources issues. His own work focuses on human resources management, compensation, organizational development, and organizational effectiveness. He is the author or co-author of over 300 articles and 30 books. His recent books include *Corporate Boards* (2001), *Designing High Performance Organizations* (2001), *Rewarding Excellence* (2000), *Tomorrow's Organization* (1998), and *Creating High Performance Organizations* (1995). He has been recognized by *BusinessWeek* as one of the nation's foremost authorities on management and human resources. He is the recipient of numerous awards for his outstanding contributions to the field of management from the American Society for Training and Development, the Academy of Management, the Human Resources Planning Society, and the Society for Industrial and Organizational Psychology.

NIGEL NICHOLSON is a professor and chairman of the Organizational Behavior Group at the London Business School. He is also director of the Center for Organizational Research and formerly held the post of research dean at the school. Before becoming a business psychologist, his first profession was a journalist. He has always sought to be a creative thinker and relevant practitioner in applying his ideas to management and organization. Most recently, he has been pioneering the application of the new science of evolutionary psychology to business, first in a widely discussed article in *Harvard Business Review* (July/August 1998), and subsequently in book form: *Executive Instinct* (Crown Business, 2000). His major research interests are in the areas of personality and leadership, risk and decision making among finance professionals, executive careers and development, and family businesses. In these and many other areas, such as innovation, organizational change, and employee performance, he has published a dozen books and over 150 articles. He has been a guest professor at German, American, and Australian universities, and been honored with an award from the Academy of Management for his contribution to the field. He is a much sought-after speaker, recently presenting the keynote address to the Forbes CEO Forum in the United States. At London Business School he directs several executive programs including Interpersonal Skills for Senior Managers.

VLADIMIR PUCIK is professor of international human resources and strategy at IMD—International Institute for Management Development, Lausanne, Switzerland. Before joining IMD, Pucik was associate professor and academic director of international programs at the Center for Advanced Human Resource Studies at the School of Industrial and Labor Relations, Cornell University, and a faculty member at the University of Michigan Business School. His research interests include international dimensions of human resource management, globalization processes, M&A and strategic alliances, and comparative management with a particular emphasis on the Far East and Eastern Europe. He has published extensively in academic and professional journals such as *Academy of Management Review, Human Resource Management, Human Resource Planning,* and *Journal of Applied Psychology,* as well as contributed to a number of books and monographs in the area of international business and human resource management. Pucik is the co-author of *The Global Challenge: Frameworks for International Human Resource Management* (McGraw-Hill) and *Accelerating International Growth* (Wiley). His other major works include *Globalizing Management: Creating and Leading the Competitive Organization* (Wiley) and *Management Culture and the Effectiveness of Local Executives in Japanese-owned U.S. Corporations.* He serves on the advisory boards of several high technology start-ups, and has consulted and conducted workshops for major corporations worldwide, including Allianz, BOC, Citibank, Canon, Daimler-Chrysler, Dentsu, DHL, GE, Gillette, Hitachi, Kodak, Nokia, Shell, Sony, and UBS. Pucik also teaches regularly in a number of executive development programs in the United States, Europe, and Asia.

EDGAR H. SCHEIN is professor emeritus and senior lecturer at the Sloan School of Management at Massachusetts Institute of Technology. He was educated at the University of Chicago; at Stanford University, where he received a master's degree in psychology in 1949; and at Harvard University, where he received his PhD in social psychology in 1952. He has taught at the MIT Sloan School of Management since 1956 and was named the Sloan Fellows Professor of Management in 1978. He is the author of many articles and books, most recently *Process Consultation Revisited* (1999) and *The Corporate Culture Survival Guide* (1999). He has consulted with many organizations in the United States and overseas on organizational culture, organization development, process consultation, and career dynamics.

SCOTT J. SCHROEDER is associate professor of management and director of business and graduate management programs at Chaminade University of Honolulu. He also teaches at the Claremont Graduate University in California. Before joining Chaminade, he was academic dean and department chairperson for the organizational management program at Antioch University's Los Angeles campus. His research focuses on personal power and influence in the workplace. He is an active consultant with a focus on executive coaching and work team facilitation.

WENDY K. SCHUTT is a human resources consultant with over 12 years of hands-on human resources management experience. She has a master's degree in labor and human resources from Ohio State University and a bachelor's degree in pre-law from Bowling Green State University. Prior to starting her consulting business, Schutt worked for Fortune 100 companies including Cardinal Health Inc., Borden, and Cargill, managing in both union and non-union environments, manufacturing and corporate settings. As a consultant, she works with a variety of industries and businesses, including privately held companies, public sector organizations, and nonprofit agencies. Her primary areas of consulting are performance management, compensation and rewards design, employee relations, recruitment, and retention.

SCOTT N. TAYLOR is a PhD student in organizational behavior at Case Western Reserve University. As an organization development consultant, he has worked with companies in travel and transportation, information technology, energy, retail, healthcare, manufacturing, nonprofit, and business services industries. Prior to pursuing a doctoral degree, he was a manager of organization development for Sabre Inc. and Ernst & Young's management consulting practice. His current research interests include voice in organizations, organizational socialization practices, emotional intelligence in leadership, and newcomer knowledge and creativity.

NOEL M. TICHY is a professor of organizational behavior and human resource management at the University of Michigan Business School, where he is the director of the Global Leadership Program. He also directs the Global Business Partnership, which links global companies and research centers in North America, Japan, and Europe. Between 1985 and 1987, Tichy was manager of management education for General Electric, where he directed its worldwide development efforts at Crotonville. Prior to joining the Michigan faculty he served for nine years on the Columbia University Business School faculty. Professor Tichy is the author of numerous books and articles. He authored *The Leadership Engine: How Winning Companies Build Leaders at Every Level* (with Eli Cohen), named one of the top 10 business books in 1997 by *BusinessWeek*. In addition, Tichy is also the co-author of *Control Your Destiny or Someone Else Will: How Jack Welch is Making General Electric the World's Most Competitive Company* (with Stratford Sherman). His most recent book is *Every Business Is a Growth Business* (1998, with Ram Charan). Professor Tichy consults widely in both the private and public sectors. He is a senior partner in Action Learning Associates. His clients have included Ameritech, AT&T, Mercedes-Benz, BellSouth, Ciba-Geigy, Chase Manhattan Bank, Citibank, Covad Communications, Exxon, Ford Motor Company, General Electric, General Motors, Honeywell, Hitachi, Imperial Chemical Inc., IBM, NEC, Northern Telecom, Nomura Securities, and 3M.

VICTOR H. VROOM is the John G. Searle Professor of Organization and Management at the School of Management of Yale University. He is an international expert on leadership and decision making. He is the author of nine books and over 50 articles. His 1964 book, *Work and Motivation*, is regarded as a landmark in that field and continues to be widely cited by scholars. In 1971 he collaborated with Professor Edward Deci in writing *Motivation in Management*. In 1973 he began his famous work on leadership with the publication of *Leadership and Decision Making*, written with Phillip Yetton. The ideas in that book have stimulated more than a hundred research studies by scholars and may be found in virtually every textbook on management and leadership published in the last two decades. His latest book on leadership, *The New Leadership: Managing Participation in Organizations*, was co-authored with Professor Arthur G. Jago and published by Prentice Hall in 1988. Professor Vroom has been actively involved in the design and execution of management development programs with General Electric, American Express, Bristol-Myers Squibb, Pfizer, Goldman Sachs, UBS, Merck, and over 50 other firms. In addition, he has received awards for his research from the American Psychological Association, McKinsey Foundation, and Ford Foundation; he is one of a select number of behavioral scientists whose autobiographies are contained in *Management Laureates*. His work was also profiled in *Life and Works of Management Thinkers*, a book dealing with the 14 foremost contributors to management theory during the 20th century. In 1998 the Society of Industrial and Organizational Psychology honored him with its Distinguished Scientific Contribution Award. Professor Vroom has also been elected President of the Society of Industrial and Organizational Psychology.

Index

8 reasons why you should read the Financial Times for 4 weeks RISK-FREE!

To help you stay current with significant
developments in the world economy ...
and to assist you to make informed business
decisions — the Financial Times brings you:

❶ Fast, meaningful overviews of international affairs ... plus daily briefings on major world news.

❷ Perceptive coverage of economic, business, financial and political developments with special focus on emerging markets.

❸ More international business news than any other publication.

❹ Sophisticated financial analysis and commentary on world market activity plus stock quotes from over 30 countries.

❺ Reports on international companies and a section on global investing.

❻ Specialized pages on management, marketing, advertising and technological innovations from all parts of the world.

❼ Highly valued single-topic special reports (over 200 annually) on countries, industries, investment opportunities, technology and more.

❽ The Saturday Weekend FT section — a globetrotter's guide to leisure-time activities around the world: the arts, fine dining, travel, sports and more.

FT FINANCIAL TIMES
World business newspaper

The *Financial Times* delivers a world of business news.

Use the Risk-Free Trial Voucher below!

To stay ahead in today's business world you need to be well-informed on a daily basis. And not just on the national level. You need a news source that closely monitors the entire world of business, and then delivers it in a concise, quick-read format.

With the *Financial Times* you get the major stories from every region of the world. Reports found nowhere else. You get business, management, politics, economics, technology and more.

Now you can try the *Financial Times* for 4 weeks, absolutely risk free. And better yet, if you wish to continue receiving the *Financial Times* you'll get great savings off the regular subscription rate. Just use the voucher below.